RADICALS AND
THE REPUBLIC

RADICALS AND THE REPUBLIC

*Socialist Republicanism
in the Irish Free State
1925–1937*

RICHARD ENGLISH

CLARENDON PRESS · OXFORD
1994

Oxford University Press, Walton Street, Oxford OX2 6DP
Oxford New York
Athens Auckland Bangkok Bombay
Calcutta Cape Town Dar es Salaam Delhi
Florence Hong Kong Istanbul Karachi
Kuala Lumpur Madras Madrid Melbourne
Mexico City Nairobi Paris Singapore
Taipei Tokyo Toronto
and associated companies in
Berlin Ibadan

Oxford is a trade mark of Oxford University Press

Published in the United States
by Oxford University Press Inc., New York

British Library Cataloguing in Publication Data
Data available

Library of Congress Cataloging in Publication Data
English, Richard, 1963–
Radicals and the republic : socialist republicanism in the Irish
Free State, 1925–1937 / Richard English.
p. cm.
Includes bibliographical references.
1. Ireland—Politics and government—1922–1949. 2. Republicanism—
Ireland—History—20th century. 3. Radicalism—Ireland—
History—20th century. 4. Socialism—Ireland—History—20th
century. I. Title.
DA963.E53 1994
941.5082'2—dc20 94–9430
ISBN 0–19–820289–X

1 3 5 7 9 10 8 6 4 2

Typeset by Graphicraft Typesetters Ltd., Hong Kong
Printed in Great Britain
on acid-free paper by Antony Rowe Ltd.
Chippenham, Wiltshire

Preface

George Gilmore—a leading inter-war Irish republican[1]—argued
that 'The oneness of the struggle against national subjection and
social oppression in a subject nation has been stressed by James
Connolly'.... 'The failure to make that essential oneness a basis
for political action has been the great weakness in the republican
movements of the nineteenth century and right down to our own
day.'[2] Gilmore's words aptly summarize the inter-war republican
socialist thesis: according to this view, the struggle of the oppressed
nation (Ireland) against the oppressor nation (England) was inextricably interwoven with the conflict within Ireland between the
oppressed classes and their social oppressors. Economic and class
interests provided the key to understanding the Irish national question, and class conflict lay at the heart of the republican struggle.

The contention of this book is that the republican socialist
argument was fundamentally incoherent. The contradictory, and
intellectually inadequate, analysis which characterized the republican left during these years explains their political failure. But the
study also aims to explore the mentality which typified republicans
—socialist and non-socialist—during the early years of the independent Irish state. Solipsistic zealotry is shown to have been
self-sustaining but, in terms of political achievement, undeniably

[1] The phrase 'inter-war' is used in this book to refer to the years on which the
study focuses, 1925–37. The term 'republican' refers to those aspiring toward
the ideal of an independent, all-Ireland republic, but refusing to participate
in majoritarian, constitutional political activity. The term 'socialism' is used in
accordance with the definition: 'a theory or policy of social organization which
advocates the ownership and control of the means of production, capital, land,
property, etc. by the community as a whole, and their administration or distribution
in the interests of all' (*The Shorter Oxford English Dictionary*, ii (1973), 2040). I
further hold that the term implies an advocacy of, and engagement in, class struggle
intended to realize the above arrangements, and that the term remains valid even
if a certain flexibility enters into the proposals for community ownership. The word
'socialist' could, for example, be used to describe an advocate of an overwhelmingly socialized programme which none the less conceded certain property-owning
rights to small farmers. The phrase 'republican left' is used to refer to republican
socialists. The word 'communist' is deployed only in reference to those who be-
longed to officially communist organizations.
[2] *The Irish Republican Congress* (Cork, CWC, 1978; 1st edn. 1935), 3.

self-defeating. Furthermore, while the arguments of the republican left were thoroughly unconvincing, scrutiny of their thesis does draw attention to the crucial relationship between nationalism and economics in Ireland during this period. In particular, the exploration of the socialist republican critique involves serious consideration of Fianna Fáil's social and economic policies and arguments. In this sense, the study of republican socialist failure clarifies the nature of Fianna Fáil success. The deficiencies of the republican left thesis reflect the importance of very different economic arguments to the dominance of de Valera's party within the young Free State. Drawing upon much new material—as well as providing the most thorough interrogation to date of more familiar sources— the book aims both to explore the subversive, dissident world of socialist republicanism and to illuminate our reading of the wider political life of inter-war Ireland.

R. E.

Belfast
Dec. 1993

Acknowledgements

John Hewitt's description of historians as 'footnote addicts'[1] has come to seem increasingly apt during the course of writing this book. As with other addictions, this one has a tendency to result in the accumulation of great debts. It is a pleasure to be able to offer—in at least partial repayment—a public expression of gratitude to those to whom I have become indebted during my work on this project.

A University of Keele Research Studentship funded the Ph.D. on which the book is primarily based. My Ph.D. supervisor, Charles Townshend, offered invaluable advice, friendship, and encouragement during (and, indeed, after) my doctoral research. Roy Foster's expertise and support were tremendously helpful. David Eastwood's encouragement and advice have been of enormous benefit throughout. The Institute of Irish Studies and the Department of Politics (both at Queen's University, Belfast) provided excellent environments in which to pursue the complementary tasks of research, writing, and teaching. Numerous libraries and other institutions have made the research both possible and enjoyable: the Archives Department, University College, Dublin (in particular, Seamus Helferty); the National Library of Ireland, Dublin; the National Archives, Dublin; Trinity College Library, Dublin (and the Board of Trinity College, Dublin); the General Register Office (Births, Deaths, and Marriages), Dublin; the British Library (Bloomsbury and Colindale), London; the House of Lords Record Office, London (papers reproduced by permission of the Clerk of the Records); the Marx Memorial Library, London; the Institute of Historical Research, London; the London School of Economics Library; the University of Keele Library; the Linen Hall Library, Belfast; the Queen's University, Belfast, Library; the University of Ulster (Jordanstown) Library; the Public Record Office of

---

[1] 'MacDonnell's Question', in F. Ormsby (ed.), *The Collected Poems of John Hewitt* (Belfast, Blackstaff, 1991), 349.

Northern Ireland, Belfast; the University of Reading Library (in particular, Michael Bott). Queen's University, Belfast, was generous in its provision of funds for research visits.

I am grateful to the following people for their kindness in allowing me access to materials in their possession, and/or in agreeing to be interviewed: Cormac O'Malley (whose archives and knowledge were particularly helpful); Anthony Coughlan; Andrew Boyd; Brendan Byrne; Nora Harkin; Gaye Poulton, at Jonathan Cape; Jennifer FitzGerald; Sean Garland; Sheila Humphreys; Joyce and Terry McMullen; Desmond Neill; Donal Nevin; John O'Beirne Ranelagh; Francis Stuart. Other people have helped greatly in a variety of ways: Paddy Byrne, Sean MacBride, Angela Crean, Kate Townshend, Deirdre McMahon, Donald and Bertha English, Marjory Ludlow, Elsie Ludlow, Mike Kenny, Ronnie Buchanan, Graham Walker, Bob Eccleshall, Vince Geoghegan, Francis Doherty, George Boyce, Tom Garvin, Alvin Jackson, Paul Bew, Margaret O'Callaghan, Paul Hayes, Ronan Fanning, Jack McCann, Joe Skelly, John Regan, Patrick Maume, David McConnell, Una O'Higgins O'Malley, Uinseann MacEoin. The support of Tony Morris, at Oxford University Press, has been greatly appreciated.

Contents

Abbreviations

ADUCD	Archives Department, University College, Dublin
BICO	British and Irish Communist Organization
CPI	Communist Party of Ireland
CUP	Cambridge University Press
CWC	Cork Workers' Club
GAC	General Army Convention (IRA)
HLRO	House of Lords Record Office, London
ICA	Irish Citizen Army
ICO	Irish Communist Organization
IHS	*Irish Historical Studies*
IIS	Institute of Irish Studies, QUB
ILP	Irish Labour Party
ILPTUC	Irish Labour Party and Trade Union Congress
IPS	*Irish Political Studies*
IRA	Irish Republican Army
IRB	Irish Republican Brotherhood
ITGWU	Irish Transport and General Workers' Union
ITUC	Irish Trade Union Congress
JCCW	James Connolly, *Collected Works*
NA	National Archives, Dublin
NLI	National Library of Ireland, Dublin
OUP	Oxford University Press
PP	Private Possession
PRONI	Public Record Office of Northern Ireland, Belfast
PSAI	Political Studies Association of Ireland
PWS	Pearse, *Political Writings and Speeches*
QUB	Queen's University, Belfast
RWG	Revolutionary Workers' Groups
TCD	Trinity College, Dublin
UCD	University College, Dublin
WUI	Workers' Union of Ireland

Introduction
Nationalism and the Class Question, 1916–1925

1916

Then came like a thunderclap the 1916 Rising.

Ernie O'Malley to Molly Childers
26 November–1 December 1923[1]

I mind the day when I followed Mr Gladstone's Home Rule policy, and used to threep about the noble, generous, warm-hearted sister nation held in a foreign bondage. My Goad! I'm not speakin' about Ulster, which is a dour, ill-natured den, but our own folk all the same. But the men that will not do a hand's turn to help the war and take the chance of our necessities to set up a bawbee rebellion are hateful to Goad and man. We treated them like pet lambs and that's the thanks we get.

Andrew Amos, in John Buchan, *Mr Standfast*[2]

Towards the end of his life, the irrepressible Irish socialist republican, Peadar O'Donnell, disputed the view 'that the Tan War and the Sinn Fein struggle arose out of the 1916 Rising'. The post-rebellion executions, he continued, did not 'promote the national uprising. I was in Donegal, and I don't believe that the executions of 1916 would have passed into ballads like '98 [the 1798 rebellion] only that the threat of conscription came on its heels and that it was the threat of conscription that forced the people onto their feet.'[3]

The threat of conscription—a proposal portrayed by the Irish

---

[1] R. English and C. O'Malley (eds.), *Prisoners: The Civil War Letters of Ernie O'Malley* (Swords, Poolbeg, 1991), 72–3.

[2] (Edinburgh, Thomas Nelson, 1923; 1st edn. 1919), 86.

[3] *Monkeys in the Superstructure: Reminiscences of Peadar O'Donnell* (Galway, Salmon, 1986), 28. Cf. O'Donnell's similar remarks in U. MacEoin (ed.), *Survivors* (Dublin, Argenta, 1987; 1st edn. 1980), 22.

Volunteers' organ, *An t-Oglach*, as one which aimed 'to inflict upon the manhood of Ireland a fate worse than death'[4]—was certainly of considerable significance. It should also be noted that the 1916 rebellion can itself be read as having accelerated discernible, preceding trends. As Terence Denman has recently noted, there was a significant decline in Irish recruitment to the British army *prior* to the Easter rebellion. The perception that the Irish soldier had received 'shabby treatment' at the hands of the authorities was complemented by the growing availability of attractive economic opportunities for non-combatants. Both ingredients helped to feed disaffection from the war effort. Denman's observation that 'Long before the Easter Rising many Catholic Irish were showing disenchantment with the war'[5] helps to establish the context within which to appreciate the 1916 rebellion and its effect. But even if one pays appropriate respect to the role both of preceding and of subsequent events, the pivotal significance of the rising must still be acknowledged. Charles Townshend's declaration that, 'in Ireland 1914 marks the beginning of processes of which 1916 was rather the symptom than the cause' is appropriately complemented by his earlier assertion: 'Undoubtedly 1916 was a critical year in Ireland. It would be pointless to deny that something like a "terrible beauty", new at least in its generation, was "born".'[6] The rebellion was a function of the First World War, but its centrality in Irish politics during this period must none the less be recognized.[7]

It is possible to dispute the view that 'Countries in the making need some fundamental epic gesture'.[8] But it would be hard to deny that, for that never-to-be-attained country of the Irish republican imagination, the 1916 rebellion did indeed come to fulfil such a role, the gesture spawning a myth of considerable power. Ernie O'Malley, one of the more charismatic republican leaders in the post-1916 revolution, was later to comment that he had 'given

---

[4] 14 Sept. 1918.

[5] *Ireland's Unknown Soldiers: The 16th (Irish) Division in the Great War, 1914–18* (Blackrock, Irish Academic Press, 1992), 130–5.

[6] *Political Violence in Ireland: Government and Resistance since 1848* (Oxford, Clarendon, 1983), 277–8.

[7] Cf. P. Bew, 'The Easter Rising: Lost Leaders and Lost Opportunites', *Irish Review*, 11 (Winter 1991–2), 9.

[8] J. Darras, 'A Man from Across the Channel: Poet with a View', in M. Crozier (ed.), *Cultural Traditions in Northern Ireland: All Europeans Now?* (Belfast, IIS, 1991), 15.

allegiance to a certain ideal of freedom as personified by the Irish Republic. It had not been realized except in the mind.'[9] The 1916 rebellion can be read as the 'fundamental epic gesture' of this republic of the mind. Seán O'Faoláin shrewdly observed that 'Few risings . . . have been conducted in any country with such a sense of the value of symbol',[10] and the rebellion itself came to assume unrivalled symbolic significance in the imagination of subsequent republican activists. O'Malley presented the events of April and May 1916 as having possessed, for him, a certain Damascus-road quality: 'Then came like a thunderclap the 1916 Rising. . . . Previous to this I had heard a little of the Irish Volunteers, but at home we always laughed at them as toy soldiers. Before [Easter] Week was finished I had changed. When I heard of the executions I was furious.'[11] Even if one is sceptical regarding such conversion stories, the fact that so many republicans felt it necessary to stress the rebellion's significance in their personal pilgrimage of faith is itself evidence of the mythic power which Easter 1916 had come to wield. O'Malley might cringe when, in the late 1920s, he was introduced at an American gathering as having 'fired the first shot in 1916'[12] but, as noted, he himself stressed the vital role which the rebellion had played in changing the direction of his life.

Indeed, many republican zealots built the rebellion into their autobiographical accounts. Maire Comerford, in Dublin during the insurrection, later recalled:

I knew a certain amount of Irish history, though I had always been taught that a successful rebellion against England was impossible. When however you saw the flag of an Irish Republic flying for the first time on the College of Surgeons, and you spoke to a young Volunteer of your own age, it began to seem quite different.

In Comerford's view, the rising not only changed her own life, but 'altered the course of the nation'.[13] Tom Barry made a similar claim: 'through the blood sacrifices of the men of 1916, had one Irish youth of eighteen been awakened to Irish nationality. Let it also

---

[9] E. O'Malley, *The Singing Flame* (Dublin, Anvil, 1978), 214.

[10] *De Valera* (Harmondsworth, Penguin, 1939), 37.

[11] O'Malley to Childers, 26 Nov.–1 Dec. 1923, in English and O'Malley (eds.), *Prisoners*, 72–3. Cf. E. O'Malley, *On Another Man's Wound* (Dublin, Anvil, 1979; 1st edn. 1936), 29–48.

[12] E. O'Malley, Diary, 13 Oct. 1928, Cormac O'Malley Papers, PP.

[13] Quoted in MacEoin (ed.), *Survivors*, 38–40.

be recorded that those sacrifices were equally necessary to awaken the minds of ninety per cent of the Irish people.'[14] Another significant Irish Republican Army [IRA] leader from the post-1916 period, Liam Deasy, sang a similar song:

> In consequence of the events that occurred in the decisive week of the Easter Rising of 1916, and more particularly of the events that followed it, thousands of young men all over Ireland, indeed thousands of men of all ages in the country, turned irrevocably against the English Government and became uncompromisingly dedicated to the cause of obliterating the last vestiges of British rule in Ireland. I was one of them. My comrades of the West Cork Brigade were others.[15]

The simplicity of such accounts renders them highly suspect, but also points to one source of their power. Just as the leading post office patriot, Patrick Pearse, derived strength from the uncompromising simplicity which limited his vision,[16] so, too, the appeal of the rebellion to subsequent republican activists in part relied upon its simplifying focus. The rebel proclamation offered a rather simplistic version of Ireland's past and present.[17] Similarly, post-1916 republican apostles filtered out the gritty sediment of Irish political complexity. James Connolly's socialist republican daughter, Nora, held that 'as a nation Ireland has never recognized England as her conqueror', and stated baldly that the Easter rebellion had been 'caused by the English occupation of Ireland'; 'For in Ireland we have the unbroken tradition of struggle for our

[14] *Guerilla Days in Ireland* (Dublin, Anvil, 1981; 1st edn. 1949), 2.

[15] *Towards Ireland Free: The West Cork Brigade in the War of Independence 1917–21* (Dublin, Mercier, 1973), 5.

[16] 'We have the strength and the peace of mind of those who never compromise' ('Why We Want Recruits' (1915), in *PWS* 121). Cf. Ruth Dudley Edwards's telling reference to 'the essential simplicity of Pearse's mind' (*Patrick Pearse: The Triumph of Failure* (Swords, Poolbeg, 1990; 1st edn. 1977), 70). See also J. J. Lee's allusion to one of the most significant issues regarding which Pearse's vision was blinkered: 'Generous and inclusive though Pearse's definition of Irish nationalism was, there was no place for a distinctive Ulster room in the house of his thought' ('In search of Patrick Pearse', in M. Ni Dhonnchadha and T. Dorgan (eds.), *Revising the Rising* (Derry, Field Day, 1991), 137).

[17] See e.g. its grandiose interpretation of minority, conspiratorial activites: 'Ireland, through us, summons her children to her flag and strikes for her freedom. Having organized and trained her manhood through her secret revolutionary organization, the Irish Republican Brotherhood, and through her open military organizations, the Irish Volunteers, and the Irish Citizen Army . . .'; 'In every generation the Irish people have asserted their right to national freedom and sovereignty' (Proclamation of the Republic, in R. F. Foster, *Modern Ireland 1600–1972* (London, Allen Lane, 1988), 597).

freedom. Every generation has seen blood spilt, and sacrifice cheerfully made that the tradition might live.' The complex and changing attitudes of Irish people throughout history were squeezed into the constricting garments of physical force republican zealotry. Thus, Nora Connolly's assertion that the Young Irelanders had 'made no secret of their belief that the freedom of Ireland must be won by force of arms' attempted to stifle a far more complicated historical reality.[18] The past was mutilated for contemporary, propagandist purpose. Simplistic readings of the rebellion's impact on Irish sensibilities merely extended this practice.

In fact, responses to the insurrection were complex. As noted, 1916 can be read as something of an accelerator, and its own impact was defined and accentuated by crucial subsequent events. The traditional picture, of an initially negative popular response followed by a sympathetic sea change of opinion, has been widely disseminated and is supported by certain eyewitness accounts.[19] But, as Lee has noted, 'It is in fact extraordinarily difficult to reconstruct the public response' to the rising.[20] The eyewitness account of F. A. McKenzie—one of two representatives of the Canadian press 'chosen to visit Ireland while the fighting was on'— suggests that, at least in the poorer parts of Dublin, Britain's post-rising severity strengthened rather than created sympathy for the insurgents:

I have read many accounts of public feeling in Dublin in these days. They are all agreed that the open and strong sympathy of the mass of the population was with the British troops. That this was so in the better parts of the city, I have no doubt, but certainly what I myself saw in the poorer districts did not confirm this. It rather indicated that there was a vast amount of sympathy with the rebels, particularly after the rebels were defeated. The sentences of the Courts Martial deepened this sympathy.[21]

[18] *The Unbroken Tradition* (New York, Boni and Liveright, 1918), pp. vii–viii, xi, and xvii–xviii. Cf. R. Davis, *The Young Ireland Movement* (Dublin, Gill and Macmillan, 1987), 244–57, 264.

[19] K. T. Hoppen, *Ireland since 1800: Conflict and Conformity* (Harlow, Longman, 1989), 137; J. Coakley, 'The Foundations of Statehood', in J. Coakley and M. Gallagher (eds.), *Politics in the Republic of Ireland* (Galway, PSAI Press, 1992), 10; MacEoin (ed.), *Survivors*, 61; W. I. Thompson, *The Imagination of an Insurrection—Dublin, Easter 1916: A Study of an Ideological Movement* (West Stockbridge, Lindisfarne Press, 1982; 1st edn. 1967), 98.

[20] *Ireland, 1912–1985: Politics and Society* (Cambridge, CUP, 1989), 29.

[21] *The Irish Rebellion: What Happened—and Why* (London, C. Arthur Pearson, 1916), 5, 105–6.

Certainly the post-rising executions did little to bolster British legitimacy in Catholic Ireland,[22] and there can be no question that there existed, in the immediate post-rebellion period, considerable nationalist sympathy for the insurgents. A Cabinet memorandum dated 15 May 1916 observed that 'Throughout Leinster popular sympathy for the rebels is growing'; in Connaught 'among all sections of nationalists hopes are generally expressed that the dupes of the revolution will be dealt with leniently'; in Munster 'general sympathy among all nationalists is becoming intensified in favour of the rebels arrested or sentenced'. But such sympathy does not necessarily validate the 'initial scepticism/subsequent conversion' thesis. Indeed, in one vital area, responses to the rebellion should be read in terms of the consolidation rather than the transformation of political opinion. The 15 May Cabinet memorandum had observed that 'public opinion generally throughout Ulster remains opposed to the rebellion' and noted the Ulster unionist view that the rising would demonstrate to English people the dangers lurking within Home Rule.[23]

The rebellion came to be viewed by many unionists as evidence of the traitorous leanings which they had held to be implicit within Irish nationalism. As Dennis Kennedy has observed:

The Somme, and the heavy sacrifices made by Ulstermen at it, came barely two months after the Sinn Fein Easter Rising in Dublin. This was a conjunction that helped cement the Unionist view that their own supreme loyalty had been in contrast to the treachery of nationalist Ireland. . . . By 1918 Ulster unionists saw nationalist Ireland's behaviour only as treachery, in stark contrast to their own heroic contribution. The Somme and the Easter Rising had become the twin symbols of loyalism and treachery.[24]

The largely Catholic rebellion of 1916[25] therefore accentuated— and, to their own eyes, validated—the anti-nationalism to which unionists already subscribed. Thus, the rebels of 1916 helped to further the process of Irish political division. John Buchan's Andrew

---

[22] T. Garvin, *Nationalist Revolutionaries in Ireland 1858–1928* (Oxford, Clarendon, 1987), 48.

[23] *Public Attitude and Opinion in Ireland as to the Recent Outbreak* (15 May 1916), Bonar Law Papers, HLRO BL 63/C/3.

[24] *The Widening Gulf: Northern Attitudes to the Independent Irish State 1919–1949* (Belfast, Blackstaff, 1988), 27.

[25] D. G. Boyce, *Nationalism in Ireland* (London, Routledge, 1991; 1st edn. 1982), 311–12.

Amos, quoted at the start of this chapter, exhibited both a loss of sympathy with Irish nationalism and also a strong sense of the difference between loyal Ulster ('a dour, ill-natured den, but our own folk all the same') and the rest of the island; crucially, the 'bawbee rebellion' had helped to produce this dual response.[26] Recent scholarship has underlined the fact that 1916 indeed strengthened the bargaining position of Ulster unionists in their relationship with the British state. Moreover, the scuppering of Home Rule, to which the rising so significantly contributed, ruined specific prospects for meaningful, structural links between unionist and nationalist Irelands.[27] In this sense, the Easter rebellion can be judged to have cast a malign shadow over much of Ireland's subsequent history.

The vital point for our current argument concerns the implications which the rebellion held for the republican left. That 1916 came to assume mythic—even paradigmatic—status for many subsequent republicans boded ill for those who sought to combine republican and socialist projects. The elevation of physical force violence as practised by a conspiratorial clique; the emphasis upon military gesture performed in the name of the people (but without their mandate) in order that the gesture should convert the people and thereby produce subsequent legitimation; the construction of a cult of willing martyrs—each of these aspects of 1916 attested to a centre of separatist gravity which rendered socialist republicans peripheral.

The most significant inter-war Irish republican socialist, Peadar O'Donnell, displayed on numerous occasions his distaste for the conspiratorial, martyrological culture of physical force—the very culture which Easter 1916 had sanctified. Looking back on the revolutionary period, he observed that 'I was not the military type',[28] and during his lengthy political career he repeatedly evinced a scepticism about the republican emphasis upon élite physical force. In 1932 he contrasted the mass revolutionary process which he himself favoured with the conspiratorial currency used by Michael Collins: 'The big thing to emphasize is that the stubborn splendour of the big mass of the people must be involved in the

---

[26] *Mr Standfast*, 86. On Buchan's own contribution to the British war effort, see J. A. Smith, *John Buchan: A Biography* (London, Rupert Hart-Davis, 1965), ch. 8.
[27] Bew, 'The Easter Rising', 10–13.
[28] Quoted in MacEoin (ed.), *Survivors*, 24.

tactics of the revolution: this heresy of the cult of armed men that brought Collins to imperialism and us to defeat must be over-come.'[29] According to O'Donnell, Collins—whose 1916 credentials were impeccable—[30] had come to suffer from 'the weakness for intrigue and conspiracy that secret societies breed'.[31]

O'Donnell's thinking was strongly influenced by Marx,[32] and certainly his attitude toward physical force carried distinctly Marxist resonances. His scepticism about the IRA's neo-Fenian cult of conspiracy echoed Marx and Engels's laments concerning the Fenians in 1867.[33] Moreover, just as Marx had stressed the im-portance of relating physical force to its wider context,[34] so O'Donnell viewed violence as an adjunct to a mass movement, the latter being the primary focus of attention and source of revolu-tionary momentum:

> It is necessary to get across the fact, the philosophy, which sees clearly that it is only as a spearpoint of a mass movement, that physical force had any meaning. Force is used only as a means of crossing the doorstep of state power. But it cannot reach the doorstep without the push of the united working mass.[35]

Writing in the republican paper, *An Phoblacht*, in 1928, O'Donnell had observed that 'Arms come into play when the mass move-ment is being stemmed, or turned back, or its leaders attacked'.[36] Similarly, O'Donnell displayed traces of scepticism concerning the republican culture of martyrdom. Writing of those who had pro-vided the main opposition to the 1921 Anglo-Irish treaty, he

---

[29] *The Gates Flew Open* (London, Jonathan Cape, 1932), 168.

[30] T. P. Coogan, *Michael Collins: A Biography* (London, Hutchinson, 1990), 32–57.   [31] *The Gates*, 31.

[32] It appears that his first encounter with Marx's writings occurred during his spell as a full-time organizer for the ITGWU, a post he assumed in 1918: 'Somebody . . . in Liberty Hall . . . gave him Marx to read. He just couldn't get over this' (Nora Harkin, interview with the author, Dublin, 4 Feb. 1988; for biographical details on Harkin—a close associate of O'Donnell's for many years—and on O'Donnell himself, see R. English, 'Peadar O'Donnell: Socialism and the Repub-lic, 1925–37', *Saothar*, 14 (1989), 47–8, 56; O'Donnell's birth is usu. given as 22 Feb. 1893, but his birth certificate records it as 12 Mar. 1893 (Birth Cert. of Peter [*sic*] O'Donnell, Office of the Register General, Dublin)).

[33] Marx to Engels (14 Dec. 1867), Engels to Marx (19 Dec. 1867) in *Ireland and the Irish Question* (London, Lawrence and Wishart, 1971 edn.), 159.

[34] D. McLellan, *The Thought of Karl Marx: An Introduction* (London, Macmillan, 1980; 1st edn. 1971), 229.

[35] Quoted in M. McInerney, *Peadar O'Donnell: Irish Social Rebel* (Dublin, O'Brien, 1974), 219.   [36] 21 Jan. 1928.

argued, 'They were the stuff that martyrs are made of, but not revolutionaries, and martyrdom should be avoided.'[37]

For O'Donnell, too great a concentration upon the culture of conspiratorial physical force or the cult of republican martyrs distracted attention from what he considered the real fire-centre of Irish republicanism—namely, the social conflicts around which a mass, socially radical, separatist movement could be mobilized. The 1916 rebellion, with its emphasis upon conspiratorial violence and redemptive death, was therefore an awkward paradigm to adopt. Yet one of the central contradictions in the inter-war republican socialist approach was that O'Donnell and his colleagues not only tried to claim the 1916 heritage for their own particular brand of republicanism, but that they also worked for years within that conspiratorial, martyrological, physical force cult, the IRA, whose centre of gravity condemned socialist republicans to the periphery. O'Donnell fought in the IRA during the Anglo-Irish and civil wars and continued to play a leading role in the organization until 1934. The IRA vehicle was one which substantially determined his ideological route. In later years, when his reputation and prestige were not dependent on the endorsement of violence, O'Donnell even questioned the wisdom of the January 1919 Soloheadbeg attack which had come to symbolize the opening of the Anglo-Irish war.[38] But, as a leading IRA figure in 1928, he had felt compelled to temper his view that physical force played a functional, secondary role in the republican struggle with the assertion that violence was inevitable: 'The use of arms can be taken for granted. Success cannot come along any line for this country without recourse to arms at some stage. So the national fathers have taught; so our sense tells us.'[39]

If 1916 was an unhelpful model for socialist republicans because of its conspiratorial and sacrificial qualities, it was also an inappropriate paradigm owing to the spiritual emphasis characteristic both of its actors and of its subsequent panegyrists. Pearse's assertions that nationality was a 'spiritual' rather than a 'material' thing, and freedom 'a spiritual necessity',[40] were echoed in the language of many who sought to build on Pearse's foundations. Terence MacSwiney declared that 'A spiritual necessity makes the true significance of our claim to freedom: the material aspect is only a

---

[37] Quoted in MacEoin (ed.), *Survivors*, 25.   [38] *Monkeys*, 28.
[39] *An Phoblacht*, 21 Jan. 1928.   [40] 'Ghosts' (1915), in *PWS* 224–5.

secondary consideration.' According to MacSwiney, 'It is a spiritual appeal . . . that primarily moves us.'[41] In Liam Deasy's view, the post-rising period demonstrated that 'The spirit of the nation was not dead. Slowly, almost imperceptibly, yet inexorably as a flowing tide, it rose, and with its rising the nation was reborn.'[42] This emphasis on a primarily spiritual conception of nationality represented Ireland in romantic, ethereal, and essentially ahistorical terms. The 'old tradition of nationhood' referred to in the 1916 rebel proclamation[43] was sufficiently abstract for it to be granted a certain unchanging quality. Thus Pearse was able to claim that, to the Irish mind, freedom had had one definition for over a thousand years.[44]

In contrast, at the heart of the republican socialist creed was the conviction that Irish nationalism was defined very firmly by particular, material, socio-economic conflicts and relations. O'Donnell and his 1930s Republican Congress colleague, Frank Ryan, reflected this difference of emphasis in a 1937 reference to the Easter rebellion. According to them, 'The 1916 Proclamation was always read to promise . . . a triumph of the poor over the small group of rich men who trafficked in their misery.'[45] Central to the republican socialist thesis was the belief that the struggle to free Ireland from English domination was inextricably linked to the class struggle fought in Ireland. The conflict between the oppressed nation (Ireland) and the oppressor nation (England) was, according to this view, mirrored by the conflict within Ireland between oppressed and oppressor classes. Thus the all-too-material question of combating capitalism and its defenders was at the very core of the republican struggle. In the words of the Republican Congress's 1934 Athlone manifesto, 'We believe that a Republic of a united Ireland will never be achieved except through a struggle which uproots capitalism on its way.'[46] Later in the same year, O'Donnell argued that the way to build towards the desired Irish republic was

to create committees of workers and small farmers to conduct working-class and small farmer struggles, and to express the political aspirations of these growing forces in increased and urgent campaign to achieve the

[41] *Principles of Freedom* (Dublin, Talbot, 1921), 4, 6.
[42] *Towards Ireland Free*, 4.   [43] Foster, *Modern Ireland*, 597.
[44] 'Ghosts', in *PWS* 228.   [45] *Irish Democrat*, 22 May 1937.
[46] *Republican Congress*, 5 May 1934.

Republic. In this way Irish capitalism will be exposed, and ever-growing power will rest in our committees of workers and small farmers. A Republic achieved that way becomes a Workers' and Small Farmers' Republic because the organs of struggle become the organs of government, to express the will of those who were the driving force to victory.[47]

The emphasis here—in terms of struggle and of end result—lies clearly in the material rather than the spiritual realm. Similarly, the socialist republican Saor Eire movement of 1931 had demonstrated in its declaration of primary objectives that social, economic, materially based conflicts and objectives defined its vision of republicanism. The movement aimed:

1. To achieve an independent revolutionary leadership for the working class and working farmers towards the overthrow of British imperialism and its ally, Irish capitalism.
2. To organize and consolidate the Republic of Ireland on the basis of the possession and administration by the workers and working farmers, of the land, instruments of production, distribution and exchange.[48]

When seeking (in 1931) to explain the partition of Ireland and the consequent frustration of republican aspirations, O'Donnell turned to economics:

In the North-East the workers are collected around industries controlled by *imperial* finance . . . For the South the rulers are a mixed assortment of bankers, industrialists, upper-tier farmers and the backing they can attach. They have organized an army, police, jails, etc., to put their will through and, to maintain themselves, they bargain with British imperialism on terms where their state will hold Ireland for the empire, but get in return freedom to raise tariffs against imperial industries breaking in on their markets. . . . Partition arises out of this uneven development of capitalism in Ireland; sentiment won't remove it.[49]

Thus, inter-war Irish republican socialists defined their republicanism in terms of material interests, conflicts, and alliances. This distanced them considerably from the spiritual romanticism so crucial to the symbolic power of 1916.

[47] Gilmore, *The Irish Republican Congress* (Cork, CWC, 1978; 1st edn. 1935), 53.   [48] *Saor Eire (Organization of Workers and Working Farmers): Constitution and Rules adopted by First National Congress held in Dublin 26 and 27 Sept., 1931*, Files of the Dept. of the Taoiseach, NA S 5864 A.   [49] *An Phoblacht*, 7 Feb. 1931.

The question of class conflict leads us to the most important difficulty facing republican socialists in relation to the Easter rebellion. The nation, as represented in the 1916 gesture, was not one defined by class conflict but rather one presented in terms of multi-class harmony. In the implausible argument of the rebels' proclamation, the Irish people were portrayed as a united group with common purpose ('In every generation the Irish people have asserted their right to national freedom and sovereignty'). The would-be republic declared its 'resolve to pursue the happiness and prosperity of the whole nation and of all its parts, cherishing all the children of the nation equally'.[50] This unconvincing rhetoric offered little to those whose republic was centrally defined by Irish class conflict. Yet, according to post-1916 socialist republican literature, the multi-class rebellion appeared to present no problems. Writing in 1936, O'Donnell claimed that 'Connolly and Pearse brought the Republican and labour forces into united front in Dublin in 1916, and this is the crowning achievement of both their lives'.[51] According to Frank Ryan, Connolly and Pearse shared the same 'ideal'.[52] George Gilmore, perhaps the flintiest of the leading inter-war republican socialists, heretically acknowledged that Pearse had been a 'backward-looking romantic'. Significantly, he balanced this with the questionable claim that 'If the Rising had ended in victory Pearse, Ceannt, and Plunkett at least would have supported Connolly in his plans for the reorganization of Irish society.' He ruefully added that 'after their defeat and death the leadership that emerged lacked any such vision'.[53]

Typically, Gilmore's argument raises an important point. Equally typically, the significance of his thesis must be called into question. As George Boyce has observed, individual sympathy among certain leaders did not necessarily provide an accurate index of broader political realities:

Pearse, Joseph Plunkett, Eamon Kent, and Sean MacDermott were all sympathetic to the cause of labour. But the dangers inherent in a combination of rebels, intellectuals and the proletariat might not prove to the

---

[50] Foster, *Modern Ireland*, 597–8.   [51] *Irish People*, 11 Apr. 1936.
[52] Seachranaidhe [F. Ryan], *Easter Week and After* (Dublin, National Publicity Committee, n.d. [1928?]), 15; for an identification of Seachranaidhe as Ryan, see S. Cronin, *Frank Ryan: The Search for the Republic* (Dublin, Repsol, 1980), 26–7.
[53] *The Irish Republican Congress* (1978 edn.), pp. iii–iv.

liking of the tenant farmers of rural Ireland; and the countryside, though it had in 1916 lost the initiative to Dublin, could not for ever be ignored by anyone engaged in the serious pursuit of political power in Ireland.[54]

It is also clear that, despite their mutual respect,[55] Pearse and Connolly remained a considerable ideological distance from one another. In contrast to Connolly, Pearse's 'conception of the nation remained . . . a comprehensive one, innocent of class conflict'.[56] As his biographer has observed, Pearse 'embraced no coherent socialist doctrine' and his 'sympathy for the workers' cause did not lead him to any desire for class conflict'.[57] Indeed, Pearse's treatment of material (as opposed to spiritual) questions showed him to be possessed of a vague, multi-class communalism which clashed with the emphasis on class struggle characteristic both of Connolly and of his inter-war socialist republican successors. In *The Sovereign People* Pearse examined the issue of the nation's jurisdiction over the people and property contained within it. Physical freedom, he claimed, was essential if 'sane and vigorous life' were to flourish. The conditions necessary for maintaining the latter were controlled through the former. These conditions were 'partly material', so national freedom involved 'control of the material things which are essential to the continued physical life and freedom of the nation'. The nation's sovereignty, therefore, extended not simply to its people, 'but to all the material possessions of the nation, the nation's soil and all its resources, all wealth and all wealth-producing processes within the nation. In other words, no private right to property is good as against the public right of the nation'. Pearse then declared the nation to be 'under a moral obligation' to exercise this right in such a way as to ensure the equal rights and liberties of all its citizens. The 'whole' was entitled to pursue its own happiness and prosperity, in order that each individual should enjoy these benefits, namely 'the maximum amount of happiness and prosperity consistent with the happiness and prosperity of all the rest'.

This notion of collective self-regulation geared towards egalitarian individual gain was an important strand in Pearse's thinking. He had insisted on 'the spiritual fact of nationality' and on

---

[54] *Nationalism in Ireland*, 313.
[55] R. D. Edwards, *James Connolly* (Dublin, Gill and Macmillan, 1981), 125.
[56] Townshend, *Political Violence*, 282.   [57] Edwards, *Pearse*, 257.

'the necessity of physical freedom in order to the continued preservation [*sic*] of that spiritual fact in a living people'. Now he was asserting 'the necessity of complete control of the material resources of the nation in order to the completeness of that physical freedom'. Again, he demonstrated that his thinking was communalist rather than socialist; for his discussion was imbued with a multi-class spirit, and was free from the dialectical conflict present in socialist analysis. No class possessed rights 'superior to those of any other class', and none enjoyed privileges denied to others, 'except with the consent of the nation'. According to Pearse, the creation and administration of laws were functions which 'the whole nation', not any particular class within the nation, had the right to perform. Only those whom the people delegated could create and administer laws, or exercise the right of control over material resources. While Pearse therefore rejected the idea that one class could dominate others in its own interests, he did not espouse class warfare. Equality, happiness, and prosperity were to be achieved not through the revolutionary actions of a vanguard class, but through the communal application of justice, by and toward members of all classes residing in the nation.

Pearse claimed that a nation had the right to determine the extent to which—and the areas within which—private property was to be permitted. It was conceivable, he continued, that land, transport, and all sources of wealth could be decreed areas in which public possession was preferable. But he was not advocating the abolition of private property, merely stating that this was one question which would arise out of the nation's obligation to use its sovereignty over material resources for the benefit of all citizens. There was nothing 'divine or sacrosanct' in the examples of public ownership to which he had referred; rather they were matters for national discussion, adjustment, and deliberation: 'I do not disallow the right to private property; but I insist that all property is held subject to the national sanction'. Both class struggle and the abolition of private ownership were, therefore, absent from Pearse's ideology. While he dismissed the right of the economically powerful to dominate society, he did not believe, as would a socialist, that their economic strength would inevitably produce their political supremacy. He therefore aimed not to eradicate class distinction, but rather to produce a community whose government would reflect all strata, being representative 'of all the men and women of the nation, the men and women of no property equally with the men and women of property'.[58]

In contrast, class conflict lay at the heart of James Connolly's version of Irish separatism. Although Irish socialist republicanism was not without its ancestors,[59] Connolly came to be by far its most famous advocate. Indeed, for inter-war republican socialists, he was unrivalled as an iconic point of reference.[60] Republican socialists celebrated the supposed genius of their hero's 1916 involvement. But close scrutiny of the evidence demolishes this approach. The divergence between the respective views of Connolly and Pearse highlights the fact that Connolly's participation in 1916 contradicted much that had been central to his version of Irish republicanism.

For Connolly, Irish republicanism had to be understood in terms of material conditions and social conflicts: 'As we have again and again pointed out, the Irish question is a social question, the whole age-long fight of the Irish people against their oppressors resolves itself, in the last analysis, into a fight for the mastery of the means of life, the sources of production, in Ireland.'[61] Associated with this approach was Connolly's view that each particular period of history had to be understood in terms of the specific economic context relevant to that period. In *Labour in Irish History* (published in 1910) Connolly openly acknowledged his debt to Marx, whom he labelled 'the greatest of modern thinkers'. In asserting that Marx had propounded the 'key to history', Connolly misleadingly attributed to the great man some words actually penned by Engels in an 1888 preface to an English edition of the *Manifesto of the Communist Party*: 'That in every historical epoch the prevailing method of economic production and exchange, and the social organization necessarily following from it, forms the basis upon which alone can be explained the political and intellectual history of that epoch'.[62] If the past was to be interpreted according to

[58] *PWS* 336–42; cf. Edwards, *Pearse*, 257–8.

[59] See V. Geoghegan, 'The Emergence and Submergence of Irish Socialism, 1821–51', in D. G. Boyce, R. Eccleshall, and V. Geoghegan (eds.), *Political Thought in Ireland since the Seventeenth Century* (London, Routledge, 1993).

[60] For Connolly's influence on the Republican Congress, see R. English, 'Socialism and Republican Schism in Ireland: The Emergence of the Republican Congress in 1934', *IHS* 27/105 (May 1990), 58–9.

[61] *Labour in Irish History* (1910), in *JCCW* i. 183.

[62] Ibid. 36; cf. F. Engels, *Preface to the English Edition of 1888* in K. Marx and F. Engels, *Manifesto of the Communist Party* (Moscow, Progress, 1977 edn.), 20.

material realities so, too, Connolly sought that the present and future should be determined by a preoccupation with social questions. In January 1897 he had stressed that Irish nationality must be shown to be more than 'a morbid idealizing of the past'. It was necessary to prove that it could formulate 'a distinct and definite answer to the problems of the present and a political and economic creed capable of adjustment to the wants of the future'. Connolly asserted that the mere removal of foreign authority would not produce genuine domestic autonomy: 'If you remove the English army tomorrow and hoist the green flag over Dublin Castle, unless you set about the organization of the Socialist Republic your efforts would be in vain.' England, Connolly argued, would still rule in Ireland, through landlords, financiers, and 'the whole array of commercial and individualist institutions she has planted in this country'.[63]

Connolly's emphasis on the primacy of material and social questions—and on the constantly changing, economically determined quality of history—stood in marked contrast to Pearse's spiritually focused romanticism, with its notion of a national ideal unchanged for over a millennium. As Ruth Dudley Edwards has shrewdly observed, Connolly 'had little in common with the largely bourgeois leadership [of the Irish Republican Brotherhood [IRB]]'.[64] This point is further underlined on close inspection of Connolly's commitment to class conflict, and of his definition of Irish separatism in terms of Irish class struggle. In contrast to the Pearsean ethos of multi-class harmony which surrounded the 1916 rebellion, Connolly had defined Ireland's struggle for independence in terms of conflict between Irish classes. In the foreword to *Labour in Irish History*, he had stated 'the two propositions' on which his book was founded. First, as societies evolved, subject nations' struggles for national liberty must keep pace with the development of 'the struggle for liberty of the most subject class' within each nation. The 'shifting of economic and political forces' which was concomitant with capitalism's development inevitably led 'to the increasing conservatism of the non-working class element, and to the revolutionary vigour and power of the working class'. Second, Ireland had witnessed the respective disappearance

[63] 'Socialism and Nationalism' (1897), in *JCCW* i. 304, 307.
[64] *Connolly*, 122.

and apostasy of 'the old chieftainry' and its descendants; the temporary national commitment but eventual anti-patriotism of the middle class; and the consequent emergence of the working class as the sole 'incorruptible inheritors' of Ireland's fight for freedom. Put more tersely, capitalism increasingly produced distinct and antagonistic classes, and this social conflict mirrored the national tussle between those who genuinely favoured Irish independence (the working class) and those who did not (everyone else).

Armed with these premises, Connolly sought to detail 'the position of the Irish workers in the past, and the lessons to be derived from a study of that position in guiding the movement of the working class today'. *Labour in Irish History* reflected Connolly's conviction that economic relations determined Irish people's attitudes towards the national issue. Those whose social interests were tied up with—and guaranteed by—British rule in Ireland, and with the capitalist system which that rule sustained, could not be relied upon in the struggle for Ireland's complete, republican independence. The Irish middle class, Connolly asserted, had 'a thousand economic strings in the shape of investments binding them to English capitalism as against every sentimental or historic attachment drawing them toward Irish patriotism'. The working class, oppressed by the capitalist system which Britain sustained in Ireland, were thus driven by their social, class interests to uproot British rule and establish a fully independent Irish republic. Economics provided the deterministic key to human history, and economic interest governed Irish attitudes to the national question: 'Only the Irish working class remain as the incorruptible inheritors of the fight for freedom in Ireland'.[65] Connolly's hostility toward capitalism[66] was thus interwoven with his Irish separatist ambitions: the social and national struggles were symbiotically related to one another. Surveying Irish history, he argued that class interests provided an index of nationalist reliability:

The lower middle class gave to the national cause in the past many unselfish patriots, but, on the whole, while willing and ready enough to please their humble fellow-countrymen, and to compound with their own conscience by shouting louder than all others their untiring devotion to

---

[65] Connolly, *Labour in Irish History*, in *JCCW* i. 24–6.

[66] 'The day has passed for patching up the capitalist system; it must go' (Connolly, *Labour, Nationality, and Religion* (1910), in *JCCW* ii. 442).

the cause of freedom, they, as a class, unceasingly strove to divert the public mind upon the lines of constitutional agitation for such reforms as might remove irritating and unnecessary officialism, while leaving untouched the basis of national and economic subjection.

The working class were, in Connolly's opinion, more dependable.[67] Indeed, Connolly tended towards a definition of the Irish people exclusively in terms of this reliable class:

We are out for Ireland for the Irish. But who are the Irish? Not the rack-renting, slum-owning landlord; not the sweating, profit-grinding capitalist; not the sleek and oily lawyer; not the prostitute pressman—the hired liars of the enemy. Not these are the Irish upon whom the future depends. Not these, but the Irish working class, the only secure foundation upon which a free nation can be reared.[68]

This quotation (dating from the same month as the Easter rebellion) brings us to the crucial point regarding Connolly's contradictory involvement in 1916. He had defined the republican struggle in terms of Irish class conflict (and had identified the working class as the real Irish people). He then proceeded to participate in a rebellion which could not be considered—in terms of ideology, personnel, or leadership—to be specifically working-class, and which endorsed a harmonious, multi-class vision of the nation which directly contradicted his own teaching. Having asserted that the working class were the only 'incorruptible inheritors of the fight for freedom in Ireland'—and having, in the words of Bew, Gibbon, and Patterson, endorsed the view that, 'there could be no national revolution without the leadership of the working class'[69]— Connolly then threw himself into a rebellion which was neither led by the working class nor characterized by a specifically working-class identity.

Thus, the celebratory attitude of inter-war republican socialists, such as the leading Irish communist, Sean Murray, was thoroughly misguided. Murray's claim ('A national independence movement allied to the working class with its ultimate goal a Socialist Republic: such was the doctrine of Connolly')[70] unwittingly directs us to

[67] Connolly, *Labour in Irish History*, in *JCCW* i. 30–1, 98–9.
[68] 'The Irish Flag' (8 Apr. 1916), in *JCCW* ii. 175.
[69] *The State in Northern Ireland 1921–72: Political Forces and Social Classes* (Manchester, Manchester Univ. Press, 1979), 17.
[70] *The Irish Revolt: 1916 and After* (n.d.), Murray Papers, PRONI D2162/J/96, 13.

the central contradiction in Connolly's behaviour. The 1916 rebellion did not have as its ultimate goal a socialist republic. Having argued strongly against republican all-class alliances,[71] he then played a leading role in a cross-class republican project. He had greatly shifted from the belief that 'the first action of a revolutionary army must harmonize in principle with those likely to be its last and . . . therefore, no revolutionists can safely invite the co-operation of men or classes, whose ideals are not theirs, and whom, therefore, they may be compelled to fight at some future critical stage of the journey to freedom'.[72]

The significance of Connolly's drastic shift in approach is that it reflects the failure of his would-be symbiotic socialist republican fusion to deal with the situation which he faced. Joseph Lee has argued that Connolly was confronted 'in a particularly acute form with the three evil geniuses of socialism—priest, patriot, and peasant' and that he possessed 'little idea how to handle them'.[73] One might, perhaps, extend the alliterative sequence by adding 'Protestant' to Lee's list of obstructive characters with whom Connolly proved unable to deal in anything approaching an adequate fashion.[74]

Connolly's famous response to Father Robert Kane[75] reflected some of the difficulties which he faced in relation to the first of Lee's three evil geniuses, the priests. Kane had asked: 'Is socialism logically incompatible with Catholicity? To this we must fearlessly answer yes; a true Catholic cannot be a real socialist.' He had also argued that there was 'no need, no excuse for socialism. But there is sore need of social reform'; and had claimed that there was 'no friend so true or so faithful to the poor as the Catholic church'.[76] According to Connolly, the Church's historical role pointed to a different conclusion. He characterized the Church's attitude in unflattering terms:

Ever counselling humility, but sitting in the seats of the mighty; ever patching up the diseased and broken wrecks of an unjust social system,

---

[71] K. Allen, *The Politics of James Connolly* (London, Pluto, 1990), 172.

[72] Connolly, quoted in D. Howell, *A Lost Left: Three Studies in Socialism and Nationalism* (Manchester, Manchester Univ. Press, 1986), 42.

[73] *The Modernization of Irish Society 1848–1918* (Dublin, Gill and Macmillan, 1973), 151.

[74] Bew, Gibbon, and Patterson, *The State in Northern Ireland*, 1–9.

[75] *Labour, Nationality, and Religion*, in *JCCW* ii.

[76] *Socialism* (Dublin, Catholic Truth Society of Ireland, 1910), 12, 68, 92.

but blessing the system which made the wrecks and spread the disease; ever running divine discontent and pity into the ground as the lightning rod runs and dissipates lightning, instead of gathering it and directing it for social righteousness as the electric battery generates and directs electricity for social use.

Moreover, the work of uprooting the capitalist system was, according to Connolly, neither inconsistent with Catholicism nor with other religious positions; in the task of abolishing capitalism,

the Catholic and the Protestant, the Catholic and the Jew, the Catholic and the Freethinker, the Catholic and the Buddhist, the Catholic and the Mahometan will co-operate together, knowing no rivalry but the rivalry of endeavour toward an end beneficial to all. For, as we have said elsewhere, socialism is neither Protestant nor Catholic, Christian nor Freethinker, Buddhist, Mahometan, nor Jew; it is only HUMAN.

In Connolly's view, history taught that 'the instincts of the reformer and revolutionists have been right, the political theories of the Vatican and the clergy unquestionably wrong. The verdict of history as unquestionably endorses the former as it condemns the latter.'[77] He had earlier made the assertion that 'in Ireland the Church denounced every Irish revolutionary movement in its day of activity, as in 1798, 1848 and 1867, and yet allowed its priests to deliver speeches in eulogy of the active spirits of those movements a generation afterwards'.[78]

But this should not blind us to the fact that, except from a tiny minority of atypical figures, Connolly's brand of revolutionary socialism failed to receive clerical endorsement even after his famous and patriotic death. The kind of clerical abuse which his daughter, Nora, records him as having experienced,[79] continued, as the present study will demonstrate, during her own inter-war republican socialist career.

Others familiar with the Irish situation in Connolly's period also tried to reconcile socialism with Catholicism.[80] But the significance of the Church's opposition should not be underestimated. As Lee

[77] *Labour, Nationality, and Religion*, in *JCCW* ii. 381, 442.
[78] 'Roman Catholicism and Socialism' (1908), in *JCCW* ii. 235.
[79] N. Connolly O'Brien, *Portrait of a Rebel Father* (London, Rich and Cowan, 1935), 134–5.
[80] L. P. O Riain, *Doctor Socialism and the Irish Hypochondriac* (Dublin, Socialist Party of Ireland, n.d. [1909?]), 16; E. Larkin, 'Socialism and Catholicism in Ireland', *Church History*, 33/4 (Dec. 1964), 477.

pithily put it, Connolly 'made a major theoretical contribution to reconciling Catholicism and socialism, but failed to get the message across to most Catholics'.[81]

Patriots embodied a problem for Connolly owing to the all-devouring dominance of contemporary nationalist politics, a dominance to which his latter-day compromises were a desperate response. The problem of the peasantry leads us to a significant gap in Connolly's thinking; the weakness of his response to the politics of the land has long been recognized.[82] Given the massive significance of the late-nineteenth, early-twentieth-century shift from tenancy to peasant proprietorship,[83] this was a vital deficiency. Connolly's endorsement of land socialization[84] met precisely the negative response which had greeted Michael Davitt's earlier espousal of land nationalization,[85] and which was later to greet similar proposals when made by inter-war republican socialists.

The problem posed for Connolly by Irish Protestants, in particular those of the Ulster unionist variety, was also of vital significance. According to Connolly, property, rather than religion, represented the pivot on which Irish politics turned: 'Class lines ... were far more strictly drawn than religious lines, as they always were in Ireland since the breakup of the clan system, and as they are to this day. ... Irish politics and divisions turn primarily around questions of property and only nominally around questions of religion.'[86] But the interweaving of religious, ethnic, cultural, economic, and political allegiances in Ireland produced divisions with which Connolly's theory and practice were simply unable to deal. Writing in 1913, Connolly argued (rather poignantly) that

According to all socialist theories North-East Ulster, being the most developed industrially, ought to be the quarter in which class lines of cleavage, politically and industrially, should be the most pronounced and class rebellion the most common. As a cold matter of fact, it is the happy

---

[81] *Modernization*, 151.

[82] Bew, Gibbon, and Patterson, *The State in Northern Ireland*, 33.

[83] R. Fanning, *Independent Ireland* (Dublin, Helicon, 1983), 73.

[84] 'Peasant Proprietorship and Socialism' (27 Aug. 1898), in *JCCW* ii. 214; cf. Howell, *A Lost Left*, 35.

[85] P. Bew, 'Parnell and Davitt', in D. G. Boyce and A. O'Day (eds.), *Parnell in Perspective* (London, Routledge, 1991), 46.

[86] *Labour in Irish History*, in *JCCW* i. 64.

hunting ground of the slave-driver and the home of the least rebellious slaves in the industrial world.[87]

Connolly rather simplistically explained socialist failure in the north-east of the island through reference to the 'devilish ingenuity of the master class'; and, as George Boyce has observed, while he 'accepted the authenticity of Irish nationalism', he was 'quick to deny any such characteristic to Ulster unionism'.[88] Another insightful commentator has noted the naïvety of Connolly's approach with regard to Ulster: 'In Connolly's view the shared experience of exploitation would eventually overcome the artificial divisions within the Belfast working class.'[89]

Connolly's view, that Irish nationalism was a progressive force, was tied both to a conviction that Irish unionism was reactionary[90] and to a rather crude assumption regarding 'the unity of the nation'.[91] His deficiencies here echoed those of his intellectual mentors, Marx and Engels,[92] and have themselves been re-echoed in more recent discussions. Thus, Ephraim Nimni states that, according to Marx and Engels:

The Irish and Polish national movements are perceived as advancing the course of progress by constituting national states capable of developing a healthy contradiction between the proletariat and the bourgeoisie. Furthermore, their state independence will be a considerable help for the proletarian struggles within the nations that subjugate them.

Nimni then immediately refers to Marx and Engels's 'perceptive discussion of the Irish question'. No mention is made here of the possibility that Marx and Engels's views are founded on crude and inadequate assumptions regarding the definition of the Irish nation. Nor is any notice taken of the significant literature challenging Marx and Engels's approach to Ireland.[93]

---

[87] 'North-East Ulster' (2 Aug. 1913), in *JCCW* i. 383–4.

[88] *Nationalism in Ireland*, 304.

[89] P. Bew, 'James Connolly (1868–1916) and Irish Socialism', in C. Brady (ed.), *Worsted in the Game: Losers in Irish History* (Dublin, Lilliput, 1989), 161.

[90] Boyce, *Nationalism in Ireland*, 305.

[91] Connolly, 'Labour and the Proposed Partition of Ireland' (14 Mar. 1914), in *JCCW* i. 393.

[92] Bew, Gibbon, and Patterson, *The State in Northern Ireland*, 2–3.

[93] E. Nimni, *Marxism and Nationalism: Theoretical Origins of a Political Crisis* (London, Pluto, 1991), 33–4; neither E. Hazelkorn, 'Reconsidering Marx and Engels on Ireland', *Saothar*, 9 (1983) nor Bew, Gibbon, and Patterson, *The State in Northern Ireland* appear in Nimni's bibliography.

The problem of division between the unionist and nationalist working classes cannot, in fact, be so easily evaded. Even William McMullen—an associate and admirer of Connolly, who was to be involved in the 1930s Republican Congress movement—openly acknowledged this. Though committedly anti-partitionist himself,[94] McMullen displayed an awareness of the depth of sectarian division, and also of the dangers of leftist self-delusion. Writing of the 1907 Belfast dockers and carters' strike, he noted that

It was a relief to those with an interest in the success of the workers['] struggle for recognition of their Union and an improved standard of life, that the 12th July celebrations passed over, without an outbreak of sectarian violence. Fears, which were well-founded, that such an outbreak would shatter the solidarity of the strikers['] ranks were strongly held by those local leaders who were natives of the city and who had an intimate knowledge of the local situation . . . The risks inherent in that situation have been little understood and grossly under-estimated by those who have romanticized the events of that occasion.[95]

Elsewhere, McMullen commented on Connolly's attempt, having settled in Belfast in 1911, to win support for the 'Marxist and nationalist' Socialist Party of Ireland. Connolly, said McMullen, strove unremittingly

to get the entire movement of the city to leave the Independent Labour Party and join the Socialist Party of Ireland. This was a much more difficult matter than Connolly, realist as he was, appeared to apprehend. In those times it was difficult enough for one to break with the unionist family tradition and embrace socialism, but much more difficult to swallow the hook, line and sinker of Irish Republicanism as well.[96]

Connolly's problems with priests, patriots, peasants, and Protestants establish the context of frustration within which his shift during the First World War must be set and appreciated. By the start of 1916 Connolly had reached a point of political desperation from which he could see no path other than violent insurrection. It is indisputable that the war acted as a crucial catalyst upon his thinking ('We believe in constitutional action in normal times; we believe in revolutionary action in exceptional times. These are

[94] See Election Leaflet for Northern Ireland Elections, 3 Apr. 1925, and also McMullen, 'An Open Letter to Eamonn [*sic*] de Valera' (n.d.), McMullen Papers, PP.   [95] Untitled MS (n.d. [1958?]), McMullen Papers, PP.
[96] Introduction to *The Workers' Republic* (1951), in *JCCW* ii. 183–4.

exceptional times').[97] But his 1916 outlook was produced by a combination of various considerations: considerations which were intimately related to the aforementioned failure of his symbiotic socialist republican thesis to deal with the problems which it faced.

His notions of the viability of Irish syndicalism had been cruelly crushed by the defeat of the strikers following the Dublin lock-out of 1913.[98] The British government's apparent capitulation before the armed threat posed by unionists had introduced the unpalatable possibility of partition and had seemed to hint at the efficacy of military gesture.[99] Moreover, Connolly held that Britain's vulnerability through wartime preoccupation presented insurrectionary opportunities unavailable in peace time.[100] In addition, as Ruth Dudley Edwards has pointed out, he 'believed that a British victory in the war would shore up the capitalist state indefinitely, and so seized the only revolutionary moment available to him'.[101] He appears to have held that Germany was a comparatively progressive power which deserved his support in the war.[102]

Most crucially, perhaps, he considered that the apostasy of the Irish working class from what he perceived to be their true, radical faith necessitated a redemptive gesture which would atone for such treachery. The class in which he had invested such hope— whose 'true interests' he had declared always to be 'on the side of progress'—[103] had, during wartime, let him down badly. In February 1916 Connolly acknowledged, with 'shame and sorrow', that 'the evil influence upon large sections of the Irish working class of the bribes and promises of the enemy cannot be denied'. This

---

[97] 'Trust your Leaders!' (4 Dec. 1915), in *JCCW* ii. 117.

[98] *Socialism Made Easy* had contained Connolly's assertion that 'the conquest of political power by the working class waits upon the conquest of economic power, and must function through the economic organization' (O. D. Edwards and B. Ransom (eds.), *James Connolly: Selected Political Writings* (London, Cape, 1973), 285). Plainly, such an approach could not survive the outcome of the lock-out.

[99] In Mar. 1914 Connolly declared his support for those who felt that partition 'should be resisted with armed force if necessary' (*Forward*, 21 Mar. 1914). Cf. Ransom's claim that, 'From Connolly's point of view, the capitulation of the elected government to the Ulster irregulars in the form of the partition scheme, made a pre-emptive counter-strike against it by the military arms of the nationalist and labour movements inevitable' (B. Ransom, *Connolly's Marxism* (London, Pluto, 1980), 78).   [100] *Workers' Republic*, 22 Jan. 1916.

[101] *Connolly*, 144.

[102] B. Clifford, *James Connolly: An Adventurous Socialist* (Cork, Labour Comment, 1984), 10; *Workers' Republic* 4 Dec. 1915.

[103] 'Ireland and Ulster: An Appeal to the Working Class' (4 Apr. 1914) in *JCCW* i. 398.

class treachery undermined the 'incorruptible inheritors' thesis and required sacrificial atonement: 'deep in the heart of Ireland has sunk the sense of the degradation wrought upon its people—our lost brothers and sisters—so deep and humiliating that no agency less potent than the red tide of war on Irish soil will ever be able to enable the Irish race to recover its self-respect, or establish its national dignity'.[104] As David Howell has observed, 'In all belligerent countries, the vast majority of socialists and trade unionists supported their respective national governments.'[105] To Connolly's regret, the trenches in Flanders had been 'the graves of scores of thousands of young Irishmen' and, moreover, 'a very large proportion of these young Irishmen were born and reared in the slums and tenement houses of Dublin'.[106] The class in Ireland whose dependability had been central to Connolly's socialist republican thesis had, in the event of war, disappointed him. In his view, redemptive action was therefore required.

Contrary to the image outlined by inter-war republican socialists, therefore, Connolly's participation in the 1916 rebellion was the result of desperation, of the lack of viable strategic paths, and of the failure of his symbiotic republican socialist thesis. His involvement in the rebellion was the product not of the triumph of his ideas, but rather of their inadequacy.

The extensive debate concerning Connolly's 1916 activities has long historical roots. In 1919, Sean O'Casey attacked what he perceived to have been Connolly's pre-rising apostasy from the socialist faith, referring to his 'determined attachment to the principles enunciated by Sinn Fein and the Irish Volunteers, which were, in many instances, directly contrary to his lifelong teaching of socialism'. Connolly had, he asserted, 'stepped from the narrow byway of Irish socialism on to the broad and crowded highway of Irish Nationalism'.[107] Numerous defences against such attacks have been offered on Connolly's behalf. Anthony Coughlan has accused academic historians of tending to forget the context—'the work-burden and immediate concerns'—within which Connolly's ideas

---

[104] *Workers' Republic*, 5 Feb. 1916.   [105] *A Lost Left*, 128.

[106] 'The Slums and the Trenches' (26 Feb. 1916), in *JCCW* ii. 147. By 1916, large numbers of the ITGWU's 1914 membership had joined the British army (E. O'Connor, *A Labour History of Ireland, 1824–1960* (Dublin, Gill and Macmillan, 1992), 91).

[107] P. O Cathasaigh (S. O'Casey), *The Story of the Irish Citizen Army* (Dublin, Talbot, 1971; 1st edn. 1919), 52, 55.

and writings developed; they 'ignore such contexts when offering criticism of a particular text or drawing some academic conclusion from minor contradictions in argument or detail'.[108] In fact, appreciation of Connolly's personal setting is not absent from the academic literature.[109] More importantly, Coughlan's argument appears to contain a certain circularity, attempting as it does to excuse the inadequacy and incoherence of a historical figure's ideas on the ground that he/she was too busy acting upon those ideas to be able to appreciate their inadequacy or incoherence.

A more direct, though equally unconvincing, defence is that offered in Kieran Allen's survey of Connolly's politics. Having been critical of many aspects of Connolly's approach, Allen tries to retain a central element of his subject's thinking: 'Connolly's view that only the working class has any real interest in seeing through the struggle against imperialism remains fundamental.'[110] But, as has been shown, it was precisely Connolly's mistaken faith in the inherent and combined radicalism and separatism of the Irish working class which had contributed so significantly to the failure of his socialist republican thesis, and to his desperate participation in the 1916 rebellion.

Desmond Greaves's endorsement of Connolly's actions centred on his belief that the socialist leader had come to espouse a 'stages' view of Irish politics. In 1984, Greaves argued that socialism 'could not be achieved until the British left the Irish free to choose their own social system'.[111] In his biography of Connolly, Greaves had asserted that the 1916 leader 'held that the national revolution was a prerequisite of the socialist revolution', that having first distinguished these as 'the political and economic *aspects* of one process' he finally 'reached the conclusion that they were two stages of one democratic reorganization of society'.[112] In trying to fit Connolly rather too neatly into a 'stages' approach, Greaves actually misquoted his man. In the *Workers' Republic* in January 1916, Connolly had written that 'as the propertied classes have so shamelessly sold themselves to the enemy the economic

---

[108] *C. Desmond Greaves, 1913–88: An Obituary Essay* (Dublin, Irish Labour Hist. Soc., 1991; 1st edn. 1990), 20.   [109] See e.g. Howell, *A Lost Left*, 86.

[110] *Connolly*, 180.

[111] 'Connolly and Easter Week: A Rejoinder to John Newsinger', *Science and Society*, 48/2 (Summer 1984), 221.

[112] *The Life and Times of James Connolly* (London, Lawrence and Wishart, 1972; 1st edn. 1961), 425.

conscription of their property will cause few qualms to whosoever shall administer the Irish government in the first days of freedom'.[113] Greaves wrongly cited Connolly as having used the phrase, 'the first stage of freedom' —[114] a slip which conveniently fitted in with Greaves's 'stages' argument.

A more sensitive, less rigid, reading of Connolly's last days would suggest that, while he retained the conviction that the causes of labour and of the nation were intimately related,[115] he was forced by circumstance to compromise his socialist republican theory in favour of a practical emphasis on non-socialist, separatist insurrectionism. The Connolly of 1916 undoubtedly did view Ireland's independence as a prerequisite for the success of the Irish socialist cause;[116] but his involvement in the rebellion was less the result of deliberate, positive 'stages' insight than of desperation, the dictation of unfortunate circumstance, and the failure of his republican socialism. He retained socialist aspirations, but in practice it was nationalism which dominated his latter-day political career.

Lengthy treatment of Connolly and of 1916 has been necessary because Connolly's attempted fusion of Irish socialism and republicanism was the ideological foundation upon which inter-war republican socialists built their theories and projects. It is essential, therefore, to recognize the deficiencies in Connolly's thinking in order to understand the feebleness of the paradigmatic foundations upon which socialist republicans in the 1925–37 period were seeking to build.

With this in mind, three final points need to be made regarding Connolly. First, it would be wrong to read his previous experiences through the magnifying glass of 1916 fame. The above discussion has highlighted the inadequacy rather than the strength of Connolly's arguments and it is as the exponent of a failed socialist republican thesis that he should primarily be remembered. Connolly's electoral record had been far from encouraging,[117] and

[113] 'Economic Conscription' (15 Jan. 1916), in *JCCW* ii. 127.

[114] *The Life and Times*, 384.

[115] 'The cause of labour is the cause of Ireland, the cause of Ireland is the cause of labour. They cannot be dissevered' (Connolly, 'The Irish Flag' (8 Apr. 1916), in *JCCW* ii. 175).   [116] Edwards, *Connolly*, 123.

[117] J. W. Boyle, *The Irish Labour Movement in the Nineteenth Century* (Washington, Catholic University of America Press, 1988), 201; P. Murray, 'Electoral Politics and the Dublin Working Class before the First World War', *Saothar*, 6 (1980), 15.

while it is vital to concentrate on him as a starting-point for any serious evaluation of inter-war socialist republicanism, it would be quite wrong to overstate his pre-1916 importance to Irish politics more broadly.

Second, it is important to note that while Connolly had famously dismissed the value of nationalist achievement if it was not accompanied by socialist reorganization, his own legacy was that of strengthening a nationalist tradition which actually lacked his socialist emphasis. As Ruth Dudley Edwards has noted, Connolly 'was assumed with the other dead men into Irish patriotic martyrology, his greatest intellectual contribution, hibernicized Marxism, overlooked or purposely ignored'.[118] Even Connolly's most eminent successor on the republican left, Peadar O'Donnell, acknowledged that it had been possible for Connolly's socialism to be drowned in nationalist tears. Writing in 1933, O'Donnell claimed that Connolly was not presented as having seen 'that the final battleground for Irish freedom must be the revolutionary struggle of the Irish workers against Irish capitalism. If his socialism is ever mentioned, it is to admit a fault which the manner of his death redeemed!'[119]

Third, it is important to consider Connolly's legacy in terms of his latter-day endorsement of republican physical force. His comrade, William McMullen, later recorded that he had 'often heard Connolly say, in explanation of what he had in mind to do if given the chance—which did come in 1916—that every generation of Irishmen had given fight against the British occupation of Ireland'.[120] But it is indisputable that Connolly, here as in other aspects of his thinking, underwent a significant shift. In 1899 he had placed before his readers

the socialist Republican conception of the functions and uses of physical force in a popular movement. We neither exalt it into a principle nor repudiate it as something not to be thought of. . . . If the time should arrive when the party of progress finds its way to freedom barred by the stubborn greed of a possessing class entrenched behind the barriers of law and order; if the party of progress has indoctrinated the people at large with the new revolutionary conception of society and is therefore representative of the will of a majority of the nation; if it has exhausted

---

[118] *Connolly*, 143.
[119] Introduction, in B. O'Neill, *The War for the Land in Ireland* (London, Lawrence, 1933), 12–13.
[120] 'Open letter to Lord Craigavon' (n.d.), McMullen Papers, PP.

all the peaceful means at its disposal for the purpose of demonstrating to the people and their enemies that the new revolutionary ideas do possess the suffrage of the majority; then, but not till then, the party which represents the revolutionary idea is justified in taking steps to assume the powers of government, and in using the weapons of force to dislodge the usurping class or government in possession, and treating its members and supporters as usurpers and rebels against the constituted authorities always have been treated.[121]

These conditions did not exist in April 1916.

George Gilmore was right in his assertion that the Easter rebellion 'did not ... "bring the gun into politics" '.[122] But it did elevate physical force through practical emphasis and through the creation of a lasting myth of redemptive, sacrificial violence. Just as Connolly, in some of his writings, endorsed the celebratory cult of martyrdom,[123] so, too, by his own leading role in 1916, he contributed towards the elevation of the physical-force approach within Irish republican thinking. This is vital to an understanding of Connolly's true legacy for the republican left. For his latter-day insurrectionism—and subsequent martyrdom—undoubtedly served to strengthen a tradition of republicanism; but it was a tradition whose primary, militaristic focus was ill-suited to the mass, social emphasis which characterized inter-war socialist republican aspirations.

1917–1921

A national movement allied to the aspiring Irish capitalists with its ultimate goal a compromise with imperialism: such was the doctrine of Arthur Griffith.

Sean Murray, *The Irish Revolt: 1916 and After*[124]

S[inn] F[ein] is not a solid, cast-iron thing like English parties. It is just a jumble of people of all classes, creeds, and opinions, who are all ready to suffer and die for Ireland...

Constance Markievicz, 17 August 1919[125]

---

[121] 'Physical Force in Irish Politics' (22 July 1899), in *JCCW* i. 337–8.
[122] G. Gilmore, *The Relevance of James Connolly in Ireland Today* (Dublin, Fodhla Printing Co., n.d. [1970?]), 3–4.
[123] Connolly, 'The Manchester Martyrs' (20 Nov. 1915) in *JCCW* ii. 106–8; Connolly, 'The Irish Flag', ibid. 173.   [124] *The Irish Revolt*, 13.
[125] *Prison Letters of Countess Markievicz* (London, Virago, 1987; 1st edn. 1934), 238.

Looking back on the Anglo-Irish war of 1919–21, Peadar O'Donnell acknowledged 'a sense of shame that we betrayed those people who entered wholeheartedly into the independence movement in the belief that the British had to go so that the Ireland of the poor could come into its inheritance'.[126] Writing in 1922, he had asserted that, under the posthumous influence of Connolly:

The Irish political struggle came under a new light. Out of the ranks of workers and peasants the Irish Republican Army grew. The imperialism of the gombeen man was plain to the workers from their new class-viewpoint, and the national inspiration merged into the social longings and hopes of the workers. The workers became the insurrectionary nation.[127]

This vision of the independence movement as the vehicle for expressing and achieving the aspirations of the socially oppressed was at the heart of O'Donnell's thinking. He himself was a full-time IRA man during the 1919–21 conflict, but he later claimed to have been imbued with an ulterior social purpose:

I went on full time IRA work in charge of an active service unit. I carried with me my Liberty Hall ideas. Indeed, I think there never was a time when I did not see the struggle 'to break the connection with England' as a preliminary to freeing the Ireland of the poor from hardship. I saw it as the necessary condition for ensuring that the poor would really come into their own.[128]

Informing O'Donnell's outlook was the view that British political control over Ireland was inextricably interwoven with her economic exploitation of the island and with the economic relations existing there. So, too, the undoing of the conquest must, according to O'Donnell, have an economic as well as a political aspect. Writing in 1932, he criticized Michael Collins on the grounds that the latter had 'confused the conquest with the mere occupation of the country with British soldiers' and 'failed to recognize that the military occupation was merely to make the imperial exploitation possible'.[129]

This emphasis on social as well as political reconquest carried with it hints of a native-versus-settler paradigm. But the direction in which O'Donnell wanted the theory to point was one which

---

[126] Quoted in McInerney, *O'Donnell*, 206.
[127] *Workers' Republic*, 26 Aug. 1922.
[128] Quoted in McInerney, *O'Donnell*, 39.   [129] *The Gates*, 31.

would lead towards a class-based reading of the 1919–21 conflict. The struggle had been given 'its mass momentum', he argued, by the 'small farm countryside and the city workers'. In contrast, 'the well-to-do farmers were on the side line; in Donegal they were hostile.'[130] With reference to a partly autobiographical character in one of his novels, O'Donnell didactically observed: 'He puzzled over it. People of property were so often against the national struggle, or joined it only in seeming. What a pity we could not collect those vitally Irish, and have the new Irish nation grow out of them.'[131] According to socialist republican theory, the Anglo-Irish war had been a period of radical potential, social as well as national. But this potential had not been developed, the rank and file having been held back by unworthy leaders. Echoing Connolly's concern that rank-and-file radicalism could be thwarted by corrupt or cautious leaders,[132] inter-war socialist republicans held that leaderships, labour and republican, had frustrated the radical potential of these years. The labour movement had, in O'Donnell's view, committed a 'national crime' by 'opting out of the leadership of the struggle in the 1918–21 period'.[133] Labour 'should have demanded their quota of seats, as part of the inheritance won for them by Connolly, but they neither had the willpower nor the calibre of women and men, necessary to demand and to fill these positions, which they should have sought from 1918 onwards'.[134]

If labour leaders had played a less than glorious role, then republican leaders were also demonized in the socialist republican thesis. George Gilmore lamented the fact that republican authorities had prevented socially radical activity during this period.[135] In O'Donnell's view, the republican government had 'worked against those changes for which the people hungered'.[136] The Anglo-Irish war had, O'Donnell argued, been 'a very innocent movement ... Radical demands that could have moved whole counties into action were frowned on. All the leadership wanted was a change from British to Irish government: they wanted no change in the basis of society.'[137]

---

[130] Quoted in McInerney, *O'Donnell*, 32, 40.

[131] *Storm: A Story of the Irish War* (Dublin, Talbot, n.d. [1926?]), 121.

[132] Howell, *A Lost Left*, 85.   [133] Quoted in McInerney, *O'Donnell*, 213.

[134] Quoted in MacEoin (ed.), *Survivors*, 23.

[135] *Labour and the Republican Movement* ([Dublin?], Repsol, 1966), 13.

[136] 'Tourists' Guide to Irish Politics', *The Bell*, 14/5 (Aug. 1947), 2.

[137] Quoted in McInerney, *O'Donnell*, 42.

Socialist republicans particularly focused their hostile attention on Arthur Griffith, who was held to epitomize the multi-class, pro-capitalist nationalism against which republican socialists rebelled. In discussing Griffith's politics, George Gilmore gave expression to a central tenet of socialist republican thinking: the conviction that capitalist interests and Irish republican aspirations were fundamentally incompatible: ' "Irish freedom", to Griffith, meant freedom for Irish industrialists to manœuvre to greater advantage within the imperial system. An independent Republic had no place in his plans.' Noting that Griffith 'placed especial emphasis upon freedom for Irish capitalists to develop industrially behind a wall of protective tariffs', Gilmore acknowledged that the Anglo-Irish war had been 'fought in a political atmosphere dominated, not by Connolly's mind, but by Griffith's mind'.[138] In O'Donnell's rueful words, there had been 'too many like Griffith in Sinn Fein'.[139] From the socialist republican perspective, this situation had proved disastrous. Sean Murray observed that Griffith had taken 'a directly opposite view to Connolly'; in describing Griffith's outlook, Murray highlighted the distance between the Sinn Fein leader's thinking and his own uncompromising, revolutionary, anti-capitalist brand of republicanism:

Griffith claimed that there was no social problem in Ireland apart from foreign rule, and that the solution was to be found in the Repeal of the Union politically and the creation of Irish industry without any change in the social system.... A national movement allied to the aspiring Irish capitalists with its ultimate goal a compromise with imperialism: such was the doctrine of Arthur Griffith.[140]

During the famous 1913 Dublin lock-out, *Sinn Fein* had carried a piece in which Griffith had addressed 'the labour question':

When a cry echoes in this country today that capitalism and not England is the enemy, the reply is obvious—the capitalism that denied its obligation to the moral law and the law of the nation—the capitalism that enunciated the doctrine of non-interference with its operations as a binding commandment on states and nations—that concept of capitalism had its germ in no Celtic or Latin civilization, but in the Teutonic Hansards and its modern development the world owes to England.

---

[138] *Labour and the Republican Movement*, 4, 7, 13.
[139] Quoted in McInerney, *O'Donnell*, 214.   [140] *The Irish Revolt*, 13.

It was not capitalism, he asserted, but 'the abuse of capitalism' which oppressed labour. It was not in the destruction of the capitalist, but in 'his subjection to the law of the state' that labour would be 'delivered from its oppression and restored to all its rights'.

I affirm that the evils of the social system, as they exist in this country and in Great Britain, are wholly due to English policy and government, and that that policy and that government are partly responsible for those evils, as they exist, though in a modified form, outside the radius of the British flag. I deny that socialism is a remedy for the existent evils or any remedy at all. I deny that capital and labour are in their nature antagonistic—I assert that they are essential and complementary the one to the other.[141]

Griffith's perspective was indeed, therefore, radically different from that of republican socialists. His opposition to the 1913 Dublin strikers brought him within range of a rather menacingly phrased statement of O'Donnell's from 1927, a statement which epitomized the latter's view of the relation between national and social questions: 'Every Irishman or woman not in sympathy with the Dublin strike was unhealthy nationally. Every active opponent was an active imperialist.'[142] Griffith was held to exemplify capitalist nationalism, with its emphasis on multi-class, patriotic harmony. His outlook represented the antithesis of the socialist version of republicanism, which stressed that anti-capitalist class conflict lay at the heart of true Irish separatism. Accordingly, republican socialists attacked the suggestion that to emphasize social conflicts and objectives in some way sullied the selfless quality of the patriotic struggle. O'Donnell later argued that

The Irish people were 'up again' in the period 1918–21, deeply stirred, gay, and therefore, easily misled. Despite the fact that it was 'the Ireland of the poor' that was 'up', they bowed to the teaching that the fight was for pure ideals—no earthly stain of greed or gain. Landlords, walled estates, in short the accumulated loot of the garrison, was safe. There was a special warning against agrarian unrest from Sinn Fein.[143]

He had expressed similar views, through a fictional medium, in his didactic novel, *The Knife*. Against the background of (Anglo-Irish war) Lagan land 'troubles', a Sinn Fein representative has been

---

[141] *Sinn Fein*, 25 Oct. 1913.   [142] *An Phoblacht*, 26 Nov. 1927.
[143] Quoted in McInerney, *O'Donnell*, 31–2.

sent from Dublin to attend a local meeting. The Dublin man claims that ' "It is only right to remind you that we are fighting for freedom, not for potatoes or oats, not to save a few pounds a year in rent, but to drive the British out of the country bag and baggage, and then the Irish government will do justice to everybody." '
To this the novel's heroine responds:

'I'm all against the Dublin man. I'm all for breaking the grip of the landlord when we have the power . . . Tell this man from Dublin to tell our government up there that it's not only the English we want to drive out, we want to throw off all the burdens the English put on our backs . . . Let us drop the burdens first and we'll fight all the better for being free from them, and all the harder to make sure they will never be put back on us.' Cheer after cheer burst from the crowd as she disappeared.[144]

Plainly, full appreciation of the socio-economic context of the Anglo-Irish war is vital if one is to grasp the roots and dynamics of the conflict. To take one obvious example, constraints on emigration (enforced by the First World War) contributed to the turbulence of the revolutionary period. In David Fitzpatrick's words, 'young men and women who would otherwise have been making their way up foreign social ladders instead devoted their enforced leisure and indignation to collective protest at home'.[145] Peadar O'Donnell himself acknowledged that 'If there had not been war in the way, I likely would have followed other members of my family to the US.'[146] Moreover, recent research has unveiled the extent and nature of important class gradations, fissures, and tensions during this period.[147]

In the 1930s, Ernie O'Malley recollected that 'Gentility flourished easily in Ireland: very little wealth nourished it. In the towns tuppence-ha'penny looked down on tuppence, and throughout the country the grades in social difference were as numerous as the layers of an onion.'[148] An earlier O'Malley comment, in reference to his time on IRA active service during the Anglo-Irish war, points in a similar direction: 'Democracy is more snobbish in its

---

[144] *The Knife* (Dublin, Irish Humanities Centre, 1980; 1st edn. 1930), 150–4.
[145] 'Ireland Since 1870', in R. F. Foster (ed.), *The Oxford Illustrated History of Ireland* (Oxford, OUP, 1989), 215.   [146] Quoted in McInerney, *O'Donnell*, 241.
[147] P. Bew, 'Sinn Fein, Agrarian Radicalism and the War of Independence, 1919–21', in D. G. Boyce (ed.), *The Revolution in Ireland, 1879–1923* (Basingstoke, Macmillan, 1988).   [148] *On Another Man's Wound*, 24.

shades of distinction than aristocracy.'[149] Not only were class distinction and tension crucial features of the 1919–21 conflict, but the socialist republican analysis was certainly accurate in so far as it identified the majority of republican leaders from those years as socially conservative. Dáil Éireann's proclamation of June 1920, 'that the present time when the Irish people are locked in a life and death struggle with their traditional enemy, is ill chosen for the stirring up of strife amongst our fellow countrymen', establishes the prevailing attitude: that class conflict would disrupt (rather than strengthen, clarify, and define) the national struggle.[150]

Socialist republicans were undoubtedly right to comment on the inadequacy of interpretations of the Anglo-Irish war which neglected social and economic forces.[151] Moreover, certain aspects of the inter-war socialist republican thesis have subsequently been endorsed by notable commentators.[152] But the fact remains that the socialist republican reading of the 1919–21 conflict can be effectively challenged at numerous points. As we have seen, O'Donnell argued that the momentum of the republican struggle in these years had been provided by oppressed classes, classes which had perceived that struggle as the vehicle through which to express and achieve the radical restructuring of Irish society. This view is simply false. Despite the anxieties expressed by the authorities, regarding the threat of social and nationalist agitation coalescing,[153] it is clear that the roots and dynamics of socially radical, militant labour activity on the one hand, and republican separatist struggle on the other, were largely autonomous. In his pithy, valuable study of Irish syndicalism, Emmet O'Connor has argued convincingly

that the explosion of industrial conflict from 1917 to 1923 stemmed primarily from social and economic forces created by wartime conditions,

[149] To Childers, 26 Nov.–1 Dec. 1923, in English and O'Malley (eds.), *Prisoners*, 77.

[150] D. Bradley, *Farm Labourers: Irish Struggle 1900–76* (Belfast, Athol, 1988), 55. Cf. Bew, 'Sinn Fein', 229–30.

[151] See e.g. Gilmore's comments concerning Dorothy Macardle in *Labour and the Republican Movement*, 10–11.

[152] E. Strauss, *Irish Nationalism and British Democracy* (London, Methuen, 1951), 264; C. D. Greaves, *Liam Mellows and the Irish Revolution* (London, Lawrence and Wishart, 1971), 147.

[153] '*War Cabinet: Sinn Fein Activity*' (24 Feb. 1918), in *Sinn Fein Activities, 1915–20: British Government Reports*, Files of the Dept. of the Taoiseach, NA S 14049; Ross to Long, 19 Feb. 1919, Bonar Law Papers, HLRO BL 96/10/8.

the post-war boom, and the slump that followed. Certainly, the break-down of political order facilitated direct action and influenced the char-acter of industrial relations; but it did not inspire or determine the nature of class conflict. In its values, its tactics, its goals, labour operated inde-pendently of the Republican campaign.[154]

Such autonomy is hardly consistent with the O'Donnellite argu-ment that the desire for radical, class-conflicting, socially revolu-tionary activity, and the aspiration towards an independent Irish republic, shared their roots and dynamics.

In his most recent book, O'Connor has made clear the de-tachment of Labour and Sinn Fein politics during this 1919–21 period.[155] George Gilmore stated that 'Ernie O'Malley has de-scribed the attitude of the IRA volunteers as being, generally speaking, vaguely sympathetic towards the cause of Labour, and that, I think, was about the size of it.'[156] In fact, O'Malley's de-claration that 'the Volunteer spirit in essentials was hostile to Labour'[157] points in a different direction. Indeed, the bulk of the evidence tends to suggest that distance (or even tension) rather than synergy characterized the labour–republican relationship of these years. Asked whether there had been much contact between republican military organizers and the labour movement in this period, O'Donnell himself emphatically acknowledged: 'No. None. None. No. None direct. No. No organized contact of any kind. It just happened to be casual. Accidental, really.'[158] Although labour forces were, on occasions, deployed to nationalist purpose, this did not indicate that the republican movement had become infused with a spirit of anti-capitalist class conflict. The famous 1920 rail-way strike was, according to Townshend, a 'notable contribution' to the republican attack on the legitimacy of British rule in Ireland. But this did not signify that labour read this republican attack in terms of the ulterior purpose of revolutionizing Irish society along anti-capitalist lines, or according to Irish class conflict. Indeed, a public appeal by the ILPTUC National Executive during the course of the strike emphasized that labour did not view this contribution

---

[154] E. O'Connor, *Syndicalism in Ireland 1917–23* (Cork, Cork University Press, 1988), pp. xviii–xix.   [155] *Labour History*, 106.
[156] *Labour and the Republican Movement*, 13.
[157] *On Another Man's Wound*, 59.
[158] Cormac O'Malley interview with Peadar O'Donnell and George Gilmore (Oct. 1970), Cormac O'Malley Papers, PP.

or the nationalist conflict in terms of class conflict. Quite the reverse: 'It is not in their interests alone, but on behalf of the whole nation, that these men have been willing to risk their means of livelihood.'[159]

Significantly, where people did endorse both revolutionary social aspirations and republican commitment, there was considerable evidence of tension and confusion in their thinking. In a latter-day interview, George Gilmore commented that 'Our whole movement was killed by the fact that we don't define things.'[160] Prior to this, he had claimed that Constance Markievicz had been unique among Dáil deputies involved in the treaty debates in her appreciation of 'the realities' behind the 1921 agreement.[161] But close inspection of Markievicz's thinking during the revolutionary period demonstrates that she was, in fact, guilty of precisely that blurred definition which Gilmore held responsible for the collapse of the republican movement. Committed to 'the Workers' Republic',[162] she none the less gave wholehearted support to Sinn Fein, an organization which, as we have seen, endorsed conservative social policies. She gushed enthusiastically when discussing Eamon de Valera, a figure whose social vision certainly did not encompass class struggle leading towards an Irish workers' republic. In a revealing passage, written in 1919, Markievicz alluded to differences over economics with an insouciance indicative of her woolly thinking: 'I belong to both organizations [Sinn Fein and Labour], for my conception of a free Ireland is economic as well as political: some agree with me, some don't, but it's not a sore point.'[163]

Just as Nora Connolly O'Brien underplayed the differences between the Irish Volunteers and her father's ICA,[164] so, too, Markievicz achieved only a blurred focus when considering the social aspects of the Anglo-Irish war. Even in the rare instances in which people did have both republican and socially revolutionary aspirations, therefore, there could be considerable tension and confusion in their thinking. The republican socialist notion that

---

[159] C. Townshend, 'The Irish Railway Strike of 1920: Industrial Action and Civil Resistance in the Struggle for Independence', *IHS* 21/83 (Mar. 1979), 268, 282.

[160] Jennifer FitzGerald interview with George Gilmore, 27 May 1985.

[161] *Labour and the Republican Movement*, 14.

[162] Markievicz, *Prison Letters*, 101. The authorities had been concerned, in 1919, by Markievicz's radical connections: *Constance G. Markievicz: Letter from Russian Consul, Glasgow, 1919*, Files of the Dept. of the Taoiseach, NA S 14058.

[163] *Prison Letters*, 238, 243.   [164] Connolly, *The Unbroken Tradition*, 7.

socially revolutionary aspirations fuelled, impelled, and determined the republican struggle implies a synergy denied by the historical evidence. Indeed, the relation between class and the national question was far more complicated than republican socialist theory suggested. The notion that working-class interests were tied to an anti-capitalist project, and that they implied a socially driven republican separatism, was most spectacularly contradicted by the case of the unionist working class in the north-east. The naïve assumption that the working class was implicitly anti-capitalist[165] was tied to a simplistic, prescriptive vision of the attitude by which northern workers ought, in the republican socialist view, to have been characterized: 'The natural, normal task for the Belfast workers in common with the workers of the rest of Ireland is to lead the struggle for freedom.'[166] That working-class interests might be identified with, rather than against, the British connection appears to have been too heretical an argument for serious consideration.

Socialist republican myopia in relation to unionism will be addressed in detail later. The vital point, at this stage, is to note that even in terms of those who were committed to the nationalist cause, the republican socialist theory is demonstrably inadequate. Much of the republican fire in these years was, in fact, generated by the Catholic middle classes, classes which—according to socialist republican dogma—could not be truly, reliably republican.[167] At an individual level it is possible to construct a variety of interpretations to explain the relation between middle-class background and republican commitment. Rebellion against bourgeois family culture;[168] romantic, literary influences drawn from a middle-class background;[169] an alternative, republican professionalism fulfilling class-influenced aspirations[170]—each of these considerations can

---

[165] Andrew Boyd, a long-time friend of O'Donnell, commented ironically and sceptically on his friend's naïve approach: 'He *believed* in the proletariat' (Interview with the author, Belfast, 24 Sept. 1992).

[166] Gilmore, *The Irish Republican Congress* (1978; 1st edn. 1935), 34.

[167] Ibid. 48–9.

[168] George Gilmore obituary, *Irish Times*, 21 June 1985; Anthony Coughlan, interview with the author, Dublin, 5 Feb. 1988; *Irish Democrat*, July 1985; *New Hibernia*, July 1985.

[169] Sheila Humphreys, interview with the author, Dublin, 26 Feb. 1987; Cronin, *Ryan*, 19.

[170] O'Malley, *On Another Man's Wound*, 27, 52–3; English and O'Malley (eds.), *Prisoners*, 25, 71–2, 77, 83–4; O'Malley to FitzGerald, 25 Aug. 1921, FitzGerald Papers, ADUCD P80; T. Donohue, 'Memorandum re Ernie O'Malley', 12 Aug.

be seen to have played a role. Nor are such individual sketches open to the charge of being exceptional: large numbers of fully committed republicans, both leaders and supporters, were drawn from classes which should not—according to socialist republican theory—have provided solid republican material. As Bew, Gibbon, and Patterson have noted, the Anglo-Irish war 'clearly demonstrated that important sectors of the rural and urban bourgeoisie could play a leading role in the national struggle'.[171] Tom Garvin has observed the importance of the petty bourgeoisie in the profile of Sinn Fein support, and has, more recently, provided useful evidence concerning the practical ways in which economic considerations could lead non-working-class people into the ranks of republican supporters.[172] Even if one is sceptical about claims such as Ernie O'Malley's, that there were 'no class distinctions' in his Dublin Volunteer company, it is clear that the ranks of the movement were drawn eclectically from a variety of classes.[173]

If the middle classes confounded socialist republican theory, so, too, did the lower orders. The spectacular failure of the republican left's thesis in relation to the unionist working class has already been mentioned. It is important to note that republican Ireland also disappointed the O'Donnellites. Even if one identified oneself with a sense of social oppression, this did not necessitate that one's republicanism would be characterized by any socially revolutionary intention. The belligerent Dan Breen firmly located himself as one of the Ireland of the poor.[174] But his attitude toward socially radical projects was anything but O'Donnellite. Breen once informed O'Donnell that, had anyone during the Anglo-Irish war talked of dividing up estates in his (Breen's) area, then he would have had them shot.[175] Plainly, allowance must be made for regional and personal variations. But the Anglo-Irish war undeniably demonstrated, as astute commentators have observed, that

1990, in the possession of the author; M. G. Valiulis, *Portrait of a Revolutionary: General Richard Mulcahy and the Founding of the Irish Free State* (Blackrock, Irish Academic Press, 1992), 8.   [171] *The State in Northern Ireland*, 36.
[172] *Nationalist Revolutionaries*, 51; 'The Takeover of Local Politics by the Dail Government, 1920–2' (unpublished MS, 1992), 3–5.
[173] O'Malley, *On Another Man's Wound*, 50–1.
[174] *My Fight for Irish Freedom* (Dublin, Anvil, 1964; 1st edn. 1924), 12.
[175] J. P. McHugh, 'Voices of the Rearguard: A Study of *An Phoblacht*—Irish Republican Thought in the Post-Revolutionary Era, 1923–37', MA thesis (UCD, 1983), 34.

the national struggle 'could enlist the support of rural and urban working classes without putting forward any socially radical aims'.[176]

The republican movement in this period reflected a desire for cross-class support and inter-class harmony.[177] Promises were made to a variety of classes[178] and over-emphasis on social questions—above all, on social conflict between Irish classes—was viewed as a disruptive distraction. The point to stress is that this was not merely the view of republican leaders, but was endorsed by vast numbers of the multi-class rank and file. A weight of research has established the socially eclectic nature of republican enthusiasm in these years,[179] and, in the *un*scholarly words of Constance Markievicz, Sinn Fein was 'a jumble of people of all classes, creeds, and opinions'.[180]

In his valuable *Dublin Made Me*, C. S. Andrews instructively claimed that 'We Catholics varied socially among ourselves but we all had the common bond, whatever our economic condition, of being second-class citizens.'[181] The influence of Catholic thinking on the republican movement in these years is indisputable,[182] and it is also true that what Garvin has referred to as 'status resentment'[183] played a significant role in the Catholic republicanism of this period. The important point is to note that, just as Andrews's telling statement would suggest, the cohesive strength of Catholic nationalist rhetoric and experience succeeded, for the most part, in overcoming the class fissures to which republican socialists longingly looked.

Popular endorsement of pan-class republican harmony brings us to the next stage in the left republican argument, namely, the contention that a radical rank and file was thwarted by unrepresentative leaders, and that, as a consequence, the revolutionary potential of these years was squandered. Traces have been identified of differing perspectives between labour leaders and their rank and file. But as an interpretative mechanism for understanding these years, the O'Donnellite thesis is simply unconvincing.

---

[176] Bew, Gibbon, and Patterson, *The State in Northern Ireland*, 36.
[177] D. Fitzpatrick, *Politics and Irish Life 1913–21: Provincial Experience of War and Revolution* (Dublin, Gill and Macmillan, 1977), 158.
[178] *Nationality*, 30 Nov. 1918.
[179] Garvin, *Nationalist Revolutionaries*, 51, 174; McHugh, 'Voices', 24.
[180] Markievicz, *Prison Letters*, 238.
[181] *Dublin Made Me: An Autobiography* (Cork, Mercier, 1979), 10.
[182] Garvin, *Nationalist Revolutionaries*, 57.   [183] Ibid. 90.

Writing in 1947 about the Anglo-Irish war, O'Donnell claimed (in relation to the social aspects of the conflict) that 'every act of the Republican government made war on the people's vision'.[184] Thus we are presented by O'Donnell with a republican movement whose fire centre and momentum were to be found among the oppressed classes—classes possessed of a vision which beheld the republic in terms of social revolution and emancipation. Yet, according to this socialist republican thesis, we are also encouraged to assume that, throughout this conflict, the republican movement was led, defined, and (ultimately) betrayed by leaders whose class background and class-determined outlook were the antitheses of those of the bulk of the movement's personnel. This rather implausible model of leader–rank-and-file relations places tremendous weight on the notion of the masses being, in O'Donnell's rather patronizing words, 'easily misled'.[185] Certainly there is evidence to suggest that, in relation to working-class militancy during these years, a more complicated leader–rank-and-file model is appropriate, with the rank and file being able, to a significant degree, to determine the pace and nature of activity.[186] As has been shown, members of the working classes were indeed prepared to endorse a republicanism which was characterized by social conservatism rather than radicalism, and by a desire for inter-class harmony rather than for class conflict. The suggestion that they did so blindly, mistakenly, or because they were misled implies a staggering degree of popular myopia regarding the social quality of the brand of nationalism which they were supporting.

In particular, the implication that the lower classes were so gullible and short-sighted with regard to social realities sits awkwardly with the simultaneous socialist republican argument that it was precisely the acute recognition, by these same people, of the intersection between social change and republican aspiration which had given the independence struggle its mass momentum. It is far more plausible to argue that the classes whose republicanism O'Donnell interpreted in terms of socially revolutionary aspirations were not, for the most part, motivated by any such social radicalism. Those who did feel that their social interests conflicted sufficiently with republican orthodoxy abstained from involvement.[187] So, too,

---

[184] 'Tourists' Guide', 2.   [185] Quoted in McInerney, *O'Donnell*, 31.
[186] O'Connor, *Syndicalism*, pp. xix, 33, 38.
[187] Fitzpatrick, *Politics and Irish Life*, 120.

those who participated in the multi-class republican movement of these years should be read as having endorsed the class-harmonious ethos which republican socialists so lamented. As Michael Laffan has observed, it was not merely the leaders of Irish nationalism who held that an emphasis on programmatic social change would have been a disruptive distraction from the national objective.[188]

Thus, the contention that 1919–21 were years of wasted, socially revolutionary potential is highly questionable. The post-1916 growth in trade union membership and the intensification of Irish strike activity from 1915 onwards[189] should not be confused with the type of socially revolutionary potential claimed in republican socialist arguments. Certainly, Bolshevism was out of the question.[190] Indeed, close scrutiny of the strike activity of these years demonstrates precisely how atypical revolutionary socialist aspirations were during the period. Peadar O'Donnell's desire for 'the complete change of society'[191] was far from representative. Mitchell has noted that Irish trade unionists 'were not socialists';[192] and O'Donnell himself hinted as much when he stated, in reference to his work as an ITGWU organizer, that 'I often settled strikes without giving up my socialism'.[193] O'Donnell claimed of the post-1916 period that 'With a rapidity that was truly marvellous town after town founded its branch of Connolly's Union and founded it more on the inspiration of the ideals his death explained than on the promise of increased wages.'[194] But, as O'Connor observes of this period, strikes were, in fact, 'usually about wages'.[195] Dan Bradley has claimed, in his discussion of Irish farm labourers, that 'the campaign for a few shillings here and the struggle to work one hour per day less there' was revolutionary in that it aimed 'to raise the standard of living of the rural worker'. This is plausible enough. But the

[188] M. Laffan, ' "Labour Must Wait": Ireland's Conservative Revolution', in P. J. Corish (ed.), *Radicals, Rebels and Establishments* (Belfast, Appletree, 1985), 220.

[189] O'Connor, *Syndicalism*, 23; D. Fitzpatrick, 'Strikes in Ireland, 1914–21', *Saothar*, 6 (1980), 28.

[190] Despite Nora Connolly's enthusiasm (Markievicz, *Prison Letters*, 257) and Desmond Greaves's rather woolly statement that 'the Irish people gave instinctive support' to the Bolsheviks after their seizure of power (Greaves, *Liam Mellows*, 142), Bolshevism was not a realistic option. As O'Connor notes, 'Bolshevism . . . was unfamiliar and rarely an effective weapon' (E. O'Connor, 'Agrarian Unrest and the Labour Movement in County Waterford 1917–23', *Saothar*, 6 (1980), 55); cf. H. Patterson, 'Fianna Fail and the Working Class: The Origins of the Enigmatic Relationship', *Saothar*, 13 (1988), 83.   [191] *Monkeys*, 9.

[192] *Labour in Irish Politics 1890–1930: The Irish Labour Movement in an Age of Revolution* (Dublin, Irish Univ. Press, 1974), 291.   [193] *Monkeys*, 24.

[194] *Workers' Republic*, 26 Aug. 1922.   [195] *Syndicalism*, 38.

amelioration of conditions within a capitalistic system, which Bradley's evidence shows to have been the central objective of most of the strike activity which he discusses, was an entirely different project from the socialistic destruction and recreation of society envisaged by O'Donnell.[196]

Claims regarding the supposedly revolutionary potential contained within these years are given superficial sustenance by the prevalence of extreme rhetoric.[197] In the context of a later struggle, O'Donnell was to note that mere declarations were useless, and that it was 'the nature of the struggle' that was important.[198] This provides the key to understanding the coexistence of socially revolutionary rhetoric with far more cautious, conservative action during the 1919–21 period. The real test of revolutionary commitment and potential was not to be found in declarations, which were often not pursued.[199] The centre of social and political gravity must be established by reference to the actions against which radical words can be tested. Liam Cahill's assertion that Dáil Éireann's 1919 Democratic Programme 'was far from being a total reflection of Sinn Fein's rather conservative economic and social thinking'[200] has recently been challenged. Referring to Cahill's argument, D. R. O'Connor Lysaght suggests: 'This was what the survivors of the Dáil would have liked people to believe in the years of political conservatism after 1923. Their papers (notably Mulcahy's) tell a different tale.'[201] In fact, the most serious student to date of Mulcahy's papers, Valiulis, has argued that the 1919 Democratic Programme 'was not actually reflective of the type of society a majority of the representatives actually envisioned'. Acknowledging that the Programme 'represented a kind of utopian vision which some nationalist leaders would cling to', Valiulis clearly points out, 'Beyond endorsing an ideal, the majority of the leaders of the revolutionary movement were unwilling to involve themselves in social and economic issues.'[202] It is also crucial to appreciate that the Programme's vague social radicalism 'steered clear of any real commitment to socialist theory'.[203]

---

[196] Bradley, *Farm Labourers*, 43–4, 47–50, 55.   [197] Ibid. 54.
[198] *An Phoblacht*, 7 Feb. 1931.   [199] O'Connor, *Syndicalism*, 67.
[200] *Forgotten Revolution: Limerick Soviet 1919—A Threat to British Power in Ireland* (Dublin, O'Brien, 1990), 28.
[201] Review of Cahill, *Forgotten Revolution*, *Saothar*, 16 (1991), 76.
[202] *Mulcahy*, 34–5.
[203] C. Townshend, *The British Campaign in Ireland 1919–21: The Development of Political and Military Policies* (Oxford, OUP, 1975), 15.

Two further points need to be made regarding the republican socialist claim of radical revolutionary potential during the independence struggle. First, the stress placed on Labour's abstention from the 1918 UK general election needs to be set in appropriate historical context. O'Donnell's suggestion that Labour should have 'demanded their quota of seats' overestimates the strength of Labour's bargaining position, particularly given the evidence of local determination, among Labour supporters, to vote Sinn Fein.[204] Moreover, the 1918 election episode tends to underline the enormous distance which existed between Labour's vision and that characteristic of O'Donnellite socialist republicanism. Anxiety at the prospect of being left out in the unconstitutional cold with Sinn Fein (and at being tied, as O'Connor puts it, to the wheel of the republic) was evident in Labour circles, but ran entirely contrary to O'Donnellite thinking.[205] Indeed, not only did the republican socialist analysis overstate the importance of the 1918 abstention in determining Labour's subsequent political weakness;[206] it also implied a greater ideological affinity than actually existed between republican socialists on the one hand and the bulk of Labour leaders and supporters on the other. O'Donnell suggested that Labour should claim the Connolly inheritance; but Connolly's republican socialism had been atypical within the labour movement—a fact reflected by Labour's awkwardness in responding to his fatal 1916 gesture.[207]

Second, republican socialist rhetoric tended to blur the regional variations vital to any proper understanding of class and social conflicts in this period. It is significant that Paul Bew, a scholar who has delineated patterns of local Irish conflict in these years, has so emphatically denied that there existed the potential for mass, collective, social rebellion of the kind envisaged by O'Donnell and by authors such as Strauss.[208]

Class was important in helping to determine and define the conflicts of the 1917–21 period; but republican socialist readings of the nature of such class influence were seriously misconceived. Looking back on the years from the Easter rebellion to the 1921 Anglo-Irish truce, O'Donnell suggested: 'The Republic having been proclaimed, the people set themselves to give it reality, asking

---

[204] Cahill, *Forgotten Revolution*, 20.   [205] O'Connor, *Labour History*, 103–4.
[206] Howell, *A Lost Left*, 153.   [207] O'Connor, *Syndicalism*, 84.
[208] Bew, 'Sinn Fein', 234.

themselves many questions. They wanted a better life, and they wanted to know how to shape the Republic to secure it.'[209] As has been demonstrated, he and his fellow socialist republicans misread the class dynamics involved in this process.

Moreover, it should be noted that two of the defining ideological forces present in the Anglo-Irish conflict, the physical force ethic and the emphasis on spirituality, were anything but class-specific. Though their appeal would be refracted through the prism of an individual's particular social background, their functional value was enhanced precisely by the fact that this appeal could straddle a variety of classes. The left republican interpretation of Anglo-Irish war republicanism—that it was driven by the class-conflicting impulses of the oppressed classes—is further undermined if one recognizes the central role played within that republicanism by the class-straddling, socially inclusive, integrative ethics of physical force and of nationalist spirituality. Furthermore, as with Connolly's incongruous participation in the 1916 rebellion, integral involvement in (and subsequent celebration of) Anglo-Irish war republicanism was an inconsistent strategy for those imbued with socialist republican vision. The weighty physical force emphasis clashed with the notion that mass social mobilization should instead take centre stage; the stress on spirituality contradicted the essentially materialist teleology of republican socialist thinking. The fact that both physical force and nationalist spirituality had a pan-class appeal and a class-integrating effect further clarifies the inappropriateness of inter-war republican socialist celebration of the war of independence.

First, then, spirituality. Terence MacSwiney's anti-material sentiments have already been noted, and are further evident in romantic passages such as the following: 'We shall rouse the world from a wicked dream of material greed, of tyrannical power, of corrupt and callous politics to the wonder of a regenerated spirit, a new and beautiful dream; and we shall establish our state in a true freedom that will endure for ever.'[210] Constance Markievicz's smug, self-deluding declaration from 1918—'Thank God we are not a materialistic nation!'—[211] establishes the flavour of much republican idealism in this period. That it was essentially self-deceiving, disguising the social realities and impulses which

---

[209] O'Donnell, 'Tourists' Guide', 1. [210] *Principles*, 25.
[211] *Prison Letters*, 188.

motivated people's actions, does not deflect the point that this self-perception significantly helped to define what republicans held themselves to be striving after. Republican socialist claims that the momentum of the independence struggle was derived from conscious, materially-oriented, class-struggling instincts are entirely contradicted if republicans themselves identified ethereal, class-inclusive, spiritual notions as lying at the heart of their republicanism. The supposed dichotomy between the spiritual and the material[212] was complemented, unhelpfully for socialist republicans, by attachment to the interwoven notions of sacrifice, suffering, the soul, and religious sensibility. In his autobiographical account of hunger striking in 1920, Frank Gallagher testified to having experienced 'a fierce joy, a sacrificial glory, a feeling of spiritual pride . . . an ecstasy'. Suffering and sacrifice were held to sanctify the national struggle, and to guarantee its victory. Gallagher's assertion, 'I feel that we have not suffered enough, that our victory has been too easy. . . . It seems unfair to have such a triumph for such little pain',[213] reflects such an outlook, as do a wealth of contemporary statements. According to Constance Markievicz, in 1919, 'without pain and self-sacrifice our country would be lost'. It was, she claimed in the following year, 'by suffering, dying and sticking out that we will win'.[214]

The religious quality of much of this thinking is significant. Just as Pearse had deployed Christian imagery in connection with nationalist sacrifice,[215] so, too, did his apostles after him. Terence MacSwiney, writing from Brixton Gaol in 1920, invoked divine assistance for his worldly endeavours:

O my God, I offer my pain for Ireland. She is on the rack . . . I offer my sufferings here for our martyred people beseeching Thee, O my God, to grant them the nerve and strength and grace to withstand the present terror in Ireland . . . that by Thy all powerful aid the persecution may end in our time and Ireland arise at last triumphant.[216]

---

[212] O'Malley, *The Singing Flame*, 86.
[213] *Days of Fear* (London, John Murray, 1928), 25, 29. See also G. Walker, ' "The Irish Dr Goebbels": Frank Gallagher and Irish Republican Propaganda', *Journal of Contemporary History*, 27 (1992).   [214] *Prison Letters*, 189, 262.
[215] Edwards, *Pearse*, 262.
[216] Quoted in M. Chavasse, *Terence MacSwiney* (Dublin, Clonmore and Reynolds, 1961), 170.

Not only was Anglo-Irish war republicanism overwhelmingly Catholic in personnel and in ideological influence, but religious language and imagery were sought in attempts to define and to further the cause. Writing in 1928 to a republican friend, Sheila Humphreys, Ernie O'Malley (with typical acerbic dissidence) accused her of holding the inaccurate view that 'we are a race of spiritualized idealists with a world idea of freedom, having nothing to learn for we have made no mistakes, and whose mission in life is to broaden the outlook of folks who do not yet quite see that point of view'.[217]

As noted, the spiritualized idealist vision of Irish nationalism was, indeed, cluttered with self-deceptions. More important, for the purposes of our current argument, is the fact that the web of spiritual, religious, sacrificial ideals revered by so many within the republican movement was deeply unhelpful to the socialist republican cause. It rendered invalid the O'Donnellite reading of a consciously, materially motivated, class-struggling republican movement. However unconvincing as an explanation of the roots and dynamics of republicanism, the articulation of national conflict in terms of spiritual struggle testified to an outlook fundamentally at odds with that imputed to the republican faithful by republican socialists.

From a republican socialist perspective, the role accorded in Anglo-Irish war republicanism to the physical force ethic was also unhelpful. That it was a central mechanism and preoccupation within the republican struggle detracted from the social emphasis essential to socialist republican advance. That its adherents tended to eschew concentration on social questions, preferring instead a class-integrative approach, further underlines the point.

The concept of soldiership was vital within post-1916 republicanism. Their journal, *An t-Oglach*, presented the Volunteers as 'a military body pure and simple', and tellingly asserted that 'the successful maintenance of the Irish Volunteer is the one thing essential to the triumph of the cause of the Irish Republic'.[218] This conviction was evident in the enthusiastic self-identification characteristic of republican soldiers. Dan Breen described himself as 'a soldier first and foremost'; Ernie O'Malley saw himself 'as a soldier',

[217] 5 Jan. 1928, Humphreys Papers, ADUCD P106.
[218] 15 Aug. 1918, 15 Dec. 1919.

and, during the 1921 truce, described himself as 'anxiously looking forward to war'; C. S. Andrews referred to the kudos which one could derive from such patriotic soldiership.[219]

The central role played by physical force thinking in the minds of republican enthusiasts must also be understood in terms of the appeal of adventure and of excitement. O'Malley suggested, of the Anglo-Irish war period: 'The lack of organized social intercourse made the young discontented, especially in the towns. The wise domination of age, to some hard and harsh in the soul as the cancer of foreign rule, made volunteering an adventure and a relief.'[220] The mixture of youthful assertiveness and glamorous adventure[221] helps to explain revolutionary military involvement. Moreover, this republican soldierly culture should be set in a wider British and European context. Owen Dudley Edwards has argued that the Easter rebellion

was an intensely *British* episode, quite apart from the British births of Clarke and Connolly, the British ancestral part-origin of Pearse, MacDonagh, Cathal Brugha, the brothers Boland, and others. In fighting against Britain, the Easter insurgents responded to the same mood which led so many to fight for Britain. The ideals were the same: militarism, honour, patriotism, self-sacrifice, manhood, adventure, and above all a desire to testify to spiritual yearnings defying the grey calculations of a secure and cautious life. Combat and death had become world-wide faiths.[222]

Post-First World War republican militarism must be placed in a similar framework. In a recent piece in the *Historical Journal*, A. D. Harvey addressed the question, 'Who were the Auxiliaries?' He argued that this force of ex-officers, deployed by the British government against the IRA during the Anglo-Irish war, was composed, in the majority, of 'men who had difficulty in returning

---

[219] Breen, *My Fight*, 167–8; English and O'Malley (eds.), *Prisoners*, 25; O'Malley to FitzGerald, 25 Aug. 1921, FitzGerald Papers, ADUCD P80; C. S. Andrews, *Man of No Property: An Autobiography* (Cork, Mercier, 1982), 9–10.

[220] *On Another Man's Wound*, 126. Cf. English and O'Malley (eds.), *Prisoners*, 17, and P. Hart, 'Youth Culture and the Cork IRA', in D. Fitzpatrick (ed.), *Revolution? Ireland, 1917–23* (Dublin, Trinity History Workshop, 1990).

[221] O'Malley to Humphreys, 9 Apr., 12 Apr. 1923, Humphreys Papers, ADUCD P106; O'Malley, *On Another Man's Wound*, 64, 134; O'Malley, *The Singing Flame*, 18; Breen, *My Fight*, 42, 55.

[222] *Eamon de Valera* (Cardiff, Univ. of Wales Press, 1987), 48.

to civilian life after the First World War'.[223] A similar reading could be offered of IRA leader, Tom Barry, who led the famous Kilmichael attack on a party of Auxiliaries in County Cork in November 1920. Barry had joined the British army in order 'to see what this Great War was like'. He had gone to the war 'for no other reason than that I wanted to see what war was like, to get a gun, to see new countries and to feel a grown man'. He remained in the army throughout the war, returning to Cork early in 1919. His subsequent construction of his post-war IRA involvement (as an ideologically motivated fight for freedom and dignity) should clearly be set against the fact that there was something which appealed to him about soldiership prior to his development of any republican ideological commitment.[224]

The culture of First World War and immediate post-war soldiership; the possibilities for expression (and employment) offered by the British forces; the prevalence of a romantic, youthful, European celebration of patriotism—each of these contextual elements should be considered part of the framework for republican militarism in this period. Thus, Ernie O'Malley celebrated Pearse,[225] but also recognized the wider, romantic pattern into which his hero fitted: 'I tried to make poems of things I had loved: mountains, rivers, trees, books and people. I found myself mingling my lines with those in a poem by Rupert Brooke, "the rough male kiss of blankets", and one of Padraig Pearse.'[226] Pearse's 'cleansing' and 'sanctifying' bloodshed and Brooke's 'red sweet wine of youth' should be considered in conjunction with one another.[227] O'Malley, prior to his 1916 conversion, had intended to join the British army, thereby following the pattern set by his older brother; once in the Irish Volunteers, he learned military tactics from British sources; and he acknowledged both a sympathy for and an affinity with Irish people in the British forces.[228]

[223] *Historical Journal*, 35/3 (1992), 669.   [224] Barry, *Guerilla Days*, 2, 10.

[225] English and O'Malley (eds.), *Prisoners*, 12–14.

[226] *The Singing Flame*, 190; cf. R. Brooke, *The Collected Poems* (London, Papermac, 1992; 1st edn. 1918), 300–2.

[227] Pearse, quoted in Townshend, *Political Violence*, 258; Brooke, *Collected Poems*, 314.

[228] English and O'Malley (eds.), *Prisoners*, 72; O'Malley, *On Another Man's Wound*, 52–3, 59; O'Malley to Gallagher, 12 Nov. 1926, copy in Cormac O'Malley Papers, PP. On this question of the extent to which British influences informed Irish republicans' culture, see: English, 'Green on Red: Two Case Studies in Early Twentieth Century Irish Republican Thought', in Boyce, Eccleshall, and Geoghegan

Significant also were the functional value of republican violence and the seductive, though misleading, simplicity of the framework which underpinned the physical-force approach. Violence was deployed as a central mechanism in this period with a threefold galvanic intention. Force was supposed to stimulate popular attachment to the separatist cause through a mixture of inspiration, intimidation, and alienation. Patriotic military gesture was supposed to stir sympathy; direct intimidation would coerce opponents into acquiescence; and republican violence was intended to provoke aggressive responses from the state, with the result that such state activity would alienate large sections of the population and lead them to sympathize with the republicans.[229] Violence was, therefore, integral to an elaborate exercise in propaganda. As with unionist cultivation of propagandist myth, republican claims were greatly disproportionate to their deeds.[230]

Furthermore, grandiose claims about the extent to which this propagandist strategy succeeded in converting popular opinion should be set against more realistic assessments both of the level of popular enthusiasm and of the marked divisions within the pre-1921 independence movement.[231] But the strengths of this militaristic galvanic theory were precisely its points of weakness. The notion that force should be central to nationalist strategy held, as we have seen, a varied appeal. But the dangers of such an emphasis were also apparent to perceptive contemporaries.[232] Moreover, the galvanic theory embodied a circularity of argument which rendered it invulnerable in terms of its own (highly questionable) logic, but which made it ultimately self-defeating. If the people were perceived to be in support, then you acted with apparent sanction; if the people were perceived not to be in support, then you acted in order to stimulate them into giving you their backing. Either way, you acted. This activist self-deception—that the people could always be won over by appropriate IRA activity—was shown to be inadequate in the years following the 1921 treaty.[233]

(eds.) *Political Thought in Ireland*; O'Donnell, *The Gates*, 147–51, 169; P. Golden, *Impressions of Ireland* (New York, Irish Industries Depot, n.d.), 60–1; Cronin, *Ryan*, 19, 153.

[229] See English, 'Green on Red' for an expansion of these points.

[230] A. Jackson, 'Unionist Myths 1912–85', *Past and Present*, 136 (Aug. 1992), 182–3; cf. English and O'Malley (eds.), *Prisoners*, 14–15.

[231] Breen, *My Fight*, 103; cf. Valiulis, *Mulcahy*, 66–7; English, 'Green on Red'.

[232] See e.g. Cathal O'Shannon's remarks, quoted in Valiulis, *Mulcahy*, 177–8.

[233] English, 'Green on Red'.

In relation to socialist republicanism, the centrality of this physical-force ethic had even more depressing implications. For some within the republican movement during this period militarism was not only autonomous from, but tended also to obscure, other forms of political expression. Anti-parliamentarian instincts overlapped with a broader hostility to politicians.[234] Notions of compromise and of possible betrayal were attached to the realm and practice of the politician, while expressly political violence was held to be a surer focus for true republican activity. The difficulty, from a socialist republican point of view, was that the concentration on physical-force methods carried with it both the ideal that pan-class involvement in the military struggle was desirable, and the accompanying notion that emphasis on social questions and conflicts would be a distraction from the national advance. Thus, Mulcahy's biographer notes that he did not want the IRA to 'involve themselves in land matters'. Mulcahy 'understood the volatile nature of the land question and did not want to cause any more friction within the army'.[235] Mulcahy's Anglo-Irish war colleague, Ernie O'Malley, not only acknowledged that he personally shared 'the pseudo-military mind of the IRA and its fear of constitutional respectability'; he also commented that the prevailing attitude was one of fear 'that any attention to [the] needs or direction [of Labour] would weaken the one-sided thrust of force'. Moreover, his initiation into the Volunteers had demonstrated the strength of the pan-class republican military ideal, the organization's objects including the aim 'to unite in the service of Ireland, Irishmen of every creed and of every party and class'.[236]

The Anglo-Irish war represented, for subsequent republicans, something of a mythic era. Just as socialist republicans tried to claim the 1916 myth for their own ideological tradition, so they attempted to read the Anglo-Irish war in terms favourable to their own class-struggling interpretation of Irish republicanism. But, just as the Easter rebellion proved an inappropriate shrine at which to kneel, so, too, the reality of the Anglo-Irish war weakened rather than strengthened the socialist republican case. Their reading of the period was, as we have seen, simplistic and seriously flawed; and the pan-class, spiritual, militaristic emphases, which did so much to colour the republican movement of these years, only served

---

[234] Markievicz, *Prison Letters*, 174; Greaves, *Liam Mellows*, 126; Fanning, *Independent Ireland*, 3; Breen, *My Fight*, 161.   [235] Valiulis, *Mulcahy*, 61, 94.
[236] *On Another Man's Wound*, 47, 59, 213.

to emphasize the marginality of the socialist republican outlook. Close scrutiny of the republican socialist attempt to claim the Anglo-Irish war inheritance demonstrates the incoherence of their arguments and the feebleness of their tradition.

1922–1925

The Free State is a British institution, and has the right of the British empire. That is: the Free State has no right in Ireland.

Peadar O'Donnell (1923)[237]

The 1921 betrayal was no accident of individual leaders being bribed or bought by the British. It was the inevitable outcome of a struggle in which the leadership was in the hands of a class who feared that the complete triumph of the national independence movement would not halt at national separation but would develop into a social revolution, resulting in the overthrow of the Irish capitalist class and the establishment of a Workers' and Farmers' Socialist Republic.

Manifesto of the Irish Communist Party (1933)[238]

In his account of his civil war incarceration, Peadar O'Donnell lamented the loss of his friend and anti-treaty colleague, Liam Mellows: 'What a pity Mellowes [*sic*] was dead: had there been such as he to assemble round there was a team of us left yet.' The focus on Mellows is instructive concerning socialist republican readings of the Irish civil war. In a document captured by the Free State authorities on its way to IRA GHQ in 1922, the imprisoned Mellows had set out what O'Donnell subsequently described as 'the bare outlines of his thoughts on a social programme'.[239] The *Irish Independent* published this embryonic manifesto, asserting that the policy which it contained involved the establishment of 'a communistic state'.[240] The notes undoubtedly did evince strong socialist influences. Mellows quoted from a document which had been printed in the *Workers' Republic* in July 1922.[241] In the new republic, industry and transport would be controlled by the state for the benefit of workers and farmers. Banks would be operated

---

[237] *Workers' Republic*, 3 Feb. 1923.
[238] *The Irish Case for Communism* (Cork, CWC, n.d.), 34–5.
[239] *The Gates*, 62, 168.   [240] 22 Sept. 1922.   [241] 22/29 July 1922.

by the state for agricultural and industrial benefit rather than for profit-making purposes. Land belonging to the aristocracy would be seized and divided among those able and willing to operate it for the nation's benefit.

Mellows here delineated the republican struggle in accordance with perceived class interests. He proposed the immediate establishment of a 'Provisional Republican Government' and asserted that the Democratic Programme of 1919 'should be translated into something definite. This is essential if the great body of the workers are to be kept on the side of independence.' He continued: 'We should certainly keep Irish Labour for the Republic; it will be possibly the biggest factor on our side.' In their efforts to win back public support, republicans had to realize that 'the commercial interests so-called—money and the gombeen-man—are on the side of the Treaty, because the Treaty means imperialism and England'. Republicans were 'back to Tone—and it is just as well—relying on that great body, "the men of no property"'.[242]

Mellows and O'Donnell had developed an intimacy during their civil war imprisonment.[243] Indeed, O'Donnell's influence over Mellows in relation to the latter's Mountjoy communication cannot be discounted.[244] What is important for our current purposes is to recognize, first, the socialist republican use of Mellows to reinforce the argument that class conflict and national conflict overlapped with one another and, second, O'Donnell's attempt to read Mellows in such a way as to claim Fenian tradition for his own particular purposes. The *Republican Congress* newspaper in 1934 referred to the civil war as having been a 'half-hearted' fight. But Mellows, the paper argued, had distinguished himself through his recognition of the true interests at stake in the conflict: he had revealed himself as 'the revolutionary thinker who saw the necessity for coming out on the side of the small farmers and workers and of making the Republican fight their fight. On the one side empire,

---

[242] *Irish Independent*, 22 Sept. 1922.

[243] O'Donnell, *The Gates*, 25, 28–9, 34, 50–1, 79–80, 82, 87–9, 168.

[244] 'De Valera and people tried to say that it was I that [induced] Mellows to write those notes . . . I didn't add anything to the content of his mind. But I certainly did make him write them' (Angela Crean interview with Peadar O'Donnell, 9 Apr. 1985). Cf. 'It's generally accepted that Mellows's *Notes from Mountjoy* were either dictated or written or certainly very much influenced by Peadar O'Donnell' (Anthony Coughlan, interview with the author, Dublin, 5 Feb. 1988). Coughlan was a close associate of O'Donnell's for many years.

capitalists; on the other Republic, workers—thus Mellowes. [*sic*] But he was a voice crying in the wilderness.'[245]

O'Donnell's reading of Mellows took this argument one stage further back into republican history. Rejecting the view that Mellows was a 'Socialist Republican', O'Donnell claimed instead that his friend had been 'a great Fenian who saw the poor as the freedom force of the nation; as Tone did'.[246] Thus Fenianism, a tradition to which O'Donnell proudly attached his own name,[247] was claimed for the class-struggling version of republicanism. Mellows (a martyred hero) and Fenianism (a tradition hallowed by other martyrs) were both appropriated by O'Donnell for what was, in fact, a minority reading of the national struggle. For O'Donnell, Fenian Ireland was 'the Ireland of the poor', 'anti-landlord, anti-rancher'.[248] Historically, however, there were problems in O'Donnell's attempted identification of his own socialist reading of republicanism with Fenian tradition. O'Donnell's preference for the revolutionizing of land and property ownership along socialistic lines, for example, sat awkwardly with much Fenian thinking.[249] There was significant evidence of socialist influence over Mellows's thought. But O'Donnell typically chose not to present him as a socialist, but instead to claim that his synergic fusion of the class and national conflicts characterized not just a particular (socialist) strain within republicanism, but rather the essence of true republicanism itself.

O'Donnell's questionable use of history here fits into a broader pattern, the validation of contemporary commitment being sought through convenient manipulation of the past. The point can be amplified through reference to Theobald Wolfe Tone. Republican presentations of Tone have tended to take the form of eulogistic celebration.[250] Socialist republican enthusiasm for Tone carried specific, class-struggling implications. Just as Connolly had sought to claim Tone's legacy, so, too, the next generation of republican

---

[245] 5 May 1934.

[246] *There Will Be Another Day* (Dublin, Dolmen, 1963), 11.

[247] McInerney, *O'Donnell*, 237.   [248] *There Will Be*, 105, 132.

[249] *An Phoblacht*, 28 Feb. 1931; Garvin, *Nationalist Revolutionaries*, 33–40; J. Newsinger, 'Revolution and Catholicism in Ireland, 1848–1923', *European Studies Review*, 9/4 (Oct. 1979), 469.

[250] Tone hagiography abounds. For examples of organizational and literary celebrations, see 'Emmet and Tone Commemoration Documents', McGarrity Papers, NLI 17641; *An Phoblacht*, 20 June 1925.

socialists identified very strongly with the prominent United Irishman.[251] The key to their enthusiasm is to be found in the phrase which Mellows had used in his Mountjoy communication: the men of no property. O'Donnell argued that 'Mellows's Ireland was that of Tone; the men of no property', and that both men had seen the poor 'as the freedom force of the nation' and had shared a 'faith in the men of no property'.[252]

In her excellent biography of Tone, Marianne Elliott notes that her subject was not

the democrat of tradition, a reputation largely based on his much misunderstood reference to 'the men of no property'.... Property in the eighteenth century meant first and foremost landed property. His 'respectable' men of no property were the middle classes who composed the Catholic and United Irish leadership alike. Irish republican separatism started out as a campaign to secure political power for the middle classes.[253]

The Mellows–O'Donnell reading rests, therefore, on shaky historical foundations. Commenting, more recently, on Tone's 'men of no property', Jim Smyth has suggested that 'irrespective of what Tone did or did not intend, his words have subsequently assumed a life and a commonly-understood meaning independent of their author. The commonly-understood meaning *might* be a popular misconception, and as such may irritate austere historians, but, whether they like it or not, that meaning is now contained in tradition.'[254]

But the point is that readings such as O'Donnell's not only misinterpreted the eighteenth century, but also helped to sustain erroneous arguments concerning the twentieth century. Tone's 'men of no property' phrase was deployed in support of the supposed key to understanding contemporary Irish political realities, namely the notion that class struggle and national struggle were neatly symbiotic. But, as we have seen, this notion does not, in fact, hold good for the 1916–21 period. Nor, as we shall see, is it a

[251] Connolly, *Labour in Irish History*, in *JCCW* i. 92; extracts from Tone's autobiography, McMullen Papers, PP; Gilmore, *The Irish Republican Congress*, pp. iii–iv.

[252] Quoted in McInerney, *O'Donnell*, 32; O'Donnell, *There Will Be*, 11–12.

[253] *Wolfe Tone: Prophet of Irish Independence* (New Haven, Yale Univ. Press, 1989), 418.

[254] Smyth rightly acknowledges the role of the middle classes in relation to the United Irishmen (*The Men of No Property: Irish Radicals and Popular Politics in the Late Eighteenth Century* (Dublin, Gill and Macmillan, 1992), p. x, 83.)

satisfactory thesis in relation to the ensuing decades. Republican socialists overplayed the reliability and significance of the working classes in relation to republican politics; they understated the role of other social groups. Just as their reading of Tone underplayed the importance of the middle class in United Irish politics, so, too, they understated the importance of the middle classes in committed, twentieth-century republicanism. What should irritate the historian of republican socialism is less the mistaken reading of the eighteenth century (regrettable though that might be) than the fact that this mistaken reading was deployed in support of a misinterpretation of contemporary politics. O'Donnell, in later life, argued that 'the habit we have in this country of taking the name and making it a slogan and attempting to revive something that has passed through history and to revive that effort in totally different conditions is one of our weaknesses'.[255] But in their treatment of Tone, socialist republicans were themselves plainly guilty of the crime of historical decontextualization.

Republican socialist responses to the 1921 Anglo-Irish treaty were marked by a firm hostility to the agreement, and by a reiteration of the thesis that Irish class and national struggles were inextricably interwoven. In 1922, *Workers' Republic* ('The Official Organ of the Communist Party of Ireland') espoused a social programme characterized by extensive state nationalization, as well as declaring firmly in favour of anti-treaty republicanism.[256] Looking back from 1933, a reincarnated Communist Party of Ireland (CPI) argued, in relation to the treaty, that

The 1921 betrayal was no accident of individual leaders being bribed or bought by the British. It was the inevitable outcome of a struggle in which the leadership was in the hands of a class who feared that the complete triumph of the National Independence Movement would not halt at national separation but would develop into a social revolution, resulting in the overthrow of the Irish capitalist class and the establishment of a Workers' and Farmers' Socialist Republic.[257]

A similar argument characterized the Republican Congress's approach in 1934, with the 1921 treaty being described as a penal

---

[255] Speech given in the Conway Street Mill, Belfast, 7 Apr. 1984. I am grateful to the West Belfast branch of the Communist Party of Ireland for allowing me access to a recording of this event.   [256] *Workers' Republic*, 16 Dec. 1922.
[257] *Manifesto of the Irish Communist Party* in *The Irish Case*, 34–5.

measure 'forced upon Republican Ireland by military terror through the betrayal of the fight for freedom by middle-class politicians acting for Irish capitalism'.[258]

Thus, while the Free State was presented as a British imposition—a 'British institution', in O'Donnell's words—[259] the compromising, treacherous, class-determined role of the Irish middle classes was stressed. As with the 1919–21 struggle, so, too, the ensuing civil war was interpreted in terms of republican interests being betrayed, or, at least, wrongly defended, by the relevant leaders. While leading members of the labour movement met with eminent representatives of the pro-treaty authorities (to discuss practical matters such as the appropriate ways in which to deal with the problem of unemployment),[260] the republican left were savaging them in print. O'Donnell, writing in August 1922, singled Thomas Johnson out for abuse:

It is England's devilish luck that at a moment when Irish Labour is faced with a situation of tremendous possibilities, the dominating influence on the National Executive should be an imperial English mind. There Johnston [*sic*] is a very excellent, able man but he is a reactionary leader. . . . The Labour Party at present champions imperialism. The dominating influence is Thomas Johnston. The duty of the Irish Citizen Army is plain. Tom Johnston must be deported. Deport him.[261]

Early in the following year O'Donnell argued that, to him, 'the National Executive of the Irish Labour Party is just a collection of imperial toadies who confuse position for themselves at the expense of the labour movement with the advancement of the labour cause.'[262] This harshly critical approach became an established part of republican socialist orthodoxy. *Republican Congress* argued, in 1934, that the Labour leadership had shown itself to be 'the lackey of Irish capitalism' when it had acquiesced under the treaty.[263]

Civil war republican leaders, too, were condemned. George Gilmore suggested that almost all of the anti-treaty speakers in the Dáil debate had failed to grasp the underlying realities of the agreement. O'Donnell likewise argued that influential anti-treaty

[258] Gilmore, *The Irish Republican Congress* (1978; 1st edn. 1935), 48–9.
[259] *Workers' Republic*, 3 Feb. 1923.
[260] *Unemployment: Conference with Labour Delegation* (1922), Files of the Dept. of the Taoiseach, NA S 740.   [261] *Workers' Republic*, 26 Aug. 1922.
[262] Ibid. 3 Feb. 1923.   [263] 5 May 1934.

republicans had displayed resolute adherence to principle, but had failed to offer a true revolutionary response.[264] The republican socialist delineation of the conflict over the treaty, therefore, resembled that of the Anglo-Irish war: the treaty had been backed by the middle classes because of their economically impelled desire to retain a link with Britain; the masses, who had provided the momentum for the Anglo-Irish war, were implicitly anti-treaty; but their leaders had again failed to lead them appropriately, and instead of tying the social revolution to the anti-treaty struggle, republican leaders had opted for physical force and martyrdom while the labour leadership had acquiesced under the pro-treaty regime.

What are we to make of this class-based reading of the civil war? In January 1923 a report sent to the Free State Minister for External Affairs referred to the delivery of dispatches from leading anti-treatyite, Eamon de Valera, to the Bolshevik Commissary in Lausanne. One of these dispatches reportedly argued that:

'Without material . . . it would be impossible to continue the struggle and failure at the present moment would mean the perpetuation of the capitalistic Free State government in Ireland for another generation.' Under those circumstances [the report continued] the 'irregular' leader felt that he could depend on the Moscow government for a loan of ten thousand pounds in English money as well as for a supply of arms and ammunition.

The notion of de Valera as anti-capitalist Bolshevik ally was recognized as having a certain propagandist value for the Free State authorities, not least in the United States.[265]

But this hint regarding the culture of international conspiracy should be set firmly in context. The essentially utilitarian nature of the republican movement's international links was, as we shall see, a persistent theme in the 1920s and 1930s. Certainly, de Valera's views conflicted with the impression given in the above report. In August 1923 he defined the Sinn Fein ideal as involving not conflict but rather 'justice between all classes',[266] and, indeed, it was central to the arguments of republican socialists themselves that

---

[264] Gilmore, *Labour and the Republican Movement*, 14; O'Donnell, quoted in MacEoin (ed.), *Survivors*, 24–5.
[265] *Civil War: Irregular Activities in France and Switzerland*, Files of the Dept. of the Taoiseach, NA S 3147.   [266] *Sinn Fein*, 7 Aug. 1923.

de Valera had not espoused a class-struggling, anti-capitalistic approach to the republic.[267]

As with the Anglo-Irish war, socio-economic considerations are plainly vital to any full understanding of the civil war conflict. In June 1922 the pro-treaty Provisional Government lamented 'grave acts' committed by anti-treaty republicans 'against the security of person and property', and asserted: 'For some months past all classes of business in Ireland have suffered severely through the feeling of insecurity engendered by reckless and wicked acts'. As Michael Laffan has argued, 'Supporters of the treaty tended to view social radicalism and republicanism as twin apparitions of anarchy.' The civil war certainly had a destructive impact on the economy, including a dislocating effect on trade union activity. It is also clear that social conflicts in some cases overlapped with the ostensibly political divisions.[268] Thus, despite Michael Hopkinson's assertion that it is 'extremely difficult to demonstrate a social basis for the divisions that led to the civil war',[269] it is undoubtedly the case that socio-economic forces played a significant part in the conflict. But the interpretation offered by groups such as the 1930s Republican Congress—empire and capitalists versus Republic and workers—is plainly inadequate to deal with the complexity of the situation. As Tom Garvin has put it:

the Treaty issue split rightists from rightists, leftists from leftists, democrats from democrats, and elitists from elitists. . . . There was some correlation between social class and support for the Treaty, with employers, big farmers and many urban middle and working class people supporting it, while other workers, small farmers and inhabitants of more remote areas opposed it. At the level of the elite itself, however, there was little obvious correspondence between class origin and position on the issue of the Treaty.[270]

Neither at the élite nor at the rank-and-file level, therefore, would a crude class analysis succeed in explaining patterns of, or motivation for, political behaviour. It was perfectly possible for labourers to break free from the pattern rigidly prescribed for

---

[267] Gilmore, *The Irish Republican Congress*, 48.

[268] *Irish Times*, 28 June 1922; Laffan, ' "Labour Must Wait" ', 219; Bradley, *Farm Labourers*, 63–4; P. Bew, E. Hazelkorn, and H. Patterson, *The Dynamics of Irish Politics* (London, Lawrence and Wishart, 1989), 25.

[269] *Green Against Green: The Irish Civil War* (Dublin, Gill and Macmillan, 1988), 45.   [270] *Nationalist Revolutionaries*, 123–4, 142.

them by socialist republicans, and to endorse the 1921 treaty.[271] It is significant that those scholars who have in recent years attempted to establish models for explaining the civil war have identified dominant themes which cut across the socialist-republican class conflict interpretation.[272]

Republican socialists assumed that there existed, during the civil war period, the potential for a socially revolutionary mass movement pursuing the republic. This interpretation can be questioned on four main counts. First, the regional particularity of, and variation between, the social conflicts of these years rendered implausible the kind of unified, national class conflict envisaged by the republican left. In terms of social and of political conflict, civil-war Ireland was a patchwork of essentially disparate struggles.[273]

Second, the proposed alliance between all the 'men of no property' implied a rather unlikely rainbow coalition. The idea that the working class, urban unemployed, agricultural labourers, and small farmers would naturally identify with one another in terms of shared interests and social vision ignores the extensive sectional conflicts and dissimilarities of interest prevalent in this period. Extensive conflict between labourers and farmers, for example, had left agricultural labourers in isolation.[274]

Third, it is hard to accept the thesis that early 1920s republicanism was the natural vehicle through which to express aspirations for radical social change. O'Connor has noted the difficulties involved in tying labour unrest to nationalism in this period.[275] If it is true that 'the working class looked on largely in apathy as Irish society was torn apart by a bitter civil war',[276] then it is difficult to see the logic in the republican socialist assumption that republican momentum and working-class social aspirations were mutually dependent. Nor can it simply be countered that republican leaders misrepresented their rank and file and bullied them into social

---

[271] S. Lawlor, *Britain and Ireland 1914–23* (Dublin, Gill and Macmillan, 1983), 149–50.

[272] Garvin, *Nationalist Revolutionaries*; J. Prager, *Building Democracy in Ireland: Political Order and Cultural Integration in a Newly Independent Nation* (Cambridge, CUP, 1986).

[273] O'Connor, *Syndicalism*, 117; O'Faoláin, *De Valera*, 97.

[274] Bradley, *Farm Labourers*, 56, 60; Bew, Hazelkorn, and Patterson, *Dynamics*, 24–5.   [275] O'Connor, *Syndicalism*, 109–10.

[276] R. Dunphy, 'Class, Power and the Fianna Fáil Party: A Study of Hegemony in Irish Politics, 1923–48', D. Phil. thesis (Florence, 1988), 46.

reaction against their true instincts. Where the local IRA sympathized with radical action, they were perfectly capable of voting with their feet.[277] The mass of the IRA's rank and file plainly did not view their republicanism in terms of O'Donnellite social radicalism. In harmony with our discussion of the 1917–21 republican movement, it is clear that by the civil-war period republicanism was, in fact, a singularly *in*appropriate vessel into which to pour socially radical hopes.

Fourth, it is highly questionable whether more than a tiny portion of the wider population sympathized at all with the revolutionary overhauling espoused by the republican left. O'Connor notes that, in 1922, soviets came to evince 'a serious revolutionary intent'. But much of the social conflict of the civil-war years centred on questions which fell far short of the revolutionary vision which characterized, for example, the contemporary *Workers' Republic*.[278]

The vast majority of political leaders—anti- as well as pro-treaty—eschewed the idea that class conflict should be the central theme of their national project. Michael Collins acknowledged the urgency of problems regarding 'housing, land hunger, and unemployment', but his message was coloured by a desire for multi-class harmony rather than for conflict between classes. Similarly, the anti-treaty leadership overwhelmingly neglected any radical socialist-republican synergy. Peadar O'Donnell acknowledged that 'We had a pretty barren mind socially; many on the Republican side were against change. Had we won, I would agree that the end results might not have been much different from what one sees today.'[279] But the vital point is that the majority of non-leaders likewise rejected the socialist republican faith. It was not a case of republican or labour leaders failing to sound the appropriate note and therefore missing the revolutionary moment. The trumpet was indeed sounded: those who sounded it found that their music failed to resonate at all with the experience, outlook, and aspirations of their would-be audience. The actual attitude of the mass of the Irish people can be detected in the symbolically

[277] Bradley, *Farm Labourers*, 60; Bew, Hazelkorn, and Patterson, *Dynamics*, 24.
[278] O'Connor, *Labour History*, 112; Bradley, *Farm Labourers*, 57, 59, 61, 65, 70–2.
[279] M. Collins, *The Path to Freedom* (Cork, Mercier, 1968; 1st edn. 1922), 15, 19, 25–6; quoted in MacEoin (ed.), *Survivors*, 25.

pathetic experience of the CPI; the overwhelming majority of those at whom the socialist republican message was preached had absolutely no sympathy with the sermon.[280]

We have established, therefore, that the 1916 and 1917–21 episodes were characterized by emphases which conflicted with the essence of the socialist republican approach. This was also true of the civil war, the third phase of the 1916–23 mythic era. The activists' culture of violence took on, during the civil war, something of a self-generating, local, and chaotic quality. The regionally varied nature of the conflict tends to reinforce this impression. So, too, does research such as that of Peter Hart, whose recent essay on the killing of Henry Wilson in 1922 underlines the confused, personalized, self-reproducing, and momentum-gathering nature of much of the violence from this period. Hart's essay also points to another vital theme. Of Reggie Dunne (one of Wilson's killers), Hart notes: 'His letters reveal a Pearse-like martyrological obsession . . . replete with references to himself as Christ. He was also a great admirer of Terence MacSwiney, who starved himself to death in the belief that such self-sacrifice would advance the revolution. Dunne clearly saw his actions in these terms.'[281] Christian (in the vast majority of cases, Catholic) thinking was important to many republicans during the civil war. There was anger at clerical hostility to anti-treatyite republicanism, and a desire to utilize clerical sympathy where possible.[282]

It is also important to recognize that religious language and imagery were deployed in direct relation to the national struggle. Thus, Ernie O'Malley not only expressed his sense of loss at having been denied the sacraments, but also linked together notions of sacrifice, suffering, and the national soul. The claim to be fighting for Ireland was tied to the claim to be fighting for God:

The country has not had, as yet, sufficient voluntary sacrifice and suffering and not until suffering fructuates will she get back her real soul. . . .

[280] O'Connor, *Labour History*, 111.

[281] 'Michael Collins and the Assassination of Sir Henry Wilson', *IHS* 28/110 (Nov. 1992), 168.

[282] 'We were all Catholics in Kilmainham except D. L. Robinson' (O'Donnell, *The Gates*, 207); cf. 'I feel of course that David [Robinson]'s outlook on life is not ours' (O'Malley to Childers, 8 Dec. 1923 in English and O'Malley (eds.), *Prisoners*, 117); 'To his Grace, the Archbishop of Dublin', 17 Oct. 1923, O'Malley Papers, ADUCD P17a/43; 'Acting President, To All Prisons and Camps', 1 Nov. 1923, O'Malley Papers, ADUCD P17a/43.

[O]ne feels that one is always fighting for God and Ireland for the spread of our spirituality, such as it is, to counteract the agnosticism and materialism of our own and other countries.[283]

Nor was O'Malley's case exceptional. The supposed efficacy of divinely blessed republican suffering is a recurrent theme in the sources for this period.[284]

From the republican socialist perspective, the prominence of physical force and of the attempted spiritualization of republicanism was deeply unhelpful. Each of these emphases led concentration away from the materialist, socio-economic argument at the heart of the republican left's approach. The October-November 1923 republican hunger strike (in pursuit of prison release) was presented not only in terms of spiritual struggle, but also as a focal point for a multi-class onslaught, with labour, manufacturers, and merchants all being woven into the fabric of the campaign.[285] As we have seen, republican socialists lamented aspects of the civil war experience. But this has to be set against their integral involvement in the military and the spiritual/sacrificial campaigns of this period and, indeed, against their enthusiasm for elements of these activities.[286] As with 1916–21, so with the civil war: actual republican experience for the most part sat awkwardly with republican socialist theory. The confused left republican mixture of participative endorsement and sceptical dissidence merely served to underline the incoherence at the heart of the socialist republican creed.

The immediate post-civil war years were bleak for labour and republican forces alike. It would be wrong to overstate the role of the individual, but James Larkin must undoubtedly figure in prominent fashion in any discussion of post-civil-war labour schism. Following his failure to regain the ITGWU leadership on his return from the USA in 1923, he came to represent an alternative focal point for labour activity. His Workers' Union of Ireland [WUI], established in 1924, won two-thirds of Dublin ITGWU members, and, although WUI success was minimal outside the

[283] To Childers, 7 Nov., 12 Nov., 5 Dec. 1923 (English and O'Malley (eds.), *Prisoners*, 42, 48, 110).
[284] See e.g. 'Aiken to All Volunteers on Hungerstrike', 30 Oct. 1923; 'Acting President: Soldiers of the Republic', 31 Oct. 1923; 'Acting President: Comrades!', 5 Nov. 1923 (O'Malley Papers, ADUCD P17a/43).
[285] 'Suggestions for Immediate Action', O'Malley Papers, ADUCD P17a/43.
[286] *Workers' Republic*, 7 Jan. 1922; O'Donnell, *The Gates*, 193; Andrew Boyd, interview with the author, Belfast, 24 Sept. 1992.

capital, the significance of the rift was considerable. Irish labour was already ruptured by partition and by the rivalry between British-based and Irish-based unions. The Larkin split exacerbated the existing fragmentation in a deeply unhelpful way. William McMullen's rather unflattering portraits of Larkin—'aggressive, domineering, and intolerant of other opinions'; 'truculent and aggressive in manner'; 'consistent logical reasoning . . . had never been a forte of Larkin's'—undoubtedly capture important aspects both of the labour leader's qualities and of labour's consequent problems. But labour difficulties in the early 1920s were not the result solely of personal conflicts.[287]

Similarly, the republican movement found itself in a tattered state after its civil war defeat. After the release of republican prisoners there occurred a republican gathering which Peadar O'Donnell subsequently described as 'a meeting of the wreckage of the IRA; to reorganize the IRA'. He recalled Ernie O'Malley's assertion at this meeting 'that the job of the IRA now was for us to restore the morale that had been endangered by all the confusion over the Treaty and so on'.[288] Wreckage, reorganization, and morale-lifting were indeed key concepts for the IRA during 1924–5.

In the broader republican movement there were other attempts to establish momentum and purpose. In March 1924 the Sinn Fein Standing Committee published *The Economic Programme of Sinn Fein*. The manifesto was embryonic rather than definitive: 'This Programme is not yet completed. Other subjects are under consideration and will be included when the Republican political leaders now in gaol have an opportunity of expressing their views upon them.' The document was declared to be 'framed in accordance with the Democratic Programme of Dáil Éireann', and it certainly displayed traces of a bias towards the less privileged. It contained a section dealing with the 'improvement of social and working conditions'. It looked toward the introduction of 'a new social order conforming to our fundamental principles of equality and opportunity'. But that crucial component of republican socialist

---

[287] O'Connor, *Labour History*, 116–20. McMullen references: McMullen, untitled MS (n.d. [1958?]); McMullen, 'The Founding of the ITGWU' (n.d.); McMullen, untitled MS. (n.d.) (McMullen, Papers, PP).

[288] Cormac O'Malley interview with O'Donnell and G. Gilmore (Oct. 1970), Cormac O'Malley Papers, PP.

politics, the explicit commitment to class conflict, was missing from the document. Indeed, the programme stated a desire to promote 'the well-being and prosperity of all classes of the Irish community'.[289]

The absence of class struggle from Sinn Fein thinking was underlined by Eamon de Valera's hostility to the notion, as expressed in 1924.[290] The 1916–25 period had, therefore, begun and ended with pan-class harmony eclipsing class conflict as the defining objective within mainstream republican thinking.

---

[289] *The Economic Programme of Sinn Fein* (1924), Coyle O'Donnell Papers, ADUCD P61/33 (3), 2–4.

[290] See T. P. O'Neill, 'In Search of a Political Path: Irish Republicanism, 1922 to 1927', in G. A. Hayes-McCoy (ed.), *Historical Studies* x (Dublin, Gill and Macmillan, 1976).

1

The New IRA, 1925–1929

PEADAR O'DONNELL

My pen is just a weapon and I use it now and again to gather into words scenes that surround certain conflicts.

Peadar O'Donnell (1933)[1]

Theory with me is the interpretation of the situation that bursts in my face; that is why my views have been developed in a series of yelps.

Peadar O'Donnell, *Salud!*[2]

On 14 and 15 November 1925 the IRA held a General Army Convention in Dalkey, County Dublin. The gathering had been preceded by rumours that certain Sinn Fein TDs were considering the possibility of entry into the Free State Dail once the latter had been purged of the oath of allegiance to the British crown. Frank Aiken, IRA chief of staff, had been questioned on this point of republican principle, and had agreed to deliver a statement at November's Convention.[3] The gathering in fact witnessed the birth of a new, autonomous IRA; its proceedings evinced many of the qualities which were to characterize—and, in certain cases, to plague—the resurgent army.

Two major changes were effected, the first containing and being influenced by the second. After the opening formalities it was 'proposed and unanimously decided that the Convention form itself into a committee for the purpose of considering an amendment to the constitution submitted by the Army Council'. The proposed

[1] To Cape, 24 Feb. 1933, Cape Archives, Univ. of Reading Library.

[2] *Salud! An Irishman in Spain* (London, Methuen, 1937), 225.

[3] *Oglaigh na h-Eireann (IRA) GHQ, Dublin: To All Units—Report of General Army Convention 14 and 15 Nov. 1925*, Blythe Papers, ADUCD P24/165 (3); MacEoin (ed.), *Survivors* (Dublin, Argenta, 1987; 1st edn. 1980), 100, 566; J. B. Bell, *The Secret Army: The IRA 1916–79* (Swords, Poolbeg, 1989; 1st edn. 1970), 52.

change was discussed clause by clause, with related resolutions being considered in conjunction with that proposed by the Army Council. After lengthy and detailed debate, seventeen amendments were approved and the altered constitution was then passed by the Convention.[4] The revised document set out four objectives: to guard the republic's honour and uphold its sovereignty and unity; to establish and uphold a legitimate government with total control over the republic; to secure and defend citizens' civil and religious liberties and their equal rights and opportunities; to revive the Irish language for daily use and promote 'the development of the best mental and physical characteristics' of the Irish race. These aspirations may be summarized under the respective headings of independence, legitimacy, liberty and equality, and Gaelicism. Significantly, they reflected the persistent republican distinction between the unfulfilled (legitimate) republican aspiration and the (illegitimate) governmental arrangements which actually obtained.

The objectives were to be obtained by:

1. Force of arms.
2. Organizing, training, and equipping the manhood of Ireland as an efficient military force.
3. Assisting as directed by the army authority all organizations working for the same objects.[5]

The new IRA's primary aim, therefore, was thirty-two-county independence; its primary method was to be violence. This military emphasis in the *Constitution* accurately reflected the movement's approach to politics: for many within the organization, politics had largely become a matter of violence. The IRA's primary role was that of a self-appointed army of national liberation and its militaristic legitimism distinguished it from those in Free State society who adhered to majoritarian political processes, and for whom politics had a non-violent centre of gravity.

This republican anti-majoritarianism was highlighted in the section of the *Constitution* which dealt with army authority. The document decreed the General Army Convention to be 'the supreme army authority', but stated that the Army Council would

---

[4] *Report of General Army Convention* (Nov. 1925), Blythe Papers, ADUCD P24/165 (3)–(5).
[5] *Constitution of Oglaigh na h-Eireann (IRA) as Amended by General Army Convention 14–15 Nov. 1925*, Blythe Papers, ADUCD P24/165 (10).

exercise this role when a Convention was not in session. It then proclaimed that

3. The Army Council shall have the power to delegate its powers to a government which is actively endeavouring to function as the de facto government of the Republic.
4. When a government is functioning as the de facto government of the Republic, a General Army Convention shall be convened to give the allegiance of Oglaigh na h-Eireann to such a government.[6]

Here the *Constitution* gave expression to the second major innovation of the November 1925 Convention. One of the numerous resolutions which had been discussed in conjunction with the proposed constitution had originated with Peadar O'Donnell. Officially put forward by the Tirconaill Battalion, this had proposed

That in view of the fact that the government has developed into a mere political party and has apparently lost sight of the fact that all energies should be devoted to the all-important work of making the army efficient so that renegades who through a coup d'etat assumed governmental powers in this country be dealt with at the earliest possible opportunity; the army of the Republic severs its connection with the Dail and act under an independent executive, such executive to be given the power to declare war when, in its opinion, a suitable opportunity arises to rid the Republic of its enemies and maintain it in accordance with the proclamation of 1916.[7]

The 'government' referred to in the resolution was the remnant of the Second Dáil, the parliament which had been elected in May 1921, and which republicans continued to view as the legitimate authority in Ireland. In 1922 the IRA had given its allegiance to an 'emergency government' comprising members of this group.[8] O'Donnell's motion sought to withdraw this allegiance, with the IRA assuming autonomous status.

The *Constitution* embodied this development: the army authorities inherited the role of representing legitimate Irish governmental power. Republican legitimism was, in this instance,

---

[6] Ibid.

[7] *Report of General Army Convention* (Nov. 1925), Blythe Papers, ADUCD P24/165 (4); O'Donnell, *There Will Be Another Day* (Dublin, Dolmen, 1963), 34–6; Bell, *Secret Army*, 52–3.

[8] *Oglaigh na h-Eireann (IRA) GHQ: To Os/C. All Units, 20 Nov. 1925—Statement by Army Council*, Blythe Papers, ADUCD P24/165 (14).

directly in conflict with majoritarian notions of democracy. The IRA was claiming the right to decide, without reference to majority opinion, which governments were legitimate and which were not. Only when a body was 'functioning as the de facto government of the Republic'—when, in other words, there existed a thirty-two-county, fully independent Ireland—would the organization hand over the keys of governmental legitimacy. In rejecting majority rule and placing itself firmly outside the democratic arena, the IRA demonstrated an élitism wholly in keeping with the recent traditions of violent republicanism. No mandate had been thought necessary in 1916, 1919, or 1922.[9] Believing their own approach to be the only legitimate one, the IRA held their actions to be justified despite the absence of popular endorsement. It was hoped—again, earlier IRA experience provided the point of reference—that republican activities which were carried out without majority support might have a catalytic effect, drawing the Irish people into the true faith and thereby creating a kind of democracy after the event.

O'Donnell's thinking undoubtedly contained elements both of a commitment to act despite a lack of support, and of a belief in the possibility of catalytic republican action. But his approach was also characterized by less traditional qualities. Indeed, there was considerable irony involved in the passing of his resolution. His aim in proposing the motion had been to lead the IRA away from what he saw as the abstract and increasingly irrelevant purism of the Second Dáil. Writing some years later about this 'Republican government', he observed that he had

very quickly formed the conviction that nothing good could come of this body, for here was the same climate of ideas as in 1918; the same impatience with every gesture towards agitation on social issues. It seemed to me that the IRA must separate itself from this political pattern, if it was to make its way into vital association with the people by giving itself a role in struggles on concrete issues, which alone could expose the interests with which the Treaty corresponded and create the forces for their overthrow.[10]

In the words of George Gilmore, who was to become O'Donnell's closest IRA ally, the latter had put forward the resolution in the

---

[9] Cf. 'If [we had consulted the feelings of the people], we would never have fired a shot.' (E. O'Malley, *The Singing Flame* (Dublin, Anvil, 1978), 25).
[10] *There Will Be*, 35.

hope 'that by breaking free from the legalistic attitudes of Sinn Fein and the remnant of Dail Eireann, the IRA would be led to involve itself instead with the realities of life, and would become a revolutionary force for the achievement of the Republic'.[11]

O'Donnell and Gilmore shared a socialist republicanism which they persistently sought to cultivate within (and eventually without) the IRA during the post-civil war era. The 1925 motion was an attempt to lead the army in a new and socially radical direction. As such, it failed to generate much enthusiasm.

An overwhelming decision against it had almost been taken when George Plunkett asked Frank Aiken whether there was any truth in a rumour of talks, on a responsible level, on the advisability of Sinn Fein TDs entering the Free State parliament if the oath of allegiance was removed. Aiken said there had been informal talks along that line.

It would be difficult to give a picture of the commotion this statement caused... There was no real discussion, just an outburst of pain and passion. OC Cork I Brigade ... declared for the shelter of my resolution, which was carried by a stampede vote, but for reasons far other than had influenced me to move it.[12]

Ironically, therefore, a resolution which had sought to steer republicans away from an obsession with questions of theoretical legitimacy was accepted precisely because it facilitated the excommunication by the legitimist faithful of those apostates who were considering acquiescence under what was perceived to be a usurping regime. O'Donnell had achieved IRA autonomy; but the new constitution's non-socialist aims, and the emphatically military means by which these were to be pursued, reflected the fact that his real objective was no nearer fulfilment.

On 20 November 1925 the IRA Army Council, of which O'Donnell appears to have been a member,[13] issued a statement which confirmed that the abstentionism which Aiken had begun to question would continue to be respected by the new IRA.

At the first meeting of the new Army Council the following decision was unanimously arrived at: 'That no member of the Army Council or GHQ Staff shall hold himself free to enter the parliaments of "Northern" or

[11] *The Irish Republican Congress* (Cork, CWC, 1978; 1st edn. 1935), 22.
[12] O'Donnell, *There Will Be*, 35–6.
[13] In 1936 O'Donnell stated that between 1924 and 1934 he had been 'practically continuously either on the Executive or Army Council of the IRA.' ('The Irish Struggle Today', *Left Review* (Apr. 1936), 298).

"Southern" Ireland, or advocate the entrance of these bodies with or without the oath of allegiance. Individual Volunteers, as citizens, are free to express their views on political questions, provided that no such issues shall arise at parades, or Staff or Council meetings.'

The statement also declared that 'loyal obedience to the spirit of the Constitution and to the instructions of the Army Council in its efforts to express them' was expected from all IRA officers and volunteers.[14] At its birth, therefore, the new IRA was a separatist body overwhelmingly military in character. It firmly established itself outside the majoritarian, constitutional arena, preferring to dwell in the increasingly marginalized realm of legitimist, military commitment. This post-1925 IRA was the vessel into which O'Donnell poured much of his revolutionary energy. The dominant, militaristic ethos of November 1925 augured ominously for his socialist republican projects: as with the movement of 1916–25, the centre of gravity was such that O'Donnell's outlook was clearly marginalized.

In the spring of 1926 O'Donnell replaced Patrick Little as editor of the republican journal, *An Phoblacht*.[15] Under its previous editor the paper had broadly adopted a socially conservative approach. In this it emulated *Sinn Fein*, the journal which it had replaced in June 1925. In contrast to O'Donnell's espousal of class struggle, *Sinn Fein* had disavowed sectional conflict between Irish people: 'Sinn Fein is the national party. It alone is not sectional. It is pro-employer and pro-employed; it is pro-farmer and pro-labourer; it is pro-Dublin and pro-Belfast ... It claims the citizens' support because of its freedom from sectionalism.' Prior to O'Donnell's editorship, *An Phoblacht*, too, avoided class struggle. In September 1925, for example, an editorial cited Connolly's hostility to patriots who were 'indifferent to the condition of the people' but, instructively, the article's own proposed remedy for unemployment and emigration lacked any class component, relying instead on a boycott of English goods.[16] Under O'Donnell's guidance, however, *An Phoblacht* became a radical revolutionary organ, its socially subversive republicanism providing a focus of alternative political culture. In later years O'Donnell claimed that his pen's primary role had always been that of 'a weapon' and that he had most

---

[14] *Statement by Army Council* (Nov. 1925), Blythe Papers, ADUCD P24/165 (14).
[15] *An Phoblacht*, 7 May 1926; MacEoin (ed.), *Survivors*, 32, 568.
[16] *Sinn Fein*, 14 Aug. 1923; *An Phoblacht*, 18 Sept. 1925.

enjoyed using it 'during my period as editor of *An Phoblacht* in the late 1920s, when I made a sort of flail of it'.[17]

O'Donnell's emergence into journalistic prominence coincided with his assumption of a more leading role within the republican movement more broadly. The schism which resulted in the foundation of Fianna Fáil in 1926 facilitated his rising profile within the republican movement which remained. Of only second-rank importance in terms of IRA leadership in 1923,[18] during the late 1920s and early 1930s O'Donnell's role in the Army Council and Executive, together with his journalistic and agitative prominence and enthusiasm, made him one of the army's most eminent figures. O'Donnell's thinking can be seen to have drawn on three main sources: labour and republican organizational experiences; theoretical and intellectual influences; and, most importantly perhaps, his particular social and regional background.

Born in County Donegal in 1893, O'Donnell trained as a teacher in Dublin and returned (in 1913) to his native county to teach, including a period working on the island of Aranmore.

When I was in Aranmore, the Gaelic-speaking children of Aranmore and of Achill went across to the tatie fields in Scotland. I went across to look at what the conditions were like. . . . People from these islands came across to earn money to pay for the shop goods that they couldn't cover from their own land. . . . In the second year I was there in a place called Girvan Lanes, a farm outside Girvan in Ayrshire. A girl burst from behind a bush absolutely vibrant with rebellion, and said to me, 'Get me out of this'. There was so much rebellion in her, that I actually lifted rebellion myself from her rebellion and went to Glasgow, and I met Manny Shinwell, who was then chairman of the Glasgow Trades Council, Willy Gallagher, [*sic*] Jimmy Ward, and a few other people. . . . In the talk that took place, the idea of the working class world of agitation and the complete change of society established itself in my mind.[19]

Referring elsewhere to this Glasgow experience, he commented that he had there 'entered an exciting world, the world of the working class struggle'.[20] O'Donnell's mother was 'a strong

[17] Quoted in M. McInerney, *Peadar O'Donnell: Irish Social Rebel* (Dublin, O'Brien, 1974), 241.

[18] T. P. Coogan, *The IRA* (London, Fontana, 1987, 1st edn. 1970), 64.

[19] *Monkeys in the Superstructure: Reminiscences of Peadar O'Donnell* (Galway, Salmon, 1986), 8–9.   [20] Quoted in McInerney, *O'Donnell*, 37.

Larkinite' and his uncle had been active in the Industrial Workers of the World while in the United States. The latter, O'Donnell contended, 'sharpened my awareness of the class struggle'. Following upon his Scottish conversion, O'Donnell himself became immersed in union work, becoming a full-time organizer for the ITGWU.[21] As a complement to his union work, he was continually 'doing odd jobs for one IRA officer or another, picking up revolvers here and there, ferrying arms from one place to the other'[22] and during the Anglo-Irish war he resigned from the ITGWU to serve full-time in the IRA. Thus, both republican and labour organizational influences formed the context for his developing outlook, his hybrid socialist republicanism reflecting the dual nature of his organizational involvement.

If figures from the organized labour movement helped draw him into the world of working-class struggle, theoretical and intellectual influences further defined his approach. As noted, it was through the ITGWU connection that he became introduced to the important influence of Karl Marx, and indeed O'Donnell presented this period in terms of an intellectual awakening: 'I was absolutely flabbergasted to find how ignorant I was. I read omnivorously, day and night, attended lectures, and prepared for the road.'[23] O'Donnell's approach to political theories had a reactive, practical quality: 'Theory with me is the interpretation of the situation that bursts in my face'.[24] In the mid-1930s one of O'Donnell's most sophisticated adversaries, James Hogan, referred to him as 'a communist in the strict sense of the word if ever there was one'.[25] This description is, perhaps, a misleading one. Certainly, O'Donnell was not characterized by any doctrinally rigid adherence to the theoretical tenets of socialism. Rather, he blended socialist theory with personal, localized, and distinctively individual observations. He displayed considerable flexibility in his interpretation of socialism as, in the words of one of his close associates, 'he applied it to the situation . . . as he found it'.[26]

O'Donnell's eclectic, manipulatory, and pragmatic approach

---

[21] O'Donnell, quoted in MacEoin (ed.), *Survivors*, 21–2.
[22] O'Donnell, quoted in McInerney, *O'Donnell*, 39.   [23] *Monkeys*, 10.
[24] *Salud!*, 225.
[25] *Could Ireland Become Communist? The Facts of the Case* (Dublin, Cahill, n.d. [1935?]), 48.   [26] Nora Harkin, interview with the author, Dublin, 4 Feb. 1988.

to intellectual sources can be illustrated through reference to his use of the nineteenth-century Irish radical, James Fintan Lalor. O'Donnell's ideas were not as locked into an urban context as Connolly's had been. He attempted—most notably in his land annuities campaign, which began in the mid-1920s—to build on rural foundations. In connection with the annuities campaign, he claimed that his intellectual point of reference had been Fintan Lalor. O'Donnell claimed to have tried to find in the works of Connolly and Pearse the kind of foundations which Marx had discovered in Smith and Ricardo. Having found nothing there upon which to base a movement, he turned to Fintan Lalor, 'the most advanced thinker of the Young Irelanders'.

Fintan Lalor had a theory that the way into a national struggle was not by just shouting patriotism, but by finding some law that was part of the very nature of government, that wasn't dependent on [a] moral code, that helped to nullify itself, and set out to nullify that law and gradually force the government to come out into warfare against the people. And it struck me that he regretted there was no tax directly payable to Britain that he could get the people to refuse . . . and I could see that the land annuity payment . . . was exactly the sort of tax that Fintan Lalor regretted wasn't in existence in his day.[27]

Here, as elsewhere, there were problems with O'Donnell's historical identification. Lalor's sympathy for 'landlord-tenant dual ownership'[28] and his inclination toward a 'peasant-proprietor system'[29] leaned in precisely the direction which, as we shall see, caused enormous problems for O'Donnell: the shift from tenancy to land ownership. But while O'Donnell's use of Lalor was therefore ironic, it remains telling in relation to his intellectual method. The adoption of a significant figure, and the adaptation, for immediate practical purpose, of aspects of their thinking, typified his agitated and agitative approach.

Crucial to O'Donnell's attempted application of ideas was his sense of local, experiential authenticity. In his novel, *The Knife*, one of the characters addresses the curate with the words: 'You may

[27] O'Donnell, speech in Belfast, 7 Apr. 1984; cf. O'Donnell, *There Will Be*, 119.
[28] R. Davis, *The Young Ireland Movement* (Dublin, Gill and Macmillan, 1987), 189.
[29] D. N. Buckley, *James Fintan Lalor: Radical* (Cork, Cork Univ. Press, 1990), 67.

be smart, and very smart, Father John, an' I be proud when I hear it said how smart ye are, but they have nothin' in the books about the Lagan because Phil Burns an' me and Denis Freel never wrote no book about the Lagan.'[30] Similarly, O'Donnell's own thinking reflected his conviction of the importance of personal experience and intimacy; 'I know that I know the insides of the minds of the mass of the folk in rural Ireland: my thoughts are distilled out of their lives.' It was not, he asserted, his task 'to say anything new', but rather 'to put words on what is in confused ferment in their minds'.[31] According to his own estimation, O'Donnell understood what was natural and instinctive among the mass of the Irish people, precisely because he was drawn from their ranks. His own projects were therefore presented in terms of drawing out what people instinctively, naturally wanted, while the opposing campaigns (led by the state, the clergy, the press, the middle classes) represented attempts to lead the mass of the people away from their natural sympathy. Thus, in reference to his 1933 play, *Wrack*, O'Donnell stated: 'I wrote *Wrack* in a rage, bottled into a corner here and there, keeping out of the way of the police in 1931, while the Irish bishops were playing havoc with the rural minds which would naturally, if left free to themselves, sympathize with those they were being incited to destroy.'[32] Similarly, he presented his 1920s role in the land annuities campaign in terms of his supposed affinity with people's pre-existing perceptions: 'My role was a simple one: I faced a few townlands with a view of a state of things which they recognized to be authentic, and their response to it was courageous, but they were influenced by what they saw and not by me directly'.[33]

This aspect of O'Donnell's approach is important, for if organizational and intellectual influences contributed to his socialist republican outlook, the third (and possibly most crucial) source for his thinking is to be found in his particular social, regional background and in his distinctive response to it. His creative writing—he published seven novels, one play, and numerous other pieces—provides a vital source for understanding both the importance of his background and the nature of his politics. The

[30] (Dublin, Irish Humanities Centre, 1980; 1st edn. 1930), 46.
[31] *The Gates Flew Open* (London, Jonathan Cape, 1932), 167.
[32] To Cape, 24 Feb. 1933, Cape Archives, Univ. of Reading Library.
[33] *There Will Be*, 6.

novelist, Francis Stuart, rather sneeringly described O'Donnell as 'a poor writer . . . very poor', suggesting that 'he wouldn't be considered by any serious critic in Ireland. He wouldn't be taken seriously'.[34] In fact, O'Donnell has been the subject of numerous literary commentators' attention,[35] though there is no doubt that his novels and play do veer towards the mawkish and suffer from a rather brutal didacticism.

But the important point for our argument lies less with the books' literary merits or demerits than with their value as historical sources regarding their author. O'Donnell himself disclaimed any literary greatness ('I have never looked on myself as a writer'),[36] stressing instead the reflective and didactic roles which he felt that creative writing should pursue. In 1947 he was to argue that the important thing was that Irish writing 'should reflect the realities of our life'.[37] A similar theme emerges from a valuable collection of O'Donnell's letters held in the Jonathan Cape Archives. Writing in the early 1930s of one of his novels, he observed, 'It is more like evidence of the way folk live in a Town-land than a novel',[38] while, in another letter from the same period, he argued: 'I think that writers today should just floodlight the facts of the life around them, when dishonest folk are inventing "facts" to serve mean purposes'.[39] This reflection of facts was to be imbued with didactic purpose. Of *Wrack*, O'Donnell observed 'I wrote it as a reply to the Irish bishops' pastoral [of 1931] when I was on the run in Jan'y '32. They said Russian gold was the cause of the [radical republican] unrest. I said such things as the slapping of wet skirts against people's legs. Therefore *Wrack*.'[40]

O'Donnell's desire that literature should teach and galvanize its audience is reflected in his critique of Sean O'Casey: 'A great dramatist he was, and his plays are very good theatrically, yet his plays do not excite or stimulate me. His *Plough and the Stars* I find nauseating. There is no character in that play from whom any

---

[34] Interview with the author, Dublin, 24 Feb. 1987.

[35] See e.g. T. Brown, *Ireland: A Social and Cultural History, 1922–85* (London, Fontana, 1985; 1st edn. 1981), 94, 184; F. Doherty, 'Windows on the World', *Fortnight*, 290 (Supplement Dec. 1990).

[36] Quoted in McInerney, *O'Donnell*, 241.

[37] 'An Unfinished Study', *The Bell*, 14/6 (Sept. 1947), 2.

[38] To Cape, n.d. [1933?], Cape Archives, Univ. of Reading Library.

[39] To Cape, ibid. 24 Feb. 1933.

[40] To Atkinson, 21 June 1933, ibid. Cf. P. O'Donnell, *Wrack: A Play in Six Scenes* (London, Jonathan Cape, 1933), 18.

revolutionary action could proceed'.[41] Like John Steinbeck—whose contemporaneous novels also focused much attention on migrant labourers—O'Donnell is less convincing as a novelist the more brutally didactic his novels become.[42] But there is no doubt about his own sense of literary purpose: 'My pen is just a weapon and I use it now and again to gather into words scenes that surround certain conflicts.'[43] O'Donnell's creative writing, therefore, unveils the importance and nature of the influence which his small-farm Donegal background had upon his thinking; in his books he draws upon his supposed intimacy with the minds of the mass of the people and attempts to direct his readers socially and politically.

His play and novels show that O'Donnell's sense both of the problems to be faced and of their solutions emerged out of his experience of his particular background. His reference to the delineation of conflict is instructive here; for just as his vision of republicanism was defined by his belief in the centrality of class conflict, so, too, his sense of literary purpose was built around the depiction of vital Irish conflicts. During his period as editor of the literary, artistic, and social journal, *The Bell*, he suggested that the periodical aimed at being 'a bit of Irish life, sharing eagerly in its conflicts'.[44] Similarly, his creative writing pointed to the problems of Irish life in terms of conflict and of consequent deprivation. O'Donnell sought to portray the hardship resulting from the economic struggles and conflicts which characterized the capitalist system. Just as he elsewhere recounted the social underprivilege of his own background,[45] so in his novels and play he sketched a similar impression.

The works are set in rural and island communities in his native Donegal,[46] and they repeatedly highlight the social deprivation

---

[41] Quoted in McInerney, *O'Donnell*, 197.

[42] e.g. O'Donnell's *The Big Windows* (Dublin, O'Brien, 1983; 1st edn. 1955) is far more convincing than *The Knife* in its depiction of character, precisely because it lacks the latter's sermonizing crudity and is marked instead by a greater narratorial distance. Similarly Steinbeck's *Tortilla Flat* (Harmondsworth, Penguin, 1950; 1st edn. 1935) and *Cannery Row* (London, Pan, 1974; 1st edn. 1945) grate far less than do *In Dubious Battle* (London, Pan, 1978; 1st edn. 1936) or *The Grapes of Wrath* (London, Pan, 1975; 1st edn. 1939).

[43] To Cape, 24 Feb. 1933, Cape Archives, Univ. of Reading Library.

[44] 'A Recognizable Gait of Going', *The Bell*, 16/2 (Nov. 1950), 7.

[45] Quoted in McInerney, *O'Donnell*, 33–4.

[46] *Storm, Islanders* (Cork, Mercier, 1963; 1st edn. 1927), *Wrack*, and *Proud Island* (Dublin, O'Brien, 1977; 1st edn. 1975) are essentially island-based, while *Adrigoole* (London, Jonathan Cape, 1929), *The Knife*, *On the Edge of the Stream* (London, Jonathan Cape, 1934), and *The Big Windows* are set on the mainland.

which their characters experience. In *Storm*, Maire Molloy and Eamonn Gallagher lament the 'hardships of poor children in mountain districts'. *Islanders* focuses largely on the Doogan family. Their poverty is made evident in the opening chapters of the novel. The ten children share three beds. The family's severely restricted diet leads the eldest son, Charlie, to complain that, 'People can't live for ever on praties'; '[Charlie's] purpose was to drive back the starvation that was crushing his mother and his folk'. Mary Doogan, the widowed mother of this impoverished clan, collapses through hunger, and the doctor who tends her observes that such incidents are common: 'I come across it again and again . . . just hunger, not a thing else . . . always the mother'. Emigration provides both a source of income for those who remain and, for the emigrant, an alternative to the stifling claustrophobia and hardship of island life. As one of the novel's characters observes, 'What chance has a child born on this island, except to go to the Lagan to be hired, or to Scotland to the pratie diggin'? . . . The island's only a nursery for foreign parts.'[47]

The hero and heroine of *Adrigoole*—O'Donnell's third novel—experience low-paid, exhausting work as migrant labourers in Scotland. They return to Donegal, marry, and work a small farm. A combination of poor land, an injury to the husband, Hughie Dalach, and the drain of constantly providing for IRA men drives the couple into poverty. Eventually, Hughie is imprisoned for brewing illicit whiskey, and during his incarceration Brigid and two of their children die of hunger. On discovering this to be the case, Hughie loses his sanity and is taken to an asylum.[48] Emigration and hardship are, again, prevalent throughout the book. O'Donnell's play, *Wrack*, presents people trapped painfully by hunger: 'Is there a house on the island with two women on the floor but there's tightness and sharpness and silence? Is there a houseful of childer but they're nagging and scratching at one another? Isn't the whole island in the fidgets? And what is at the root of it all? I'll tell you, it's hunger; aye, it is, hunger.'[49] *The Big Windows* sets out a similar pattern and also, along with O'Donnell's

---

[47] *Storm*, 54; *Islanders*, 13, 16, 26–7, 42, 75.

[48] Regarding the actual case which inspired O'Donnell's novel, see: McGilligan Papers, ADUCD P35b/185, esp. J. D. McCormack, *Influenza at Adrigole* (1927). O'Donnell transferred the setting from the Cork/Kerry border to his 'native Donegal': 'the drama of Adrigoole was simply the local setting of a world play.' (O'Donnell, *Adrigoole*, 7.)

[49] *Wrack*, 16.

final novel, *Proud Island*, reflects the economic pull towards emigration felt in poor western communities.[50]

O'Donnell's writings reflect the fact that his perception of social problems had roots in his personal observation of, and concern for, the underprivileged communities with which he was familiar. Similarly, his approach to the improvement of these social conditions was weightily influenced by local and personal observations, rooted, again, in his Donegal experience. In the same way as his recognition of social deprivation developed from first-hand knowledge of suffering communities, so his faith in the possibility of social redemption grew out of a belief in the resilience and inherent 'neighbourliness' of those whose communities were disadvantaged. Francis Stuart commented on O'Donnell's 'great compassion for the victims',[51] and O'Donnell himself argued that 'In the roots of us all there is a pity which is all-embracing, a deep, eternal pity which kindles on a love of life for all things that walk in the sun.'[52] But the overall weight of evidence suggests that O'Donnell preferred to stress people's self-reliance rather than try to evoke pity on their behalf.[53]

C. S. Andrews, having been shown around the Donegal Rosses by O'Donnell, commented that 'what struck me most forcefully was the atmosphere of independent self-reliance'.[54] It was precisely this resourceful, self-reliant quality which O'Donnell identified in his fictional Donegal characters, and it was upon just such a quality that much of his socialist hope was pinned. For the communities which O'Donnell depicts in his writing display a self-regulatory, communal toughness. Custom and code govern huge areas of his characters' life and experience.[55] Moreover, these communities are presented in terms of survival achieved through mutual help. A townland can be interpreted as having one communal mind and heart,[56] and the communal mind directs its thoughts toward mutual aid. In *Storm*, Eamonn Gallagher claims

---

[50] *Big Windows*, 16, 35, 106, 153; *Proud Island*, 25.

[51] Interview with the author, Dublin, 24 Feb. 1987.   [52] *Salud!*, 92.

[53] P. O'Donnell, 'The Dumb Multitudinous Masses', *The Bell*, 2/4 (July 1941), 67; 'People and Pawnshops', ibid., 5/3 (Dec. 1942), 207.

[54] *Dublin Made Me: An Autobiography* (Cork, Mercier, 1979), 199–200. Cf. Brody's comment that 'self-reliance lies at the very heart of peasant life.' (H. Brody, *Inishkillane: Change and Decline in the West of Ireland* (London, Faber and Faber, 1986; 1st edn. 1973, 131.)

[55] *Storm*, 32–3; *Islanders*, 37, 109; *Adrigoole*, 220; *Proud Island*, 74, 76, 79, 91; *Big Windows*, 193–5.   [56] O'Donnell, *On the Edge*, 190; *Proud Island*, 8.

that poor rural people possess 'the strongest sympathy knitting them all together' and that 'the hardest pressed of them would somehow manage to spare a naggin of milk when a neighbour's cow was dry, or there was a sick child in the house'.[57] In *Islanders*, the entire community automatically makes the Doogan family its primary priority after Nellie's death. Practical and moral support and co-operation are presented as integral parts of communal existence.[58] The same picture of societal intimacy and mutual aid emerges throughout O'Donnell's literary world.[59] As Francis Doherty has observed, O'Donnell's community 'can be seen to act, when at its best and most united, in ways which reinforce the deep sense of sharing and belonging'.[60]

The vital concept on which O'Donnell draws, and which he in turn develops for his own particular purposes, is that of 'neighbourliness'. This is O'Donnell's leitmotif, running through his books, and it does much to explain the origin and nature of his thinking. In the opening chapter of *Adrigoole* it is claimed that 'The diffused neighbourliness of the open fields collected in pools of eager folk in special houses that varied from night to night'. It is also asserted that this communal spirit manifested itself through acts of practical co-operation, such as 'gatherings'—the 'voluntary coming together of neighbours for part of a day to do special work without pay for some family without men-folk'.[61]

Just as he autobiographically described his background as having been 'rich in neighbourliness'[62] so, too, his partly autobiographical creative writing told the same tale. Hughie's townland, in *Adrigoole*, is described as one 'where neighbours and nature cooperated in the routine of life and there were few clashes'.[63] While O'Donnell acknowledged the divisions which could exist in these communities—within families, for example,—[64] and stressed that his folk suffered as a result of the class-based conflict and exploitation implicit within capitalism, he tended to present the suffering communities themselves in terms of good neighbourly behaviour

[57] O'Donnell, *Storm*, 55.
[58] O'Donnell, *Islanders*, 19, 40, 47–9, 107, 110. Cf. Brody, *Inishkillane*, 134.
[59] *Proud Island*, 32–4, 54, 59, 106; *Big Windows*, 37, 210.   [60] 'Windows', 10.
[61] *Adrigoole*, 12, 114. For a full examination of this practice, and of rural co-operative labour in general, see A. O'Dowd, *Meitheal: A Study of Co-operative Labour in Rural Ireland* (Dublin, Folklore Council of Ireland, 1981).
[62] Quoted in McInerney, *O'Donnell*, 34.   [63] *Adrigoole*, 77.
[64] *Big Windows*, 134.

and of its benefits.[65] 'Always put heed,' declares one of the characters in *Wrack*, 'in what might be the shout of a neighbour wanting you.'[66] While much of O'Donnell's writing evinced a romantic—at times, an extremely sentimental—approach to his subject, his conception of neighbourliness did have a hard edge to it. One of the women in *The Big Windows*, Mary Manus, suggests that 'The be-all of neighbourliness is to ask and to give.'[67] But, according to O'Donnell's vision, it was also crucial to guard against too generous a stance. Mary Manus also advises that 'It is right to be good-neighbourly. It is wrong to be soft. A man needs to have a good greed for the world in him. . . . A body has to have a hard face on him for the world, and go against his own feelings by times.'[68] In an earlier novel, it had been suggested that 'Roguery was deep in people; hadn't your neighbour on each side of you done his best to eat in on your mearn?'[69]

O'Donnell's vision of the path toward radical social change was rooted in his faith in this tough-minded, communal, mutually supportive neighbourliness. His journalistic writings reinforce the impression that his socialism owed much to the influence of this sense of neighbourliness which he had culled from his own rural experience. Writing in *An Phoblacht* in 1927, he referred to the Donegal land annuities campaign as 'entirely an affair of neighbours'. As a 'representative of the people', he argued, he would have little influence; 'but as the son of a man who owes nine years' rent, I can talk to my neighbours'.[70] A year later he expressed his belief that even the acrimonious division between Free Staters and republicans was in certain instances capable of being overpowered by the neighbourly bond: 'no peasant farmer, however much he was Cumann na nGaedheal, would buy his neighbour's cow, seized at the instance of the British Treasury'.[71]

His own background provided O'Donnell, therefore, with a sense of the gravity of the social problems to be addressed; the notion of neighbourliness, drawn from the same source, offered the means of salvation. O'Donnell held that 'in many ways the small farm countryside has a great radical tradition of Fenianism, rural socialism in its most militant sense'.[72] As this quotation suggests,

---

[65] *Islanders*, 41; *Big Windows*, 51.   [66] *Wrack*, 82.   [67] *Big Windows*, 100.
[68] Ibid. 29–30.   [69] *On the Edge*, 144.   [70] *An Phoblacht*, 14 Jan. 1927.
[71] Ibid. 14 Jan. 1928; cf. O'Donnell, *There Will Be*, 24, 26, 33, 61, 66, 86, 95.
[72] Quoted in McInerney, *O'Donnell*, 209.

O'Donnell's vision of social redemption was tied, as ever, to his republican aspirations. He claimed to 'love making restless folk aware of themselves'.[73] Convinced that he knew the nature of the social problems to be solved, that he was intimate with people's radical instincts, and that he could rely on their communal toughness and neighbourliness, O'Donnell aimed to galvanize his Irish masses around a radical republican project which he perceived to be the natural line of advance for his rural folk.

The state, according to O'Donnell's revolutionary prescription, would emerge recreated out of a struggle which had its origins among the oppressed. Thus refashioned, it would serve an emancipatory, facilitatory role. As he wrote in 1927:

I am convinced that the hard-pressed peasantry and the famishing workless are the point of assembly . . . it is not by appeasing hunger by crusts of bread, nor relieving cold by doled out cast-off clothing, but by the organizing of the people to seize power to make bread and clothing available, according as the labour of the nation and our resources can afford them.

That, then, is our task—to seize power so that the people may be worthy of themselves. . . . But such organization will only spring from the collecting of the hardest pressed to drive hunger out of their lives.[74]

In similar vein he referred, later in the same year, to 'the conquest and its capitalist system', arguing that:

The question of undoing the conquest is . . . much more than merely getting rid of the Governor-General, and the oath, and outside dictation. It is a question of releasing the native stock . . . It is about time we heard the last of the childish talk of uniting all classes to free the country. Such balderdash is ages out of date. . . . I have been attacked in Dublin by a babble of chattering tongues because I have been seeking to take the movement 'down to the gutter'. Any movement that is to raise the people out of the gutter must pick up there. Revolutionary movements must reach down to the gutter, if they are to mean anything to the workers. Until Ireland drops all this wordy cant about sovereignty and gets to work to make that sovereignty active against the forces of the conquest that are now exacting tribute from our toiling, hard pressed, working folk, all we can say is that Ireland is jabbering in her sleep.[75]

This passage is a classically O'Donnellite one, stressing the dual social and political nature of the conquest and vehemently

---

[73] *The Gates*, 51.   [74] *An Phoblacht*, 25 Mar. 1927.   [75] Ibid. 24 Dec. 1927.

denouncing the theory of pan-class nationalism. Social conflict is presented, as ever, as the fire centre of the republican struggle.

Terence Brown has argued that 'In the 1920s a number of literary works were published which attempted a more realistic treatment of the western island and the Gaeltacht'. Novels such as O'Donnell's *Islanders* and *Adrigoole*, Brown contended, were works 'not of romantic discovery but essays in rural naturalism and social criticism'. Coupling O'Donnell with Liam O'Flaherty, Brown argued that

What is striking about the work of both these writers who wrote their novels with a vigorous socialist concern to unmask social injustice in the Irish countryside through literary realism is that they both seem tempted by the vision of an Irish rural world that exists beyond political reality. At moments the Irish rural scene in both their works is allowed to occupy the same primal, essentially mythic territory as it does in the conceptions of purely nationalist ideologues. In both O'Donnell and O'Flaherty's writings there are passages of epic writing therefore which obtrude in their realistic settings. At such moments class politics and social analysis give way before an apprehension of the west as a place of fundamental natural forces, of human figures set passively or heroically against landscapes of stone, rock and sea in a way that makes their works less radical than they perhaps thought they were. There is implicit therefore in their writings a sense that Gaelic Ireland in the west is the authentic heroic Ireland in a way that confirms rather than contradicts the conventional image of the west as 'certain set apart'. The power of this conventional image was perhaps so great that it affected as intelligent a social commentator as Peadar O'Donnell and overwhelmed the turbulent anger of Liam O'Flaherty's social criticism.[76]

Brown's argument is worth quoting at length because it points to an important strain in O'Donnell's thinking. O'Donnell expressed his disgust at sentimental preservation: 'I hate to see spinning-wheels, thatched cottages, small farms and handicraft kept alive to make a show. A fishing-village carefully preserved within a holiday resort appals me as only exhausted forms can appal.'[77] He also evinced a slightly patronizing scepticism regarding the romantic fantasies harboured by outsiders in relation to his native culture. In *Islanders* it is observed that 'Doctor Wilson was in his third year as dispensary doctor in the Rosses. His sister, Ruth, spent a great deal of her time with him. She had long wished to live in the

[76] *Ireland*, 94.   [77] *Salud!*, 22.

Rosses and to know its people. It was a desire born of the Abbey Theatre, and fostered by short trips to Kerry and Connemara'.[78]

Yet, as Terence Brown notes, O'Donnell's books do contain passages of sentimental, heroic, and romantic writing. While much of his narrative deals with hardship and all-too-realistic drudge, there are also lengthy excursions into the realm of mythic, epic depiction. *Storm* begins with the bravery of fishermen involved in 'the unequal struggle' against appalling weather conditions which, were it not for extreme financial exigency, would prohibit any attempt to take boats out.[79] *Islanders* contains an episode in which, despite atrocious storm conditions, Charlie Doogan rows to the mainland in a curragh in order to contact a doctor on behalf of his sick sister. Doogan is drawn in epic, heroic terms:

It was a mighty tussle...Once clear of the surf, he drove before the storm, delaying, hurrying, once or twice trusting blindly, but racing, racing across the waters. His black, hatless head, his set, granite-hued face dripping wet; strong, supple arms, fingers of steel....He shouted; he knew not why, but he shouted...just opened his mouth and roared, plying his paddle with grand stroke, and god-like confidence. He growled when a swell slipped water into the curragh; laughed when he broke the face of a crumbling wave....He drove his bending paddle deeper into the tossing water, and forged forward, using strength mostly, almost scorning to use caution.

At a regatta, later in the novel, Doogan and his rival are described as being engaged in 'a battle of evenly matched giants'. Charlie rebels 'against the helplessness' by which he appears to be surrounded. At the end of the novel he and his partner, Susan Manus, having separately contemplated emigration, resolve to remain on the island. O'Donnell portrays the couple as examples of a breed resisting the pressure which threatens to force their community out of existence.[80] *Wrack* and *Proud Island* both contain displays of bravery on the part of fishermen facing ferocious elements,[81] and also portray uncowed widows, stoically endeavouring to fend for their families despite poverty and bereavement.

But while Brown's argument illuminates this important aspect of O'Donnell's writing, it does rather misinterpret the nature of O'Donnell's socialism. It is not that romanticism, myth, and

[78] *Islanders*, 65–6. [79] *Storm*, 7–23. [80] *Islanders*, 32, 65, 84, 124.
[81] *Wrack*, 81–4; *Proud Island*, 81 ff.

heroicism 'obtrude' into O'Donnell's hard-headed, realistic, socialist world; it is rather that his socialism, in substantial measure, had grown out of that very romantic, heroic perception in the first place. It is precisely because O'Donnell's Donegal is peopled, in his view, with characters who are heroic, resilient, courageous, and endlessly resourceful that he is able to build an optimistic vision of the potential lying within this instinctive 'rural socialism'. That his literary portrayal of such characters was naïve and romantic appears to have been (belatedly) recognized even by O'Donnell himself. Whereas his inter-war novels present an unyielding courage which will provide the basis for rural regeneration—'god-like' Charlie Doogan's refusal to acknowledge the death of Inniscara Island, for example—in later life he conceded that there had, in fact, been no hope for such communities. Asked in 1985 whether he felt that governments had let down the rural west, allowing it to suffer avoidable decline, O'Donnell replied with pessimism.

INTERVIEWER. Do you think the west of Ireland was treated badly under the Free State ... and do you think there was maybe a bit of hypocrisy in that they [were saying that the west] was the real Ireland ... and yet at the same time they weren't prepared to help it that much?

O'DONNELL. Well, what could they do? What could they do?

INTERVIEWER. You don't think they could have done more?

O'DONNELL. No, I don't think that at all.

INTERVIEWER. Why was that?

O'DONNELL. Because there was no basis for them to do anything more. There was nothing that could be done with the farms and as far as industry was concerned, they could never hope to organize industry there.[82]

The origins of O'Donnell's socialist thinking cannot be understood without reference to his particular social background. His belief in a pre-existing form of rural socialism, and in the communal courage and toughness of his rural constituency, determined his faith in the possibility of socialist reconstruction in Ireland. Declan Kiberd has suggested that 'it is easy to see why socialist authors, from Peadar O'Donnell to George Thomson, have chosen island life as a theme'.[83] In relation to O'Donnell, however, this perhaps

---

[82] Angela Crean interview with Peadar O'Donnell, 9 Apr. 1985.

[83] 'Irish Literature and Irish History', in R. F. Foster (ed.), *The Oxford Illustrated History of Ireland* (Oxford, OUP, 1989), 333.

leads in the wrong direction. In O'Donnell's case, it was not so much that a socialist author found in island life themes that suited his purposes, as that a socialist author had emerged out of small farm and island Donegal. O'Donnell's vision of his Donegal world was coloured by romantic misconception. Similarly, the political project which he intended his literature to serve was itself marred by incoherence and contradiction. But, whatever O'Donnell's misconceptions, it is vital to recognize that, in his case, the Donegal background helped to forge the socialist, just as the socialist unsurprisingly recreated—with didactic purpose—the Donegal world which had done so much to produce and define his socialism.

THE LAND ANNUITIES CAMPAIGN

Are the remnants of the Gaelic stock to be sought out among the rocks and stripped naked under a cruel winter? Can these homes stamped unmistakably with the personality of these Gaelic folk—and they are yet a vital, unbroken set of people—be razed because tribute to Britain is not being paid?

Peadar O'Donnell (1927)[84]

Does every farmer in Ireland pay Annuities?
Yes, and the amount is a heavy burden to him.
Why are these paid?
They are paid to the British Government instead of the rent formerly paid to landlords.

Catechism of Land Annuities (1928)[85]

James Connolly's weakness with regard to rural Ireland has already been commented upon, and it should also be acknowledged that, in the words of one of his more critical biographers, he 'never seriously considered achieving social or political objectives by uniting urban and rural workers (not even in 1914–16)'.[86] In contrast, the pursuit of rural and urban radical co-operation was central to Peadar O'Donnell's inter-war political projects. With

---

[84] *An Phoblacht*, 17 Dec. 1927.
[85] *Catechism of Land Annuities* (Oct. 1928), Moore Papers, NLI MS. 10,560.
[86] A. Morgan, *James Connolly: A Political Biography* (Manchester, Manchester Univ. Press, 1988), 31.

O'Donnell, indeed, specifically rural struggles were of vital importance and he devoted much of his energy toward them.

Most significantly, perhaps, O'Donnell used his talents during the 1920s in connection with the land annuities campaign which he himself had done much to instigate. The money in question related to the 1891 and 1909 Land Acts, and represented the repayment by farmers of the advances which had facilitated their participation in the process of land purchase. Under section 26 of the Government of Ireland Act, both north and south were to have retained the annuities paid in their respective territories. This situation was held to have been superseded as a result of the 1921 treaty and subsequent arrangements. On 12 February 1923 a secret agreement was arrived at between the British and Free State governments, under which it was accepted that the latter would collect annuity payments from tenants and place the money in a Purchase Annuities Fund, the nature of which was highly ambiguous. This arrangement was confirmed under section 12 of the Irish Land Act of 1923. On 3 December 1925 a financial agreement arrived at in London between Britain, Northern Ireland, and the Free State released the 26-county state from its liability to contribute to the British national debt. The following March, the Free State government's undertaking to pay the land annuities over to Britain was confirmed under the terms of the Ultimate Financial Settlement.[87]

Characteristically, however, O'Donnell, the irritant around which the annuities campaign formed, took little interest in this complicated legal tangle. The struggle began in his home region of Donegal. According to O'Donnell, it had its roots in the years of the Anglo-Irish war, during which period a bailiff 'seized a few head of cattle for arrears of rent due to the estate of the Marquess of Conyngham'. Some local people opposed this, declaring that from that day onwards 'the bailiff's office was abolished'. A subsequent meeting saw 'wild ideas' expounded:

Landlordism was a worn-out, historical myth. It was binding nowhere, and least of all in Ireland. The land annuity was only the other side of the rent penny. People should disown that too. Henceforth let no man pay

[87] D. McMahon, *Republicans and Imperialists: Anglo-Irish Relations in the 1930s* (New Haven, Conn., Yale Univ. Press, 1984), 38–9; R. Fanning, *Independent Ireland* (Dublin, Helicon, 1983), 112, *The Irish Department of Finance, 1922–58* (Dublin, Institute of Public Administration, 1978), ch. 4.

rent for land. The people raised their hands and pledged themselves to practise and protect this freedom . . . people came to look on it that loyalty to the Republic was, somehow, involved in the repudiation of landlordism; as if it was an aspect of the refusal to recognize the British court.

In 'late 1925 or early 1926' O'Donnell discovered on a visit to his local district that one local man, Jack Boyle, had been informed that his continued non-payment of annuity arrears would result in court proceedings. O'Donnell suggested that legal costs be avoided by making the required payments, but Boyle explained that he could pay nothing anyway without selling his cattle and that there was, therefore, nothing to be lost by non-payment. O'Donnell managed to ascertain that others were in a similarly difficult plight: 'I was a native of the district and it was easy for me to wander around and pick up enough to give myself an idea of the state of things, on the level of neighbourly gossip'. On the Sunday following Boyle's revelation, O'Donnell addressed people outside the local chapel after Mass. His message

was a simple one: the bailiff would soon be on the rampage through the townlands. Nothing was to be gained by asking whether people did the right or the wrong thing in witholding rents in 1919, nor whether what was right in the setting of 1919 was wrong now. The rent itself was no great burden on people then, but the arrears were not so simple a matter now and there was a neighbour, here and there, who just could not pay them, and already such people were threatened with the bailiff. I told them that I did not know whether the recent strife had broken the pattern of neighbourliness among us so much that neighbours would not gather round the neighbour in trouble and save his cattle.[88]

O'Donnell later claimed that 'The only person who ever acknowledged my role in the [land annuities] thing was Paddy Hogan [Cumann na nGaedheal Minister for Agriculture]'.[89] In fact, Seán O'Faoláin had publicly noted, in the 1930s, that O'Donnell, 'in rousing his native Donegal people against the Free State government bade them refuse to pay their Land Annuities, or rent.'[90] Deploying *An Phoblacht* ('as near as no matter the official organ of the agitation'), O'Donnell brought his oratorical and organizational talents to the campaign against payment of the annuities.[91]

[88] *There Will Be*, 20–4.   [89] *Monkeys*, 27.
[90] *De Valera* (Harmondsworth, Penguin, 1939), 124.
[91] O'Donnell, *There Will Be*, 24–5, 38.

The campaign spread.[92] O'Donnell employed a typical combination of wit and menace in his efforts to build the movement. In his engaging account of the agitation, O'Donnell refers to an occasion on which he was arrested[93] and charged in connection with the campaign. He refused to recognize the Free State court and, characteristically, defended himself with impish enjoyment. His words reflected his willingness to employ IRA menace in support of his social campaign:

When the State rested its case and my turn came, I explained to the jurors that refusing to recognize the court simply meant I didn't recognize 'the lad in the wig'. I did recognize the jury, however. They were neighbours of mine and I had a word to say to them. I recited the background to this case against me. I told them of the continuous clashes between militant Republicans and the State forces and I emphasized 'militant Republicans' in hopes they would think I had the IRA in mind. I asked the jury not to take sides in those clashes; the government had no right to involve them. The way for them to keep out of it all was find me not guilty ... The jury found me not guilty.[94]

O'Donnell's approach to the land-annuities agitation centred on the hope that social struggle and republican momentum could exist in symbiotic relation to one another. He presented the threat of Donegal evictions in terms of national conscience:

Have we come to this then? Are the remnants of the Gaelic stock to be sought out among the rocks and stripped naked under a cruel winter? Can these homes stamped unmistakably with the personality of these Gaelic folk—and they are yet a vital, unbroken set of people—be razed because tribute to Britain is not being paid? The national conscience will be tried out in these cases, and if the nation does not cry halt, then indeed we have fallen very low, very low.[95]

At a Comhairle na dTeachtai[96] gathering in December 1926, O'Donnell had argued that he

---

[92] Ibid. 58; M. M. Banta, 'The Red Scare in the Irish Free State, 1929–37', MA thesis (UCD, 1982), 16–17.
[93] O'Donnell's pioneering involvement in the land annuities struggle led to regular conflict with the Free State authorities: see e.g. *An Phoblacht*, 25 Mar., 1 Apr., 8 Apr. 1927.   [94] *There Will Be*, 56–7.
[95] *An Phoblacht*, 17 Dec. 1927.
[96] Comhairle na dTeachtai [Council of Deputies], set up in 1924: 'Excluded by dogma from [the Free State Dail], the Sinn Fein TDs organized the Comhairle, which included all TDs elected by Sinn Fein since 1921.... [T]he Comhairle na

thought it would be well to take up some particular activity. . . . Comhairle na dTeachtai could be useful if it took up a certain activity. To my mind, the question of payment of annuities to England is a thing for it to take up. When you do things of this sort the people will understand you and the [republican] government position will be assured again. The Free State army will have to be forced out. We have an opportunity today of definitely choosing a particular law and rely [*sic*] on yourselves to put it into force.[97]

Shortly after O'Donnell's assumption of the paper's editorship in 1926, an *An Phoblacht* editorial argued that rural agitation represented the natural focal point and fire centre of the national advance:

The conquest is pressing heaviest in the enforcing of the 'Rights' of conquest over our lands. The point of attack should be the point of rally. Such a concentration is not moving away from the full programme of ending the conquest. It is challenging the conquest and moving nationally in opposition to it . . . We recognize that it is no wandering from our supreme purpose to undo the conquest absolutely to put ourselves into the defence of the peasant farmers against this robbery of children to meet the call of British interests.[98]

In O'Donnell's view, there existed the potential for the land annuities issue to become 'transformed into an overwhelming uprising of Republican feeling'.[99] Moreover, 'the Republic if restored through a struggle on this level, would be a Republic of the poor, achieved by the poor, for the poor'. The republican defeat over the 1921 treaty could, he believed, be overturned: 'Republicans could roast the Treaty in the fire from this kindling'; 'This skirmish we were conducting could lead into a land war which could restore the independence movement that the Treaty had wrecked.'[100]

Within sections of the republican movement, however, there was considerable hostility to this O'Donnellite vision. With specific reference to O'Donnell's land annuities agitation, Austin

dTeachtai, with only the Second Dail members voting, was [according to republicans] the *de jure* government of Ireland' (Bell, *Secret Army*, 49; cf. O'Faoláin, *De Valera*, 117).

[97] Comhairle na dTeachtai, 18–19 Dec. 1926, *Evolution of Fianna Fáil Party and New Sinn Fein Party*, Files of the Dept. of the Taoiseach, NA S 5880, 59–60.

[98] *An Phoblacht*, 4 June 1926.   [99] 'Irish Struggle', 299.

[100] *There Will Be*, 34, 52, 86.

Stack's biographer observed that 'Stack was haunted by the spectre of the Republican, physical-force, separatist tradition destroying itself in a welter of greed and self-seeking'. He was convinced 'that involvement by the IRA in agrarian trouble would lead only to disaster.'[101] Although O'Donnell was not without some local IRA backing, he had failed to persuade either the Army Council or the Army Executive to give him their support in the project.[102] O'Donnell himself acknowledged that top-level IRA endorsement had not been forthcoming.[103] George Gilmore—O'Donnell's 'only constant support' on the issue within the IRA—[104] argued that there had been 'enough determination to avoid division within the army on class issues, and to avoid the loss of what middle class support it still retained, to make it impossible to involve the army organizationally in that agitation'.[105] It was a telling and typical obstacle to O'Donnellite progress.

Another significant problem emerged in relation to Fianna Fáil. Colonel Maurice Moore had offered 'sustained protest in the Free State Senate against the payment of land annuities to Britain, on the ground that the Free State was under no legal obligation to pay them'. Moore and O'Donnell colluded on the issue and it became clear to both men that 'it would greatly help us in the countryside if we could bring Fianna Fáil TDs onto our platform there'.[106] But O'Donnell's and de Valera's respective approaches to the annuities issue differed greatly from one another.[107] O'Donnell himself recognized the divergence: 'If Fianna Fáil were allowed off on their own they would drift into soft talk of the burden of those payments on the national economy, and of the good use they would make of this money when they got into office.'

O'Donnell, indeed, came to find himself marginalized on the radical wing of a campaign which increasingly took on a moderate aspect. From its early stages the annuity struggle had been waged

---

[101] J. A. Gaughan, *Austin Stack: Portrait of a Separatist* (Mount Merrion, Kingdom Books, 1977), 259–60.
[102] Bell, *Secret Army*, 58; O'Donnell, quoted in MacEoin (ed.), *Survivors*, 33.
[103] O'Donnell, *There Will Be*, 87–8.
[104] O'Donnell, quoted in MacEoin (ed.), *Survivors*, 33.
[105] *The Irish Republican Congress* (1978; 1st edn. 1935), 23.
[106] O'Donnell, *There Will Be*, 79, 89.
[107] H. Patterson, 'Fianna Fáil and the Working Class: The Origins of the Enigmatic Relationship', *Saothar*, 13 (1988), 85.

by people drawn from a wide spectrum of political opinion. Maurice Moore, for example, had given valuable backing to O'Donnell without sharing his socially subversive purpose. Moore thought the annuity payments illegal, immoral, and a burden on the economy. But he had suspected O'Donnell of 'acting for the IRA', and their alliance was based on a temporary intersection of purpose rather than on a common political philosophy. The Donegal socialist sought to use Moore's Fianna Fáil connections in order to strengthen the campaign. But the attitude of Fianna Fáil leaders was doubly problematic for O'Donnell. First, there was the difficulty of persuading them to endorse a campaign so redolent of social extremism. In O'Donnell's own words, the agitation had been portrayed as 'a communist activity with Peadar O'Donnell as its high priest',[108] and some of those who opposed the campaign did show traces of having been infected with the anti-socialist virus. In December 1928 the *Irish Independent* quoted Bishop Michael Fogarty's 'stern rebuke' to those county councils which endorsed the view that farmers were neither legally nor morally bound to pay their annuities: 'The first remark one is tempted to make is that it is not for enunciating Bolshevist principles of this kind that the Co. Councils are maintained by the rates of the people'. It was, he continued, 'very regrettable to see men who should know better propounding subversive principles of that kind, which strike at the very basis of social life'.[109] O'Donnell's charming indifference to such opposition is evident in his claim that as he was not widely known by appearance, except in Dublin and Donegal, he was 'often able to join in the talk, at the next table to me in a provincial hotel, on this blackguard Peadar O'Donnell'. But his insouciance should not be allowed to obscure the gravity of the problem. Although de Valera, for example, was 'impressed by the case [Moore] made on the legal aspect of the annuity issue', there was some anxiety that an agitator as red as O'Donnell should enjoy a high profile in a movement in which Fianna Fáil was to participate.[110]

Second, there was the subtler, though ultimately more serious, problem reflected by the divergence between O'Donnell's perspective and that of his more moderate anti-annuity colleagues.

---

[108] *There Will Be*, 49, 86–90.   [109] *Irish Independent* 19 Dec. 1928.
[110] O'Donnell, *There Will Be*, 49, 89–90.

The irony—tragic, from O'Donnell's perspective—was that although he had galvanized people into action and done much to organize, publicize, and strengthen the annuities campaign, the movement was actually to gain its fullest political significance as part of a socially conservative package marketed by Fianna Fáil.[111] On 14 February 1928 the 'No Tribute' campaign was launched at a Rotunda meeting chaired by Maurice Moore.[112] A resolution was passed declaring the land annuities 'to be neither morally nor legally due to the British Treasury' and asserting that 'all decrees for annuities already issued, or about to be issued, against farmers should be suspended pending a national settlement of what payments Irish farmers are to make to the national revenue'.[113] O'Donnell spoke at the meeting, yet his own demands went much further than those expressed in the above resolution. The gulf between his socialist ambitions and the more limited aspirations of the moderates is made clear through a reading of Moore's tract, *Catechism of Land Annuities*. The senator gave greater prominence than did O'Donnell to legal arguments. He cited the Government of Ireland Act to prove that the British government regarded the land purchase funds as part of Britain's national debt. He added as further evidence that 'the repayment of the capital is being retained by the British National Debt Commissioners'. He referred to the 1925 agreement by which Britain 'agreed to abolish clause five [of the 1921 treaty]', thereby freeing the Free State 'from payment of any part of the British National debt, which included the Annuities'. This agreement was absolute and final, and yet in March 1926 it had been agreed 'to pay the annuities, local loans, and other sums to Britain'.[114]

Moore was an energetic evangelist in relation to the annuities issue.[115] In a 1931 piece, his arguments again clarified the distance between his own stance and that of O'Donnell. The burdens on farmers were, he asserted,

[111] *Irish Press*, 6 Feb., 8 Feb., 9 Feb., 10 Feb. 1932; E. Rumpf and A. C. Hepburn, *Nationalism and Socialism in Twentieth Century Ireland* (Liverpool, Liverpool Univ. Press, 1977), 101–2.

[112] Moore to Fogarty, 19 Dec. 1928, Moore Papers, NLI MS 10,560.

[113] *Irish Times*, 15 Feb. 1928.

[114] *Catechism of Land Annuities*, Coyle O'Donnell Papers, ADUCD P61/32 (8), 3.

[115] Fintan Lalor Cumann, *Fianna Fáil: Minute Book*, 13 Dec. 1928, Byrne Papers, PP.

too heavy to bear; the annuities and the rates are crushing the farmers;
they are everywhere demanding relief. The Northern farmers have se-
cured derating, why not the Free State?

The total sum required for derating all the agricultural land will be
about £2,100,000.... The retention of the Land Annuities in the Free
State is the key to the whole situation; the Land Annuities amount to
£3,000,000 a year, so that after completely derating the agricultural land
(£2,100,000) there remains a substantial sum for the improvement of the
people.[116]

Retention, rather than O'Donnellite scrapping, was therefore
Moore's prescription. Like O'Donnell, he located the annuities
issue in the context of historical English wrongs:

It is not generally remembered that the Irish land purchase annuities are
nothing more or less than the old rents imposed by landlords and their
predecessors; that the titles to those lands were based on confiscation
from the original inhabitants of the country by English kings mainly of
the Tudor and Stuart dynasties; that the original occupiers of the soil
were reduced to a position of servitude the most degraded ever imposed
on a helpless people.[117]

But the two men's respective projects were, none the less, distinct
from one another. Where O'Donnell wanted to attack the notion
of rent and opposed any payment of annuities, Moore argued that
the money should still be paid but that the Free State government
should retain it. Admittedly, he intended that the amount paid
should be reduced. But he did not envisage the kind of radical
social emancipation for which O'Donnell was hoping, nor did he
seek to reactivate republican separatism through the annuities
campaign. Indeed, in contrast to O'Donnell, Moore stressed that
retention of the annuities would not cause a clash with Britain.[118]

Such distinctions were telling, for they epitomized the crucial
divergence between Fianna Fáil's more socially conservative nationalism, and O'Donnell's full-throated, uncompromising socialist republicanism. O'Donnell himself noted that de Valera's land
annuity policy fell far short of his own aspiration: 'he reduced the
annuity by half, without extending the period of payment. He
funded arrears of three years, and forgave arrears with deeper

---

[116] *Derating and the Land Annuities* (1931), Moore Papers, NLI MS 10,560.
[117] *Short Notes on the Irish Land Purchase Annuities: How They Originated and
the Present Position* (n.d.), ibid.
[118] *Catechism*, Coyle O'Donnell Papers, ADUCD P61/32 (8), 4.

roots.'[119] But the pattern of Fianna Fáil success at the expense of O'Donnellite ambitions was to reassert itself forcefully throughout the 1930s. The annuities issue was helpful to Fianna Fáil in their successful 1932 election campaign. Ironically, therefore, by helping to build the land annuities agitation, O'Donnell gave a boost to the very political force whose capitalist nationalism was to eclipse his own socialist republicanism.

FIANNA FÁIL

De Valera was still President of the Irish Republic, a shadow government which governed nothing. He was President of Sinn Fein, a shadow political party which took no part in practical politics. He decided that this situation must end.

Robert Briscoe[120]

Mrs Mulhall moved and Mr F. Carty (senior) seconded the following resolution: 'That the Fianna Fáil party consider the introduction of a Bill to control the price of food'. After a good discussion the resolution was passed unanimously . . .

Fintan Lalor Cumann, *Fianna Fáil: Minute Book* (1929)[121]

Speaking in Belfast in 1984, Peadar O'Donnell referred to a telephone conversation which he had had with Eamon de Valera during the latter's presidency in the Republic. ' "You've got to remember, Dev," '—said O'Donnell—' "that damn nearly a million Irish people left there while you were Taoiseach." "Ah, be fair now," '—said de Valera—' "if you had been in my place there'd have been emigration, too." "Yes, Dev, that's quite true;" '—O'Donnell claims to have replied—' "if I had been in your place there'd have been a great many people who would have left the country. But they would not have been the same people!" '[122]

The story epitomizes O'Donnell's cheeky intimacy with the powerful. But it also reflects the gulf which existed between his own outlook and that of the party which was to dominate independent Irish politics during (and beyond) the 1930s. In later life, O'Donnell described the 1926 formation of Fianna Fáil as 'a burst

---

[119] *There Will Be*, 131–2.
[120] (with A. Hatch), *For the Life of Me* (London, Longmans, 1958), 224.
[121] 18 Apr. 1929, Byrne Papers, PP. [122] Speech in Belfast, 7 Apr. 1984.

of political realism'.[123] De Valera's withdrawal from Sinn Fein to found Fianna Fáil was 'a breath of fresh air into a world of make-believe'.[124] But the crucial points to stress are, first, the massive differences between O'Donnell's socialist republican outlook and the outlook which characterized Fianna Fáil and, second, the fact that the latter's conservative nationalism was the force which triumphed over and obscured republican socialism during this period. Both the means and the end result of their respective nationalist projects demonstrated the divergence between socialist republicanism and Fianna Fáil nationalism.

De Valera, 'the tall, professorial figure of nationalist Ireland's conscience',[125] was to lead his party during the 1930s on a nationalistic pilgrimage which resulted in the 'untreating' of the Irish Free State. But it is the economic and social aspects of his and his party's approach which are of greatest relevance to our argument. Even in the earliest years of the new state's existence, economic policies were of vital importance in determining the pattern of party politics. Cumann na nGaedheal's policies, for example, favoured large farmers at smallholders' expense,[126] and right from its inception Fianna Fáil's project was framed with a view to its economic appeal. In April 1926 de Valera issued a press statement regarding the aims of his newly emerging political party. These included the aspirations to develop 'a social system in which, as far as possible, equal opportunity will be afforded to every Irish citizen to live a noble and useful Christian life', to arrange land distribution 'so as to get the greatest number possible of Irish families rooted in the soil of Ireland', and to make Ireland 'an economic unit, as self-contained and self-sufficient as possible— with a proper balance between agriculture and the other essential industries'.[127]

Such rhetorical pieties can (and perhaps should) be scoffed at, but there is no doubt about the seriousness of Fianna Fáil's sense of economic purpose even during its early years. As Mary Daly has recently observed, 'In its founding constitution Fianna Fáil

---

[123] Quoted in McInerney, *O'Donnell*, 101.   [124] O'Donnell, *There Will Be*, 36.
[125] D. G. Boyce, *The Irish Question and British Politics 1868–1986* (Basingstoke, Macmillan, 1988), 74.
[126] M. E. Daly, *Industrial Development and Irish National Identity 1922–39* (Dublin, Gill and Macmillan, 1992), 17.
[127] Fanning, *Independent Ireland*, 96–7.

showed its continuity with traditional Sinn Fein thinking, reiterating the belief that Ireland could flourish under independence and calling for industrial development behind protective tariffs, programmes of reforestation, transport, land distribution, and a state development bank.'[128] As its courting of élites and its distinctive profile of social support demonstrate,[129] Fianna Fáil were very sharp in recognizing the importance of economic questions to their chances of political success. De Valera famously wrote to the influential Clan na Gael figure, Joe McGarrity, in 1926, justifying his new departure:

You perhaps will wonder why I did not wait longer. It is vital that the Free State be shaken at the *next* general election, for if an opportunity be given it to consolidate itself further as an institution—if the present Free State members are replaced by Farmers and Labourers and other class interests, the national interest as a whole will be submerged in the clashing of the rival economic groups.[130]

Where socialist republicans defined the national struggle in terms of class conflict, de Valera feared that class conflict would drown 'the national interest as a whole'.

This passage, therefore, reflects the differences of emphasis between O'Donnell's and de Valera's contrasting approaches to nationalism. It also shows that de Valera, 'the most significant figure in the political history of modern Ireland',[131] was keenly aware during these years of the importance of economic issues in determining the pattern of party political life. Consequently, he and his party set out to build economic strategies which would appeal to as wide a section of the people as possible in order that Fianna Fáil would be able to achieve hegemony in the young Free State. Cross-class alliances, rather than inter-class conflict, and capitalism, rather than anti-capitalism, were to characterize de Valera's party. As Richard Dunphy has rightly observed:

from its inception the Fianna Fáil party fought on the basis of an economic and social programme with specific appeal to broad sections of the

---

[128] *Industrial Development*, 38.
[129] D. Keogh, 'De Valera, the Catholic Church and the "Red Scare", 1931–2', in J. P. O'Carroll and J. A. Murphy (eds.), *De Valera and His Times* (Cork, Cork Univ. Press, 1986; 1st edn. 1983), 155; Rumpf and Hepburn, *Nationalism and Socialism*, 107. [130] 13 Mar. 1926, McGarrity Papers, NLI MS 17,441.
[131] J. A. Murphy, 'The Achievement of Eamon de Valera', in O'Carroll and Murphy (eds.), *De Valera and His Times*, 1–2.

98 *The New IRA*

electorate . . . from the outset, [the party] sought to articulate its nationalism in concrete economic and social terms which *combined* a development strategy geared to the vital interests of important strata such as the small farmers and petty bourgeoisie with welfarist policies and overtures to the trade union movement designed to secure working class support . . .[132]

This project was emphatically capitalist. Protection was celebrated as the condition upon which Irish capitalist success would be built. The cross-class alliance—'petty bourgeoisie (small farmers included), home-market-oriented bourgeoisie . . . , urban workers, unemployed, and agricultural labourers'—[133] was, therefore, to be forged on the basis of a diametrically opposed project from that which characterized republican socialists. Where socialist republicans looked for anti-capitalist class conflict as the motor of national advance, Fianna Fáil, from its very inception, sought class harmony and capitalist success.

Both Fianna Fáil and the republican left aimed to relate nationalist objectives to economic policies; but their respective economic projects were mutually antithetical. De Valera might bathe, as in May 1926, in the prospect of 'cutting the bonds of foreign interference one by one until the full internal sovereignty of the Twenty-Six Counties was established beyond question',[134] but it is indisputable that the untreating of the state was inextricably interwoven in Fianna Fáil thinking with economic policies. In this sense, Fianna Fáil's adoption of the land annuities campaign neatly epitomized the party's approach: the campaign was anti-British, involved the breaking of links with the old enemy, and simultaneously offered economic advantage to a significant section of supporters. Commenting on the differences between Cumann na nGaedheal and Fianna Fáil, Mary Daly has argued that 'The economic divisions were of a piece with those on the national question: between continuity and change; between retaining close links with Britain and asserting independence; between introspective isolation—even breaking with economic conventions—and a more international outlook. The contrasting positions

132 Dunphy, 'Class, Power and the Fianna Fail Party', 11, 20.
133 Ibid. 121, 132–3.
134 M. Moynihan (ed.), *Speeches and Statements of Eamon de Valera, 1917–73* (Dublin, Gill and Macmillan, 1980), 135.

may have served to entrench each party in its particular ideological camp.'[135]

The degree to which economic interests defined and determined Fianna Fáil's political project can be seen in the valuable Minute Books of the party's Fintan Lalor Cumann in Dublin. Social and economic concerns repeatedly surface in the record of the branch's meetings. On 13 December 1928 Maurice Moore 'delivered, to a large number of members and their friends, a very interesting lecture on "The Land Annuities" '. The following month, it was suggested that another lecture be delivered: 'Senator J. Connolly: "Irish finance and its relations to Irish industry and Irish civilization" '. In February 1929 the branch secretary 'was instructed to write for some leaflets dealing with the tariff on woollen cloths'. On 11 April the question was raised 'of the Fianna Fáil party bringing a Bill in the Dáil re the standardizing of prices of the necessities of life'. The following week, a resolution was proposed, ' "That the Fianna Fáil party consider the introduction of a Bill to control the price of food". After a good discussion the resolution was passed unanimously'.[136]

Later in 1929, a resolution was passed at a meeting of this Fintan Lalor branch to the effect, 'That this Cumann is of opinion that the Fianna Fáil party should take official action in relation to the Tram Strike and we draw attention to the fact, that in [the] ranks of Fianna Fáil are many Tramway workers, and we suggest that a public meeting be called immediately to protest against the lockout.' The following week, 'On behalf of the Tramway workers of the Cumann Mr Dan O'Hanlon thanked the members for their Resolution.' In October 1929 the Cumann heard a lecture on 'The Housing Problem', a topic which was to recur in their discussions.[137]

Locally as well as centrally, Fianna Fáil were, from their earliest years, focusing attention on a range of economic questions of relevance to various sections of the electorate. This pattern, as we shall see, was to continue throughout our period. The party derived strength from this economic focus. Labour's electoral organizers noted, for example, 'that the workers expected Fianna Fáil to fulfil

[135] *Industrial Development*, 38.
[136] Fintan Lalor Cumann, *Fianna Fáil: Minute Book*, 13 Dec. 1928, 10 Jan., 7 Feb., 11 Apr., 18 Apr. 1929, Byrne Papers, PP.
[137] Ibid. 12 Sept., 19 Sept., 10 Oct. 1929, 18 Sept. 1930.

all their wishes'.[138] But the radical flavour of Fianna Fáil's early years must not be allowed to blind us to the massive differences which existed between this capitalist, pan-class nationalism and the class-struggling republican socialism of O'Donnell and his comrades.

Another crucial difference distinguishing the two would-be hegemonic groupings was the question of participation in the machinery of the existing Free State. During the late 1920s and the 1930s Fianna Fáil were to lead the anti-treaty constituency from abstentionist alienation to dominant participation in the twenty-six-county state. In the 1923 general election, republicans had been supported by 27.4 per cent of those who voted. Fianna Fáil won by 26.1 per cent in June 1927, but this figure increased to 35.2 per cent in September 1927, and to 44.5 per cent in 1932. In 1933 49.7 per cent of those who voted supported de Valera's party, in 1937 the figure was 45.2 per cent and in 1938 it reached 51.9 per cent. In 1923 only 58.7 per cent of the electorate had voted, and only 27.4 per cent of these people had voted republican. In the 1938 election 75.7 per cent of the electorate voted, and 51.9 per cent of these votes were cast in favour of Fianna Fáil. Anti-treatyites were being brought back, by de Valera's party, into the electoral arena.[139]

Robert Briscoe, 'a founder and member of the Executive Committee of ... Fianna Fáil', commented of de Valera's resignation from the presidency of Sinn Fein and of the supposed Irish republic that, as a consequence, 'he was free to enter the arena of action'. Regarding the position on the eve of the split from Sinn Fein, Briscoe observed: 'De Valera was still President of the Irish Republic, a shadow government which governed nothing. He was President of Sinn Fein, a shadow political party which took no part in practical politics. He decided that this situation must end.'[140] It is precisely this question of pragmatic participation in 'the arena of action' that it is important to stress. This is the point which was missed by the neo-Pearsean Brian Murphy when he defended those

---

[138] Quoted in Rumpf and Hepburn, *Nationalism and Socialism*, 107.

[139] Between 1923 and 1933 the percentage of the electorate actually voting increased in successive elections. Fianna Fáil's share of the votes cast rose at successive elections between June 1927 and 1933 (T. Garvin, 'Nationalist Elites, Irish Voters and Irish Political Development: A Comparative Perspective', *Economic and Social Review*, 8/3 (Apr. 1977), 173). [140] *For the Life*, 224, 226.

republicans who did not join de Valera's Fianna Fáil departure in the 1920s. These people, Murphy argued, tend to be 'dismissed as of inferior calibre' to those who followed de Valera. Murphy's assessment differed: 'The names and records of those who resisted de Valera's initiative gives the lie to such a contention.' Citing republicans like Mary MacSwiney, J. J. O'Kelly, Austin Stack, and Peadar O'Donnell, he argued that 'Given the opportunity, there is no reason to believe that this body of people would, at the very least, have performed any worse than the Fianna Fáil party that came to power in 1932.'[141] The point, however, is that it was by refusing to recognize the importance of participation that such people ensured that they were not given 'the opportunity'. Participation in the Free State's political machinery involved a compromise of absolutist republican principle. But this compromise facilitated the pursuit—in de Valera's case, the successful pursuit—of empowering majoritarian endorsement.

Republican purists like Mary MacSwiney could luxuriate in uncompromising self-righteousness, but their absence from 'the arena of action' would increasingly determine their marginality. MacSwiney's words reflected her self-deluding idealism: 'We are feeling sore that de Valera has split our forces on a mere hypothesis, and that he and his followers are taking a course, to our minds, incompatible with practical allegiance to the existing Republic, which hitherto we thought they believed in as we do.'[142] In 1929 Sinn Fein were unrealistically celebrating the 1919 Declaration of Independence as the touchstone of popular political commitment.[143] But Sinn Fein's deployment of republican rhetoric was impotent compared with that of the pragmatic Fianna Fáil usurpers. Also in 1929, de Valera argued that while the Dáil was 'faulty', he and his colleagues had entered it 'because we thought that a practical rule could be evolved in which order could be maintained'.[144] Practical rule and order indeed set Fianna Fáil apart from the extra-constitutional republican rump.

It has been noted that there was considerable distance between the republicanism of a purist such as Austin Stack, and the socialist

---

[141] *Patrick Pearse and the Lost Republican Ideal* (Dublin, James Duffy, 1991), 178.   [142] S. Cronin, *The McGarrity Papers* (Dublin, Anvil, 1972), 143.
[143] Sinn Fein Standing Committee, 'To All Republican Citizens' (Jan. 1929), *Evolution of Fianna Fáil Party and New Sinn Fein Party*, Files of the Dept. of the Taoiseach, NA S 5880.   [144] Moynihan (ed.), *Speeches and Statements*, 162.

republicanism which is our primary focus in this study. But they shared, in the late 1920s, a rejection of the compromising, constitutional path upon which Fianna Fáil were successfully embarking. In retrospect, O'Donnell argued that, during the late 1920s, republican socialists should have joined de Valera: 'In those days, the alternative to Fianna Fáil *was* Fianna Fáil'.[145] But, despite a certain degree of collusion,[146] O'Donnell's attitude at the time was very different. This is illustrated if one examines the attempts during the late 1920s to establish sufficient common ground for combined action by the IRA, Sinn Fein, and Fianna Fáil. O'Donnell was integrally involved in this process.[147] But it is vital to realize that, just as O'Donnell himself was not prepared to work through the pragmatic, post-republican nationalism of Fianna Fáil and to participate in the Dáil, so, too, the proposals for IRA/Sinn Fein/ Fianna Fáil co-operation stipulated that de Valera's party must not participate in the Free State's structures. A decade earlier, at the October 1917 Sinn Fein Convention, de Valera had found the words to mask (albeit temporarily) the differences which existed within the contemporary independence movement.[148] In 1927, no such sense of nationalist unity could be manufactured. Indeed, one of the most important lessons to be drawn from the study of inter-war republican socialism is precisely that there existed within Irish nationalist ranks divergent, mutually contradictory definitions both of objectives and of methods. But the fiction that nationalist unity could be achieved was evident in IRA thinking even in the 1927 proposals for joint action with Fianna Fáil and Sinn Fein.

In May 1927 the IRA Army Council issued a circular to its unit commanders. This argued that 'if unity could be restored to the extent of getting the two political organizations [Sinn Fein and Fianna Fáil] and the army' to agree to work together at elections and to agree a policy to be pursued should they achieve electoral success, then 'the present imperial colonial authorities could be defeated'. A meeting of the IRA's GHQ Staff and unit commanders was held, at which the Army Council put forward proposals which it hoped would prove 'acceptable to all Republicans' and 'a basis

---

[145] Quoted in McInerney, *O'Donnell*, 104.

[146] Fianna Fáil were, for example, allowed to advertise in *An Phoblacht* during O'Donnell's editorship of the paper (*An Phoblacht*, 10 Sept. 1927).

[147] O'Donnell to Secs. Sinn Fein, 27 Apr. 1927, MacSwiney Papers, ADUCD P48a/43 (34); Bell, *Secret Army*, 59.   [148] Murphy, *Patrick Pearse*, 92–3.

for agreement'. These proposals had included the suggestion of a joint panel of candidates to stand in elections, and a commitment by each candidate not to acquiesce under an oath to the British crown or to its representatives. These proposals had been put both to the Standing Committee of Sinn Fein and to Fianna Fáil's National Executive. Sinn Fein had stipulated that, if discussions were to continue, Fianna Fáil would have to pledge never to enter 'any foreign-controlled parliament' as minority or majority, with or without an oath of allegiance. They further demanded, with unrealistic purism, that 'the government of the Republic is recognized as the only lawful government of the country'.

If Sinn Fein's response was characteristically stubborn and impossibilistic, Fianna Fáil's was simply humiliating. De Valera's party replied with the statement: 'It was unanimously decided that the proposals were not acceptable as a basis for discussion.' When the IRA Army Council enquired whether all of the proposals had been judged unacceptable, Fianna Fáil offered an even more deflating rebuff: 'We have to inform you that the proposals were not discussed in detail.' The Army Council had therefore 'decided that nothing further could usefully be done in the way of endeavouring to achieve co-ordination, and so ceased their efforts in this direction'. Tellingly, they argued that, in the absence of republican unity, IRA Volunteers who might secure election would be in danger of finding their energies 'frittered away in futile political agitation'. Having vainly tried the co-operative path, the IRA leaders wanted to impress on their Volunteers that the army's chief aim, 'to establish and to uphold a lawful government in sole and absolute control of the Republic', could more surely be achieved by the means set out in the organization's constitution: 'Force of arms. . . . Organizing, training, and equipping the manhood of Ireland as an effective military force.'[149]

Fianna Fáil's cutting rejection of these republican proposals was given even sharper edge by the party's success in securing electoral endorsement. The June 1927 general election decisively established Fianna Fáil's strength: 'Among the outgoing deputies twenty-three had stayed with Sinn Fein and twenty-two had joined the new party. Now the latter doubled its size to forty-four

---

[149] Army Council Circular to the Commander of Each Independent Unit (20 May 1927), McGarrity Papers, NLI MS 17,532.

while the former collapsed to a humiliating rump of five.'[150] As O'Donnell himself later acknowledged, by remaining aloof from the party which was emerging into dominance, republican socialists contributed to their own marginalization. His suggestion that had they joined de Valera then the left could have 'acted as a platform—and the alternative—against the policies of the right-wing in Fianna Fáil'[151] misunderstood the true nature of Fianna Fáil's politics. It would not have been possible for the small forces of socialist republicanism to have deflected de Valera's party from its wholly different approach simply by means of vociferous ranting, even had they been members of the party. The gulf was simply too wide, Fianna Fáil's success being based on precisely that 'childish talk of uniting all classes to free the country' which O'Donnell so deplored.[152] But there can be no doubt that by remaining in the extra-constitutional cold during the years in which Fianna Fáil were building their formidable parliamentary strength, republican socialists did contribute to the process of their own marginalization.

Fianna Fáil's participation in the Free State parliament was, in the event, precipitated by the killing, in July 1927, of Kevin O'Higgins (Free State Minister for Justice, Minister for External Affairs, and Vice-President of the Executive Council).[153] The IRA swiftly denied responsibility for the shooting.[154] The killers were, in fact, republicans,[155] and the incident is a telling one. There had existed for some years a strong desire for vengeance against civil war opponents,[156] of whom O'Higgins was, perhaps, the toughest and most able. If it was as 'the chief moral architect of the Free State' that he was recognized by mourners at his funeral,[157] then some similar recognition was afforded him by his enemies, with fatal consequences. The irony was that, as so often, republican violence had an impact very different from that which its brutal agents foresaw. O'Higgins's killing helped to stabilize the Free State which his killers so despised. Responses to the assassination reflected the distance which separated adherents of physical force

---

[150] K. T. Hoppen, *Ireland Since 1800: Conflict and Conformity* (London, Longman, 1989), 178.   [151] Quoted in McInerney, *O'Donnell*, 104.
[152] *An Phoblacht*, 24 Dec. 1927.   [153] *Irish Times*, 11 July 1927.
[154] *An Phoblacht*, 15 July 1927.
[155] T. de V. White, *Kevin O'Higgins* (Dublin, Anvil, 1986; 1st edn. 1948), 256; MacEoin (ed.), *Survivors*, 34; Gannon statement, NA 999/951.
[156] O'Donnell, *The Gates*, 75.
[157] George Russell, quoted in White, *O'Higgins*, 232–3.

from the dominant majoritarian political culture. President Cosgrave claimed in the Dáil that a blow had fallen 'not merely upon a particular political party, not merely upon a particular governmental group, but... upon this assembly and through it upon the nation—a blow too recent to be fully realized in all its grievousness'.[158] Labour's Thomas Johnson endorsed Cosgrave's attitude, referring to the shooting as 'an exhibition of decadence'.[159] Most significantly, de Valera also reacted in a negative way to the killing (though he did seek to exonerate republican organizations from blame):

> The assassination of Mr O'Higgins is murder, and is inexcusable from any standpoint. I am confident that no Republican organization was responsible for it, or would give it any countenance. It is the duty of every citizen to set his face sternly against anything of the kind. It is a crime that cuts at the root of all representative government, and no one who realizes what crime means can do otherwise than deplore and condemn it.[160]

The point about the brutal killing of O'Higgins is that this majoritarian consensus was further enabled to undermine marginal republicanism as, in Professor Foster's words, the assassination 'gave the government the opportunity to pass emergency legislation enforcing the Oath as a *sine qua non* of entering constitutional politics on any level'.[161] Fianna Fáil thus entered the democratic ring and provided the counterweight necessary to stabilize a previously lop-sided parliamentary contest. Despite the fears voiced by Cosgrave, O'Higgins's gruesome killing had, in fact, facilitated Fianna Fáil's entry into the Dáil and had thereby contributed toward the strengthening of the twenty-six-county state. The 're-storation of order and peace' which O'Higgins had celebrated in December 1924,[162] ironically, became all the surer as a result of his death.

While purist republicans scorned constitutionalism, therefore,[163] Fianna Fáil pragmatically entered the constitutional arena. The starkness of the contrast is emphasized through examination of

---

[158] *Dáil Debates*, 20/755.   [159] Ibid. 20/757.   [160] *Irish Times*, 12 July 1927.

[161] R. F. Foster, *Modern Ireland, 1600–1972* (London, Allen Lane, 1988), 526.

[162] 'O'Higgins's Message to Nation' (8 Dec 1924), *Independence Day 6 Dec.*, Files of the Dept. of the Taoiseach, NA S 4178.

[163] 'Parliaments are for museums. They will here and forever betray revolutions' (*An Phoblacht*, 5 May 1928, quoted in Rumpf and Hepburn, *Nationalism and Socialism*, 91).

the organization and publicity orchestrated by de Valera's new party in its bid for hegemony. Sophisticated, efficient local operations[164] were complemented by a shrewd awareness of the importance of effective propaganda.[165] The launching of the *Irish Press* in September 1931 provided a valuable platform from which to broadcast the party's approach. Quickly achieving its ambitious circulation target, the paper was, in Lee's words, 'a brilliant journalistic success'.[166] But the launch marked the culmination of a lengthy period of detailed preparation. The *Minute Book* of the Rathmines Fintan Lalor Cumann noted in December 1928: 'Subscriptions for the first allotment of shares in the new paper were taken, and in connection with the second allotment, the following resolution . . . was carried: "That members give a small contribution each week to pay off the shares in the paper" '. The following month, it was decided to pay the second allotment on the shares 'out of Cumann funds'. In April 1929, 'The treasurer mentioned that notice had been received from the Irish Press Ltd. that the last allotments . . . were due and it was decided to take the amount from the profits made by the amusements committee.' This payment was duly made.[167]

Other valuable manuscript evidence also attests to the degree of enthusiastic, energetic planning which preceded the 'brilliant journalistic success' of the 1930s *Irish Press*. In 1928 Ernie O'Malley went with Frank Aiken to the United States on a fundraising trip on behalf of the forthcoming paper. In O'Malley's papers there are records of amounts raised across North America between October and December 1928, citing funds amassed in New York, Massachusetts, California, Pennsylvania, Illinois, Connecticut, New Jersey, Michigan, Missouri, Colorado, Ohio, Nebraska, Kansas, Arizona, Iowa, Tennessee, Canada, Montana, New Hampshire, Minnesota, and New Mexico.[168] Aiken conveyed the desire of the

---

[164] T. Garvin, 'Democratic Politics in Independent Ireland', in J. Coakley and M. Gallagher (eds.), *Politics in the Republic of Ireland* (Galway, PSAI Press, 1992), 227.

[165] On the propagandist role of Frank Gallagher during the later 1920s, see G. Walker, ' "The Irish Dr Goebbels": Frank Gallagher and Irish Republican Propaganda' *Journal of Contemporary History*, 27 (1992), 158–9.

[166] *Ireland, 1912–85: Politics and Society* (Cambridge, CUP, 1989), 217.

[167] Fintan Lalor Cumann, *Fianna Fáil, Minute Book*: 6 Dec. 1928, 10 Jan., 11 Apr., 9 May 1929, Byrne Papers, PP.

[168] Summary of Amounts of Money Collected (Oct.–Dec. 1928), Cormac O'Malley Papers, PP.

Directors (of Irish Press Limited) 'that the American quota should be raised as quickly as possible'.

The people at home have already raised their quota of $500,000. If you realize the economic state of the people at home you will appreciate the hard work and enthusiasm required to raise the sum. As soon as the American quota is forthcoming, everything is ready to procure premises and plant, and the first issue of the newspaper will be on the newsstands within a few months afterwards.[169]

According to a publicity document on behalf of the forthcoming paper, there was (in 1928)

no National daily paper in Ireland. The three daily papers circulating in the twenty-six counties comprising the Irish Free State, are pro-British in outlook. They opposed the fight for Irish freedom during the Black and Tan war. The *Irish Independent*, the largest of them, actually called on the British to execute James Connolly and Sean M[a]cDermott, two of the leaders of the revolution who were put to death by the British after the rising of 1916. They applied the British epithets of murderers, assassins, looters, etc., to Irish patriots. They have always opposed policies which were directed to making Ireland a self-contained country independent of England.

De Valera intended the new paper to be 'devoted to the building up of Irish industries, the promotion of Irish culture, and the supporting of Irish interests generally against the domination of any foreign power'. The directorate backing the new venture, so the document continued, consisted 'of some of the best and most progressive business men in Ireland', and indeed the list of directors reflected Fianna Fáil's important links with the Irish bourgeoisie. To complement the money raised in Ireland, committees had been formed 'in nearly all the principal cities in the United States':

Influential friends of Ireland in America promised Eamon de Valera that they would raise $500,000 for the Irish Press, Ltd. . . . On the 13th of October, 1928, over $80,000 had been raised in sums of $100 up to $2,500 each and the committees are actively at work raising the balance. They have found most of the old friends of Ireland whom they have approached willing to invest because this project gives them a good opportunity of making a remunerative investment for themselves, as well as a chance of helping Ireland.[170]

---

[169] Letter (n.d. [1928?]), Cormac O'Malley Papers, PP.
[170] Irish Press Ltd., Publicity Document (1928), Cormac O'Malley Papers, PP.

In emissary O'Malley's opinion there was no doubt either about the need for, or about the national purpose of, the new organ. 'There is little need', he argued, 'to stress the necessity for the paper: anyone who is at all familiar with the present day Irish press can see that it does not represent the country, that it does not interpret our national aspirations, that it has not a dignified independent outlook'. O'Malley continued by arguing, 'As a nation we are not a reading people, not a nation of serious readers, hence newspapers influence our outlook more so than they do that of most other countries.'[171]

Whether or not one agrees with this last point, there is no doubting the energy, planning, commitment, and organization which lay behind Fianna Fáil's assault on constitutional politics in the Free State. The pragmatic decision to opt for actual power via the functioning machinery of the state was complemented by the meticulous construction of strong social foundations upon which to build. The party skilfully and realistically adapted the Irish nationalist tradition of multi-class harmony, thereby appealing to important and varied sections of the population, including those whom O'Donnellite socialism inevitably alienated; and further momentum was acquired through the party's preparedness to grasp power through the actual—as opposed to the imaginary, republican—mechanisms of government. In both cases (economic appeal and constitutional pragmatism) Fianna Fáil had access to crucial reservoirs of strength unavailable to republican socialists.

'THE DEVELOPMENT OF LEFTWARD TENDENCIES'

> The worsening conditions among the rural and urban population helped the development of leftward tendencies within the IRA, and this was increasingly apparent in its propaganda.
>
> George Gilmore[172]

> Our existence is not the aftermath of a past revolt; it is the presage of a future one. Over and above any consideration of future success or failure, the resumption of the fight is for us

---

[171] O'Malley, untitled MS (n.d. [1928?]), Cormac O'Malley Papers, PP.
[172] *The Irish Republican Congress* (1978; 1st edn. 1935), 23.

a sacred duty. Let us this Eastertide—those of us who have
not already done so—pledge ourselves that we will, in this
generation, raise the flag of the Irish Republic in battle.

Frank Ryan (1928)[173]

Even within the extra-constitutional republican movement, however, socialist republicans found that they were unable to establish
the dominance of their own, class-struggling vision. It is true that
a high profile was given during the late-1920s to socially radical
rhetoric. In May 1929 the belligerent Frank Ryan took over as
editor of *An Phoblacht*.[174] The journal continued—radically and
ineffectually—to hew at the conservative rock face of Free State
society. Its style did differ under Ryan. O'Donnell's prose had
possessed jovial and witty qualities, with geniality and humour
colouring his radical polemicism. On 8 October 1926 *An Phoblacht*
published a telegram which O'Donnell had received from John
Sweeney, agent for the trustees of the Marquis of Conyngham,
Donegal. The telegram stated that republicans had stolen rent
books, and asked that O'Donnell use any influence he had to try
and have them returned. *An Phoblacht* also published O'Donnell's
reply: 'I will not use any influence to have the books returned; I
could not promise to use any influence to have even the landlord's
agent returned should he happen to serve a useful purpose by
following the books.'[175] Ryan was less prone to disguise aggressive
attitudes with wit, and his writing elicited fewer smiles than did
O'Donnell's.[176]

But the same mixture of social radicalism, Gaelicism, militaristic separatism, and anti-majoritarianism characterized the paper's
rhetoric under its new, and less witty, editor. An editorial of
December 1930 set out the journal's stance. The objective was

---

[173] Seachranaidhe [F. Ryan], *Easter Week and After* (Dublin, National Publicity
Committee, n.d. [1928?]), 16.

[174] *An Phoblacht*, 25 May 1929; S. Cronin, *Frank Ryan: The Search for the Republic* (Dublin, Repsol, 1980), 25.   [175] 8 Oct. 1926.

[176] Compare the respective ways in which the two men expressed a similar attitude on the question of free speech for their opponents (both comments at the
same meeting, in Dublin, on 10 Nov. 1932): (Ryan:) 'No matter what anyone said
to the contrary, recent events showed that while they had fists, hands, and boots
to use, and guns if necessary, they would not allow free speech to traitors';
(O'Donnell:) 'The policeman who put his head between Mr Cosgrave's head and
the hands of angry Irishmen might as well keep his head at home' (*An Phoblacht*,
19 Nov. 1932; *Irish Independent*, 11 Nov. 1932).

the Irish Republic of thirty-two counties, politically united as one nation, having no link with the British empire whether in politics, finance, or by way of alliance . . . an Irish Republic, supplying its own needs, fashioning its own distinctive culture out of the wealth of our Gaelic tradition—a Republic in which every citizen alike contributes to the production of the necessaries of life and, alike, participates in the enjoyment of them.

The paper had 'no use for parliamentary agitation'. Indeed, the physical-force strategy was thoroughly endorsed: Ireland had never obtained any concessions except 'by armed revolt or by the threat of armed revolt'. But militarism was tinged with anti-capitalist ambition: 'Our policy is to work with the people, and for them, preparing for an armed rising for the overthrow of imperialism and capitalism in Ireland.'[177]

During the late 1920s, indeed, there had been significant hints that republican socialists were making considerable headway in their efforts to draw republicanism to the left. An IRA Army Council statement in 1928, for example, declared that 'In addition to the aim of recruiting and maintaining an efficient military force, we are simultaneously encouraging the growth and spread of revolutionary principles and action with a view to producing amongst the civilian population a revolutionary feeling and atmosphere, which would be favourable to military action.' The army control's 'general outlook and policy', said the statement, must be 'broadly revolutionary rather than bigotedly military'.[178]

The new IRA's international links also seemed to suggest increasing radicalization. In 1927 Michael Fitzpatrick was among trade union delegates who went to Moscow 'to join in the celebration of the tenth anniversary of the Russian revolution'.[179] Fitzpatrick, who had briefly commanded the IRA's Dublin brigade during the civil war, was both a leading IRA figure and the president of the Friends of Soviet Russia.[180] As such, he appeared to some to epitomize the IRA's conversion to socialism.[181] On 13 February 1929, he presided over a meeting held in the Dublin Rotunda commemorating 'the second anniversary of the world

[177] *An Phoblacht*, 6 Dec. 1930.
[178] Statement for Clan na Gael Convention, 1928, McGarrity Papers, NLI MS 17,533.   [179] *An Phoblacht*, 5 Nov. 1927; *Irish Times*, 29 Oct. 1927.
[180] *Revolutionary Organizations* [memorandum circulated to each member of the Executive Council, 5 Apr. 1930], Blythe Papers, ADUCD P24/169, 2; Rumpf and Hepburn, *Nationalism and Socialism*, 91.
[181] Hogan, *Could Ireland Become Communist?*, 37.

congress against imperialism, founded in Brussels in 1927'. Fitzpatrick stated that 'the national revolutionary, as well as the trades union movement, were represented on the platform'.[182] Peadar O'Donnell had also been present at the Brussels gathering and, in July 1929, he and Sean MacBride 'attended the second world congress of the League against Imperialism and for National Independence', held in Frankfurt-on-Main. The declaration which they managed to elicit from the congress drew on social as well as national rhetoric: 'the world congress of the Anti-Imperialist League calls on the organized workers of Great Britain to force the British Labour government to withdraw the threat of war against Ireland and to allow Ireland freely to organize her own life in accordance with her working-class ideals'.[183] The statement typified republican lazy-mindedness concerning the assumption that Ireland should automatically be treated as one political unit; more remarkably, its suggestion that Ireland adhered to 'working-class ideals' displayed the extent of convenient self-delusion characteristic of contemporary republican radicals.

In March 1930 O'Donnell further established his international credentials when he 'formally opened' and chaired the 'European Congress of Peasants and Working Farmers'.[184] There is no doubt that some of the Irish republicans who forged these international links and marketed themselves as anti-imperialists possessed socialist views. O'Donnell was accused by the *Irish Rosary* of having been 'sent, in 1929, with six students, to the Lenin College in Moscow to study the technique of revolution'.[185] Despite his denial of this particular charge,[186] there is no question that O'Donnell's forging of international radical links did indeed fit neatly with his own hybrid socialist republican thinking. At the February 1929 Rotunda meeting, to which reference has already been made, O'Donnell had made clear his socialist allegiances and aspirations. In connection with the land annuities campaign, he stated that the Donegal people's vanguard against 'bailiffs and process servers' were not the wealthy; they were 'the working farmers'. These were the people around whom O'Donnell sought to build his Irish anti-imperialist struggle.

---

[182] *An Phoblacht*, 23 Feb. 1929.
[183] Coogan, *The IRA*, 124; *An Phoblacht*, 10 Aug. 1929.
[184] Ibid. 5 Apr. 1930; cf. O'Donnell, *Monkeys*, 23.
[185] Editorial, 36/4 (Apr. 1932), 245.   [186] *Salud!*, 135.

The workers in the towns and those that till the land must get closer and make common ground. All that was wrong was that the imperialists, who were exploiting the town workers and raiding peasant Ireland, had hired armed bands. If the peasant and town workers could only disarm the imperialists and then exercise the power seized to minister to the wants of the masses as definitely as power today is used for the few, then the native would be back in control in Ireland and Ireland would be free. Organize industrially and arm had been Connolly's teaching, and it sounds good sensible teaching when one looks round at how the enemy is organized and armed.[187]

A Free State Department of Justice memorandum of March 1930 reported a Galway meeting at which O'Donnell had exhorted his audience of farmers and labourers 'to organize to fight against capitalism. He spoke of Russia and referred in glowing terms to the government there.'[188]

But, despite some ensuing radical rhetoric, it would be wrong to assume that the IRA's association with foreign 'anti-imperialists' necessarily reflected the organization's conversion to socialism. Emotionally, financially, and militarily punctured,[189] it is unsurprising that the post-civil war IRA should have welcomed the prospect of foreign allies or supporters, and non-socialist republicans were perfectly willing to visit Moscow if it was thought that arms could be acquired there.[190] Indeed, Michael McInerney's rather flattering reading of republican connections in these years ('The IRA of those days had a world consciousness. It sent delegates to international anti-imperialist conferences.') is rather undermined by the cynical reflection of Sean MacBride, one such delegate. Referring to the aforementioned 1929 Frankfurt League against Imperialism gathering, which had produced a radical republican declaration on Ireland, MacBride commented that this 'was one of those high-sounding organizations that we felt we had to support'.[191] Not all those engaging in international contacts were

---

[187] *An Phoblacht*, 23 Feb. 1929.

[188] *Communist Activities: Peasant Farmers' Organization (Kristertern)* [memorandum circulated to each member of the Executive Council], 29 Mar. 1930, Blythe Papers, ADUCD P24/168.

[189] Chairman of Army Council to McGarrity, 3 Aug. 1927, McGarrity Papers, NLI MS 17,532; C. S. Andrews, *Man of No Property: An Autobiography*, ii (Cork, Mercier, 1982), 15, 19; M. Hopkinson, *Green Against Green: The Irish Civil War* (Dublin, Gilland Macmillan, 1988), 259–60; Bell, *Secret Army*, 50–1; Gaughan, *Stack*, 242–3.   [190] Cronin, *Ryan*, 173; Bell, *Secret Army*, 65.

[191] McInerney, *O'Donnell*, 110; quoted in MacEoin (ed.), *Survivors*, 122.

socially radical, and even when radical rhetoric resulted it is far from clear how seriously this should be taken.

International anti-imperialism could certainly appeal in Ireland on separatist, anglophobic terms without necessarily possessing any socialist aspect. On 10 November 1930 a meeting 'was held in College Green, Dublin . . . under the auspices of the Irish section of the League against Imperialism and for National Independence'. The gathering was an emphatically anti-British gesture, coming on the eve of armistice day and concluding with the lighting in Foster Place of 'a bonfire of Union Jacks'. The main speaker was Eamon de Valera, certainly no socialist, and he used the occasion to claim that the following day would witness 'a demonstration by a section of Irishmen flouting the feelings of their fellow-citizens by the flaunting of a foreign flag in their midst'. This, he asserted, was the reason for the College Green gathering. It was 'because the imperialists in this country had abused that demonstration and tried to turn it into a political demonstration for the British empire that they had to protest'.[192] The 'anti-imperialist' alliance in the Free State was united not by socialism, but rather by the desire for Irish independence from Britain. The IRA's socialists had not succeeded in effecting a genuine shift to the left within the republican movement of the late 1920s.

Socially radical ideas had, admittedly, gained greater prominence in IRA circles than had been the case during either the Anglo-Irish conflict or the civil war. But the army's socialists were a definite minority within the organization. O'Donnell and Ryan were the two most influential IRA journalists of the period,[193] and they produced propaganda which was often more radical than the movement on whose behalf it was issued. Thus, as we have seen, O'Donnell used *An Phoblacht* in order to trumpet out his socially radical land-annuities message, despite the reservations of most of the IRA leadership, and in spite of the official non-involvement of the organization. This tension, between the class-struggling radicalism of certain leading republican publicists and the less radical centre of gravity of the movement, was, in the early 1930s, to result in the attempted silencing of the IRA left-wing by the organization's authorities. For the moment, the ambiguity persisted. But it is important to note that non-socialists within the army

---

[192] *Irish Times*, 11 Nov. 1930.   [193] MacEoin (ed.), *Survivors*, 568.

sometimes employed rhetoric during these years which misleadingly seemed to suggest a harmony of radical purpose with people such as O'Donnell, Gilmore, and Ryan. It has been noted that the Army Council in 1928 endorsed a 'broadly revolutionary' approach. But, more tellingly, the Council's 1928 Clan na Gael statement declared an allegiance to the doctrine which represented the real foundation of the IRA's philosophy: the conviction of the supremacy of legitimist physical force.

The reasons and necessity for maintaining a military organization are based primarily on the admitted right of the Irish nation to full and complete control of its affairs . . . and on the principle that any section or proportion of the citizens have the right, and it is their duty, if they feel they can do so, to assert the sovereignty of the nation. It is the belief of the army that it is only by military action that the sovereignty of the Republic can be asserted.[194]

The latter sentence contains within it the key to understanding the way in which the IRA functioned politically during the late 1920s; the former expressed the ideological foundation upon which such an approach rested. The army remained an army, despite its inability to give any momentum to the war in which it considered itself to be engaged. Attempts to modify the IRA's physical-force emphasis met with considerable scepticism. In November 1929, chief of staff Moss Twomey[195] commented, in a letter to Joe McGarrity, that there existed within the IRA 'a prejudice against good speakers, no matter how good their military records have been, or the services they still render'. Twomey's automatic assumption that the accepted source from which to derive republican kudos was military activity is as revealing as is his subsequent statement that it was being claimed within the IRA 'that soldiers of the Republic are becoming politicians and spouters'.[196] That such

---

[194] Statement for Clan na Gael Convention, 1928, McGarrity Papers, NLI MS 17,533.

[195] The sequence of post-Liam Lynch IRA chiefs of staff was: Frank Aiken (1923–5), Andy Cooney (1925–6), Maurice (Moss) Twomey (1926–36), Sean MacBride (1936), Tom Barry (1937), Michael Fitzpatrick (1937–8), Sean Russell (+1938) (MacEoin (ed.), *Survivors*, 20, 100–1, 121, 123, 275, 373; Cronin, *Ryan*, 105–6, 178, 182, 192; Bell, *Secret Army*, 53, 133, 136–7, 146, 159; Coogan, *The IRA*, 56, 85, 176; M. MacEvilly, 'Sean MacBride and the Republican Motor Launch *St George*', *Irish Sword*, 16/62 (1984) 50; M. Farrell, 'The Extraordinary Life and Times of Sean MacBride', *Magill*, 6/3 (Christmas 1982), 28).

[196] Twomey to McGarrity, 21 Nov. 1929, McGarrity Papers, NLI MS 17,534 (3). Twomey was later (1933) to argue that 'everybody is agreed that force must be the ultimate weapon' (quoted in Townshend, *Political Violence*, 379).

accusations were being levelled is, of course, an indication that certain voices were challenging the IRA's physical-force orthodoxy. But Twomey's words seem to suggest that such dissidence was still treated with suspicion.

One point subsequently made by IRA socialists regarding this period was that a preoccupation with organizational matters obstructed the movement's development along socially radical lines. Referring to his chief of staff's attitude toward the land annuities struggle, Peadar O'Donnell commented that 'Moss Twomey was closer to me than any of the rural men. The thing that held him back was that he was a great organizer, and the unity of the organization was all-important to him.'[197] A spirit of respectful disagreement was also evident in George Gilmore's latter-day critique, *The Irish Republican Congress*: 'The IRA, under Maurice Twomey's highly efficient and wholly dedicated leadership, made a wonderfully successful recovery as an organization in those post-war years of weariness and disappointment, but when it balked at involvement in the growing agrarian struggle it threw away its opportunity of leading the national advance.'[198] In practice, organization tended to mean military organization, and it undoubtedly did consume considerable energy.[199]

The Army Council were certainly far more concerned with maintaining an intact army than with attempting to inject socialism into the republican philosophy. Indeed, the position of socialists such as O'Donnell and Gilmore within the IRA leadership was an extremely awkward one. Despite their membership of the republican inner circle, they were unable to draw their organization toward an endorsement of their own, class-struggling understanding of republicanism. The wide spectrum of contemporary republican opinion[200] had a non-socialist centre of gravity.

Close inspection of IRA rhetoric and action during these years certainly emphasizes the atypicality of Gilmore and O'Donnell's

---

[197] Quoted in MacEoin (ed.), *Survivors*, 33.   [198] (1978; 1st edn. 1935), 24.

[199] Bell, *Secret Army*, 73–4.

[200] Illustrative of the diversity of this spectrum was a conference held in Nov. 1929 in connection with the republican political organization, Comhairle na Poblachta. The delegates ranged from the socially radical Gilmore and Ryan to conservatives such as Mary MacSwiney and Brian O'Higgins (Executive Council memorandum of a conference held under the auspices of Comhairle na Poblachta in Wynn's Hotel on 3 Nov. 1929, Files of the Dept. of the Taoiseach, NA S 5864 A; Bell, *Secret Army*, 77–8; S. Cronin, *Irish Nationalism: A History of its Roots and Ideology* (Dublin, Academy Press, 1980), 158.)

version of republicanism within the movement through which they chose to work. Although the army was unable to engage in a second civil war during the late 1920s, violence remained a crucial component not only of its philosophy but also of its practice. An *An Phoblacht* editorial of May 1926 asserted that 'Should freedom come to this country as a gift in any generation not on edge for an opportunity to snatch it in armed revolt we should no longer be a people who could use it'.[201] Although no sustained, systematic campaign emerged, the physical-force assumptions evident in the above statement pervaded the organization. Calls for action were indeed complemented by military activities,[202] and frustrated expectation overlapped with sporadic paramilitary brutality. The recollection of one contemporary IRA man is revealing both for his casual attitude toward fatal violence and for his depiction of stifled revolutionary expectation:

Some silly things happened; I suppose that is inevitable at times. [An IRA] volunteer went to disarm a Free State soldier, and shot dead the girl who was with him. Then there was a raid on pawn shops, for binoculars of all things, and a pawn shop assistant was shot. . . . I did not bother seriously about my job, getting married, or anything. I remember a bloke came to me selling insurance. When I saw in the fine print that it would all be invalidated in the event of a revolution, I told him to take it away. I was sure we would be on the hills by 1928, but the years went by and still 'we were on the verge'.[203]

That republican violence was inchoate and stuttering should not divert us either from the horror of such 'silly things', or from the centrality of physical-force thinking within the IRA: military activity remained the organization's primary, practical focus.

Moreover, while the killing of Kevin O'Higgins demonstrated that violent republican action was still a realistic possibility, it should also be noted that the threat, as well as the application, of violence was itself an important feature of the physical-force approach. During the late 1920s Cumann na mBan, the women's republican organization, began to organize an anti-juror campaign, with jurors' names being acquired through a contact at a Dublin courthouse. Letters were sent to jurors involved in cases dealing with republicans; the message was that the accused should not be

[201] 21 May 1926.   [202] Bell, *Secret Army*, 52, 57–8.
[203] Frank Edwards, quoted in MacEoin (ed.), *Survivors*, 5–6.

found guilty. The majority of these bullying epistles appear to have been written by the truculent Sheila Humphreys. Their style matched the aggressiveness of their threat:

The enemies of Ireland are imprisoning the men and women who are carrying out the only practical programme to attain freedom. Unfortunately some of Dublin's degenerate and slavish citizens assist them in this work. Last month the following [names and addresses given] helped . . . to send the Irish patriot Con Healy to penal servitude for five years. These men are traitors to their country. (Death would be their fate in any free country in the world).

That the IRA did indeed shoot the foreman of the jury in the Healy case underlined the seriousness of this intimidatory strategy.[204]

It is possible, therefore, to distinguish between two rival visions of politics: the first, characteristic of IRA orthodoxy; the second, characteristic of socialist republicanism. Just as inter-war republican socialists celebrated myths which emphasized their own marginality—the 1916 rebellion being the most famous example—so, too, their choice of the IRA as a post-civil-war vehicle locked them into an organization within which their philosophy was destined to be peripheral. In August 1929 Moss Twomey described the separatist problem as being 'essentially military in character': 'The volunteer organization is engaged in a continuation of the task of endeavouring to organize at this stage the most consciously national elements of the nation, around whom it is hoped later to rally the entire manhood of the country.'[205]

But where Twomey wanted people to rally to the militaristic faith, IRA socialists wanted exponents of the republican faith to rally to the people. An *An Phoblacht* editorial published early in O'Donnell's reign at the paper asserted that 'Our first activities should be among those who suffer most . . . If we are in earnest we shall enter the struggle along the line of starvation and work forward from that point'.[206] The army's socialists sought that people should become involved in activities which had a less purely military aspect than those which IRA traditionalists were offering. During the late 1920s and early 1930s the latter tended, according to

[204] M. Ward, *Unmanageable Revolutionaries: Women and Irish Nationalism* (London, Pluto, 1983), 206–8; Bell, *Secret Army*, 76.
[205] *An Phoblacht*, 10 Aug. 1929.   [206] Ibid. 17 Sept. 1926.

George Gilmore, 'to think in terms of gaining the support of the people for the army rather than of the army spear-pointing a popular struggle'.[207] The view of the IRA left was that the development of such a popular struggle would necessitate republican involvement in activity which would go beyond the rather stifling, traditional blend of military purism and legitimist decree.

But, suggestive rhetoric notwithstanding, it was very much toward the latter, more orthodox position that the late-1920s IRA clearly leaned. O'Donnellite infuriation with abstract, legitimist posturing had, as we have seen, ironically led to the newly autonomous status of the post-1925 IRA. But the traditionalists within the army maintained precisely that impractical allegiance to alternative, republican legitimacy against which O'Donnell had raged. The thrust of his argument had been that galvanic, socially radical action would provide the only means of establishing republican momentum. In fact, official republican claims to legitimacy continued to lack any practical complement in the realm of social agitation. Pious declarations—increasingly absurd when contrasted with the ever-strengthening foundations of the *actual* state—spewed forth self-righteously, and confirmed the gap between republican orthodoxy and socialist republican heterodoxy.

Legitimist commitment was, for example, given typically uncompromising expression in an Army Council letter written in January 1930. Rather pathetically, the IRA's leading body stated that it recognized itself to be 'the supreme national authority in Ireland', and that it considered itself not to be 'subservient to, or subject in any way to any other body'. With unjustified confidence, the Army Council recognized its own 'right, at any time, to proclaim itself the provisional government of the Republic of Ireland. It has not formally done this. As a matter of fact the General Convention of November 1927 explicitly gave it this authority, should the Council believe the situation demanded or warranted it doing so.'[208] This letter serves as an indication of the gulf which separated the IRA's rather arrogant vision of politics from that

---

[207] *The Irish Republican Congress* (1978; 1st edn. 1935), 23.

[208] Army Council to McGarrity, 27 Jan. 1930, McGarrity Papers, NLI MS 17,535 (1). Republican pomposity was widely prevalent during these years; see, for example, the words of the ever-zealous J. J. O'Kelly in a letter to Ramsay MacDonald in 1929, in reference to the republican governmental rump: 'in the full confidence that it speaks the mind of the Irish people, the government of the Republic of Ireland will be glad to hear in due course that you are prepared to withdraw the

enshrined in what had, by this time, become a majoritarian main-stream culture in which the bulk of the electorate participated. In place of such concepts as majority rule and parliamentary power, the IRA held to notions of *de jure* authority and Army Council decree. Moreover, according to the official army line, no social action, no practical economic project, was considered necessary in order to inject life into alternative republican legitimacy. It is this latter point which emphasizes republican socialists' marginality.

As with the 1916–25 period, therefore, the culture prevailing in the movement through which O'Donnellite socialists worked was ill-suited to their class-struggling project. This is underlined if one examines the frequent summoning up by republicans, in these years, of eminent spirits from the past. Often, such hagiography had an eerie tendency to imply that true republican greatness was only to be found among the dead.[209] For socialists within the move-ment this represented, perhaps, the unwelcome verification of Marx's assertion regarding the tradition of all the dead genera-tions weighing like a nightmare on the brain of the living.[210] Cer-tainly, it tended not to be the social radicalism of past heroes which earned them contemporary esteem. Even where such radi-cal tendencies had formed a significant part of a person's polit-ical approach, these tendencies did not necessarily receive any prominence. Thus, for example, a 1929 Cumann na mBan docu-ment dealing with Liam Mellows was able to stress his military heroism without paying any attention at all to his radical leanings.[211]

Indeed, the republican undead tended far more often to be celebrated in connection with some act of political violence. The ritualistic quotation of the words of figures such as Tone, Emmet, Pearse, Connolly, Plunkett, Casement, and MacSwiney[212] served not merely to elevate the dead, but also to strengthen the contemporary

---

threat of immediate and terrible war..., evacuate our ports and our whole ter-ritory..., and abide by the result of the free expression of the will of the people of all Ireland' (O'Kelly to MacDonald, 26 Aug. 1929, McGarrity Papers, NLI MS 17,474).

[209] Cf. Ernie O'Malley's comment that, 'As a Republican one was... never suf-ficiently tested until one had died in the Republican faith' (O'Malley, *The Singing Flame*, 276).

[210] K. Marx, *The Eighteenth Brumaire of Louis Bonaparte* (Moscow, Progress, 1954 edn.), 10.

[211] *The Story of Liam Mellowes* [*sic*] (1929), Coyle O'Donnell Papers, ADUCD P61/6 (2).   [212] *An Phoblacht*, 7 May, 4 June, 11 June, 6 Aug., 27 Aug. 1926.

cult of republican violence. Just as the Pearsean ethos of 1916 had rendered the rebellion an ill-fitting paradigm for republican socialists to adopt, so the fact that Pearse rather than Connolly enjoyed especial prominence in 1920s hagiography reflected the true balance of contemporary republican opinion.[213]

At certain points during this period, republican socialists seemed to lean towards a native-versus-settler model which clashed with their primary, class-based, definition of the nation. Thus, in 1929, O'Donnell talked about putting 'the native . . . back in control in Ireland',[214] while he had earlier argued that the undoing of the conquest was 'a question of releasing the native stock'.[215] This again raises the question of socialists endorsing certain trends within contemporary republican culture which, in fact, tended to contradict their own central theses. The identification of the nationalist struggle with Gaelic identity had been an important element of the post-1916 independence movement. Aodh de Blacam, for example, had argued that

The sole bond of Irish nationality is—and always was—the native Gaelic culture, and whatever the changing details may be, the underlying motive of every strong national movement can be traced to *the restoration of Gaelicism*. Movements and causes in Ireland may always be observed to succeed or fail in proportion as they approximate to Gaelic tradition.[216]

Even allowing for de Blacam's desire that Gaelicism should not be thought of as 'a narrow racial cause', there remained obvious problems. Certainly, the linkage of nationalist and Gaelicist enthusiasms led, not surprisingly, to a unionist hostility toward Gaelicist ambition. Dennis Kennedy rightly draws attention to the obsessional interest which northern politicians and journalists took in the 'elevation of Irish to a key position in Sinn Fein nationalism'. He also stresses Protestant concern regarding compulsory Irish in schools, and this draws attention to the important point that

---

[213] Pearse's words were given gospel-like status: *An Phoblacht*, 7 May, 28 May, 4 June, 18 June 1926. The fact that O'Donnell, as editor of *An Phoblacht*, facilitated such a trend points again to the fundamental incoherence of the republican socialist approach; they not only worked through an essentially unsuitable movement, but they also contributed to some of those aspects of the movement which, by contradicting their own emphasis, rendered it unsuitable.

[214] Ibid. 23 Feb. 1929.   [215] Ibid. 24 Dec. 1927.

[216] A. S. de Blacam, *Towards the Republic: A Study of New Ireland's Social and Political Aims* (Dublin, Kiersey, 1918), 13.

Gaelicization was understandably viewed in a negative light by those who found early twentieth-century Gaelic identification threatening, backward-looking, and exclusive.[217]

Similarly, the late-1920s endorsement of Gaelicism gave a divisive edge to republican thinking. That socialist republicans occasionally drifted down such paths themselves ran contrary to their central, non-ethnic, and, by implication, secular, class-determined thesis. Broader republican culture, however, once again left socialists clearly on the periphery. For while the latter occasionally 'went native' in their definition of the nation, the broader republican culture, much less ambiguously, identified the national struggle with Gaelicism and with the celebration of all things Gaelic. Like Flann O'Brien's orator, but without the sense of irony, republicans sometimes gave the impression during this period that 'There is nothing in this life so nice and so Gaelic as truly true Gaelic Gaels who speak in true Gaelic Gaelic about the truly Gaelic language'.[218] There was, indeed, a marked tendency to stress the positive qualities of Gaelic culture more generally. *An Phoblacht* carried a column ('Our native games and pastimes') which offered weekly news and comment on culturally sound leisure activities.[219]

The paper was not exclusively concerned with traditional Gaelic forms. But, despite O'Donnell's claim that it was 'not parochial; we turned our minds to other nations, to happenings in the world of art, literary criticism, and the theatre',[220] the paper was undoubtedly marred by the traces which it bore of a revanchist racism.[221] As ever, the picture is far from straightforward. O'Donnell and Ryan[222] were both literate, literary figures, and the paper

[217] De Blacam, quoted in S. Deane (ed.), *The Field Day Anthology of Irish Writing*, ii (Derry, Field Day, 1991), 983; E. O'Malley, *On Another Man's Wound* (Dublin, Anvil, 1979; 1st edn. 1936), 57–8; D. Kennedy, *The Widening Gulf: Northern Attitudes to the Independent Irish State, 1919–49* (Belfast, Blackstaff, 1988), 175–6.

[218] *The Poor Mouth* (London, Paladin, 1988; 1st edn. 1941), 54–5; see e.g. *An Phoblacht*, 18 Mar., 25 Mar. 1927.

[219] *An Phoblacht*, 7 May, 14 May, 21 May, 28 May 1926. Gaelicism was not, of course, peculiar to republicans: their enemies in the government were themselves committed to language revival (O. MacDonagh, *States of Mind: A Study of Anglo-Irish Conflict 1780–1980* (London, Allen and Unwin, 1983), 117–19).

[220] Quoted in MacEoin (ed.), *Survivors*, 32.

[221] See e.g. the scarcely veiled anti-semitism of a theatre review published in December 1927: '*An Phoblacht* at the play', *An Phoblacht*, 31 Dec. 1927.

[222] Cronin, *Ryan*, 19, 21, 153.

under their editorship certainly did carry some considered, intelligent artistic comment.[223] But there is no question that pro-Gaelicist orthodoxy prevailed among many republicans in these years, and that these assumptions involved a sneering, supremacist view of other cultures. Bitter Anglophobia formed an important part of this picture:

How can we hit England? What desire of hers can we thwart; what mean scheme—and all her schemes are mean—can we expose? On such questions we should periodically examine our conscience. We are prone to let our minds laze on the idea that whenever the British Empire is caught up in a war the Irish people will 'do something' to take advantage of it. We forget that England is ever reaching out to grab and cheat, that she is ever guilty of murder and loot against our people, and that we are never at peace with England while the military occupies our shores and forces her rule in our nation.

The war against England was, according to this 1926 *An Phoblacht* article, 'continuous', varying 'in form only'. It was the duty of every Irish person 'to hit England'.[224] The belief in an English propensity towards meanness, grabbing, cheating, murdering, and looting therefore complemented the positive republican stereotyping of all things Gaelic. Moreover, inter-war Gaelic supremacism extended beyond anglophobia.[225] This emphasis on a cultural definition of the nation had not only a stifling and exclusive quality to it, but it also clarified the problems facing those who sought to build Irish nationalist momentum on the strength of class-based criteria. Socialist republicans occasionally lapsed into nativist discourse, and this reflected a degree of incoherence in their thinking. More significantly still, the essentially non-ethnic,

---

[223] See e.g. the review of Patrick Trench's work: *An Phoblacht*, 24 Sept. 1927.

[224] Ibid. 2 July 1926. Cf. 'The Empire in India: England's Dark Work', 'Imperial Economy', 'Heaven-sent Britain: Her Rights in Africa', 'Why Ireland is Destitute: Confiscation and Absentee Drain' (ibid. 7 May, 18 June, 25 June 1926).

[225] Hostility to the non-Gaelic Gaelic culture of jazz came to be expressed in rather frantic terms. In 1934 *An Phoblacht* reported a meeting held under Gaelic League auspices to protest against 'the wave of jazz which is sweeping through the country to the detriment of national music and dances'. One Gaelic Leaguer, dealing with complaints of jazz programmes from broadcasting stations, asserted: 'Our Minister for Finance has a soul buried in jazz and is selling the musical soul of the nation for the dividends of sponsored jazz programmes. He is jazzing every night of the week. . . . As far as Nationality is concerned, the Minister for Finance knows nothing about it. He is the man who will kill nationality, if nationality is killed in the country' (ibid. 6 Jan. 1934).

non-cultural thesis which lay at the heart of their philosophy was emphatically established as being marginal to mainstream republican thinking, by the predominance of Gaelicist assumptions within the broader republican fold. Once again, republican socialists were peripheralized by thinking to which they incoherently gave a degree of endorsement.

2

Class Struggle and Coercion, 1930–1932

'CAPITALISM CAN'T LAST'

If we decide to continue the system of competition and struggle of man against man for existence we must make up our minds to put up with the consequences, and the consequences are slums and unemployment and misery for a large proportion of the community.

George Gilmore (1931)[1]

Beat the landlord out of life, beat the capitalist out of industry, smash the state machine, arm the workers. Rest in them, in alliance with working farmers, all the powers over production.

Peadar O'Donnell (1931)[2]

At the start of the 1930s there was fierce debate within the republican movement concerning social radicalism. The creation of a socialist republican political organization, to which the name Saor Eire [Free Ireland] had become attached, had been 'in prospect since 1929', with Peadar O'Donnell as its most prominent sponsor.[3] At the turn of the decade, republican discussion developed around the question of social philosophy. In November 1930 Moss Twomey, using the pseudonym Manus O'Ruairc,[4] published a draft constitution under the heading, 'The Sovereignty of the People: Suggestions for a Constitution for an Irish Republic'. In harmony with his Pearsean title, Twomey supported the view that the nation or community possessed extensive rights over natural resources and economic life.[5]

This aspect of the proposals provoked lively discussion within the republican movement, the focus of attention being the issue of

---

[1] *An Phoblacht*, 31 Jan. 1931. [2] Ibid. 7 Feb. 1931.

[3] R. Fanning, *Independent Ireland* (Dublin, Helicon, 1983), 103; J. B. Bell, *The Secret Army: the IRA 1916–79* (Swords, Poolbeg, 1989; 1st edn. 1970), 77.

[4] S. Cronin, *Frank Ryan: The Search for the Republic* (Dublin, Repsol, 1980), 170. [5] *An Phoblacht*, 29 Nov. 1930.

private property. In response to criticism, the IRA chief of staff clarified his social ideas at the start of 1931.

The principles of government which I suggest do definitely insist that the means of production in agriculture and industry shall be nationally owned, that the means of distribution shall, accordingly, be nationally directed, and that government shall primarily be based on those who produce and distribute to the detriment of the parasitical and non-producing elements within the state. This is the matter to be debated, and references to '-isms' and class-war are uncalled for and misleading.

It was to Pearse that Twomey turned in his attempt to deny the allegation that his policies were borrowed from Russia. *The Sovereign People* had been 'written and published ... before we Irish had so much as heard the name of Bolshevism'. The IRA chief of staff quoted from Pearse's tract, citing the 1916 leader's assertion of the nation's right to determine 'to what extent private property may be held by its members, and in what items of the nation's material resources private property shall be allowed'. Twomey defiantly argued that an attack on poverty necessitated that 'private ownership' would have to be 'very severely curtailed'. But he also felt able to assert that private ownership was not 'inherently or fundamentally wrong'.[6] He did not endorse class struggle, but rather espoused a Pearsean communalism according to which individual rights could, where necessary, be curtailed for the benefit of the poorer sections of the community.

Some republicans, however, were less equivocal in their hostility to private ownership. Sean MacBride—whose stance was to change dramatically during the ensuing years—asserted in February 1931 that the toleration of private capitalism 'in any form' would lead to the inevitable exploitation of the poor to the advantage of the rich.[7] In typically uncompromising fashion, George Gilmore also took a hard line against private ownership.

The elimination of private property in the means of production of the necessaries of life will do much more than abolish such results of capitalism as unemployment and miserable conditions of life for the workers.

Not only will working conditions be better, but work also will be better, because the necessity to turn out cheap and shoddy articles to undersell competitors will not exist. When articles are manufactured for use rather than for profit, the manufacturer will be able to follow his natural desire

[6] Ibid. 3 Jan. 1931.   [7] Ibid. 14 Feb. 1931.

to make a good article. He will take pride in doing good work, and in that pride will find a truer self-respect than even the financially successful victim of the competitive system can ever find in increasing his bank balance by selling shoddy goods.[8]

Not all within the republican movement, however, were as convinced as Gilmore by the socialist remedy for alienation. Reflective of the Catholic ethos which characterized the contemporary IRA were arguments such as those employed by Michael Price. The right to acquire and own property, Price asserted, grew out of ecclesiastical insistence 'that the natural law demands the existence of private property'; Catholic social principles supported the notion of a society 'in which the greater part of citizens own land and capital in small quantities (diffusion of ownership to the maximum)'.[9] But Price's more conservative scruples did not carry the day. Speaking at the annual Bodenstown pilgrimage in June, Peadar O'Donnell outlined the approach which was, rhetorically at least, to characterize IRA policy during most of 1931. Employing, once again, his historically questionable interpretation of the man at whose grave the oration was given, O'Donnell

summarized the work to be done: to recognize with Tone that the movement of freedom must be based on that large and respectable section of the community—the men of no property and their allies who are being crushed into misery in the land; based on them and with a leadership collected right in among those on whom the movement is based. Every struggle that rises, every strike in the cities, every fight on the land must be interpreted in this light so that the mass of the people of this country may be led into revolt against the machinery of the state on the whole front, not merely against the police on occasions like this, but against the whole order of life that the state enforces.[10]

At an IRA Convention earlier in the year the Saor Eire project had been sanctioned,[11] and on 26 and 27 September 1931 a national Congress was held in the Iona Hall, Dublin.[12] Saor Eire's literature was emphatically socialist,[13] as is made resoundingly clear

[8] Ibid. 31 Jan. 1931.   [9] Ibid. 7 Feb. 1931.   [10] Ibid. 27 June 1931.
[11] Bell, *Secret Army*, 81; T. P. Coogan, *The IRA* (London, Fontana 1987; 1st edn. 1970), 83; Cronin, *Ryan*, 34.
[12] *Irish Times*, 28 Sept. 1931; *An Phoblacht*, 3 Oct. 1931.
[13] Saor Eire's rhetoric appears largely to have originated with Peadar O'Donnell and David Fitzgerald (Seán Nolan, interview with the author, Dublin, 3 Feb. 1988; U. MacEoin (ed.), *Survivors* (Dublin, Argenta, 1987; 1st edn. 1980), 32; Bell, *Secret*

by the *Constitution and Rules* adopted at the September Congress. The new group's objectives were declared to be threefold:

1. To achieve an independent revolutionary leadership for the working class and working farmers towards the overthrow of British imperialism and its ally, Irish capitalism.
2. To organize and consolidate the Republic of Ireland on the basis of the possession and administration by the workers and working farmers, of the land, instruments of production, distribution, and exchange.
3. To restore and foster the Irish language, culture, and games.

Socialism, republican separatism, and Gaelicism, therefore, defined the movement's typically ambitious aims. The ethnic emphasis reflected in the third objective again rather clashed with the class-based definition at the heart of the organization's philosophy.

The same hybrid and rather incoherent thinking was also evident in Saor Eire's proposed methods. The group would achieve its objectives:

1. By organizing committees of action among the industrial and agricultural workers to lead the day-to-day struggle of the working class and working farmers.
2. By striving to bring about the closest co-operation between workers in agricultural and rural districts and those in cities and towns, to bring them to realize that their interests are mutual and, therefore, they should be allies, as they are all victims of the same exploiting agencies.
3. By the mobilization of the mass of the Irish people behind a revolutionary government for the overthrow of British imperialism in Ireland and the organization of a Workers' and Working Farmers' Republic.
4. By using the Irish language in as many spheres as possible, particularly in this organization.[14]

Army, 81). Fitzgerald's republicanism, like O'Donnell's, was defined by notions of class conflict. Seán Nolan, an associate of Fitzgerald's active in inter-war Irish communist circles, claimed that Fitzgerald's work on the Saor Eire programme had been 'influenced heavily by communist literature' (Nolan, interview with the author). For biographical details on Fitzgerald, see *An Phoblacht*, 9 Sept. 1933.

[14] Saor Eire (Organization of Workers and Working Farmers), *Constitution and Rules Adopted by First National Congress Held in Dublin, 26 and 27 Sept. 1931*, Files of the Dept. of the Taoiseach, NA S 5864 A.

In elaborating upon the movement's aims, Saor Eire's *Constitution and Rules* stated that there were 'two phases' to the struggle. Class-conscious, socially revolutionary activity was integral to both. First, there was to be 'intensive organizational, propagandist and day-to-day activity, knitting the mass of small farmers, agricultural labourers and industrial workers into a solid front', which would provide 'mass resistance' to exploitation. The exploited would be gathered into a 'programme of activity and resistance in the field of rents, annuities, evictions, seizures, bank sales, lock-outs, strikes, and wage-cuts'. Imperialism and capitalism would thus be challenged 'along the whole front of their attacks', creating a situation in which power would pass 'from the imperialist into the hands of the masses of the Irish people'.

This energetic and class-cohesive revolutionary agitation was, according to the millenarian thinking of Saor Eire's proponents, to be followed by a 'second phase' which would involve the consolidation of power 'by the organization of the economy of the workers and working farmers' Republic'. Having achieved power, 'the revolutionary toilers will have reached a point in the struggle from which the attack upon the imperialist state and the capitalist system will take the aspect of supplanting the old forms of organization and administration by new forms'. Control of 'the key positions of capitalist economy' would be of primary importance. Banking, credit, export, and import would, therefore, be run as state monopolies. Landlordism 'in land, fisheries, and minerals' was to be 'abolished without compensation'. Agricultural productivity was to be raised 'by making credits, machinery, seeds, and instruction available to the agricultural population'. On 're-stored lands', state and co-operative organization would prevail. The main forms of public transport were to be taken over by the state.[15]

James Hogan's observation that Saor Eire's 'publicly declared aims and methods' provided evidence of the organization's 'common character with revolutionary communism' was a fair one.[16] Saor Eire offered class conflict which would dismantle Irish capitalism: 'Control of exports, imports, credits, and transport with the development of state co-operatives will gradually eliminate

---

[15] Ibid.
[16] *Could Ireland Become Communist? The Facts of the Case* (Dublin, Cahill, n.d. [1935?]), 99.

the forms of capitalist profit-making distribution'. There were to be 'industrial workers' co-operatives under state direction and management, the workers to regulate internal working conditions'. Sea fisheries were to be 'reorganized in co-operatives and developed by state credits'. Adequate housing was to be provided through the state's organization of workers' co-operatives within the building trade. Rents were to be 'fixed in ratio to wages'.[17] The unemployed were to be guaranteed a minimum standard of living, and free education was to be provided for all.

In addition to this blueprint for a socialist society, Saor Eire's *Constitution and Rules* also provided details of the movement's own organizational structures—structures which, in the event, were to prove largely theoretical. Given that Saor Eire was very much the IRA's radical alter ego, it was natural that it should carry echoes of army organization. Thus the new group's National Congress was its 'supreme governing body' while in session, and its National Executive was to act as the governing authority between Congresses.[18]

As will be seen, Saor Eire was not deeply rooted in the soil of republican thinking; as a consequence, it quickly withered. But it was a telling episode in regard to republican socialist aspiration and assumption. Central to the project—and, indeed, to socialist republican failure more generally in these years—was the question of the land. There was a certain ambiguity evident in republican socialist land policies during the inter-war period. Peadar O'Donnell openly stressed the importance of the bond between individual farmers and their individual holdings,[19] and at times trumpeted the rights of the small farmer. In his account of his experiences during the Spanish civil war he stated that some in Barcelona favoured 'rapid collectivization', and commented that he found himself 'a considerable distance from their views on land issues'. He noted that, 'when acting on their own [peasants] striped the land into small farms', and he thought it important that farmers be assured 'that no man working his own land will lose it'. He found the proposed socialization policy 'the hardest of the new notions to understand'. At an Anarchist Farmers' congress he clearly sided with those delegates who favoured the retention of small-scale private ownership, but the reallocation of land on large estates:

---

[17] *Constitution and Rules*, Files of the Dept. of the Taoiseach, NA S 5864 A.
[18] Ibid.   [19] *Adrigoole* (London, Jonathan Cape, 1929), 21.

'Everything must be simple. You live on a farm. You and your family work it. Very well. We all confirm everybody in possession of his farm.'[20]

He had made a similar assertion in an Irish context in February 1931, but had on this occasion implied that collective farming was the model which he held to be superior:

Nobody will interfere with the man who prefers to remain aloof in his own holding with his spade or his two horses. Undoubtedly, security of free tenure to the working farmer is assured. He will stay out until he sees that a safer, surer, better condition of living is waiting for him inside the collectives.[21]

The Saor Eire experiment which took place later in the year bore traces of the same tension between private and public agriculture. A resolution to the September Congress pledged Saor Eire to 'confirm the working farmer in the possession of his holding'. It also declared that the movement endorsed 'the right of the landless men and working farmers to organize the agricultural industry and to bring within the scope of their administration the unbroken ranches'.[22] There was nothing necessarily socialist here: breaking up ranches and guaranteeing the possession of individual holdings smacked more of small-scale agricultural capitalism than of its dialectical opposite. But Saor Eire also espoused the establishment of 'state and co-operative groupings',[23] and, in the words of Rumpf and Hepburn, 'collectivization was declared to be the only land policy for the nation worth considering: a daring, not to say suicidal, policy in a country of small peasant proprietors.'[24] Just as James Connolly had argued that farmers would come to recognize the limitations of peasant proprietorship and would therefore willingly embrace a socialized system,[25] so, too, inter-war republican socialists assumed that private ownership and individual farming would be superseded by nationalized structures.

Unfortunately for the republican left, however, the Connolly

[20] P. O'Donnell, *Salud! An Irishman in Spain* (London, Methuen, 1937), 43–4, 118, 147, 166–70.   [21] *An Phoblacht*, 28 Feb. 1931.

[22] *Resolutions to be Submitted to the Congress*, Files of the Dept. of the Taoiseach, NA S 5864 B.

[23] Saor Eire, *Constitution and Rules*, Files of the Dept. of the Taoiseach, S 5864 A.

[24] *Nationalism and Socialism in Twentieth Century Ireland* (Liverpool, Liverpool Univ. Press, 1977), 92.

[25] 'Peasant Proprietorship and Socialism' (Aug. 1898), in *JCCW* ii. 213–14.

reference was all too apt. As noted, Connolly's socializing approach towards the land had fallen on the same stony ground of popular rejection which had earlier greeted Michael Davitt's nationalizing proposals. Predictably enough, when inter-war socialist republicans displayed a similar preference for land socialization, their project also failed to resonate with the masses whom they intended to lead. An appealing agricultural programme was essential for anyone who sought to establish political dominance during these years. The Free State census for 1926 lists 672,129 people as being engaged in agricultural occupations, and 263,334 as being engaged in industrial occupations.[26] The equivalent figures for 1936 were, respectively, 643,965 and 280,431.[27] Thus industrial workers were considerably outnumbered within the twenty-six counties by those in agricultural occupations.

During the period between the end of the mid-nineteenth-century famine and the establishment of independent Ireland, 'the peasant proprietor came to dominate rural society'.[28] Moreover, as one commentator has put it, 'Peasant proprietorship seemed to further reinforce the post-famine tendencies to greater conservatism, unwillingness to part with land and general peasant caution'.[29] It was indeed crucial to the failure of Saor Eire—as it was to the failure of inter-war socialist republicanism more generally—that so many of those to whom the republican left looked for support existed within the orbit of small farm private ownership. If small-scale proprietors or landless labourers did desire change, then such aspirations unsurprisingly developed around the conservative theme of land ownership rather than around the more radical project of socialization. Anti-rancher rhetoric was part of an emotive tradition,[30] feeding as it did on understandable and persistent

[26] Irish Free State, *Census of Population 1926, vol. ii*, 1–13. The industrial figure comprises those listed under 'mining and quarrying occupations' (2,599), 'other industrial occupations' (186,617), 'transport and communication' (64,952), 'warehousing, storekeepers, and packers' (6,935), and 'stationary engine drivers' (2,231).

[27] Eire/Ireland, *Census of Population 1936, vol. ii*, 2–15. The latter figure comprises those listed under 'mining and quarrying occupations' (3,042), 'other industrial occupations' (196,104), 'transport and communication' (69,043), 'warehousing, storekeepers, and packers' (9,853), and 'stationary engine drivers' (2,389).

[28] M. E. Daly, *Social and Economic History of Ireland Since 1800* (Dublin, Educational Company of Ireland, 1981), 26. On the change from tenancy to ownership, see Rumpf and Hepburn, *Nationalism and Socialism*, 227.

[29] Daly, *Social and Economic History*, 51.

[30] F. S. L. Lyons, *Ireland Since the Famine* (London, Fontana, 1973; 1st edn. 1971), 216.

resentment. But the proposed breaking up of the ranches was not automatically a radical policy—not, at least, in socialist terms—and Saor Eire was crippled by a paralysis suffered throughout these years by socialist republicans. If one espoused socialist land programmes one was rejected by those who owned (or who wished to own) land. If one recognized the importance of peasant pro-prietorship and consequently offered more conservative policies, then one was again rejected, this time in favour of forces whose promises of guaranteed private ownership were less ambiguous. The more limited radicalism of Fianna Fáil once again trumped the genuinely revolutionary approach of republican socialists. Saor Eire was unable to attract people either by its pledges of support for small farmers or by its promises of co-operative agriculture; its equivocal answer to the land question satisfied virtually nobody.

Saor Eire proposed an alliance of rural and urban workers, and here, too, it is possible to trace weaknesses in the thinking which lay behind the organization. Republican socialist conviction that the interests of rural and urban workers were 'mutual' and that therefore 'they should be allies' did little to offset the difficulties involved in attempting to build synergic revolutionary activity involving these two sectors. O'Donnell himself acknowledged the tensions which existed between urban labour and 'the small farmer countryside',[31] and, as Townshend observes in direct relation to the Saor Eire proposals, ' "Working farmers" have little in common with workers'.[32] Moreover, among industrial workers themselves the picture was, to the Saor Eire zealot, an extremely depressing one. Henry Patterson has suggested that while Fianna Fáil, La-bour, and the republican left all attempted to win the affections of the Free State working class in the early 1930s, there was 'never any doubt which would be chosen'. Fianna Fáil, Patterson argues, managed to identify itself as 'the only realistically "national" party',[33] and succeeded in outflanking both the reformist and the revolutionary left. Saor Eire's proposal to revolutionize indus-try (and, indeed, society) belly-flopped into a pool of working-class indifference. Trade-union opinion tended overwhelmingly

---

[31] *There Will Be Another Day* (Dublin, Dolmen, 1963), 87.

[32] *Political Violence in Ireland: Government and Resistance Since 1848* (Oxford, Clarendon, 1984; 1st edn. 1983), 380.

[33] 'Fianna Fáil and the Working Class: the Origins of the Enigmatic Relation-ship', *Saothar*, 13 (1988), 85.

toward 'a sensitive, mild, parliamentary socialism',[34] and the extra-constitutional, millenarian fanaticism of socialist republicans was eschewed as a consequence.

The aspirations of the republican left were also overwhelmingly rejected in that part of Ireland in which the urban working class was most significant. In 1926, 38.8 per cent of the Northern Irish work-force were engaged in industrial occupations.[35] But if the six-county state's political composition was 'scarcely appropriate to the normal provisions of democracy', it was also ill-suited to the needs of republican socialists. The Catholic population of Northern Ireland accounted for only 33.5 per cent of the region's inhabitants in 1926,[36] and the unionist commitment of the majority of the six counties' non-Catholics effectively nullified republican hopes of developing any dominant mass movement there. Saor Eire's brand of republicanism combined socialist commitment with irredentist aspiration. In 1930 O'Donnell had been organizing rurally 'to break the British connection and to set up a free independent Irish Republic, with power resting in the working farmers and town workers'.[37] So, too, in June 1931 he had stated his purpose in similar terms: 'To break the connection with England and vest all power in a free Republic in the Irish working class and working farmers.'[38] The Saor Eire programme for which O'Donnell was in part responsible reflected the same dual desire for social change and national reunification. The republican socialist ambition in 1931 was to effect a changeover from one age into another; in O'Donnell's words, 'Always one age merges in another with some leading and some holding back.... But inevitably the cross-over takes place. Capitalism can't last'.[39] The important point, in relation to Northern Ireland, was that the social transformation from one age to the other was to be accompanied by the ending of Irish partition.

Republican socialist thinking in relation to partition was distinctive within nationalist circles in that it emphasized the role which class struggle would supposedly play in bringing about

---

[34] C. McCarthy, 'From Division to Dissension: Irish Trade Unions in the Nineteen Thirties', *Economic and Social Review*, 5/3 (Apr. 1974), 360.

[35] D. W. Harkness, *Northern Ireland Since 1920* (Dublin, Helicon, 1983), 46; in the same year, only 20.1% of those occupied in the Free State were engaged in industrial occupations (Irish Free State, *Census of Population 1926, vol. ii*, 1–13).

[36] Harkness, *Northern Ireland*, 43, 48.   [37] *An Phoblacht*, 8 Feb. 1930.

[38] Ibid. 27 June 1931.   [39] Ibid. 28 Feb. 1931.

reunification. In February 1926, William McMullen had argued that it was 'not possible in either the orange or the green camp to form homogeneous parties in which the component units will have common interests, but conversely ... there is an alignment of interest between the Protestant employer and the Catholic employer, as there is between the Protestant worker and the Catholic worker'. It was, he asserted, 'on this basis' that the battle 'must be fought'. Class interests and class unity would, according to this view, provide the incentive and the mechanism by which unification would be achieved:

As an economic necessity, we must complete the unity of the country, for the future of the North is inextricably bound up with the rest of Ireland, for as standing alone or as an appanage of Great Britain, we have no future, and while recognizing this, we must organize on a class basis, regardless of creed, driving employers of different creeds into a common organization in defence of their common interests, so that we may have a perfect setting for our fight for the conquest of political and economic power.[40]

McMullen was typical of republican socialists in that he identified class interests as the key to reunifying Ireland and to establishing an all-Ireland, independent republic; he was atypical in that he was a Protestant. His own explanation of his progress to the socialist republican position merely emphasized his fundamental dissidence when considered within the context of contemporary Irish Protestantism. He had, he claimed, recognized 'that something was radically wrong with the social and economic system of society, and it was but a step from such a conviction, that the land-owning and property-owning class that held the workers in thraldom were the same class that opposed any change in Ireland's [constitutional] status'.[41]

This dual determination—that the social oppressors opposed Irish nationalism and that, therefore, the socially oppressed should support it—distinguished McMullen from the bulk of his Irish co-religionists. Socialist republicanism, whether in the form of Saor Eire or of any of its other inter-war manifestations, was fundamentally a branch of Catholic nationalism, mavericks like McMullen notwithstanding. The irredentism of the republican left

---

[40] *Voice of Labour*, 6 Feb. 1926.
[41] Untitled MS (n.d.), McMullen Papers, PP.

in these years reflected, and could only realistically be expected to appeal to, a Catholic nationalist constituency. Indeed, socialist republican attitudes toward Northern Ireland bore witness to this essentially inward-looking approach. In common with many others in the nationalist tradition, the republican left failed to address seriously the problems inherent in their 'one island, one nation' assumption. Responding to the suggestion that there might be more than one, uncomplicated nation in Ireland, Peadar O'Donnell was stubbornly myopic: 'I think it is nonsense to suggest that we are two peoples. We are the same people with different relatives.'[42] O'Donnell displayed a casual, self-deceiving optimism character-istic of much socialist republican thinking on this subject. Frank Gallagher records in his prison diary for December 1922 that O'Donnell 'thought unity between Ulster Specials and IRA on national freedom not impossible'.[43] Such misguided thinking was complemented by his acceptance, and, indeed, propagation, of caricatures regarding unionists.[44]

The inadequacy of O'Donnell's thinking in relation to northern Protestants is, perhaps, clearest at those points at which he claimed distinctive insights on the subject. At times he stressed his Ulster identity,[45] and he also publicized the fact that his ITGWU work had covered 'all the northern counties—except Donegal'.[46] Armed, therefore, with a supposed expertise, he was prepared to sermonize on the failings of other nationalists in relation to the north-east of the island. But his preaching, in fact, only demonstrated his own blind spot on the subject. Thus, in January 1950, he stated that he had 'often thought it would be well worth somebody's while to make his way through half a dozen typical unionist working-class homes in Belfast to search out and set down a plain statement of the beliefs and fears which are tied up in their minds with partition'. It might be thought that, by 1950, enough evidence already existed on which to base at least a preliminary sketch! But O'Donnell was not to be deterred from his knuckle-rapping message: 'Ireland as a whole needs educating on aspects of the problem of this minority

[42] Quoted in M. McInerney, *Peadar O'Donnell: Irish Social Rebel* (Dublin, O'Brien, 1974), 201. [43] Gallagher Papers, NLI MS 18356.
[44] See esp. P. O'Donnell, *The Knife* (Dublin, Irish Humanities Centre, 1980; 1st edn. 1930).
[45] See e.g. his dedication to John Hewitt and Micheal MacLaverty in O'Donnell, *Proud Island* (Dublin, O'Brien, 1983; 1st edn. 1955), 6.
[46] Quoted in MacEoin (ed.), *Survivors*, 22.

in revolt in north-east Ulster'. O'Donnell claimed to have outgrown 'the idea that these work-a-day Protestants of north-east Ulster were merely a resident garrison holding a bridge-head for the empire in Ireland'. But his rather smug assumption that he was in advance of most nationalist opinion could not disguise the deficiencies which existed within his own thinking. He emphasized the 'thorough Irishness' of a unionist whom he had recently met, and argued that 'the differences that separate the minority from the majority are purely cultural; they have been built in and they can be taken down and cast away'.[47] However, these descriptions underline O'Donnell's fundamental misconstruction of the problems regarding partition. He assumed that the difficulty was one of dealing with a minority within an Irish context. The counter-argument—that this rigid encasing of unionists within the inevitability of one-island, all-Ireland separatism was simply unacceptable—lay entirely beyond O'Donnell's thinking. That the framework for understanding and responding to unionism might be one of 'islands', rather than of 'the island', simply escaped him.

Such myopia left republicans of all hues bankrupt of ideas with regard to the north. Frank Ryan noted in November 1930 that, 'We seem to have no remedy for [partition]',[48] and certainly the republican left found the northern question too difficult to answer in any adequate fashion. The approach evident in the Saor Eire project amply demonstrated this.[49] James Hogan, one of Saor Eire's harshest critics, noted rightly in 1935 that the growth of support for the IRA among northern nationalists would mean 'still another obstacle in the path of Irish unity'.[50] It is also true that, through its approach to partition, the IRA's leftist self, Saor Eire, managed to avoid a pragmatic response to the important economic questions of the period in Northern Ireland. As Buckland has noted of the inter-war years, 'In Belfast . . . unemployment was of as much concern as the border, and in Co. Antrim the fate of land purchase worried many farmers'.[51] Thus Saor Eire's impossibilist, millenarian approach would not only make Irish reunification an even less

---

[47] *Sunday Press*, 1 Jan. 1950.   [48] *An Phoblacht*, 8 Nov. 1930.

[49] See e.g. the absurd analysis offered in *An Phoblacht*: 'The function of the six and twenty-six counties [*sic*] governments is to beat down the mass resistance to the efforts of the ruling classes to pass the burdens of today's crisis on to the backs of the poor' (ibid. 10 Oct. 1931).

[50] To Henry, 18 Apr. [1935?], enclosed with QUB library copy of Hogan, *Could Ireland Become Communist?*, QUB Special Collections Room.

[51] *A History of Northern Ireland* (Dublin, Gill and Macmillan, 1981), 57.

likely prospect; it also clouded practical thinking on economic issues, and tied proposals for social change to a polarizing and
unrealistic irredentist project.

The republican socialist orthodoxy typified by Saor Eire contrasted sharply with the insight apparently reached by its leading
sponsor earlier in 1931. In February of that year O'Donnell had
argued that partition resulted from the 'uneven development
of capitalism in Ireland'.[52] This took him near to an important
point. As Mary Daly has observed, 'While Ireland's economic per-
formance under the Union was not the sole factor fuelling the
movement for independence, it is hardly a coincidence that Ulster,
the most successful province under the union, rejected independence'.[53] Henry Patterson has rightly noted Peadar O'Donnell's
'capacity for sharp insights within a fundamentally fuzzy and
ambiguous conceptualization of the Irish social order',[54] and
O'Donnell's comments of February 1931 tend to reinforce such a
judgement. The basic O'Donnellite thesis was, as we have seen,
that class interest determined the nature and quality of one's attitude to the national question; those from the classes oppressed
under capitalism had, according to this argument, anti-capitalist
and, as a consequence, pro-separatist interests and instincts. As a
result, working-class Belfast, Protestant as well as Catholic, could
be expected to join in the republican advance. O'Donnell had,
however, recognized the important role played by divergent regional economic development, and this insight should have had
important consequences for the republican socialist argument. For
the unionist working class, the logic of economic interests did
indeed affect their stance in relation to the national question, but
it did so in exactly the opposite fashion from that enshrined in
O'Donnellite orthodoxy. Rather than inclining them toward republican separatism, economic interests tied them even more tightly
to the link with Britain. Yet, rather than adjusting the theory to
suit the economic insight, O'Donnell returned to an unaltered
orthodoxy later in the year in his work for Saor Eire. This infu-
riating ability—to achieve sharp focus and then wholeheartedly
to ignore the vision thus acquired—was evident in much of
O'Donnell's activity, and it repeatedly crushed the life out of his
more interesting, intelligent observations.

[52] *An Phoblacht*, 7 Feb. 1931.
[53] *Industrial Development and Irish National Identity, 1922–39* (Dublin, Gill and
Macmillan, 1992), 3. [54] 'Fianna Fáil and the Working Class', 85.

Even among the Northern Irish IRA, whom one might consider to have been Saor Eire's most promising six-county audience, the socialist republican message failed to resonate. Munck and Rolston's research for their oral history of 1930s Belfast led them to conclude: 'The outlook of the average IRA volunteer at that period was relatively uncomplicated: it was a question of securing a British withdrawal and "politics" could be left till later.' 'Politics' provoked little excitement, the preference being for military activity. Peadar O'Donnell criticized the northern IRA, commenting on 'the great weakness of the republican movement in the north, that they never managed to hold their religious services apart from their political commemorations. I always maintained and repeatedly said it to the Army Council, "We haven't a battalion of IRA men in Belfast; we just have a battalion of armed Catholics" '. O'Donnell rather smugly asserted that he had been 'probably the only person on the Army Council so aware of the need to bring Protestant workers of the north-east to our side'.[55] But Saor Eire's emphasis on the Gaelicization of Ireland, enshrined in literature which O'Donnell himself had co-drafted,[56] was hardly destined to rally the Ulster Protestant masses in 1931. Indeed, O'Donnell's suggestion that northern Protestants 'had no opposition to the existence of the IRA' (but that they simply had 'a lot of impatience' with the IRA's idea that they could achieve Irish unity through force of arms)[57] demonstrates once again his capacity for misguidedly optimistic thinking on the question of partition. Neither with northern republicans, nor with unionist anti-republicans, was Saor Eire calculated to win many recruits.

'UNLAWFUL AND DANGEROUS ASSOCIATIONS'

It is of interest to note that O'Donnell is . . . actively working to promote relations with the communist movement.

> Free State Executive Council memorandum
> (1930)[58]

---

[55] R. Munck and B. Rolston (with G. Moore), *Belfast in the Thirties: An Oral History* (Belfast, Blackstaff, 1987), 171, 183–4.

[56] Saor Eire, *Constitution and Rules*, Files of the Dept. of the Taoiseach, NA S 5864 A.   [57] Munck and Rolston, *Belfast in the Thirties*, 184.

[58] *Communist Activities: Peasant Farmers' Organization (Kristertern)* [memorandum circulated to each member of the Executive Council] (27 Mar. 1930), *Communist Activities 1929–30, Saorstat Eireann*, Files of the Dept. of the Taoiseach, NA S 5074 A.

The red scare of 1931 was nonsense, in relation to Irish life,
but it was necessary to make a climate for new, terrorist
legislation. . . . The government raised a great din, press and
pulpit forming a jazz band that bare throats could not cut
through to reach the people.

Peadar O'Donnell[59]

Saor Eire's prospects were not significantly better in the neighbouring Free State than they were in Northern Ireland, but the
Cumann na nGaedheal government responded to the organization with tenacious hostility. The slump at the end of the 1920s
had stifled opportunities for emigration to the United States,[60] and
the depressing social and economic context at the turn of the decade
appeared to some to increase the possibility of widespread radical
activity. *An Phoblacht* certainly broadcast incitements to social
subversion. In January 1931 it depicted grotesque social inequali-
ties with the intention of stimulating revolt.

Never were the great shops of Dublin and the provincial capitals more
well-stocked than this Christmas—yet not for years have the mass of our
people endured greater want. . . . The minority have all that they desire—
aye, they have to invent new desires . . . Pampered parasites and starving
slaves—that is the Irish nation today. Why starve? Why be slaves, ye
people of proud memories? All that you want is here in your own land
if you but have the courage of men, and take it![61]

There was considerable official anxiety during this period concerning the possibility that such revolutionary exhortations might
actually stimulate serious subversion. A Department of Justice report compiled later in 1931, dealing with 'unlawful and dangerous'
organizations operating within the Free State, had estimated that
the IRA comprised approximately 1,300 officers and 3,500 rank
and file.[62] Although the 'names, addresses, and ranks of practically

---

[59] *There Will Be*, 126.
[60] H. Patterson, *The Politics of Illusion: Republicanism and Socialism in Modern Ireland* (London, Hutchinson Radius, 1989), 44.
[61] *An Phoblacht*, 3 Jan. 1931.
[62] *Dept. of Justice Report on the Present Position (Aug. 1931) as Regards the Activities of Unlawful and Dangerous Associations in the Saorstat with a Summary of Similar Activities in Recent Years*, Files of the Dept. of the Taoiseach, NA S 5864 B. It should be noted that a memorandum sent to Cardinal MacRory in Sept. 1931 claimed that the 1,300/3,500 estimate related to Jan. 1931, and that the numbers had 'increased rapidly since that date' (*Copy of Enclosure to Letter Addressed by the President to the Cardinal on 10 Sept. 1931. Memorandum Regarding the Activities of Certain Organizations*).

all these men who are of any importance' were known to the police, it was 'not possible to bring them to justice'. The IRA's jury intimidation and silence under interrogation rendered the prosecution of political offenders virtually impossible: 'The cumulative result of these conditions is to put the police in a hopeless position'.[63] In the previous month the Garda Commissioner, Eoin O'Duffy, had argued the need for greater legal freedom in dealing with 'the Irregulars [IRA]',[64] and official concern was in particular focused on the supposed fusion of republican and left-wing energies.

The frustration exhibited by O'Duffy—the 'scare-maker-in-chief on the communist danger', according to O'Donnell—[65] was woven into governmental fears about the possibility of socialist republican revolution. In May 1929 a Department of Justice memorandum reported 'that Russian Oil Products, Dublin, now employ Roddy Connolly, . . . the Dublin communist'; in April 1929, the memorandum asserted, Connolly had 'outlined a scheme for the formation of a Workers' Defence Corps'. This body was to be 'a complementary unit to the IRA, and would, at first, work in co-operation with the IRA, and later absorb that body'. The alarm generated by the prospect of communist/IRA links was further expressed in a memorandum of July 1929: 'The formation of a Workers' Defence Corps would now appear to be definite and close attention will have to be paid to that body. There is a likelihood that they may attempt to openly arm and drill on the same lines as the Citizen Army and in such an event the IRA would take shelter within that body.'[66]

The dread of republican socialist revolt led to close supervision of supposedly threatening subversives during the early 1930s. The Irish version of the Friends of Soviet Russia was thoroughly scrutinized, and its leading figures identified as having both communist and republican sympathies.[67] In August 1930, attention was directed by the Department of Justice towards specifically Russian

[63] *Dept. of Justice Report on the Present Position*, Files of the Dept. of the Taoiseach, NA S 5864 B.

[64] Keogh, 'De Valera, the Catholic Church, and the "Red Scare" 1931–2', in O'Carroll and Murphy (eds.), *De Valera and His Times*, 136–7.

[65] *There Will Be*, 122.

[66] *Russian Oil Products* [memorandum circulated to each member of the Executive Council] (7 May 1929); memorandum dealing with the Workers' Defence Corps (16 July 1929) (*Communist Activities 1929–30 Saorstat Eireann*, Files of the Dept. of the Taoiseach, NA S 5074 A).

[67] Dept. of Justice memoranda (6, 19 Mar. 1930).

influence over the republican left. The Executive Council was circulated copies of 'a draft letter purporting to be a message from the Communist Party in Russia to Irish communists'. This document did, indeed, present republicanism in terms of working-class revolutionary potential:

The ECCI [Executive Committee of the Communist International] considers the work of the Irish comrades for the organization of the revolutionary elements in Ireland marks an important advance on the road to the organization of the revolutionary party of the proletariat. The direct approach made to the workers resulting in the establishment of a number of contacts in the factories, in the establishment of relations with the IRA; the unemployed demonstrations on March 6, the organization of the peasants' delegation to the Berlin Conference, and . . . the appearance of the *Workers' Voice*, all indicate the existence in Ireland of wide possibilities for the formation and development of a revolutionary working-class party.

The accompanying memorandum stated that the *Workers' Voice* was 'in close touch with the Communist Party in Russia' and that there existed 'some kind of working understanding between the communists as represented by the *Workers' Voice* and the Irregulars'.[68] A previous Department of Justice memorandum had dealt with the Workers' Revolutionary Party (the body behind the *Workers' Voice*) and had stated that 'Every effort has been made by Peadar O'Donnell to entice members of the Irregulars to join the organization and in that respect he has been very successful'. It was obvious, continued the memorandum, 'that the Workers' Revolutionary Party and IRA are closely allied and information received is to the effect that GHQ Irregulars have encouraged members of the Dublin brigade to join the Workers' Revolutionary Party'.[69]

This fear of republican and leftist synergy pervades much official material from the early 1930s. The August 1931 Department of Justice report, to which reference has already been made, pointed to the number of groups in the state which sought a Russian-style revolution and a 'working-class republic', and noted the overlap between these organizations and the IRA.[70] A cabinet

---

[68] Dept. of Justice memorandum (1 Aug. 1930), *Communist Activities in Saorstat Eireann 1929- [sic]*, S 5074 B.

[69] Dept. of Justice memorandum (16 June 1930), ibid.

[70] *Dept. of Justice Report on the Present Position (Aug. 1931)*, Files of the Dept. of the Taoiseach, NA S 5864 B.

memorandum from the previous year had listed and given details regarding fifteen 'Revolutionary Organizations' operating in the Free State. This document made much of links between the listed organizations and the Soviet Union. Kathleen Price, secretary of Friends of Soviet Russia, had been 'one of the delegates to Russia from Ireland for the celebrations in connection with the anniversary of the foundation of the Union of Socialist Soviet Republics'. Robert Stewart and Helena Moloney, also involved with the Friends, were likewise branded with Russian connections. The object of the movement was 'to promote Soviet propaganda in An Saorstat'. Other groups were also tarnished with the stains of Soviet association. Thomas Bell (of the Irish Communist Party and Workers' Revolutionary Party) had 'studied revolutionary methods at the Lenin College, Moscow' and had been 'appointed Irish agent by the Communist Internationale in September 1928'. The Irish National Unemployed Movement was 'a branch of the Communist Internationale'.[71]

Towards the end of this survey of nefarious groups, it was suggested that 'the number of these revolutionary organizations . . . is bewildering and each week so to speak gives birth to new ones'.[72] This subversive fecundity prompted drastic state repression, anxiety at paramilitaristic activity[73] blending with concern 'that the extremist movement in this country is a strange mixture of political revolutionaries and social revolutionaries'.[74] Indeed, the Cumann na nGaedheal government had begun the move toward stern action prior to Saor Eire's September 1931 debut Congress. Anxious to secure Catholic hierarchical support before engaging in any drastic assault on subversion, President Cosgrave had written in August 1931 to Joseph MacRory, Primate of All Ireland. The facts, he argued, made it imperative that the Cardinal 'be given the fullest information about a situation which threatens the whole fabric of both Church and state'.[75]

On 10 September Cosgrave again wrote to MacRory, this time

[71] *Revolutionary Organizations* [memorandum circulated to each member of the Executive Council] (5 Apr. 1930), Blythe Papers, ADUCD P24/169, 1–4.

[72] Ibid. 11.

[73] *Summary of Outrages and Activities by members of Irregular Organization since 1 Jan. 1931, Anti-State Activities Apr. 1929–Oct. 1931*, Files of the Dept. of the Taoiseach, NA S 5864 A.

[74] *Revolutionary Organizations*, Blythe Papers, ADUCD P24/169, 1.

[75] To MacRory, 13 Aug. 1931, Files of the Dept. of the Taoiseach, NA S 5864 B.

enclosing a memorandum and appendices intended to convince him 'of the real gravity of the situation' and to encourage him

> to request the general body of the bishops to consider whether the most effective manner of dealing with the pernicious teachings which are sapping the bases of all authority in this country would not be joint episcopal action in the form of a concise statement of the law of the church in relation to the present issues, and the penalties attached to its violation.[76]

The first appendix stressed IRA and communist links,[77] and this point was also emphasized in the attached memorandum. While the active membership of the communistic organizations was recognized to be 'comparatively small', it was suggested that 'the acceptance of communistic doctrines by the other organizations is alarmingly rapid'. With specific reference to the supposedly emerging threat from Saor Eire, it was argued

> that a class war is being organized, a revolutionary struggle in which every needy or aggrieved or dissatisfied or destructive element is to be encouraged and exhorted to provide for its needs and to avenge its grievances by attacking social and political institutions in general and all who may support or direct them.

Faced with a menacing array of subversives, the government felt it their duty 'to take every step practicable to them to stem the growth of these forces of anarchy while they are yet sufficiently undeveloped to be grappled with'. They intended, when parliament resumed, to introduce legislation giving them 'more effective powers to curb the activities of these organizations'.[78] This they did. On 14 October 1931 Cosgrave introduced into the Dáil 'a Bill entitled an Act to amend the Constitution by inserting therein an Article making better provision for safeguarding the rights of the people and containing provisions for meeting a prevalence of disorder'. The Constitution (Amendment No. 17) Bill was passed in the Dáil on 16 October, coming into effect after the Seanad's approval and the Governor-General's signature the following day.[79]

The amendment was, in one historian's apt description, 'a stringent public safety act establishing a five-man military tribunal

[76] Ibid. 10 Sept. 1931.
[77] *Copy of Report Submitted to Government by Dept. of Justice on Alliance Between IRA and Communists.*
[78] *Copy of Enclosure to Letter Addressed by the President to the Cardinal on 10 Sept. 1931.*   [79] *Dáil Debates*, 40/24, 385–7; *Irish Times*, 19 Oct. 1931.

with sweeping powers (including the death penalty) to deal with all political crime and empowering the Executive Council to declare organizations unlawful'.[80] The police were given extensive powers of search, seizure, arrest, and detention[81] and, as republicans were to discover, the legislation undeniably established a formidable armoury of repressive weapons.[82] The government's public safety act was complemented by a Pastoral (read at Masses throughout Ireland on 18 October 1931) in which 'Cardinal MacRory, and the archbishops and bishops of Ireland' expressed their 'grave anxiety' at 'the progress made by anti-social and anti-Christian organizations in this country'. The statement demonstrated the depth of episcopal commitment to majoritarian constitutionalism. The Free State government had been 'entrusted with office by the votes of the people' and represented 'the only lawful civil authority'. Majority disapproval could remove it from power through the electoral process, but nobody was free 'to resist its decrees or its officials by armed force, violence, or intimidation'. Such a situation would result in 'anarchy, the destruction of personal liberty and the material as well as the spiritual ruin of the country'. The IRA's 'methods and principles of action' were stated to be 'in direct opposition to the law of God', coming 'under the definite condemnation of the Catholic Church'.

The bishops also, however, shared the government's concern about socialism. Saor Eire's intention was 'to impose upon the Catholic soil of Ireland the same materialistic regime, with its fanatical hatred of God, as now dominates Russia and threatens to dominate Spain'. There was no equivocation: 'materialistic communism, in its principles and action, wherever it appears, means a blasphemous denial of God and the overthrow of Christian civilization... You cannot be a Catholic and a communist. One stands for Christ, the other for Anti-Christ.'[83] The bishops had

[80] Fanning, *Independent Ireland*, 104.

[81] *Constitution (Amendment No. 17) Bill, 1931*, Files of the Dept. of the Taoiseach, NA S 4469/17. An important aspect of the legislation was the way in which it was used to censor the press, with *An Phoblacht, Irish World, Workers' Voice, Irish Worker*, and *Republican File* all having issues declared 'seditious' by the Military Tribunal (*Constitution (Amendment No. 17) Act, 1931: Important Data*, S 9249.)

[82] See e.g. *George Gilmore: Sentence by Constitution (Special Powers) Tribunal*, Files of the Dept. of the Taoiseach, NA S 2745; *Sheila Humphreys: Trial by Constitution (Special Powers) Tribunal*, S 2846.

[83] *Irish Catholic Directory and Almanac, 1932*, 621–4. The more positive side of Catholic anti-communism—both within and outside Ireland—should not be ignored. In particular, class-harmonious vocationalism was offered as a way of

responded precisely as Cosgrave had wished; 'the gentlemen that they are, they are always helpful', as one communist was ironically to express it.[84] In the view of IRA GHQ, the events of 1931 fitted a historical pattern: 'Again, as in 1922 the hierarchy are lending their sanction to brutal and repressive measures against Republicans'.[85]

The assault on socialist republicans was particularly keen. According to Saor Eire's Sheila Humphreys,[86] that organization was 'the most abused organization that was ever started in Ireland or indeed anywhere'.[87] The theme of Saor Eire's supposed godlessness, played resoundingly in the October 1931 bishops' pastoral, had indeed been picked up elsewhere. The *Irish Rosary* argued that the group represented 'in reality a wild cat of Anti-Christian and Anti-Irish hatred', and while certain of the organization's adherents tried to counter such claims,[88] there is little doubt both that Saor Eire was widely perceived in anti-Christian terms, and also that its project did in fact imply conflict with the Church. O'Donnell might try to put some distance between himself and his anti-clerical image,[89] but this should not disguise the fact that his state socializing projects did indeed represent a challenge to clerical authority and vision. If the state perceived him to be 'a very dangerous individual',[90] then he himself also recognized the conflict with the Church into which his campaigns would unavoidably bring him. This was reflected in his suggestion in 1930 that 'a good many bishops in Ireland had earned gaol', and his hope that 'they would get their deserts'.[91]

---

achieving social justice (J. H. Whyte, *Church and State in Modern Ireland 1923–79* (Dublin, Gill and Macmillan, 1980; 1st edn. 1971), 67–8; Lyons, *Ireland Since the Famine*, 528).

[84] Sean Nolan, interview with the author, Dublin, 3 Feb. 1988.

[85] Oglaigh na h-Eireann: GHQ to the Commander of Each Independent Unit, 27 Oct. 1931, *The Coercion Act: Our Attitude and Tasks*, Mulcahy Papers, ADUCD P7/C/88 (2).

[86] Humphreys was a member of Saor Eire's Executive (quoted in MacEoin (ed.), *Survivors*, 349).

[87] To O'Malley, 5 Apr. 1932, Cormac O'Malley Papers, PP.

[88] *Irish Rosary*, 36, 4 (Apr. 1932), 245–7. Cf. the suggestion by Humphreys: 'We've always had the Church against us. And why, I don't know . . . because if you go back to our Lord . . . he would have been called a socialist in his time' (interview with the author, Dublin, 26 Feb. 1987).   [89] *Salud!*, 36.

[90] *Revolutionary Organizations*, Blythe Papers, ADUCD P24/169, 2.

[91] *Communist Activities: Peasant Farmers' Organization, Communist Activities 1929–30 Saorstat Eireann*, Files of the Dept. of the Taoiseach, NA S 5074 A. O'Donnell's jabbing clashes with the clergy continued long after the inter-war

The O'Donnellite reading of the 'red scare' period reflected his awareness of the extent of the conflict between socialism and the Church: 'The Irish bishops were playing havoc with the rural minds which would naturally, if left free to themselves, sympathize with those they were being incited to destroy';[92] 'The government raised a great din, press and pulpit forming a jazz band that bare throats could not cut through to reach the people.'[93] But his plaintive suggestion that 'there must be some way of settling social struggles without involving churches any more than we involve schools of medicine'[94] could not be considered realistic in the context of inter-war Ireland. Fianna Fáil's emphatically Catholic self-presentation[95] reflected the usefulness to Free State political groups of playing a Catholic card, and there is no doubt that the 'new-found respect' which de Valera had managed to acquire among many churchmen[96] reinforced his success, just as clerical hostility contributed toward O'Donnellite failure. Yet Church influence should not be overstated. Indeed, the Saor Eire episode clarifies both the complexity and the limitations of the Church's impact on Free State politics.

'ONE OF OUR MISTAKES'

I thought Saor Eire, when it came, was a wonderful organization. On paper, it sounded marvellous. Unfortunately it remained only on paper.

Sheila Humphreys[97]

Saor Eire . . . was not so revolutionary as it seemed to be. It was academic really, and constituted, in effect, an IRA alibi enabling it to slide out of doing something practical to implement its aims.

Peadar O'Donnell[98]

---

period; see e.g. *Activities of Peadar O'Donnell in Relation to Irish Centre, London*, Dept. of Foreign Affairs, Secretary's Office Files, NA A 87.

[92] O'Donnell to Cape, 24 Feb. 1933, Cape Archives, Univ. of Reading Library.
[93] O'Donnell, *There Will Be*, 126. [94] *Salud!*, 101.
[95] Whyte, *Church and State*, 41.
[96] Keogh, 'De Valera, the Catholic Church, and the "Red Scare"', 155.
[97] Quoted in MacEoin (ed.), *Survivors*, 349.
[98] Quoted in McInerney, *O'Donnell*, 116.

The Saor Eire episode has often been presented, by enemies and supporters alike, as a moment containing revolutionary potential. James Hogan suggested that the organization 'spread like wild-fire', and celebrated the fact that the government's Public Safety Act had nipped this flourishing, poisonous growth 'in the bud'.[99] Noel Browne, an Irish dissident of a later generation, lamented the crushing of Saor Eire, 'the one and only manifestation of re-publicanism in its true sense, in the south of Ireland, throughout the last 75 years'.[100] Rumpf and Hepburn have Saor Eire meeting 'with instant success, converting IRA units into Saor Eire branches almost overnight'.[101] But Sean Nolan's more sceptical, alternative formulation—'What there *was* of an organization was the IRA units'—[102] is probably nearer the mark. For the point about Saor Eire is precisely its shallow-rooted feebleness. It is true that col-lusion between state and Church led to the delivery of a crushing blow towards the end of 1931. On 20 October Saor Eire, along with the IRA and ten other revolutionary groups, was proscribed by the government under the provisions of its new Public Safety Act,[103] and the republican movement undoubtedly experienced considerable harassment during the height of the 'red scare' pe-riod.[104] Saor Eire, indeed, did not have long to live. At an IRA Convention in 1932 it was decided, in the words of Moss Twomey, that 'there should be no attempt to revive Saor Eire'.[105]

Yet it would be misleading to imply that Saor Eire was a men-ace which government and hierarchy just managed to stifle before the bud began to flourish. Certainly, it is mistaken to claim that this episode demonstrated the mechanical power of the Catholic Church over Irish politics. Noel Browne asserts that 'In 1931, a pastoral letter from the bishops of Rome condemned Saor Eire, because it was republican, and socialist. So ended [Saor Eire]'.[106] Yet both Saor Eire and the IRA had been attacked in the bishops' pastoral, and only the former dissolved as a result. The repression of 1931 only succeeded in destroying Saor Eire so effectively precisely because the movement lacked any political sturdiness in

[99] *Could Ireland Become Communist?*, 101, 104.
[100] *Church and State in Modern Ireland* (Belfast, QUB Politics Dept, 1991), 17.
[101] *Nationalism and Socialism*, 92.
[102] Interview with the author, Dublin, 3 Feb. 1988.
[103] *Irish Times*, 21 Oct. 1931.
[104] *Republican File*, 28 Nov. 1931–13 Feb. 1932; Banta, 'Red Scare', 44–8.
[105] Cronin, *Ryan*, 42.   [106] *Church and State*, 17.

the first place; episcopal condemnation of the new organization was, in the words of one distinguished scholar, 'taking a sledge hammer to crack a nut'.[107] Saor Eire had been destined for a short and fruitless life whether or not Cosgrave or MacRory had noticed its existence. Socialist class struggle was simply not a popular brand of politics in the contemporary Free State; and, given our survey of the deficiencies in the thinking which underpinned Saor Eire, such lack of popular enthusiasm is, perhaps, hardly surprising.

Committed adherence to particular forms of Irish nationalism had withstood clerical disapproval on numerous occasions during the modern period.[108] In 1931 the IRA survived such disapproval, whereas Saor Eire did not. Had the Church possessed the power mechanically to silence those of whom it disapproved—a power ascribed to it, for example, by Noel Browne—then the condemnatory pastoral would surely have resulted in the demolition of the IRA.

Indeed, far from demonstrating the strength of the Catholic Church's hold on Irish politics, this episode in fact demarcates the limitations of clerical power in terms of direct influence in the political realm. Episcopal condemnation only had an 'annihilating effect'[109] on Saor Eire because the organization was such a soft target for abusive bullying in the first place. The lesson of the 'red scare' was that republicans robustly adhered to their convictions despite episcopal disapproval. Socialist republicans remained both socialist and republican; non-socialist republicans were willing to shed their supposed attachment to a class-struggling creed to which they had not been truly committed anyway. When condemned by the bishops for anti-majoritarian physical force and for godless socialism, the IRA dropped the latter and maintained the former. While it is important to recognize that the Cosgrave-MacRory alliance led the IRA to drop its allegiance to Saor Eire in this way in 1932, it is surely more important to stress that the hybrid ideology of the short-lived experiment had never truly been absorbed into IRA orthodoxy to begin with.

For close scrutiny of the evidence demonstrates just how shallow-rooted the Saor Eire plant was, even within the organization from which it had sprung. Looking back on Saor Eire, Peadar O'Donnell

---

[107] J. J. Lee, 'Irish Nationalism and Socialism: Rumpf Reconsidered', *Saothar*, 6 (1980), 63.   [108] Whyte, *Church and State*, 8–12.
[109] Rumpf and Hepburn, *Nationalism and Socialism*, 95.

argued that the venture had represented 'an IRA alibi enabling it to slide out of doing something practical to implement its aims'.[110] This certainly fits with Sheila Humphreys' evaluation of Saor Eire, that 'On paper, it sounded marvellous. Unfortunately it remained only on paper.'[111] In a letter written in 1932, Humphreys noted that priests, bishops, employers, Sinn Fein, 'and in short the great majority of the country' were opposed to Saor Eire and that, consequently, 'it needs some enthusiasm to go ahead with it'. She also added a comment which was telling in its depiction of the degree of commitment which Saor Eire actually commanded in the republican movement: 'As a matter of fact since the election [of February 1932] everyone has been so busy with other matters that it [Saor Eire] has been neglected.'[112]

In February 1931, Peadar O'Donnell had argued that mere declarations were useless and that it was 'the nature of the struggle' that was important.[113] In this he was undoubtedly right. If socialist republicanism were to flourish, then class struggle would have to become integral to the republican crusade. O'Donnell's problem was that the IRA would not allow class struggle to become a fundamental, determining component of its republicanism in practice, Saor Eire rhetoric notwithstanding. That this was so is clear from the IRA's response to the attacks of the pious and the powerful at the end of 1931. And the distance which republican socialists had to travel in terms of winning nationalists to their class-struggling vision was, again, reflected in Humphreys' contemporary thoughts.

The truth of the matter is that most people see red when you mention 'worker'. And all our opponents say we are introducing class warfare into holy Ireland where rich and poor stood together in the national struggle! etc. etc.! This argument makes me sick, as if there wasn't at present an intensive war being carried out by the rich against the poor whom they regard as a different species of human kind.... [T]he only hope I see is in a revolution by the workers themselves. And unfortunately we have a good distance to travel before the people are ready for that.

Humphreys' condescension toward those with, perhaps, a more typical outlook than her own is instructive regarding those of her

[110] Quoted in McInerney, *O'Donnell*, 116.
[111] Quoted in MacEoin (ed.), *Survivors*, 349.
[112] To O'Malley, 5 Apr. 1932, Cormac O'Malley Papers, PP.
[113] *An Phoblacht*, 7 Feb. 1931.

zealous cast of mind. She quoted a struggling small farmer (with whom she had recently spoken) as having argued: ' "Sure it's only right for the man who was born rich that he should profit by the labour of others as only for his brains and his money there would be no work." What hope is there', Humphreys asked, 'for such a mentality?'[114] Humphreys' exasperation here rather resembles that of Liam O'Flaherty's Dan Gallagher with regard to his rank and file: 'Their damn superstitions always stand in the way of revolutionary beliefs. They talk at International Headquarters about romanticism and leftism and all sorts of freak notions. What do they know about the peculiar type of hog mind that constitutes an Irish peasant?'[115] The prospects for the class-based revolution sought by Humphreys and her comrades were, indeed, dismal. Cumann na mBan, the organization with which Humphreys herself had been heavily involved, displayed a telling caution with regard to Saor Eire: 'Members of Cumann na mBan entered Saor Eire as individuals; the organization did not formally endorse the actions of those who joined. To have done so would have precipitated a disastrous internal crisis as many completely disapproved of this "socialistic trend".'[116]

Even the IRA, from which Saor Eire had itself emerged, was not in fact committed to the project. Our preceding discussion of late-1920s IRA culture renders this unsurprising; there were significant, and obvious, divergences between the socialist republican offspring and its IRA parent. Saor Eire espoused class struggle in unequivocally socialist language. The vague social aspirations of IRA orthodoxy were replaced by calls for a socially revolutionary, rural and urban alliance. The aim was a new republic founded on the principle and practice of class-conscious social ownership. The method was to be class-based organization: Saor Eire's 'committees of action' engaging in 'the day-to-day struggle of the working class and working farmers'[117] contrasted starkly with the IRA's 'manhood of Ireland' employing 'force of arms'.[118] Although Saor

---

[114] To O'Malley, 5 Apr. 1932, Cormac O'Malley Papers, PP.

[115] L. O'Flaherty, *The Informer* (London, Jonathan Cape, 1925), 238.

[116] M. Ward, *Unmanageable Revolutionaries: Women and Irish Nationalism* (London, Pluto, 1983), 214.

[117] Saor Eire, *Constitution and Rules*, Files of the Dept. of the Taoiseach, NA S 5864 A.

[118] *Constitution of Oglaigh na h-Eireann* (Nov. 1925), Blythe Papers, ADUCD P24/165 (10).

Eire emerged from the womb of the IRA, therefore, it was characterized by objectives and proposed methods which cut at the root of army orthodoxy.

George Gilmore later argued that Saor Eire had been 'one of our mistakes. I didn't think so at the time, but do now. It was an attempt to push the labour movement from outside and for the IRA instead of labour to give a political lead.'[119] Certainly, the IRA's approach rendered it unsuitable for the project envisaged by those truly committed to Saor Eire. The speed with which the army abandoned the socialist project causes one to doubt that it had undergone the conversion suggested by Rumpf and Hepburn. Indeed, one striking fact about the 1931 IRA was the amount of traditional, physical-force activity which it generated. If practical rather than verbal evidence gives the truer indication of genuine commitment, then the 1931 IRA was a far from appropriate vehicle in which to make O'Donnellite progress. Republican commitment to violence was noted in official sources,[120] and the army itself was far from reticent on the subject. In August 1931 the *Daily Express* published a report of an interview given in Dublin to its 'Special Correspondent' by Frank Ryan and Geoffrey Coulter.[121] In typically bellicose vein, Ryan had stated that the IRA was 'still at war with Britain ... We shall not lay down our arms until we have achieved the object Irishmen have been fighting for these many years—a completely independent republic for all Ireland ... We have to meet force by force. That is why the IRA will not surrender their arms.'[122] Physical force continued to represent the IRA's primary method and its most instinctive mode of political activity. The army GHQ's response to the Public Safety Act reflected the organization's true centre of gravity: 'At the present time, discipline and cohesion are of vital importance. It may be expedient, in units which have been very active, to curtail training activities, in public, but companies and sections must continue to parade frequently, for orders and instructions.'[123]

[119] Anthony Coughlan, 'Notes on his Conversations with George Gilmore' (7 Mar. 1982), Coughlan Papers, PP.
[120] *Summary of Outrages and Activities, Anti-State Activities Apr. 1929–Oct. 1931*, Files of the Dept. of the Taoiseach, NA S 5864 A.
[121] Ryan was to be influential in the Republican Congress movement, but had not been one of Saor Eire's founders; Coulter acted as Ryan's assistant editor at *An Phoblacht* (Cronin, *Ryan*, 25, 35). [122] *Daily Express*, 24 Aug. 1931.
[123] *The Coercion Act: Our Attitude and Tasks*, Mulcahy Papers, ADUCD P7/C/88 (2).

Why, then, given this manifest lack of commitment, did Saor Eire emerge at all? Peadar O'Donnell subsequently claimed that the movement had represented 'evasive action', a social policy which masked the army's actual 'hesitation to embark on concrete struggles'.[124] Certainly, Saor Eire never went far beyond the politics of rhetorical gesture, and there was advantage in the experiment for IRA leaders like Twomey if such a gesture could be used to mollify O'Donnellite left-wingers. As the early-1930s debates demonstrated, there was a variety of opinion developing within the republican movement concerning the relation between separatism and social argument. There was undoubtedly reason to fear another damaging split, based on social outlook, in what remained of the extra-constitutional republican movement; indeed, just such a schism occurred in 1934, resulting in the emergence of the Republican Congress.

In 1931 there already existed an ideological fault line between those for whom republicanism was defined by class struggle, and those for whom it was not. The evasive-action thesis serves further to emphasize the marginality of O'Donnellite ideas within republican culture, underlining as it does the fact that people were simply not prepared to *act* in accordance with the class-conflicting vision of republican struggle. But this thesis is indeed plausible in relation to the genesis of Saor Eire. Patrick Pearse's 1916 communalism had taken the form of rhetoric accompanying military–separatist action. So, too, Moss Twomey's 1931 neo-Pearsean republicanism involved vague statements about the panacean social qualities of republicanism, without such social argument coming to define the republican project in practice. As noted, in Twomey's case, as in that of Pearse, republican radicalism did not necessarily involve even verbal endorsement of class struggle. Thus Saor Eire's rhetoric itself marked a new development. That it was endorsed by an IRA which, in the main, had no serious commitment to its principles should not, however, surprise us. Not only was there the hope that thoroughgoing socialists could be soothed by a gestural venture of this kind; more importantly, the hazy nature of much republican social thinking makes the 1931 episode unsurprising.

The republican tendency to endorse high-sounding rhetorical declarations had been evident on many occasions during and after

---

[124] *There Will Be*, 121.

the revolutionary period. It was certainly not the case that such verbal enthusiasm necessarily provided a true index either of genuine, detailed aspiration or of practical commitment. As noted earlier, the 1919 Democratic Programme—a celebrated republican text—did not, in fact, represent the practical orientation of the republican movement. So, too, the 1930–1 debate within republican circles involved the espousal of many grand schemes and objectives connected to radical social change. But these should be assessed in relation to the fact that social programmes, in practice, did not for the most part figure in contemporary republican culture. Thus, while support for Saor Eire involved the new departure of giving official, explicit backing to class struggle, it can also be seen as fitting into a pattern of support for movements whose aims never engaged one's practical (as opposed to vague and rhetorical) commitment. To give theoretical support to an O'Donnellite project, while having no serious intention of pursuing it, required no greater act of doublethink than had been involved in giving theoretical (but not practical) support to other social blueprints. Thus, for example, the IRA's (1925) constitutional commitment to 'secure and defend civil and religious liberty and equal rights and equal opportunities for all citizens'[125] had not resulted in anything serious, programmatic, or practical emerging as a consequence. It simply reinforced the organization's smug self-image.

The difference with Saor Eire was, first, that O'Donnell did actually define his republicanism according to social argument and, second, that (as a result of this class-struggling commitment) the organization attracted massive ecclesiastical and state hostility. When Saor Eire consequently became a liability, the clouds of republican thinking cleared sufficiently for the IRA to establish that it had never, in fact, intended to commit itself to socialist class struggle in the first place.

The Cumann na nGaedheal 1931 Public Safety Act had been opposed by Fianna Fáil. Speaking in the Dáil on 14 October, de Valera had stated his party's view that there was 'no need whatever, beyond the present powers that the Executive have, for any further powers to deal with any situation that we know of'; the 'ordinary law' was 'quite sufficient' to deal with the dangers which

---

[125] *Constitution of Oglaigh na h-Eireann* (Nov. 1925), Blythe Papers, ADUCD P24/165 (10).

Cosgrave had outlined. The President had warned that the right to private property was threatened by a 'new patriotism based on Muscovite teachings with a sugar coating of Irish extremism'. For his part, de Valera openly endorsed the 'right to private property', but argued that it was not under any immediate threat.[126] Without doubt, the IRA's lack of commitment to Saor Eire, and the latter's thoroughgoing feebleness, demonstrate that governmental fears regarding republican-socialist revolution were, in fact, overstated. Even from official documents cataloguing the supposed threat, there was evidence suggesting that, on this front at least, the authorities had little reason to worry. A Department of Justice memorandum dealing with the Irish Communist Party in March 1930 commented on a series of meetings held under the Party's auspices. It suggested: 'It would appear that the idea [of these meetings] is to obtain the opinion of the Irregular leaders as to the feasibility of joining forces with the Communist Party'. Significantly, however, the report added: 'It is understood that nothing tangible resulted from these meetings'.[127]

Again, the *Revolutionary Organizations* memorandum of April 1930 had reflected the marginal status of the subversive fringe on which it focused rather over-anxious attention. The numbers involved were small. The Friends of Soviet Russia was held to possess a membership of 'about twelve'. The Irish Labour Defence League had 190 members. The Women Prisoners' Defence League numbered 'approximately' twenty. The Irish National Unemployed Movement had slightly over 300 members. Cumann na mBan was 'approximately fifty strong' in Dublin city and county. The memorandum noted that at one of the early meetings held by the Workers' Revolutionary Party in March 1930, there had been 'about fifty persons' in attendance. The paucity of subversives was made even more obvious by the fact that there was considerable overlap of membership between the Free State's various anti-state bodies. Of the 122 people named in association with the revolutionary organizations, 33 (or 27 per cent) were listed in connection with two or more groups. Of these, 5 were involved with three groups each, 1 with four organizations, and the indefatigable Maud Gonne

---

[126] *Dáil Debates*, 40/25–6, 49, 51–2, 58.
[127] Dept. of Justice Memorandum Concerning a Meeting Held Under the Auspices of the Irish Communist Party (19 Mar. 1930), *Communist Activities 1929–30 Saorstat Eireann*, Files of the Dept. of the Taoiseach, NA S 5074 A.

MacBride topped the list through her association with five separate bodies. With the exception of Larkin's Workers' Union of Ireland, all of the named organizations contained people known to be associated with other subversive groups. Also significant was the fact that a number of the organizations (the Irish Communist Party, Anti-Imperialist League, Workers' Union of Ireland, Clann na Gaedheal, Sinn Fein, Fianna Eireann) were plainly floundering in a serious way.[128]

Government literature, therefore, reflected both the degree of official anxiety concerning the threat of revolution and also the fact that such anxiety was unnecessary. The real threat to Cumann na nGaedheal's power came not from republican socialist revolutionaries, but rather from Fianna Fáil. The growing strength of de Valera's party also represented a potentially fatal threat to extraconstitutional republicans. Writing to Joe McGarrity as editor of *An Phoblacht* in January 1930, Frank Ryan expressed his keenness to dispel the impression that 'all Irish-American support is behind either Cosgrave's party or Fianna Fáil'. He blamed the prevalence of this impression on wide-circulation Irish-American papers.

The *Irish World*, for instance, seeks to give the impression that all who supported the Republic have transferred their allegiance to the Fianna Fáil party. I do not think I could over-estimate the importance to the revolutionary movement—and the consequent strengthening of its morale—if that wrong impression were dispelled. . . . I would suggest that you show the extent and the continuity of support by Irish-America to the revolutionary movement in Ireland, and its faith in the efficacy of militant action alone as a means of achieving full freedom. . . . I am hoping you will see your way to do as I request, and I assure [you] that if you do, you will be making a big contribution to the old cause.[129]

The vulnerability of 'the old cause' as sponsored by those relying on 'militant action' was reflected in an *An Phoblacht* editorial some months later. In contrast to Fianna Fáil's increasingly strong-rooted electoral power base, revolutionary republicans relied on the much feebler hope that violent revolution would provide the mass momentum which they sought. The increasingly irrelevant 1916 rebellion was their point of reference: 'The men of Easter Week waited for no mandate to take to arms—otherwise they would

---

[128] *Revolutionary Organizations*, Blythe Papers, ADUCD P24/169, 2–6, 8–10.
[129] 25 Jan. 1930, McGarrity Papers, NLI MS 17535.

have been waiting to this day . . . On the policy of revolution they could not have won a single constituency in Ireland.'[130] But while *An Phoblacht* sought to build preparations for revolt, Fianna Fáil was advancing along more relevant, serious paths to power.

The contrast between de Valera's party and O'Donnell's Saor Eire is of particular pertinence to our argument. Fianna Fáil's constitutional and social pragmatism left it better-placed to build solid foundations within the southern Irish state. Saor Eire's Sheila Humphreys observed, in reference to one particular Fianna Fáil scheme during the early 1930s, that it was 'a plan beset with all the difficulties that a compromise has always to face',[131] and this provides a valuable insight into the impossibilistic cast of mind characteristic of such hard-line republican figures. There is considerable irony in Humphreys' later suggestion that, via Saor Eire, 'we could have some impact on the ordinary people and show them what freedom really meant'.[132] As has been shown, what in fact characterized Saor Eire was precisely its lack of relevance to 'ordinary people' and, indeed, its lack of any real substance as a committed project.

In terms of constitutional change, of social policy, of religious culture, and of the practical pursuit of power, Fianna Fáil represented the force most capable of resonating with popular opinion. Admittedly, the party's approach gained it twenty-six-county nationalist support at the cost of rendering Irish reunification even less likely than was already the case. But, as noted, the uncompromising simplicities of republican socialists on the subject of partition hardly left them in a position to gloat on this score; and, in terms of building support among twenty-six-county nationalists, the nature of Fianna Fáil's success illuminates the extent of socialist republicans' hopeless marginality. In the same month in which the Department of Justice was maligning O'Donnellite 'Revolutionary Organizations', Fianna Fáil's Fintan Lalor Cumann was emphasizing the overlap between its Catholicism and its nationalism by proposing 'a mass for all those who died for Irish freedom'. And while Saor Eire was having to come to terms with harsh episcopal condemnation, the Fintan Lalor Cumann was discussing the provision of flags for the forthcoming Eucharistic Congress.

[130] *An Phoblacht*, 26 Apr. 1930.
[131] To O'Malley, 5 Apr. 1932, Cormac O'Malley Papers, PP.
[132] Quoted in Cronin, *Ryan*, 36.

The implicit sectarianism of branch-level Fianna Fáil activity is, of course, of the utmost significance with regard to the broader themes of Irish (especially Northern Irish) politics in this period. It is also true that, for the purposes of building a solid, popularly resonant nationalist movement, a Catholic-soaked approach offered definite advantages within the confines of the independent Irish state. So, too, did Fianna Fáil's crafty approach to economics. The question of the Eucharistic flags serves here as an indication of the way in which Irish nationalism's Catholic and economic aspects could, on occasions, become interwoven. One member of the Fintan Lalor Cumann had

called the attention of the Cumann to the question of Irish-made flags for the Eucharistic Congress. He stated that the Congress had given him a licence to make flags on which he had been engaged for some time. The Catholic Truth Society, however, had for sale flags which were made in Manchester, and these flags were being sold as Irish-made.[133]

The suggestion that the Catholic Truth Society was being rather less than truthful is as delightful, perhaps, as the rather more important evidence which this passage provides of the connections which could exist between economic self-interest, economic nationalism, and Catholic triumphalism in the young state. Two days after Saor Eire had been proscribed by the government, the discussions of the Fintan Lalor Cumann again reflected the gulf between Fianna Fáil's capitalistic nationalism and the left-wingers' aspirations. The Cumann 'reaffirmed the policy of Fianna Fáil to give protection to *all* Irish industries by tariffs or prohibition'. Thus, the project of building up Irish capitalism was endorsed. Telling, too, was the commitment to energetic electoral participation. On 17 December 1931 a special meeting of the Cumann was 'summoned to hear the statement to be made by Mr Eamonn Donnelly, chief organizer':

Mr Donnelly gave an account of the position of the Fianna Fáil Cumainn in the twenty-six counties and of the preparations made by the organization to contest the coming general election. So far as his information went, the election would not take place as early as next February; but

---

[133] Fintan Lalor Cumann, *Fianna Fáil: Minute Book*, 24 Apr. 1930, 26 Nov. 1931, Byrne Papers, PP. On Fianna Fáil's identification with the Eucharistic Congress, see Whyte, *Church and State*, 47–8 and Fanning, *Independent Ireland*, 129.

nevertheless not a moment's time should be lost by the Rathmines Cumann in completing its election arrangements for this area . . .

An 'Organizer and Director of Election for Rathmines' was appointed, and frequent meetings planned.[134] Catholic, capitalistic, and constitutional, Fianna Fáil was clearly better placed to reflect and to guide popular twenty-six-county nationalist opinion than was its revolutionary O'Donnellite rival.

Two further points should be made regarding the Saor Eire episode. First, there is evidence, in relation to the early 1930s, of the same blurred conception of supposedly overlapping nationalist purpose which had lain behind the vain attempts by republicans to forge pan-nationalist unity in the late 1920s. Thus, despite her scepticism about Fianna Fáil's tendency to compromise, and despite the fact that that party represented an irreconcilably different project from that embodied in her own Saor Eire, Sheila Humphreys still shared in the celebrations at de Valera's 1932 election victory.[135] In part, this was explicable in terms of an overwhelming desire to see the removal of a Cumann na nGaedheal government which had been hostile toward zealots such as Humphreys. As Peadar O'Donnell put it, 'To put Fianna Fáil in was the only way to put the Cosgrave gang out'. But while O'Donnell himself was clear that Fianna Fáil 'cannot achieve the Irish Republic nor can it free the mass of the Irish people',[136] there are traces—from contemporary as well as from subsequent evidence—that the republican left could, at times, blur its focus in regard to the differences between Fianna Fáil's nationalism and its own. Looking back on the 1932 election, George Gilmore suggested that Fianna Fáil had won power 'as the party facing the great depression of those years as champion of the smaller capitalist interests and of the tillage farmers'.[137] But in the days immediately after the election, Gilmore had actually been one of the IRA's representatives in discussions with Fianna Fáil on the possibility of synergic action.[138] Gilmore had supported Saor Eire

---

[134] Fintan Lalor Cumann, *Fianna Fáil: Minute Book*, 22 Oct., 17 Dec. 1931, Byrne Papers, PP.
[135] Humphreys to O'Malley, 5 Apr. 1932, Cormac O'Malley Papers, PP.
[136] *An Phoblacht*, 12 Mar. 1932
[137] *The Irish Republican Congress* (Cork, CWC, 1978; 1st edn. 1935), 5.
[138] D. McMahon, *Republicans and Imperialists*: Anglo-Irish Relations in the 1930s (New Haven, Yale Univ. Press, 1984), 22.

and had taken an unambiguously anti-capitalist stand in the preceding debates within the republican movement.[139] Yet he, who had openly challenged the rights of private property, now tried to find common ground for political co-operation with de Valera, who, in February 1932, had declared, 'I believe in the rights of private property'.[140]

This fuzziness regarding the stark differences between socialist republicanism and Fianna Fáil's capitalistic nationalism is again evident in Sheila Humphreys' later claim that 'We were delighted, of course, when Fianna Fáil won the election in February, 1932, and we were doubly delighted when they came officially as part of our contingent to Bodenstown'.[141] Similarly hazy thinking was also evident in the latter-day suggestion by O'Donnell, noted at an earlier stage, that socialist republicans should have joined with Fianna Fáil and attempted to draw the party in a more radical direction. For this fundamentally misses the point that de Valera's party built its massive strength in substantial part upon an economic programme which diametrically opposed Saor Eire's ambitions. To imply the possibility of synergic action between those who defined their nationalism in terms of anti-capitalism and those who were building their nationalism on capitalistic foundations required considerable blurring of vision.

Second, there are strains, in O'Donnell's account of this period, of the 'failed leadership' thesis which socialist republicans had deployed in relation to the revolutionary period. With a typical mixture of reinvention and optimism, O'Donnell argued that

Fenian Ireland, the Ireland of the poor, came to the very doorstep of a struggle for power twice in ten years; in 1922 and again in 1931. In each case it failed to achieve a leadership to correspond with its needs and was driven back in confusion. It has paid a heavy price in mass emigration for those failures. It has, however, gained sharp, political lessons; the lesson of 1922, even only half-learned, is apparent in the IRA search for a policy in 1931. Other men, in other days, will contemplate those mistakes, for of course the Ireland of the poor will be back. There will be another day . . .[142]

Here, again, is the suggestion of a radical mass, simply waiting for the appropriate leadership in order that it should follow its

[139] Anthony Coughlan, 'Notes on his Conversations with George Gilmore' (7 Mar. 1982), Coughlan Papers, PP; *An Phoblacht*, 31 Jan. 1931.
[140] *Irish Press*, 6 Feb. 1932.   [141] Quoted in MacEoin (ed.), *Survivors*, 350.
[142] O'Donnell, *There Will Be*, 132.

supposedly natural revolutionary path. As our preceding discussion has demonstrated, such a reading of the events of 1931 is scarcely plausible. Not only had the IRA's 'search for a policy' shown, even according to O'Donnell himself, how distant his own revolutionary vision was from that of the army; more importantly still, Saor Eire—O'Donnell's own project—was characterized by an approach to political aims and to political methods which showed no sign whatsoever of resonating with anything but a tiny minority of the Irish people. O'Donnell's smug assumption that he knew the minds of the masses, and Humphreys' equally self-righteous condescension toward those who opposed her, could do nothing to offset the crushing fact that their radical views and objectives were those of an atypical, and unavoidably marginal, cult.

3

'Increasing Strains and Stresses within the IRA', 1932–1934

But that there *is* a distinct social flavour about De Valera-ism there can be no question.

Sean O'Faolain[1]

To be frank, it is apparent that an agreement between your forces and the forces of the IRA is a national necessity. They can do the things you will not care to do or cannot do in the face of public criticism, while the IRA pay no heed to public clamour so long as they feel they are doing a national duty.

Joseph McGarrity to Eamon de Valera[2]

Despite their attempts to present Fianna Fáil as ambivalent regarding gunmen (and as possessed of a social radicalism which leaned toward state control),[3] Cumann na nGaedheal were defeated by de Valera's party in the general election of February 1932. Fianna Fáil's constitutional crusade of the 1930s is familiar, a programme which relied for much of its coherence on the undoing of the treaty against which republicans had fought in 1922–3. By attempting to rid the Free State of features which he found repellent—annuity payments to Britain, the oath of allegiance to the British crown, the office of Governor-General, the right of appeal to the Privy Council, British access to Irish naval facilities,

---

[1] *De Valera* (Harmondsworth, Penguin, 1939), 167.

[2] 2 Oct. 1933, McGarrity Papers, NLI MS 17441.

[3] See Keogh, 'De Valera, the Catholic Church, and the "Red Scare", 1931–2', in O'Carroll and Murphy (eds.), *De Valera and his Times*. Cf. 'How will *you* vote tomorrow? The gunmen are voting for Fianna Fáil. The communists are voting for Fianna Fáil.... Irishmen who want peace and prosperity at home, and peace, friendship and increased markets abroad will vote for the Government Party' (*Irish Times*, 15 Feb. 1932).

the 1922 constitution—de Valera embarked on a parliamentary second round of the 1922–3 struggle, albeit in a way which proved the validity of Michael Collins's original argument.[4]

This process of untreatying the Free State helped Fianna Fáil to draw support from the large anti-treaty constituency upon which it built its electoral strength, and this 1930s neo-nationalism had harsh implications for those aiming to establish extra-constitutional republican momentum. As Ronan Fanning has put it, 'While de Valera was witholding the land annuities, tearing up the oath, degrading the office of Governor-General, taking the crown out of the constitution, getting back the ports and defending neutrality against all comers, the IRA had scant hope of winning ground among the unconverted.'[5] And as Sheila Humphreys observed, with regard to the same period, 'There were a lot of people that thought [de Valera] was going slowly, but he was going somewhere—and they were happy with it.'[6] The pursuit of sovereignty was thus crucial, and it had a distinctly symbolic aspect. As de Valera stated in 1933, 'Let it be made clear that we yield no willing assent to any form or symbol that is out of keeping with Ireland's right as a sovereign nation. Let us remove these forms one by one'.[7]

But it is vital to realize the extent to which Fianna Fáil's 1932 triumph resulted from, and itself contributed towards, a political project rooted in economic and social policies. Just prior to the February general election, de Valera had argued that:

The achievement of independence was not the real aim of Fianna Fáil: their real aim was to get for their country the happiest and best conditions of life . . . the people were entitled to get an opportunity of earning their daily bread without being dependent on other people. Why was it that the number of people existing on home assistance had increased from forty odd thousand to seventy thousand? . . . It was not right that such conditions should continue, especially when there was a remedy, and Fianna Fáil proposed to apply the remedy.

De Valera 'did not say that they should neglect the foreign market, but he did say that they should not keep their eyes on the

---

[4] J. A. Murphy, *Ireland in the Twentieth Century* (Dublin, Gill and Macmillan, 1975), 40.

[5] ' "The Rule of Order": Eamon de Valera and the IRA, 1923–40', in O'Carroll and Murphy (eds.), *De Valera and His Times*, 170–1.

[6] Interview with the author, Dublin, 26 Feb. 1987.

[7] Quoted in Fanning, *Independent Ireland* (Dublin, Helicon, 1983), 116.

ends of the earth all the time'. There was, he said, 'a tremendous home market available in agricultural produce' and it was Fianna Fáil's policy 'to develop and expand that market'.[8]

Indeed, the party's election manifesto had made clear that its policy included the aims of organizing manufacturing industry to meet community needs, preserving the home market, and encouraging self-sufficiency in food supplies.[9] Fianna Fáil continued to target a range of social classes, as was made clear in the pre-election attitude of leading party figure, Sean MacEntee. Speaking shortly before the election, MacEntee had stated that 'if the workers of the country wanted a change of government', then they would have to have 'the courage of their convictions' and give their first preferences to his party. He 'stressed the importance of the land annuities to the farmers and the agricultural labourers', and he also made a direct attack on the outgoing government's electoral record:

> Mr MacEntee . . . referred to the promises made by President Cosgrave's government during the past eight years. Where, he asked, were the employment and the happy homes that had been promised through the cultivation of beet, the manufacture of sugar, and other schemes promoted by Mr Cosgrave's government? These things did not materialize . . . All the countries of the world—America, France, Germany—had protected their home markets. The Free State had not. Surely the nations that had done so could not all be wrong, and the Free State alone be right. Tariffs would be one of the principal means of curing the present unemployment problem, and they would be introduced by the Fianna Fáil government if the people returned them to power.[10]

Workers, farmers, agricultural labourers, the unemployed: all were explicitly targeted.

Fianna Fáil's 1932 election manifesto, in which 'emphasis was placed on economic, social, and health policies',[11] resonated with the various social groups at which it was primarily aimed. The concerns which it reflected were certainly given expression in the deliberations of the party's Rathmines Fintan Lalor Cumann during this period. In April 1932, for example, concern was expressed about 'the present widespread unemployment', which caused 'semi-starvation for so many of our people'. These anxieties were close

---

[8] *Irish Times*, 15 Feb. 1932.
[9] D. McMahon, *Republicans and Imperialists: Anglo-Irish Relations in the 1930s* (New Haven, Yale Univ. Press, 1984), 4.   [10] *Irish Times*, 15 Feb. 1932.
[11] Dunphy, 'Class, Power, and the Fianna Fáil Party', 11.

to home; later in the same month it was recorded that unemployed members of the Cumann had applied to the manager of the *Irish Press* 'for employment on the proposed evening paper'. Further concerns were noted, on other occasions, with regard to local joblessness.[12]

Similarly, the Cumann gave explicit support to the policy of tariffs, and displayed a definite pro-Irish-goods bias. Indeed, it is clear from the Cumann Minutes that economic concerns and national ambitions were inextricably intertwined. As was noted earlier, the 1922-3 civil war had been influenced by important social and economic forces. So, too, the early 1930s Fianna Fáil project represented a nationalism infused with social and economic concerns. Members of the Cumann were still angry in relation to civil-war events; in September 1932 a resolution was passed, for example, calling on the government 'to set up at once a tribunal to investigate all outrages ... committed by members of the "National" army during the civil war with a view to the punishment of the criminals concerned in those outrages'.[13] But if the early 1930s are to be read as a kind of parliamentary re-enactment of the civil war, then, just as with the 1922-3 conflict itself, it is vital to understand this second round in terms of its economic features. De Valera had, in Rumpf and Hepburn's words, 'promised that Fianna Fáil would end the clamour for land', and his party certainly spent more on land distribution during its early years than had its Cumann na nGaedheal predecessor. The land annuities issue, moreover, further demonstrated the interrelated quality of Fianna Fáil's economic and nationalistic appeal. The attraction of not having to pay annuities, or, at least, that of paying smaller sums, was complemented by the sense that the retention of payments which were to have been made to Britain involved a victory in the battle for Irish nationalist independence.[14]

Mary Daly has noted that the 1930s economic war with Britain 'showed that given the choice between economic and nationalist objectives, the latter took priority, at least for de Valera'. But,

[12] Fintan Lalor Cumann, *Fianna Fáil: Minute Book*, 13 Apr., 27 Apr., 3 Aug., 3 Nov. 1932, Byrne Papers, PP; cf. Gallagher to Briscoe, 29 Nov. 1928, Gallagher Papers, NLI MS 18353.

[13] Fintan Lalor Cumann, *Fianna Fáil: Minute Book*, 29 June, 8 Sept., 29 Sept. 1932, 9 Feb. 1933, Byrne Papers, PP.

[14] E. Rumpf and A. C. Hepburn, *Nationalism and Socialism in Twentieth Century Ireland* (Liverpool, Liverpool Univ. Press, 1977), 123-4.

significantly, she also observes, 'In 1932 much of Fianna Fáil's attraction lay in its appearing to offer *both* greater independence and material advancement for the masses.'[15] Whatever the contradictions and controversies involved in Fianna Fáil's approach,[16] there is no doubt that economic policies and nationalistic ambitions could be presented, and—by some, at least—received as complementary rather than conflicting. Thus Sean Lemass, Minister for Industry and Commerce, not only assumed that industry required and should get protection, but also held that 'the agitation for the protection of industries . . . is identical with the struggle for the preservation of our nationality'. Accompanying the sharp rise in the number of tariffs,[17] however, was the growing awareness that tariffs alone would not guarantee prosperity for native firms. The 1932 and 1934 Control of Manufactures Acts had the primary aim of preventing 'the establishment in a protected Irish market of firms which were merely branches of external concerns and hence incapable of ever exporting'.[18] The 1932 Act stipulated that companies lacking majority native shareholding 'were required to obtain a licence which could be made subject to conditions concerning size and composition of output, labour force, and location'.[19] 'Licences would be granted where the minister was satisfied that native manufacturers would not be endangered by the new plant.'[20] The 1934 Act required that a majority of all shares (and two-thirds of ordinary ones) should be Irish-held. It further stipulated that a majority of directors be Irish.

While the twin aims of self-sufficiency and native control can be seen to have come into conflict with one another by the later 1930s, it is also clear that Fianna Fáil's early 1930s political project carried with it the belief that national ends could and should be furthered by such autarkic aspirations. The tradition that British rule in Ireland had brought with it the stifling of Irish economic development—evident, for example, in Arthur Griffith's thinking —[21] was mirrored in the 1930s by Fianna Fáil's assumption that

---

[15] *Industrial Development and Irish National Identity, 1922–39* (Dublin, Gill and Macmillan, 1992), 62–3.
[16] M. E. Daly, 'An Irish-Ireland for Business? The Control of Manufactures Acts, 1932 and 1934', *IHS* 24/94 (Nov. 1984), 270.
[17] Daly, *Industrial Development*, 64, 66–7.
[18] Daly, 'An Irish-Ireland for Business?', 246, 271.
[19] Daly, *Industrial Development*, 72.
[20] Daly, 'An Irish-Ireland for Business?', 254.
[21] Daly, *Industrial Development*, 5, 73.

the assertion of economic self-reliance formed a part of the ongoing struggle for national independence from Britain. Economic strategy and anglophobic instinct were certainly mingled in the collective mind of the Fintan Lalor Cumann. In May 1932, the Rathmines group unanimously passed a resolution calling on the party's National Executive 'to organize a series of meetings throughout the country, at which prominent speakers would explain to the people the benefits of the government's policy, as regards the budgets and tariffs, and agriculture'. Such action was deemed necessary because of a campaign of 'lying and scurrilous propaganda' directed 'against the members of the Executive Council and the Fianna Fáil organization generally'. It was suggested that the banks—'which represented the English mind'—were substantially responsible for this propaganda.

The conflict between national and English minds was therefore held to be occurring in relation to economic policy. This view was further underlined by the Cumann's tendency to present governmental 'National and Economic Policy' as though its two elements were fused and inseparable. And in September 1932, the Cumann adopted a resolution which reflected their approach to the brewing economic conflict with Britain; they rejected as part of an 'inferiority complex' the view 'that we cannot hold out to British arrogance, or win this fight against British dictators who would wish to make us pliable and reliant on the goodwill of their economic programmes'. Possibly the clearest indicator of this mingling of economic and nationalistic assertiveness came in a unanimously adopted resolution from later in the same month. The Cumann disapproved

of the giving of preferences to English goods or English materials in the imposition of tariffs by the Free State government, as long as England continues to act as our national enemy by dividing our country by force into two separate portions and by persisting in occupying six of our counties and many of our important ports by her armed forces.[22]

As with republican socialists, therefore, economics played a significant part in Fianna Fáil nationalist thinking. But the respective economic arguments were emphatically different and it is vital to stress the diametrically opposed visions which these rival versions

[22] Fintan Lalor Cumann, *Fianna Fáil: Minute Book*, 18 May, 1 June, 15 Sept., 29 Sept. 1932, Byrne Papers, PP.

of nationalism involved. Seán O'Faoláin argued, with justification, that there was 'a distinct social flavour about De Valera-ism'. He further argued that 'In the course of time Republicanism in politics may well be expected to develop into socialism in economic affairs, and that clause in De Valera's Constitution . . . which seems to protect private property may be "interpreted" to suit that development'.[23] Indeed, the 1930s Fianna Fáil project has been described in terms both of favouring the less privileged classes and of having a socialistic flavour to it. Thus, Mary Daly has argued both that the party's policies favoured 'the low paid at the expense of the rich, the small farmer rather than the rancher', and also that de Valera's agenda was 'an amalgam of nationalist and quasi-socialist policies often stolen from the manifestos of left-wing republican organizations'.[24]

Plainly, Fianna Fáil's radicalism should not be ignored when studying these years, but it should not be exaggerated either. Indeed, one of the most useful aspects of studying inter-war socialist republicanism is that it helps to clarify the essentially conservative nature of Fianna Fáil's project, even during the party's phase of early-1930s populism. Fianna Fáil's 1932 election manifesto had stated unequivocally that 'the individual will be protected in his person and in his property with all the resources at the government's command':

Ordinarily such promises would not be necessary. Apprehensions, however, have been aroused and it is necessary to allay them. We may add that we have no leaning towards communism and no belief in communistic doctrines. We believe in the diffusion of property and ownership and are convinced that this would lead to much more satisfactory social conditions and to a much higher life for the individual.[25]

The contrast between 'De Valera-ism' and republican socialism was certainly as marked as the above dissociation from communism might suggest. Rumpf and Hepburn present Fianna Fáil support in terms which resemble socialist republican argument; in direct reference to de Valera's party, they state that 'economic dependence could only be broken by a party which looked for its

---

[23] *De Valera*, 141, 167.   [24] *Industrial Development*, 60–1.
[25] McMahon, *Republicans and Imperialists*, 5. Cf. de Valera's assertion that 'I have never stood for communism in any form. I loathe it and detest it' (*Dáil Debates* 50/2495–6).

support to those classes with no apparent feeling of economic interest in the British connection, i.e. small farmers and workers'.[26] But this omits the vital point, discussed above, that Fianna Fáil looked for significant support from an indigenous bourgeoisie which it explicitly sought to foster and to develop. This raises two points of divergence between republican socialist thinking and that which characterized the post-1932 government: first, Fianna Fáil did not endorse O'Donnellite class conflict as the foundation upon which nationalist advance should be constructed, and, second, the overriding structure envisaged in Fianna Fáil's outlook was emphatically capitalistic. Thus, where O'Donnellites sought to use revolutionary class conflict to demolish capitalism and establish a socialized republic, de Valera aimed to build wider class alliances on the way toward capitalistic development.

Peadar O'Donnell was scornful of the approach adopted by Fianna Fáil with regard to class relations. In 1933, he claimed disdainfully that there had returned a situation

when a middle class leadership is busy uniting all the people of Ireland to overthrow the common enemy, England. Anything in the nature of class warfare is to be suppressed because it would weaken the national forces. The solution of Ireland's political aim is to be sought in this unity.[27]

The leadership of Fianna Fáil represented, in George Gilmore's view, 'business interests'; but Gilmore noted that de Valera built on an appeal not only to indigenous capitalists but also to industrial and rural workers and to small farmers.[28] This particular pan-class approach was anathema to socialist republicans. O'Donnell's pugilistic tract, *For or Against the Ranchers?*, aimed to state the issue 'in very clear terms'. 'Classless nationalism' (according to O'Donnell) was destined to fail, 'no matter how extreme its separatist phrases'. For O'Donnell, the 'rancher-based cattle trade versus tillage fight' involved class conflict which underlay the national struggle. Drawing on his radical European credentials, he sought to place Irish conflicts in an international context:

The News Bulletin of the European Peasant Committee . . . shows that small farmers everywhere are in dire need and forced to fight for their

---

[26] *Nationalism and Socialism*, 114.
[27] Introduction, in B. O'Neill, *The War for the Land in Ireland* (London, Lawrence, 1933), 12.
[28] *The Irish Republican Congress* (Cork, CWC, 1978; 1st edn. 1935), 6.

lives against the big farmers, who, in alliance with the capitalist bosses, try to pass the growing burdens of the crisis more and more on to the backs of the small farmers and workers . . .

But the conflict over alternative agricultural strategies was, in O'Donnell's view, a nationalist issue.

The thinning down of rural life and the organized dependence on the British, of what persists, was the economic organizing for our national enslavement. It is the national issue that is in the forefront in breaking down that dependence and in increasing rural employment. . . . It is in their role as imperialists that the ranchers and big farmers are warring now, and it is in their role as nationalists that the mass of the Irish people must overwhelm them. Any leadership that does not take its stand on the full separatist platform must, therefore, fall short of the needs of the situation.[29]

O'Donnell's programme here involved an explicit celebration of class conflict as lying at the heart of his nationalist vision. Nationalist Ireland was 'the submerged Ireland; the road to freedom is the road of the submerged class in submerged Ireland to freedom'. The rurally submerged must, according to this self-appointed prophet, ally with 'the wage earners of the towns and cities' and 'the workers and small farmers of the North-East'. This class alliance was emphatically not inclusive of bourgeois nationalists: classless nationalism was rejected in favour of an explicitly anti-capitalist separatism based exclusively on the working classes. The 'fight against capitalism' was openly proclaimed, as was the preference for state farms rather than for smallholdings. O'Donnell's rousing climax left no room for doubt concerning the class-conflicting, socialist version of republicanism which he was espousing: 'Take over the ranches: they are yours. Workers and Working Farmers—Unite! Long live the Workers' and Working Farmers' Republic!'[30]

In stark contrast lay de Valera's declared inclination toward 'justice between all classes', toward projects which would be 'of advantage to all', and toward a 'national programme for the common good' rather than 'a class programme'.[31] Indeed, O'Donnell was openly scathing about de Valera's social vision, referring

[29] *For or Against the Ranchers? Irish Working Farmers in the Economic War* (Westport, Mayo News, n.d. [1932?]), 3, 5, 6.   [30] Ibid. 7–8.
[31] Quoted in T. R. Dwyer, *Eamon de Valera* (Dublin, Gill and Macmillan, 1980), 78–9.

to the latter's 'St Patrick's Purgatory outlook' and arguing with regard to rural Ireland that 'A little less frugality would be a blessing'.[32] O'Donnell's approach relied far less than did de Valera's upon a spiritual emphasis. Thus, while de Valera could argue that 'The Irish genius has always stressed spiritual and intellectual rather than material values', O'Donnell took the view 'that the greatest spiritual tonic a man can get is a job in which he can take pride, wages that make him feel adequate to the tasks of his home' and 'that the best step towards a new cultural life is a sharp rise in the standards of living'.[33]

Yet, whatever the rhetorical casing, it is clear that Fianna Fáil's approach, as well as that of republican socialists, was imbued with definite economic objectives and strategies. The key difference between the two outlooks was in the divergent ways in which economic argument influenced and determined their respective nationalisms. As noted, de Valera's party sought to build a cross-class alliance which comprised classes between which O'Donnell sought to foment conflict. Fianna Fáil's supposedly complementary relationship between indigenous bourgeoisie and working classes played no part in O'Donnell's vision. It is also true that the overriding philosophies which governed these rival economic projects were diametrically opposed.

While Fianna Fáil's 1932 election manifesto contained what Deirdre McMahon has described as 'heady, if vague, expectations of social and economic revolution',[34] these should be set against an understanding of what Fianna Fáil were *not* aiming to achieve. De Valera had promised in 1932 that his party's policies contained 'nothing that interfered with the rights of private property',[35] and, as one perceptive commentator has observed, 'The Fianna Fáil agricultural policy, which has often been hailed as a radical assault upon the big estates, actually reinforced the private ownership of land more than ever'.[36] More broadly, Fianna Fáil's acceptance of a capitalistic approach to economics was never really in doubt.[37]

[32] 'Teachers Vote Strike', *The Bell*, 11/2 (Nov. 1945), 671.
[33] De Valera, quoted in Fanning, *Independent Ireland*, 127; P. O'Donnell, 'At the Sign of the Donkey Cart', *The Bell*, 12/2 (May 1946), 96.
[34] *Republicans and Imperialists*, 16.
[35] De Valera, quoted in D. G. Boyce, *Nationalism in Ireland* (London, Routledge, 1991; 1st edn. 1982), 348.
[36] Dunphy, 'Class, Power, and the Fianna Fáil Party', 29–30.
[37] Ibid., 132–3.

Fianna Fáil's radicalism should not, therefore, be confused with the anti-capitalist, socialist radicalism characteristic of the republican left. Where O'Donnellites sought to define nationalism according to anti-capitalist class conflict, Fianna Fáil sought to build a capitalistic alliance which drew together classes viewed by republican socialists as mutually hostile.

As noted, such clarity of vision was not consistently achieved by contemporary republican socialists. According to O'Donnell, 'It was to the cry of "Release the Gilmores" and the rest that the masses pelted Cosgrave into obscurity in 1932';[38] once released, George Gilmore was among those IRA representatives who met with Fianna Fáil in the hope of achieving synergic co-operation between the two organizations. Given their respective visions of the relation between economics and Irish republicanism, such hopes on Gilmore's part could only have been sustained by a blurred conception of the forces involved. But the relationship between the republican left and Fianna Fáil was merely part of a wider pattern of hazily defined relations between the new government and the old believers. The IRA, non-socialists as well as socialists, entertained some unjustified hopes regarding the possibilities of combined action with Fianna Fáil. Euphoria at the ousting of Cumann na nGaedheal was further boosted by the new government's benevolent attitude toward those who had been incarcerated by the previous regime; republican prisoners were emancipated at the first opportunity. On 10 March 1932, an order was made 'freely pardoning' seventeen prisoners who had been convicted by the Special Powers Tribunal. A further three prisoners had the balance of their sentences remitted, and the cases of three other people 'were referred to the Minister for Justice for investigation'.[39] The IRA had made a contribution to Fianna Fáil's 1932 victory, but the party's 'close, if uneasy, links' with extreme republicans[40] should not blind us to the enormous differences which existed between the constitutional and the extra-constitutional nationalists —differences which were quite obvious from the evidence available at the time.

[38] 'The Irish Struggle Today', *Left Review* (Apr. 1936), 298.
[39] Meeting of the Executive Council (10 Mar. 1932), Dept. of the Taoiseach: Govt. and Cabinet Minutes, NA G 2/9, 1–2. George Gilmore was among those pardoned (cf. *George Gilmore: Sentence by Constitution (Special Powers) Tribunal*, Files of the Dept. of the Taoiseach, ibid., S 2745).
[40] McMahon, *Republicans and Imperialists*, 6–7.

The relationship between Fianna Fáil and the republicans was soon to deteriorate both openly and acrimoniously. De Valera showed himself willing to use Cumann na nGaedheal's Article 2A against the IRA, and such actions led to his being compared, by some republicans, with the despised Cosgrave himself.[41] But the deteriorating relationship was entirely in keeping with the massive gulf which separated the political approaches respectively characteristic of the IRA and of de Valera's party. The crucial axis here was that stretching between alienated legitimism and integrated majoritarianism: the IRA and the president were now at opposite ends. De Valera had long talked of majority rule.[42] Once in power, this ideological predilection was strengthened by the convenient fact that it was now he who possessed the majority.

The IRA certainly had no excuse for mistaking the Fianna Fáil leader's policy. In a revealing series of meetings between the army's Sean MacBride and de Valera (shortly after Fianna Fáil first came to power),[43] de Valera had repeatedly stressed that 'the recognition of majority rule was essential'; that 'once the oath [of allegiance to the British crown under the 1921 Anglo-Irish treaty] was removed there could be no objection to such a recognition of majority rule and to recognizing the Free State parliament as a legitimate body upon which rested the function of leading people'; and that even if the IRA 'did not recognize majority rule as right *per se*', they should 'recognize it as a rule of order and progress'. De Valera's consistent attitude was 'that the most important thing of all was to ensure recognition of majority rule by all parties'. If the IRA objected to his policy, he informed MacBride, then they 'could go and seek the votes of the people, to put [their] policy into effect'.[44]

---

[41] R. F. Foster, *Modern Ireland, 1600–1972* (London, Allen Lane, 1988), 547; *An Phoblacht*, 4 Nov. 1933. Regarding Fianna Fáil's establishment of the Special Powers Tribunal, see 'Statement Given to Press' (22 Aug. 1933), Files of the Dept. of the Taoiseach, NA S 2437; as under Cumann na nGaedheal, Article 2A came to be used by Fianna Fáil as a mechanism by means of which to censor the press (Files of the Dept. of the Taoiseach, S 8093).

[42] Fanning, ' "The Rule of Order" ', 160.

[43] In an Oct. 1933 letter to Joseph McGarrity, MacBride gives details of these five meetings with de Valera; he gives no exact dates for the conversations, but they must have occurred after July 1932, as he states that he referred at each of the meetings to a communication of that date from the IRA Army Council to the Fianna Fáil Executive (MacBride to McGarrity, 19 Oct. 1933, McGarrity Papers, NLI MS 17456). [44] Ibid.

MacBride—who had written in 1923 that he beheld de Valera with 'confidence', 'trust', 'respect', and 'love'—[45] now found himself in strong disagreement with the Fianna Fáil leader. He responded to de Valera's arguments by asserting that while majority rule might be beneficial 'in a free country', it could not be enforced in one 'which was not free and was not even a single unit, under the control of one majority'. Historically, he contended, 'it had been found that progress towards national freedom could not be made through majority rule'. The majority had been wrong in 1916 and 1922. But de Valera's emphasis upon majority opinion reflected his sounder grasp of political realities. MacBride's appeal to de Valera 'to take the situation as it is' was, in fact, rather pathetic, given that his own approach relied on self-legitimation rather than on any serious appraisal of political attitudes beyond the bounds of his own zealous, self-referential clique.[46]

The recipient of MacBride's October 1933 epistle, Joseph McGarrity, had evinced something of this self-legitimizing approach in a letter of his own to de Valera earlier in the same month.

To be frank [McGarrity had written], it is apparent that an agreement between your forces and the forces of the IRA is a national necessity. They can do the things you will not care to do or cannot do in the face of public criticism, while the IRA pay no heed to public clamour so long as they feel they are doing a national duty.[47]

In a sense, the leading Irish American had captured the essence of republicans' self-sustaining approach to politics. According to this view, the IRA could rely solely, and with a self-important confidence, on the fact that *they* felt themselves to be fulfilling a national duty. McGarrity plainly saw nothing problematic in this. De Valera, however, did. In January 1934 he famously, and exasperatedly, replied to McGarrity's letter:

I refrained from replying to your letter of October 2nd. The fact is that to reply to it would require a book, that is, if I wished the reply to be convincing.... You talk about coming to an understanding with the IRA. You talk of the influence it would have both here and abroad. You talk as if we were fools and didn't realize all this. My God! Do you not know that ever since 1921 the main purpose in everything I have done has been

[45] Handwritten notes (Apr. 1923), Cormac O'Malley Papers, PP.
[46] MacBride to McGarrity, 19 Oct. 1933, McGarrity Papers, NLI MS 17456.
[47] 2 Oct. 1933, ibid. MS 17441.

to try to secure a basis for national unity[?] How can you imagine for one moment that I don't realize what division in the Republican ranks means at a time like this[?] But is this need and desire for unity to be used as a means of trying to blackmail us into adopting a policy which we know could only lead our people to disaster[?] It has taken us ten long years of patient effort to get the Irish nation on the march again after a devastating civil war. Are we to abandon all this in order to satisfy a group who have not given the slightest evidence of any ability to lead our people anywhere except back into the morass[?][48]

McGarrity's 'deep reverence' for de Valera[49] could not disguise the clear gulf which existed between himself and his hero. The self-legitimizing approach which McGarrity approvingly identified as characteristic of the IRA had become tiresome to de Valera. The Fianna Fáil leader's January 1934 letter reflected his shrewd appreciation of the IRA's political destructiveness. While he deplored 'division in the Republican ranks', de Valera was clear about the insuperable obstacles which stood in the way of unity with irreconcilables such as the IRA. Indeed, through their reliance on popular sanction, their realistic approach to the attainment of power, their adoption of detailed, practical policies, and their acceptance of the compromises necessitated by such behaviour, Fianna Fáil might be considered to have broken with much that was central to early-twentieth-century Irish republicanism. That, in practice, at least, the party also preferred twenty-six-county achievement to irredentist aspiration lends further weight to the argument that hopes of unity 'in the Republican ranks' could only be based on a blurred appreciation of the forces involved. To use the term 'republican', in reference both to the IRA and also to Fianna Fáil renders the term imprecise and, therefore, largely useless for analytical purposes. If, with Fianna Fáil's 1932 victory, parliamentary democracy 'had come of age in independent Ireland',[50] then it had only been able to do so because Fianna Fáil had politically grown up. Arthur Aughey has convincingly argued that an 'adolescent quality' was evident in the thought of Patrick Pearse: 'What informs the adolescent mind, and is the substance of the romantic and bohemian attitude, is that one's individual sufferings are at once uniquely intense and of universal significance

---

[48] 31 Jan. 1934, ibid., MS 17441.
[49] Connie Neenan, quoted in U. MacEoin (ed.), *Survivors* (Dublin, Argenta, 1987; 1st edn. 1980), 250.   [50] Fanning, *Independent Ireland*, 109.

to mankind.'[51] A similar reading could persuasively be offered with regard to many of the neo-Pearsean faithful at the heart of the revolutionary republican tradition.[52] De Valera continued to be of enormous symbolic importance in relation to the rituals of republican culture;[53] but he had, in fact, broken free from this Pearsean adolescence, and now thoroughly diverged, in his political approach, from the IRA's old believers. At times, republicans made it plain that they disapprovingly recognized his apostasy. In both 1932 and 1933, the army declared itself fundamentally at odds with Fianna Fáil's approach to politics.[54]

But, as noted, IRA republicans simultaneously entertained unjustified hopes for synergic action with their one-time colleagues; Tom Barry and Sean Russell, for example, held that de Valera would redeclare the republic, thereby restoring momentum to the 'national advance'.[55] In republican terms, however, de Valera was out of reach; his majoritarianism and twenty-six-county governmental pragmatism cut him irretrievably adrift from irreconcilable republicans. Hopes of achieving unity in republican ranks missed the point that there was now no combined purpose and assumption. Post-republican Fianna Fáil could only be viewed as potential allies because republican vision was so ill-focused.

'THE COMMUNISTS ARE STILL ACTIVE'

Today, in the Irish working class, is joined the fight of the Irish nation for freedom and of the exploited for social emancipation from capitalism.

Sean Murray[56]

[51] 'What is Living and What is Dead in the Ideal of 1916?' in M. Ni Dhonnchadha and T. Dorgan (eds.), *Revising the Rising* (Derry, Field Day, 1991), 75–6.

[52] A sense of the wider relevance of one's own (romantically conceived) sufferings can be detected, for example, in the writings of Ernie O'Malley and of Frank Gallagher (R. English and C. O'Malley (eds.), *Prisoners: The Civil War Letters of Ernie O'Malley* (Swords, Poolbeg, 1991), 48, 110; F. Gallagher, *Days of Fear* (London, John Murray, 1928), 13).

[53] O. D. Edwards, *Eamon de Valera* (Cardiff, Univ. of Wales Press, 1987), 11–12.

[54] Oglaigh na h-Eireann, Army Council to Commander of Each Independent Unit (12 Jan. 1932), Files of the Dept. of the Taoiseach, NA S 5864 C; Banta, 'The Red Scare', 106–7.

[55] S. Cronin, *Frank Ryan: The Search for the Republic* (Dublin, Repsol, 1980), 44.

[56] Preface (1933) to *Manifesto of the Irish Communist Party: Ireland's Path to Freedom* (1933) in Cork Workers' Club, *The Irish Case for Communism* (Cork, CWC, n.d.), 31.

Communism is not dead in Ireland, neither is it sleeping.

Catholic Mind (February 1934)[57]

If the IRA retained certain blurred hopes regarding relations with Fianna Fáil, greater clarity characterized their attitude toward the Communist Party of Ireland [CPI]. On 4 and 5 June 1933 the CPI was established in Dublin. The latest in a series of Irish communist incarnations, the party set itself the task of 'leading the Irish masses against imperialist oppression and capitalist exploitation'.[58] *An Phoblacht* promptly reported IRA GHQ's claim that 'no member of the Irish Republican Army had authority to be present [at the CPI's inaugural gathering], nor had anybody authority to represent or speak for the army there'. A week later the paper went further, asserting that 'there is a definite order which forbids volunteers being members of the Communist Party or of any other political organization. There has not, and has never been, any connection between the Irish Republican Army and the Communist organization.'[59] The CPI was condemned by the IRA's Army Council for holding 'a dogma of atheism',[60] while *An Phoblacht* made it quite clear that the army did not favour a policy of land nationalization.[61]

The Saor Eire experience had demonstrated the weight of condemnation which socialist ideas could provoke, and the severe anti-communism prevalent in inter-war Ireland strengthened IRA resolve to establish a clear distance between itself and communism. Clerical anti-communism was widespread. In December 1932 Joseph MacRory stated, in St Patrick's Cathedral, Armagh, 'that the Pope had urged him to be vigilant in regard to the communist evil, and to warn priests and people against the poisonous doctrines of communism'. The following month, Patrick Collier, Bishop of Ossory, declared in a New Year pastoral that 'No Catholic can be a communist; no communist can be a Catholic'; and he further stated the whole communistic organization and programme in his diocese to be 'under the ban of the Church'. In February 1933, John Harty (Archbishop of Cashel) said that 'in the recent election they had the grand spectacle of all the political parties expressing their opposition to communistic and materialistic ideals.

---

[57] Feb. 1934, 23.   [58] *Irish Workers' Voice*, 17 June 1933.
[59] *An Phoblacht*, 10 June, 17 June 1933.   [60] Cronin, *Ryan*, 52.
[61] *An Phoblacht*, 17 June 1933.

He thanked God that, no matter how they might differ in Ireland, their Faith was secure.'[62]

Sean Murray, soon to be the CPI's first General Secretary, complained in a pamphlet published in January 1933 that 'The capitalist press, daily and weekly, lay and clerical, belches forth a steady torrent of propaganda against communism'.[63] Certainly, there is no shortage of anti-communist literature from this period. *Catholic Mind* declared early in 1934 that 'Communism is not dead in Ireland, neither is it sleeping.' Communists were 'organizing and consolidating their position daily'. Every effort should be made to stop the importation and distribution 'of all forms of communist propaganda and intelligence'.[64] In the same period, the *Standard* argued that

The communists are still active. They will never cease to work as long as they are tolerated. . . . It is a thousand pities to let a movement of such virulence, of such cunning, of such persistency, develop in a Catholic country like ours. The government is optimistic in this matter. Pessimism would be a wiser and a safer policy.[65]

Anti-communist sentiments were given not merely rhetorical, but also practical and violent, expression in these years. On 27 March 1933 Connolly House in Dublin, which contained the offices of the Revolutionary Workers' Groups [RWG],[66] was set upon 'by a large crowd'. Windows were smashed 'and a quantity of literature was burned on the street'. Two days later, another crowd attempted to set fire to the building and sang religious songs (accompanied by a piano) while besieging the house for two hours.[67] The same day saw the Workers' College in Dublin's Eccles Street attacked, and on 30 March police guarded both buildings as large crowds gathered and were repelled by baton charges.[68] The bizarre quality of the images generated by these incidents—a mob singing 'God Bless Our Pope' and 'Hail Glorious St Patrick' while

---

[62] *Irish Catholic Directory and Almanac, 1934,* 568, 572, 578.

[63] S. Murray, 'The Irish Case For Communism' (1933), in CWC, *The Irish Case,* 4.   [64] *Catholic Mind* (Feb. 1934), 23.

[65] 19 Jan. 1934.

[66] It was out of the RWG that the 1933 CPI had emerged (CWC, *The Irish Case,* 18).

[67] *Irish Press,* 28 Mar., 30 Mar. 1933; Sean Nolan, interview with the author, Dublin, 3 Feb. 1988; P. Byrne, *Memories of the Republican Congress* (London, Connolly Association, n.d.), 8–9.   [68] *Irish Press,* 31 Mar. 1933.

engaging in rather less than charitably Christian behaviour—should not be allowed to disguise the serious, witch-hunting potential of Catholic anti-communism in this period.[69] The IRA's zeal to distance itself from communism must be understood in this context and, indeed, it was amid this far from benevolent setting that the CPI had been launched. Bold claims that, in establishing the party, 'the vanguard of the Irish toiling masses' had 'hurled down their class gauntlet'[70] have to be set against the fact that they had been forced to throw down their gauntlet in secrecy: the CPI's June 1933 inaugural congress took place in a room which, owing to the prevalent anti-communistic atmosphere, had had to be hired under a false name.[71]

Though many republican socialists were not CPI members, the latter organization's outlook overlapped massively with republican socialist orthodoxy. The CPI offered an explicitly communistic version of O'Donnellite, class-struggling republicanism. Though organizationally distinct, the CPI should be read as part of the wider inter-war socialist republican movement. The party was to merge with socialist republicans in the Republican Congress movement, and the close personal links between CPI members and non-party socialists[72] reflected the ideological common ground which existed between these different schools of left-wing republicanism. The CPI was characterized by the same explicit, uncompromising hostility to capitalism ('The fight of the workers to live is in conflict with the fight of the capitalist system to live'), coupled with the assertion that there existed 'a general crisis of

[69] Ibid. 30 Mar. 1933; T. P. Coogan, *The IRA* (London, Fontana, 1987; 1st edn. 1970), 106.   [70] CWC, *The Irish Case*, 27.

[71] Veteran communist, Sean Nolan, recalled that the premises had been booked under the name of a total abstinence group, and noted wryly that most of the communist delegates *were* total abstainers—not through principle, but because 'we had no bloody money!' (Interview with the author, Dublin, 3 Feb. 1988). Cf. 'The new party [CPI] is of no great numerical strength. It consists of a handful of professional agitators ... It has no real existence outside of Dublin and Belfast' (*Notes on Communism in Saorstat Eireann* (Nov. 1936), MacEntee Papers, ADUCD P67/523 (5)).

[72] Peadar O'Donnell was particularly close to Sean Murray, having been involved with him through the RWG, and referring to him as 'really the greatest thing we in Ireland produced since Connolly'. Andrew Boyd, who knew both men, claims that O'Donnell not only greatly respected Murray, but also allowed him to write pieces for *The Bell* on international affairs, which would then be amended slightly by O'Donnell and printed under O'Donnell's name (M. McInerney, *Peadar O'Donnell: Irish Social Rebel* (Dublin, O'Brien, 1974), 24, 97; Andrew Boyd, interview with the author, Belfast, 24 Sept. 1992).

the entire capitalist system'.[73] There was the same conviction that the separatist and class-struggling crusades were symbiotically interlinked: 'the task of winning Irish independence from British imperialism is directly linked with the struggle to abolish the rule of the present ruling class in Ireland—the Irish capitalists'. The working classes were held to be those upon whom the nationalist advance rested: 'The working class and working farmers are the only classes in Ireland faithful to the Irish national cause'.[74] According to Sean Murray, the CPI's 1933 manifesto laid down

two central propositions. The first is that the main barrier to a unified and independent Irish nation is the Irish capitalist class and its dominance of the national movement. The second is that the Irish working class backed by the working farmers can alone carry the national struggle to victory. The entire work of the Irish Communist Party is based on these two propositions of the manifesto.[75]

Such an outlook raised the issue of appropriate leadership, an issue which was vital, as we have seen, in republican socialist thinking: 'The national struggle is a class question and victory or defeat will depend upon which class is at the head of the struggle'.[76] The 1933 manifesto declared confidently that

The whole history of the Irish national movement proves that the capitalist class has been disloyal to the national cause, bargained and made agreements with the British government at the expense of the interests of workers and peasant masses, time and again betrayed the struggle for freedom. . . . Only an alliance of the proletariat and the peasants, under the leadership of the former, can produce sufficient power for the victory of the revolution.[77]

'What class', asked Murray, 'is to lead the struggle? Only the class which can fight the capitalists—the Irish working class in alliance with the working farmers and all toilers.'[78] The emphasis here is interesting; for, while O'Donnell had concentrated much attention on the peasantry, it was none the less an important feature of socialist republican orthodoxy in this

---

[73] Murray, 'The Irish Case', 5–6.   [74] Ibid. 4, 11.
[75] Preface to *Ireland's Path to Freedom*, 31.
[76] Murray, quoted in 'The Congress Report' in CWC, *The Irish Case*, 29.
[77] *Ireland's Path to Freedom*, 33, 36.   [78] 'The Irish Case', 4.

period that the struggle could only be won if urban working-class leadership was established. The CPI manifesto asked:

Are the peasant farmers capable of leading the revolutionary national struggle and carrying it to a finish? No, they are not capable. . . . The revolutionary farmers' movement in Ireland can become a powerful and decisive force only under the leadership of another revolutionary class which is in such conditions that it can organize its forces . . . [The working class] is the only revolutionary class capable of an irreconcilable struggle for national freedom, and, therefore, capable of standing at the head of this movement as its leader. The working class has become able to assert itself as an independent class force through its growing concentration in the factories and the towns, its property-less nature, and therefore its freedom from adherence to private property and its ability to move independently and exert its leadership over the other national forces.[79]

Despite the impression given by Patterson,[80] this emphasis on the central role of the urban working class was in fact shared by O'Donnell himself. In 1933, O'Donnell argued that 'In the absence of a strongly organized party of the working class to provide a revolutionary leadership for the urban and rural masses, rural struggles can never achieve their objective'. He lamented that 'The alliance of workers and working farmers behind such a leadership has never come into view in Ireland so backed and urged that it became a fixed factor in the struggles of both'.[81]

The authorities, north and south, regarded Murray-style radicalism as something of a threat,[82] and the communists, in line with other socialist republicans, were hostile to the established mainstream political parties. Labour and trade union leaders were denounced as 'the most reliable agents of the capitalists in their attack on the working class, and the cringing flunkeys of British imperialism in the Free State'.[83] Fianna Fáil were also condemned: 'The national struggle against Britain is being directed by the Fianna Fáil party along the line of compromise, capitulation, and betrayal.'[84]

[79] *Ireland's Path to Freedom*, 35–6.
[80] 'Fianna Fáil and the Working Class: The Origins of the Enigmatic Relationship', *Saothar*, 13 (1988), 84–5.
[81] Introduction, in O'Neill, *The War for the Land*, 18.
[82] See e.g. the material on Murray in Box 3 (uncatalogued papers), Henry Papers, QUB.
[83] 'The Constituent Congress of the Irish Communist Party', in CWC, *The Irish Case*, 18.   [84] *Ireland's Path to Freedom*, 37.

But, like Saor Eire before it and the Republican Congress after it, the new CPI in fact presented no serious threat to the established political parties. Like Saor Eire and the Congress, moreover, the party's weakness could be gauged from the crudity and misguidedness of its political analysis. Having labelled Cosgrave 'Big Capitalism' and de Valera 'Small Capitalism', for example, Sean Murray made the assertion, preposterous in its 1933 context, that 'The working class and working farmers stand in opposition to all sections of Irish capitalism in the fight for complete independence and in defence of their own class interests'.[85] That the IRA should dissociate itself from such ludicrous views might be considered a testimony to its good sense, had the army's own approach not been marred by similarly crippling analytical deficiencies. An IRA Convention held in March 1933 adopted a *Governmental Programme* which advocated radical social change; the republic which the IRA aimed to create was to be organized along largely communal lines. The nation's 'soil' was declared to be 'the property of the people', with the state favouring 'the co-operative organization of the agricultural industry'. Similarly, 'rivers, lakes, and inland natural waterways' were held to belong to the people, and the state was pledged 'to promote the development of the fishing industry on co-operative lines'. Irish industry was also to be state-directed. Distribution, banking, credit, marketing, export, import, transport, and insurance were to come under state control and the state was also to be responsible 'for the provision of adequate housing'.[86]

Such aspirations overlapped, to an extent, with the aims of the party's socialists. But there was undoubtedly a division between communalist rhetoricians and class-struggling activists. Of the latter group, O'Donnell and Gilmore argued that the IRA should forge an alliance with other separatist and radical groups. Their aim was to produce a 'convention or congress' which would provide the starting point for a campaign towards a socialist republic.[87] This proposal was defeated at the 1933 General Army Convention. Moreover, an order was also issued 'that no individual member of

[85] 'The Irish Case', 8–9.
[86] Oglaigh na h-Eireann, *Constitution and Governmental Programme for the Republic of Ireland: Adopted by a GAC of Oglaigh na h-Eireann, Mar. 1933* (1934), Coyle O'Donnell Papers, ADUCD P61/11 (1), 5–8.
[87] O'Donnell, 'Irish Struggle', 299; Cronin, *Ryan*, 57.

the IRA should attempt to popularize any view not endorsed by the Convention, either by writing or lecture'.[88] In particular, O'Donnell, Gilmore, and Frank Ryan were subject to censorship, Ryan even having *An Phoblacht* editorials dictated to him by Moss Twomey. O'Donnell was to claim, in March 1934, that 'We, myself and Gilmore, have been muzzled for the past twelve months. I hold views which should be useful to the Republic. Gilmore has ideas that are vital. We were not allowed to write for the *Phoblacht*. We were muzzled.'[89]

The radical words of the IRA's 1933 *Governmental Programme* must, therefore, be evaluated in the light of simultaneous efforts to prevent IRA socialists from advocating socially revolutionary *action*. The document's communalistic rhetoric was accompanied by the IRA leadership's attempts to stifle those who sought to turn the republican struggle into a class-struggling, socialist one. The IRA remained an unsuitable vehicle for socialist advance. On close reading, the *Governmental Programme* itself, published with the army's constitution in January 1934, indicated as much. The programme contained no discussion of class struggle, so central a feature of the O'Donnellite definition of republicanism. Social revolution was presented by the IRA document in millenial terms, with economic change and social justice descending automatically at the appropriate, apocalyptic moment. Nothing was said of the way in which immediate activities should be orchestrated in order to bring about these changes. Indeed, taken as a whole, the *Constitution and Governmental Programme* supports the view that the IRA's overwhelming preoccupations remained those of legitimist separatism and physical force. The former was given primacy of emphasis as an objective, the latter as a method of action. Unsurprisingly, given the fact that republicans considered their nation's freedom to have been suppressed for centuries and further compromised since 1921, national sovereignty was something of an obsession:

The national sovereignty of the Republic of Ireland resides under God in the citizens of the entire nation. It is non-judicable and inalienable. It

[88] O'Donnell, 'Irish Struggle', 299; Gilmore, *The Irish Republican Congress* (1978 edn.), 29; cf. his depiction of 1933–4 as a period of 'increasing strains and stresses within the IRA'.

[89] Cronin, *Ryan*, 46; Ryan resigned as editor of *An Phoblacht* early in 1933 (*An Phoblacht*, 1 Apr. 1933); O'Donnell, in IRA General Army Convention (17 Mar. 1934), *Minutes*, MacEntee Papers, ADUCD P67/525.

cannot be surrendered or transferred to an external authority or power; any attempt made to surrender or transfer it shall be treason. It shall be the right and the duty of every citizen of the Republic to defend and maintain the nation's sovereignty.[90]

Socialist republicans were no less committed than the rest of the IRA to the realization of national sovereignty; they simply wished to challenge republican orthodoxy with an alternative, class-struggling version of the separatist faith. Such an attitude was considered by many in the movement to involve the dilution of republican effort. In the rueful words of Sheila Humphreys,

They thought we were dissipating our energies, I think. They thought that we should get Ireland free first, get what we want *that* way, and *then* . . . but, sure, that doesn't happen. . . . They just thought . . . that, well, if we have freedom we'll have social freedom as well. But it doesn't follow. Not at all.[91]

Humphreys' reservations were not, however, characteristic of the dominant republican ethos in the early 1930s. A pamphlet published in June 1932 by the Republican Information Bureau more accurately reflected the prevalent assumptions. Peppered with Pearsean quotations, the tract bore traces also of Pearse's uncompromising attitude, declaring that 'The abandonment of a principle for which men had fought and died must always react unfavourably'. The pamphlet endorsed the primacy and sole efficacy of physical force, arguing that British aggression and the denial of Irish rights 'can only be effectively challenged by the Irish people, when Irish manhood is armed and trained'. The army was, therefore, to act as the (self-appointed) national vanguard, drilling, training, and considering that it would be needed until the Irish Republic had been 'freed from foreign aggression' and could 'function freely'. When the tract turned, at last, to economics it exhibited precisely that prioritizing approach lamented by Sheila Humphreys. An economic aspect to the struggle was recognized, and then immediately relegated to the status of a secondary objective: 'The achievement of real independence means more than the breaking of the military grip of England. While striving for that immediate objective we must also aim at the overthrow of the institutions and social conditions imposed on Ireland under the

---

[90] *Constitution and Governmental Programme*, Coyle O'Donnell Papers, ADUCD P61/11 (1), 4, 11.   [91] Interview with the author, Dublin, 26 Feb. 1987.

conquest.' Military objective and military method were to define the republican advance, with economic concerns left, vaguely, on the sidelines.[92]

Again, therefore, the IRA's centre of gravity was such as to marginalize those whose nationalism was defined by class struggle. The arguments used in the IRA's *Governmental Programme*, however, cost the organization more support than they gained. James Hogan, the articulate conscience of anti-communist Ireland, argued that the IRA had become wary of full-blooded socialism after its experience with Saor Eire, 'when socialism, running in single harness, came within an ace of upsetting the IRA cart into the ditch'. According to Hogan, the post-Saor Eire IRA preferred a more ambiguous approach:

What was needed was a programme which would retain the essentials of socialism without causing uneasiness in right wing supporters, or without frightening off possible recruits from the middle classes; a programme which would be socialist enough for Mr George Gilmore, and which would not appear too socialist to Miss MacSwiney.

The result, he asserted, was 'the present double-faced programme [*Constitution and Governmental Programme for the Republic of Ireland*]'.[93] In fact, the IRA's programme lacked the central socialist component of class struggle, and it is also true that its commitment to 'the co-operative organization of the agricultural industry' would alone have been enough to scare off many right-wing or middle-class people from the army's blueprinted future. Indeed, the point about the IRA programme is not that it simultaneously appealed in both directions, but rather that it failed to appeal in either. The Irish masses at whom such documents were ostensibly aimed were hardly likely to rally to a project so riddled with state-controlled, co-operative features. But the army's socialists were themselves unconvinced of the merits of the IRA's official approach; they recognized that the programme's rhetoric lacked their own crucial doctrinal tenet regarding the definitive importance of class struggle, and they also saw that the document's left-leaning words were contradicted by the IRA's simultaneous attempts to

[92] Oglach, *Oglaigh na h-Eireann* (1932), in Coyle O'Donnell Papers, ADUCD, P61/11 (2), 12–14.

[93] *Could Ireland Become Communist? The Facts of the Case* (Dublin, Cahill, n.d. [1935?]), 2–3.

stifle their practical efforts to move forward. That the army did not offer a viable route for republican socialist advance was finally to be confirmed in March 1934 when, as a result, the IRA was fractured.

REPUBLICAN CONGRESS

We believe that a Republic of a united Ireland will never be achieved except through a struggle which uproots capitalism on its way.

Athlone Manifesto[94]

Our policy and Fianna Fáil's are as far apart as were Connolly and Griffith; as irreconcilable as the Dublin workers in 1913 and Martin Murphyism; the vanguard of our movement as unyielding as the Irish Citizen Army.

Republican Congress[95]

On 17 and 18 March 1934 an IRA General Army Convention [GAC] was held in Dublin. There was a motion on the agenda in the name of the Army Council, to the effect:

That the GAC empowers the Army Council to form a public auxiliary organization to the army based on the *Constitution and Governmental Programme for the Republic of Ireland.* That the aims of the organization shall be to promote the political education of volunteers, to popularize this constitution and programme, and to mobilize the people behind the army.

Michael Price, called upon to propose this resolution, stated that he could not do so until the GAC passed a declaration asserting

That we, authorized delegates from all units of the army and Britain, assembled in GAC of the IRA, redeclare our allegiance to the Republic of Ireland, based upon production and distribution for use and not for profit, and in which the exploitation of human beings, with all the attendant miseries and insecurity shall not be tolerated, as shown in the pamphlet headed *Governmental Policy and Constitution of Oglaigh na h-Eireann.* We again declare . . . that the IRA shall not be disbanded until such time as the government of the Irish Republic, based upon the

[94] Manifesto issued from the Athlone conference (8 Apr. 1934), quoted in *Republican Congress* 5 May 1934.   [95] Ibid.

political and social principles set out in the pamphlet referred to, is functioning freely.

Standing orders were suspended in order that Price's resolution be debated. The thrust of Price's argument was that, as the army had verbally committed itself to social revolution, it should not disband until such revolution had been effected. In this sense, he was seeking that IRA rhetoric should be matched by practical commitment.

Tellingly, however, voices were raised in opposition to this approach. The IRA's *Governmental Programme* notwithstanding, it was held by some at the GAC that to commit the army to remaining in existence until social revolution had been achieved would involve a new and unhelpful departure. In practice, at least, the army was still not prepared to define the republic in terms of social revolution. Instead, it was preferred that the army should be prepared to disband once an all-Ireland republican government was functioning. Michael Fitzpatrick argued:

The propaganda which is being used against us by Fianna Fáil and the *Irish Press* is that we are not the army that fought the Black and Tans. We can definitely state that we are . . . We are defending the constitution—the constitution which the IRA always fought for. We should be proud to be still holding fast to that programme. What we have to gain by supporting this resolution (M[ichael] P[rice]'s) I cannot see. . . . No one has shown what advantage this resolution gives us. Now our enemies say that we are a new army. If we adopt a new policy it will also be used against us.

Continuity and a refusal to define republicanism according to radical social ambition were also evident in the approach adopted by Sean MacBride. He suggested an amendment to the effect that 'this Convention reapproves of the governmental policy and of the constitution of Oglaigh na h-Eireann as they stand', and argued, with reference to Price's resolution:

I oppose the resolution. . . . The end of this declaration is an amendment to the constitution. If this resolution is passed the clause providing for our co-operation with a government which is endeavouring to function as the de facto government of the Republic goes by the board. I accept every single word in the economic programme, which the army has adopted.

This was a telling intervention; for while MacBride claimed to agree with the radical prescriptions of the IRA's official programme, he was plainly unwilling that such economic aspirations should be considered central to republican objectives. Whether or not any functioning, *de facto* government of the republic took a radical social line, MacBride held that the IRA should co-operate with it. This was why he opposed Price, to whom he protested, 'You hold that we cannot support any government that will not accept your resolution'.

It could be argued, however, that Price was merely taking the army's official policy seriously. As George Gilmore contended at the Convention: 'Mick Price is not suggesting an alteration [to the existing constitution], but clarifying a very important point in it'. The IRA had offered verbal commitment to radical social aims; given this, it might have been judged consistent that it should stipulate that any government to which it would give its allegiance should itself accept the social dimension to the army's expressed republican aspirations. What this debate clarified was the emptiness of the IRA's existing rhetorical commitment to social radicalism. MacBride's amendment was accepted (35 in favour, 25 against). Price then moved again for the suspension of standing orders, 'to permit of the ruling—by this Convention—that a declaration that I want is not an alteration to the constitution'. When this motion was defeated, Price left the Convention with dramatic utterance: 'At this stage I must leave. I have no other alternative. I cannot be of this Convention.'

The gathering then witnessed another attempt to tie IRA rhetoric to genuine, committed action. Peadar O'Donnell (seconded by George Gilmore) proposed an amendment to the Army Council's original motion. The O'Donnell–Gilmore proposal sought

that the GAC charge the A/C [Army Council] with the task of raising the issue of the Republic as the dominating political consideration for the Irish people and direct that this should be achieved through the rallying by each unit of the backing of Republican opinion to which it has access, the selection of delegates by these gatherings to a Republican Congress which will restate the whole Republican standard and confront the imperialists with a solid form of nationalist masses pledged to the achievement of the Republic of Ireland and to the revolutionary struggle in solid association with the IRA.

This gained support from Frank Ryan: 'I am in favour of P. O'Donnell's amendment. . . . Sean MacBride wants a continuation of the present army policy—inactivity. He wants this inactivity to continue.' But the O'Donnell–Gilmore amendment was in fact defeated (39 against, 30 in favour), and the two men then left the Convention.[96]

Following this defeat, the O'Donnellites embarked on the new departure themselves. 'George Gilmore, Frank Ryan, and I,' recalled O'Donnell, 'resigned from the IRA and set about organizing a republican congress with the backing of a very powerful section of the IRA'.[97] Enthusiasts for the new venture toured Ireland, trying to generate support for a gathering to be held in Athlone over the weekend of 7 and 8 April 1934.[98] The Athlone conference marked the birth of the new movement. A manifesto was produced, the opening paragraph of which revealed the movement's most fundamental doctrine, its most influential source of inspiration, and its crippling tendency to claim as existing reality that which it desired to be the case:

We believe that a Republic of a united Ireland will never be achieved except through a struggle which uproots capitalism on its way. 'We cannot conceive of a free Ireland with a subject working class; we cannot conceive of a subject Ireland with a free working class.' This teaching of Connolly represents the deepest instinct of the oppressed Irish nation.[99]

If Pearse was the inspiration for much IRA orthodoxy, then Connolly was the socialist republicans' ideological reference point. The group's paper, *Republican Congress*,[100] carried as a subheading his words, 'We cannot conceive of a free Ireland with a subject working class'. It advocated the purchase and digestion of his works, and shared his faith in separatist socialism. On 12 May 1934 it published a lecture which had been given in Waterford on 30 April by Nora Connolly O'Brien. It was rather hagiographical ('he pointed the way, he planned the road, he strove to reach the goal'),

---

[96] 'To: All Camps: The General Army Convention of the IRA . . .', McGarrity Papers, NLI MS 17539; IRA General Army Convention (17 Mar. 1934), Minutes, MacEntee Papers, ADUCD P67/525.   [97] 'Irish Struggle', 299.

[98] J. B. Bell, *The Secret Army: The IRA 1916–79* (Swords, Poolbeg, 1989, 1st edn. 1970), 113; McInerney, *O'Donnell*, 137.

[99] *Republican Congress*, 5 May 1934.

[100] The first edn. of the paper appeared on 5 May 1934. This number seems to have been edited by O'Donnell (Cronin, *Ryan*, 54), and subsequent issues by Frank Ryan. Patrick Byrne—who became one of the Congress's joint secretaries—observed that, except for the first issue, the paper 'was the sole editorial responsibility of Frank Ryan. He had a completely free hand and the full trust of us all' (To the author, 12 Apr. 1988; Cronin, *Ryan*, 54).

but it did succeed in identifying what was perceived to be the central ideological link between the Congress and Connolly, namely the belief that national and social freedom were two parts of the same whole: 'Ever and always he preached the doctrine that the economic freedom of the nation was an integral part of the freedom of the nation—that one was bound up in the other.'[101]

This was, indeed, the leitmotif of the Congress. There was, however, room for differing emphasis within the socialist republican philosophy. At times, it seemed that the republican, rather than the socialist, component predominated within the new movement. In the words of one Athlone signatory and member of the original Organizing Bureau, Sheila Humphreys, 'it was really a *republican* organization, but socially minded'.[102] Yet, in an address given in Dublin on 20 April 1934, Michael Price noted one critic's suggestion that the Athlone conference had arisen 'because there was fear that an Irish Republic would see Irish workers still exploited', and denied that this was the primary motive in people's minds:

The truth of the matter is that the decision of the conference [to endorse the Republican Congress campaign] was influenced, not so much by the fear of exploitation under an Irish Republic as by the recognition of the fact that the independence and unity of the Irish Republic can only be achieved by struggles which aim at uprooting Irish capitalism which is the ally of British imperialism here.[103]

As portrayed here by Price, anti-capitalist struggle appears almost as a functional means toward the greater end of united independence.

Differences of emphasis regarding the Congress's hybrid philosophy were, indeed, to cripple the young movement before its first year was finished. The influence of socialist thinking on the new movement, however, is not in question. The Congress's anti-capitalist, class-struggling ideology testified to this, as does the typically ebullient statement by Patrick Byrne that 'The Congress was from beginning to end *socialist.* . . . We never stopped talking about Marx, Lenin, Engels, and the others. We openly discussed Marx, and wrote about him. . . . We all regularly quoted Marx.'[104]

---

[101] *Republican Congress*, 5 May, 12 May, 19 May, 2 June 1934.
[102] Interview with the author, Dublin, 26 Feb. 1987.
[103] *Republican Congress*, 5 May 1934.   [104] To the author, 12 Apr. 1988.

William McMullen, who was to chair the movement's Rathmines Congress in September 1934, similarly acknowledged Marxist influences.[105] Indeed, the language of the new organization made plain the socialist sources upon which it had drawn. *Republican Congress* openly advocated the establishment of an 'Irish Workers' Republic' and even those, such as George Gilmore, who were subsequently doubtful about the phrase, could openly endorse it at the start of the movement's campaign.[106]

For the Congress was unambiguously anti-capitalist. O'Donnell was to argue that 'the well being of the many cannot be finally organized and guaranteed within the capitalist system',[107] and in the view of Patrick Byrne, the aim of the movement was to abolish capitalism 'and in its place put socialism'.[108] George Gilmore, shortly before the inauguration of the Congress, had claimed that the capitalist system was 'breaking down all over the world',[109] and the movement's new paper carried the same message.[110] But the anti-capitalist fight was, as ever, tied in with the Irish republican struggle: the Athlone manifesto stated, with reference to the Free State, that Irish capitalism was 'the holdfast' for 'the imperial connection', and that 'the forces which defend Irish capitalism are the forces which in the final push for freedom will be called out to maintain the connection'. The document called for a 'Congress of Republican opinion', and simultaneously argued that the republican struggle could only be successful if it were aimed at the uprooting of capitalism.[111]

The nation was effectively defined in terms of Ireland's oppressed,[112] and the government of the new republic was envisaged accordingly:

Have you ever pictured what the government of the Irish Republic must be if it is to secure this country against imperialist attacks and end poverty in town and countryside? . . . It must be government by the workers. Just see how they stand today. They manufacture clothes which they cannot afford to buy. They build houses in which they cannot afford to live. They raise crops in abundance and yet are bogged in poverty. To change all this they must achieve a government of their own to rescue the oppressed common people.[113]

[105] Untitled lecture (n.d.), McMullen Papers, PP.
[106] *Republican Congress*, 5 May, 12 May 1934.   [107] Ibid. 6 Apr. 1935.
[108] To the author, 29 Apr. 1988.   [109] *An Phoblacht*, 3 Mar. 1934.
[110] *Republican Congress*, 12 May 1934.   [111] Ibid. 5 May 1934.
[112] Ibid. 12 May 1934.   [113] Ibid. 5 May 1934.

The anti-capitalist nature of the struggle for the Irish republic was held to be crucial in determining its outcome. As O'Donnell argued in July 1934, regarding a speech made by IRA leader, Sean MacBride:

Extreme views like promising to make revolutionary changes when they are in power is exactly the same trick played by constitutional leaders .... MacBride here is promising, and promising is good, but this Republic he sees in the sky can only be reached on earth through struggles that smash up capitalism en route. You don't become a revolutionary merely by the things you promise ... but by the nature of the organizational activities through which you seek your goal.[114]

The symbiotic relation between separatism and anti-capitalism was, therefore, central to the Congress's approach. Indeed, the connection between the two strands of the socialist republican faith was held to be axiomatic: 'Being socialist we were naturally Republicans.'[115] As with much republican socialist thinking, this ideological relationship was perceived through the medium of assumption: more sure because unquestioned, unchallenged because apprehended at the level of galvanizing faith. Indeed, religious comparisons are unavoidable. Patrick Byrne, describing his own political progression toward socialism, claimed that he 'saw the light' during the early 1930s.[116] William McMullen presented left-wing assumptions in terms which distinctly resemble the evangelist:

In the labour movement there were so few people free to undertake public duties that once a person became a full time trade union official he was hall-marked as a candidate for either municipal or parliamentary honours or both. I was not ambitious in this direction, being perfectly content to do my trade union work and remain a rank and file worker in the wider labour movement but in whatever branch of the movement one found oneself there was always a strong urge to contest whatever vacancies occurred, even if they were forlorn hopes, in the belief that the labour or socialist message only required to be repeated often enough, to find acceptance by an increasing number, until the stage was reached when it would hold sway and we would be on the way to the socialist millennium.[117]

Perhaps the most lucid evangelist in the movement was George Gilmore. On 5 May 1934 *Republican Congress* published an article

---

[114] Ibid. 28 July 1934.   [115] Patrick Byrne to the author, 12 Apr. 1988.
[116] To the author, 29 Apr. 1988.
[117] W. McMullen, untitled MS (n.d.), McMullen Papers, PP.

of his, in which he argued that people engaged in any 'forward move in the political sphere' find themselves criticized for creating disruption, and that such accusations had been levelled at the Congress. Indeed, he continued, the new movement *would* cause 'a very considerable amount of disruption of existing political parties'. But this was highly desirable:

Consider for a moment the political parties as they stand at present. The body politic is divided into a number of parties and organizations by what I shall take the liberty to describe as 'vertical' division lines. The leaderships of these parties have real dividing interests reflected in the policies of the different parties. But the rank and file of all of them are divided in a very artificial way—very largely by the memory of their war alignments, which themselves were usually pretty meaningless.

The members of this 'rank and file', Gilmore argued, were Irish working people whose exploitation at the hands of 'Irish capitalism and British imperialism' gave them a natural and logical place in the movement for a workers' republic. The 'Blueshirt Party' and the 'Unionist Party' represented, in their respective territories, 'the interests of British imperialist capitalism'. Fianna Fáil ruled 'in the interests of Irish capitalism'. The 'Free State Labour Party', the 'National League of the North', and the IRA played the part of 'supports behind Fianna Fáil'. Each of these groups had followers whose natural place, according, at least, to Gilmore, was with the socialists of the Congress. Across these 'vertically divided' organizations the Republican Congress was going to cut a 'horizontal' line, to forge into 'one great forward movement all those of the oppressed classes in all the parties'.[118]

Fianna Fáil was subjected to fierce criticism by the new movement. An *Irish Press* editorial was, for example, singled out by *Republican Congress* in May 1934 for having endorsed the view that one should be determined ' "to achieve freedom, that with it we may in turn free the oppressed amongst us" '. This was, according to the Congress's organ, 'the most insidious (and incidentally the most common) form of anti-working-class propaganda', for it entailed the view that one should concentrate on the attainment of national freedom and that only then all else, including social emancipation, would follow. According to *Republican Congress*, such an approach was 'pernicious': 'Such teaching

[118] *Republican Congress*, 5 May 1934.

deplores rousing Ireland of the poor to seek its own and the nation's freedom in a struggle to uproot exploitation. Such teaching marshals the national forces behind industrialists and brings the Republican struggle to a halt at their signal.' The Congress's reaction was that the poor should 'see in themselves the enslaved Ireland and . . . see in their own freedom the freedom of [the] Irish nation'.[119]

The early Republican Congress, indeed, set out to differentiate itself in unambiguous terms from the governing party of the state: 'Our policy and Fianna Fáil's are as far apart as were Connolly and Griffith; as irreconcilable as the Dublin workers in 1913 and Martin Murphyism.' It had not been recognized in 1932 'that a Fianna Fáil government could only serve Irish capitalism'.[120] In the words of Michael Price, 'We see in the Fianna Fáil government the entrance of Irish industrialist capitalism organizing its field for exploitation. This section of interests could not lead the fight for the unity and independence of Ireland.'[121] Again, therefore, the socialist republican critique focused on the question of which forces would be able to lead the republican struggle successfully to a conclusion. In his valuable article dealing with Fianna Fáil and the working class, Henry Patterson argues that 'The hegemony of [Fianna Fáil] can be measured by the fact that its most militant critics from the left challenged not its objectives but rather its capacity to attain them given the social composition of its leadership'.[122] This view has been branded by Kieran Allen as 'undoubtedly correct',[123] and Patterson's argument does indeed raise a crucial point. George Gilmore later reflected that the Congress movement had involved 'an effort to free the republican-minded people of Ireland in the trades unions and in the countryside generally from the illusion that Fianna Fáil leadership was leading towards their freedom in Ireland'.[124] Patterson has further argued that Peadar O'Donnell 'himself saw his agitational and ideological work as aimed at pushing Fianna Fáil to the left rather than displacing it', and that at the core of the socialist republican analysis there existed 'a central ambiguity about the nature of Fianna Fáil.

---

[119] Ibid. 12 May 1934.   [120] Ibid. 5 May 1934.   [121] Ibid.
[122] Patterson, 'Fianna Fáil and the Working Class', 84.
[123] K. Allen, 'Forging the Links: Fianna Fáil, the Trade Unions, and the Emergency', *Saothar*, 16 (1991), 55.
[124] *The Irish Republican Congress* (1978 edn.), p. iii.

Although labelled a middle-class party, it was reckoned to have progressive tendencies within it'.[125]

Again, this raises an important point. But the focus of these arguments could, perhaps, be sharpened with regard to the period currently under scrutiny. First, while it is true that socialist republicans shared with Fianna Fáil an aspiration toward an all-Ireland, independent republic, it is also true that the republics respectively envisaged were, in fact, vastly different from one another. In Saor Eire and the early Republican Congress this was made clear by the words used by republican socialists to describe their own objective ('Workers and Working Farmers' Republic'; 'Workers' Republic'). As noted, the republican left laid great stress on the notion that the republican struggle could only be effective if it were anti-capitalist; Patterson is right to note that this view involved the assumption that Fianna Fáil could not achieve the republic, precisely because the party was not anti-capitalist. But what Patterson's argument overlooks is the republican socialist conviction that the nature of the republican struggle determines and defines the nature of the republic thus achieved. It was not just a case of taking a different (and, therefore, successful) route to the same place; the anti-capitalist route would determine that one ended up at an anti-capitalist republic, wholly different from the endpoint envisaged by Fianna Fáil. Both Saor Eire and the Republican Congress entailed visions of a republic governed by different class alliances from those involved in Fianna Fáil's future, and infused with an entirely different social philosophy from that which characterized the republic of de Valera's dreams. In order properly to understand the factions within inter-war Irish nationalism, it is important not to blur this distinction.

Second, the suggestion that O'Donnellites sought to draw Fianna Fáil to the left rather than to displace it requires some fine tuning, at least with regard to the early days of the Republican Congress movement. George Gilmore's horizontal levelling article of May 1934 made clear that he—'the Congress chief organizer', according to Sean Cronin—[126] entertained the prospect, not only of displacing, but of cutting in two de Valera's party. Having argued that the 'Fianna Fáil party has a very class-conscious leadership

[125] 'Fianna Fáil and the Working Class', 86.
[126] *Irish Nationalism: A History of its Roots and Ideology* (Dublin, Academy Press, 1980), 158.

ruling in the interests of Irish capitalism', Gilmore then prophesied that, once the Congress's horizontal levelling had occurred, 'the political leadership, representative of the capitalist interests—Irish and British—will be outside our unity and will probably form a united front of their own to oppose the advance of the risen people'. This, Gilmore argued, was

> to be expected. It is only in accordance with political developments every-where. It is foreshadowed in Mr de Valera's statement that, should the necessity arise, he is prepared to unite with the Blueshirts to 'preserve order'. The question at issue is—which united front is to prevail—the united front of British and Irish capitalism and all that they stand for, or the united front of the working farmers and other workers of Ireland which this Congress will create.[127]

Clearly, Gilmore here envisages Fianna Fáil being cut in two, with its pro-capitalist leadership being part of a new grouping opposed to the Republican Congress, while the party's rank and file participated enthusiastically in the Congress's united front. Again, the Congress's espousal of the setting up of 'government by the workers' certainly implies the displacing of Fianna Fáil from its hegemonic perch; even in September 1934, when O'Donnell was at his most ambiguous with regard to Fianna Fáil, he was arguing that 'the organs of struggle become the organs of government', and that these organs of struggle were 'committees of workers and small farmers' conducting 'working-class and small-farmer struggles'.[128] The suggestion that these groups should form the government in the new republic again clearly implies the dis-placement of Fianna Fáil.

At the start of the Congress, it was undoubtedly desired that rank and file Fianna Fáil supporters might be drawn in large num-bers to follow the Congress's anti-capitalistic approach. It was held that, given the capitalistic interests governing the leaders of Fianna Fáil (and, indeed, of other political parties), there would emerge new alignments which would cut the old party structures in pieces. Later in 1934, the Republican Congress was to be characterized by greater confusion and ambiguity regarding relations with de Valera's party. But it is crucial to recognize, first, that the initial Congress view *did* involve the notion of displacing—indeed,

---

[127] *Republican Congress*, 5 May 1934.
[128] Quoted in Gilmore, *The Irish Republican Congress* (1978 edn.), 53.

destroying—Fianna Fáil and, second, that republican socialists' objective, as well as their means of attaining it, were fundamentally divergent from those of de Valera.

What of the Congress's specific programme? In June 1934 *Republican Congress* carried Peadar O'Donnell's assertion that 'the road to the Republic goes through the ranches'.[129] Earlier, the paper had made clear the movement's unambiguous hostility to large farming culture; referring to the large landholders' 'no rates' campaign, *Republican Congress* argued that 'the ranchers want to pass their burdens on to us all. Very well, let them pass on their ranches too. That is a solution—the only solution. So, the demand of the small farmers today must be not for relief for ranchers and big farmers, but for their complete elimination.'[130] The Congress endorsed 'a system of peasant ownership where appropriate, but especially the development of co-operatives on a large scale'.[131] The rate of land redistribution under Fianna Fáil was criticized, and the suggestion of state farms supported.[132]

Industrial conflict was also deemed crucial. On 19 May 1934 *Republican Congress* proclaimed that 'No industrial struggle should be let go by without our workers drawing close to it to help. The Congress committees will work for solidarity in every worker's fight'.[133] Through publicity and participation the Congress supported all forms of industrial struggle which were believed to advance the workers' cause. In particular, backing was given to wage campaigns and to efforts to improve working conditions.[134] Housing was another of the Congress's preoccupations. Both Gilmore and Byrne made much of the movement's work in this field,[135] and, indeed, it probably was the organization's most successful arena. On 30 June 1934, a *Republican Congress* editorial outlined the movement's attitude to housing struggles. 'Dublin City Congress committees' were focusing public attention on the 'ghastly conditions' in the city's slum areas. As a result, the writer asserted, people would spend a period feeling concerned about the subject. Such concern, however, should not be allowed to 'distract the inhabitants and the Congress committees from their

---

[129] *Republican Congress*, 9 June 1934.   [130] Ibid. 12 May 1934.
[131] Patrick Byrne to the author, 12 Apr. 1988. A similar mixture of state farms on the one hand, and land division among landless labourers and small farmers on the other, was envisaged by the CPI (Murray, 'The Irish Case', 12).
[132] *Republican Congress*, 5 May 1934.   [133] Ibid. 19 May 1934.
[134] Ibid. 12 May, 19 May 1934; cf. Byrne. *Memories*, 5–6, and Gilmore, *The Irish Republican Congress* (1978 edn.), 44.   [135] Ibid. 40–4; Byrne, *Memories*, 6–7.

real task'. Here, again, the ambitiously radical nature of the movement was made evident. The committees had 'entered not merely on a skirmish, nor even a battle, but on a whole campaign. The campaign for adequate, economic housing for the Dublin working class still to be fought and won.' A plan of campaign was outlined, comprising data-collection, the formulation of assertive demands, and the immediate, organized pursuit of these aims. The article's conclusion reflected the socialist impetus which lay behind its assertions, referring to the Congress committees as 'the advance-guard of the working-class army moving forward to fight for houses that can be homes'.[136] It had earlier been made clear that the organization's approach to housing fitted in with its wider anti-capitalist stance: 'Capitalism blocks the way to any peaceful solution of the problem of housing Ireland's workers.'[137]

The issue of partition was addressed by the Congress with a mixture of naïvety and patronizing smugness. Admittedly, Northern Ireland presented problems for all flavours of inter-war Irish nationalism. Seán O'Faoláin commented that, 'About partition [Fianna Fáil] could do nothing—nobody could';[138] and, as John Murphy has observed, de Valera's 'approach to the "partition" question, in particular his assumption that it was primarily a matter for Britain to resolve, remained consistently inadequate throughout his political career'.[139] Inadequate, too, was the Congress's approach to partition; though, yet again, the republican left was possessed of a clearly different analysis from that which characterized Fianna Fáil. O'Donnell lamented the historical fact that the north-east of the island had deviated from the path laid down for it in socialist republican orthodoxy. The workers in the industrial north-east had, he argued, 'played a very unfortunate role. Here, where the great weight of the Irish proletarian population is concentrated, the owning class were able not merely to hold these workers apart from the national struggle, but actually to make them available for imperial reaction.'[140] Northern Protestant workers, in the eyes of socialist republicans, ought to recognize

---

[136] *Republican Congress*, 30 June 1934. While such revolutionary promise was to prove unfulfilled, the Congress's housing struggles did possess a certain practical quality, and some progress was made through the combination of publicity work with physical involvement (ibid. 23 June, 7 July, 25 Aug., 1 Sept. 1934).
[137] Ibid. 12 May 1934.
[138] *The Irish* (Harmondsworth, Penguin, 1980; 1st edn. 1947), 156.
[139] *Ireland in the Twentieth Century*, 94.
[140] Introduction in O'Neill, *The War for the Land*, 13.

that their true class interests linked them to the republican movement; in the words of *Republican Congress*, 'The natural, normal task for the Belfast workers in common with the workers of the rest of Ireland is to lead the struggle for freedom.'[141]

If the republican left deluded themselves in assuming, rather patronizingly, that northern Protestant workers had existed in a state of mass false consciousness, they further deceived themselves in thinking that a sea change of opinion was occurring. The Athlone manifesto declared that

The fight for freedom in our day has been weakened by the failure of the workers in the north-east to see that their freedom is inseparable from the national struggle for freedom. Now that deep wedges of workers there are freeing themselves from the illusions which so long held them in bondage to their imperial exploiters the national issue must be brought sharply forward.[142]

Much was made of the 1932 Belfast Outdoor Relief disturbances,[143] during which Catholics and Protestants were temporarily united, sharing anger at the inadequacy of relief payments, the humiliation of means testing, and the inappropriateness of taskwork.[144] Much was also made of the appearance at the republican gathering at Bodenstown (in June 1934) of a contingent of Belfast Protestants.[145] Subsequent commentators have, on occasions, similarly stressed the achievements of the Congress in regard to the north. According to Michael McInerney, for example, the movement 'made inroads into Northern Ireland that few organizations had made before'.[146]

It was claimed, in the movement's paper in May 1934, that the Congress was the one force that could smash partition, 'because it goes to the root of the evil and because it springs from the conditions under which the people subjected to that evil suffer'. But despite all the confidence ('At last it has come. A movement that can break the border has been born'),[147] the organization's approach to partition was severely deficient, and its failure to make any serious progress on the issue was entirely predictable. The supposed sea change in unionist opinion, self-deludingly

---

[141] *Republican Congress*, 5 May 1934.   [142] Ibid.
[143] Gilmore, *The Irish Republican Congress* (1978 edn.), 19–21.
[144] D. W. Harkness, *Northern Ireland Since 1920* (Dublin, Helicon, 1983), 69–70.
[145] Byrne, *Memories*, 10.   [146] O'Donnell, 233.
[147] *Republican Congress*, 12 May 1934.

hailed by the Congress, was in fact merely a mirage. The atypical cross-sectarian unity of October 1932 was, in reality, but a 'fleeting peak of Orange-Green collaboration',[148] with the outdoor relief riots being 'short-lived in their impact on working-class politics'.[149] Far from indicating that the Catholic and Protestant working classes in Northern Ireland were 'waking up to realities' and becoming comrades,[150] the events of 1932 came and went without class unity lastingly overriding sectarian division in the north-east of the island. As Henry Patterson has rightly noted, O'Donnellite republican socialists demonstrated an 'incapacity to gauge the depth of Protestant working-class antagonism to "the national struggle"'.[151] Preposterous claims, such as that 'the erection of the border was made possible by the separation of the Republican from the working-class movement',[152] merely reflected the inability of the republican left to acknowledge the genuine, sturdy anti-republicanism of most northern Protestants.

Recent scholarship has tended overwhelmingly to endorse the view that Ulster unionism must be understood in terms of a self-generated, deep hostility toward Irish republican separatism. John Whyte, in his masterly *Interpreting Northern Ireland*, observes that 'On the whole, recent historians have been struck by the depth of Ulster unionist opposition to a united Ireland separate from Britain, and the independence of that opposition from British support'. He also demonstrates the flaws in the arguments of those who have tried, in the modern period, to sustain a Connollyite approach, and who have argued that 'Northern Ireland was governed by a capitalist class which kept the working class repressed and divided' by means of beating 'the sectarian drum' and by using 'differential discrimination'. Such an approach, as Whyte observes, involves 'brushing aside all the other reasons for Protestant attitudes', and requires one 'to ignore the whole thrust of recent historiography on Ulster under the union period'.[153] In his recent work dealing

[148] P. Buckland, *A History of Northern Ireland* (Dublin, Gill and Macmillan, 1981), 71.

[149] P. Bew, P. Gibbon, and H. Patterson, *The State in Northern Ireland, 1921–72: Political Forces and Social Classes* (Manchester, Manchester Univ. Press, 1979), 100. [150] *Republican Congress*, 12 May 1934.

[151] H. Patterson, *The Politics of Illusion: Republicanism and Socialism in Modern Ireland* (London, Hutchinson Radius, 1989), 65.

[152] *Republican Congress*, 12 May 1934.

[153] *Interpreting Northern Ireland* (Oxford, Clarendon, 1990), 125, 179–81.

with Protestant paramilitarism, Professor Steve Bruce has stressed the inadequacy of those explanations of the modern Ulster Volunteer Force which fail to acknowledge its origins as 'a self-recruiting, working-class movement'.[154] Similarly, the inter-war socialist republican critique of Ulster unionism failed to appreciate the true nature of its subject; the power of the 'owning class' to create working-class opinion was grossly exaggerated, with the result that workers' culture, interests, attitudes, and influence were hopelessly misinterpreted. The flawed analysis rightly challenged by Bruce for the modern period fits, therefore, into a broader historical pattern of nationalists misunderstanding unionist politics.

Thus, republican socialist analysis of Northern Irish politics was seriously marred and, predictably, no progress was made. Misguided optimism was forced to coexist with a recognition of the fact that Ulster unionism continued to present difficulties. Thus, William McMullen referred to his own 'insistence that anything short of one parliament for the entire country could never be a final settlement of the Irish question', and asked, 'When the border is an evil memory, what shall I be hailed, a "firebrand"—or prophet?' He commented elsewhere on Protestant naïvety in thinking that 'while the Catholic they knew was decent, it was the one they didn't know that was conspiring to encompass their downfall'. Yet, as we have already seen, McMullen was shrewd enough to acknowledge the depth and problematic persistence of sectarian division: 'Belfast is inexorably slow to change in sectarian matters'; 'Northern intransigence . . . never has been a monopoly of either side, as has been so often mistakenly thought'. But rather than reading partition as a response to existing Irish divisions, McMullen took the more convenient line that the divisions were sustained by partition: 'the separation that divided Protestant from Catholic into two warring and distinct unions persisted, and does so even to the present day, and looks likely to continue as long as the division of Ireland lasts'.[155] Sheila Humphreys recalled an occasion on which Moss Twomey had been informed that a particular Protestant republican had converted to Catholicism; Twomey responded: 'That's the limit. We *can't* keep a bloody Protestant in

---

[154] *The Red Hand: Protestant Paramilitaries in Northern Ireland* (Oxford, OUP, 1992), 24–6.

[155] 'A Reply to a Series of Articles in the *Irish Times*' (May 1950); untitled MS (n.d.); 'The Suffering Ducks' (n.d.); untitled MS (n.d.) (McMullen Papers, PP).

the movement'. Humphreys herself also recognized that a difficulty existed: 'You can't convince the unionists in the north that we wouldn't annihilate them all . . . if they came in with us. Isn't it very, very difficult?'[156] Yet the 1930s republican left did nothing to suggest that they had appreciated the depth and nature of the roots of unionist anti-republicanism.

Indeed, Peadar O'Donnell's criticism of the Belfast IRA for its failure to attract Protestants missed the fundamental point that the inter-war northern IRA largely defined itself in terms of sectarian rationale. As Michael Laffan has observed, 'For most of the 1920s and 1930s the Northern units of the IRA saw their role as a defensive one, protecting the Catholic minority against the Protestant majority'.[157] The only constituency from which the IRA could realistically hope to draw support in Northern Ireland was comprised by Catholic communities. And the shift of northern Catholic support to the IRA would, as O'Donnell's critic, James Hogan, recognized, further obstruct progress toward a united Ireland.[158] Despite the expression of great claims and hopes, therefore, the republican left was unable to leave any significant imprint on Northern Irish politics during the inter-war period. 'Sectarianism burns out quickly where there is team work in common struggle,' declared the Congress movement.[159] But during these years there in fact appeared no likelihood of any ideological, cultural, economic, or political argument converting large numbers of northern Protestants to the notion of a united Irish republic.[160]

The Republican Congress's case in relation to Northern Protestants was further weakened owing to the Gaelic flavour which the movement regularly evinced. Gaelic culture was specifically celebrated,[161] while Irish emigrants were identified (simplistically) as 'Gaels'.[162] Such celebration and identification were unlikely to strengthen the supposedly emerging Protestant working-class

---

[156] Interview with the author, Dublin, 26 Feb. 1987.

[157] 'Violence and Terror in Twentieth Century Ireland: IRB and IRA', in W. J. Mommsen and G. Hirschfield (eds.), *Social Protest, Violence, and Terror in Nineteenth and Twentieth Century Europe* (London, Macmillan, 1982), 169.

[158] See Ch. 2, n. 50.

[159] Gilmore, *The Irish Republican Congress* (1978 edn.), 21.

[160] On the overwhelming unionist domination of 6-county electoral politics, see Harkness, *Northern Ireland Since 1920*, 184.

[161] See, e.g. *Republican Congress*, 12 May 1934, and the 'Gaelic Games' column, ibid. 16 June, 23 June, 30 June, 7 July 1934.   [162] Ibid. 5 May 1934.

republicanism. But this merely underlines an important deficiency in the Congress's proposed strategy: the rainbow alliance which it aimed to create in fact consisted of groups whose common interests and identification were hard to recognize. The Athlone manifesto had listed the sections of Irish society from which the Congress had hoped to recruit its class-struggling followers. First, there were Northern Irish workers. In 'the south of Ireland' there were industrial workers, Gaeltacht inhabitants, small farmers, and petty traders. Referring to the latter two groups, the manifesto argued that 'this section of the nation can only free itself as the ally of the working class'.[163] But the deeply differing circumstances of industrial workers on the one hand, and of small farmers, traders, and Gaeltacht inhabitants on the other, rendered it unlikely that the four groups would coalesce in the automatic fashion envisaged by the Congress. Similarly, while appeal was made to northern workers on the basis of class identification—interpreting the nation, effectively, in terms of class—an ethnic (Gaelic) motif was simultaneously used. This not only cut across the class-based definition, but was singularly unlikely to appeal to northern Protestant sensibilities in the mid-1930s.

In addition to policies relating to land, industry, housing, Northern Ireland, and the political parties of the Free State, the Congress also placed great emphasis on the fight against fascism. The fascist menace was, at times, presented as the most important focal point for the movement: 'Every task comes secondary to the great one of keeping this menace beaten back. Meetings, publicity, lectures, demonstrations—all the forms of mass struggle must be called forth to keep us free from this steel jacket. As the war danger rushes nearer fascism will strive fanatically for power.'[164] O'Donnell had earlier argued that, when war arrived, the appropriate motto should be that of 'England's war being Ireland's opportunity'.[165] When war involved England fighting against fascism, the twin imperatives, of opposing fascism and of fighting England, therefore came into collision. As we shall see, some republicans—including some on the republican left—found themselves able to sympathize with the fascists during the Second World War, making nonsense of the casual assumption peddled by the

---

[163] Ibid.   [164] Ibid.

[165] 'Communist Activities: Peasant Farmers' Organization', in *Communist Activities*, NA S 5074 A.

republican left that Irish republicanism formed part of a wider, international struggle for freedom,[166] of an international fight 'for a better world'.[167] The situation was more complicated than such simplifications would allow.

In the 1934 Republican Congress, however, the anti-fascist cause was strenuously supported. The movement's paper directed its raucous bawling against the forces of international fascism.[168] But the focus of much attention was the (Irish) Blueshirt organization, with whom republicans regularly came into conflict. During the early 1930s the Army Comrades Association had been established, 'an organization of ex-Free State army members [whose] principal objective seemed to be the promotion of its members' welfare'.[169] The movement was, however, to develop into a more ambitious political creature. In July 1933, Eoin O'Duffy took over the group's leadership, and the title 'National Guard' was adopted. In September a further change occurred when the Guard (more commonly known as the Blueshirts) joined with Cumann na nGaedheal and the Centre Party to form the United Ireland Party, with O'Duffy as president.[170] The Blueshirts had their own journal, the first edition of which had contained a constitution outlining the movement's objectives. These included opposition to communism, the promotion and maintenance of social order, and the espousal of a class-harmonious approach to industrial conflict. While the charge of fascism was explicitly denied by the paper,[171] certain of the organization's supporters seemed less clear on this point, and openly drew comparisons with European fascists.[172] Indeed, while some authors have sought to play down the fascistic nature of the Blueshirts,[173] it would be quite wrong to overlook the genuinely fascistic aroma given off, at least, by significant figures associated during this period with Fine Gael (as the United Ireland Party came more popularly to be known). Thus, James Hogan, whose sophisticated attack on the republican left represents one of the

---

[166] Cronin, *Ryan*, 24, 84.   [167] O'Donnell, 'Irish Struggle', 300.

[168] *Republican Congress*, 26 May, 2 June, 9 June, 7 July 1934.

[169] Murphy, *Ireland in the Twentieth Century*, 78.

[170] Ibid. 79; *Irish Press*, 21 July 1933; *Irish Times*, 9 Sept. 1933.

[171] *Blueshirt*, 5 Aug. 1933.

[172] *United Ireland*, 30 Dec. 1933; *Dáil Debates*, 50: 2237 (J. A. Costello, 28 Feb. 1934).

[173] Cf. 'The Blueshirts are frequently described as fascists. They were not' (J. J. Lee, *Ireland, 1912–85: Politics and Society* (Cambridge, CUP, 1989), 181).

most valuable sources for this entire period,[174] was explicit in his enthusiasm for the 'fascist state'.[175]

Hogan was to argue that the post-First World War period had witnessed 'the rapid spread of two criticisms of democracy, one coming from the left, the other from the right'. The challenge from the right repudiated French Revolutionary ideals and liberal democratic ideas: 'This new anti-liberal creed was at once more logical and more dynamic than the creed of communism and it has embodied itself in the formidable Nazi and Fascist regimes.' According to Hogan, the challenge from the right was both more revolutionary and more sturdy than its left-wing opponent: 'In essence the so-called reactionary fascist movements are far more revolutionary than communism, and the logic of events proves that communism has no answer to them'. Hogan's own vision was significantly coloured by Christian conviction. The French Revolutionary ideals of liberty and equality having come into conflict with one another, it was, he asserted, through the largely ignored third ideal, that of fraternity, that a resolution of the conflict could be achieved. Democracy had been caught by the dilemma that 'a society of equals cannot be at one and the same time a society of freemen'. What therefore arose was oligarchy. But this democratic dilemma had arisen, Hogan claimed, 'only because the main movement of modern democracy turned its back on Christianity. Liberty and equality are reconcilable in terms of fraternity. . . . For fraternity is in its essence central to Christianity. Without the fatherhood of God the brotherhood of men is a meaningless abstraction.'[176]

Hogan's views, therefore, drew on religious inspiration in a way fundamentally at odds with the essentially materialistic emphasis of republican socialists, and in the battle between left and right Hogan and the O'Donnellites inhabited opposing ends of the ideological spectrum. But both refused to fetishize either free speech or parliamentary process,[177] and they further shared the

[174] Hogan, *Could Ireland Become Communist?* See also an intriguing contemporary letter from Hogan in which he outlines aspects of his thinking: Hogan to Henry, 18 Apr. [1935?], enclosed with QUB Library Copy of Hogan, *Could Ireland Become Communist?* QUB Special Collections Room.

[175] P. Bew, E. Hazelkorn, and H. Patterson, *The Dynamics of Irish Politics* (London, Lawrence and Wishart, 1989), 64.

[176] *Modern Democracy* (Cork, Cork Univ. Press, 1938), 6–7, 17, 20.

[177] Ibid. 15; *An Phoblacht*, 19 Nov. 1932; *Irish Independent*, 11 Nov. 1932.

conviction that their own case was particularly urgent, given the seriousness of the threat posed by the opposing evils which they respectively claimed to face.[178]

The battles between republicans and Blueshirts formed the focal point for much Congress argument. The state was condemned for proceeding against those who militantly combated Irish fascism, and for providing protection for Blueshirt meetings.[179] Indeed, the clashes between republicans and Blueshirts in these years set a street-fighting context for the Congress's activities. While there were undoubtedly certain echoes here of continental street violence, it is also important to note that the Republican Congress protagonists simultaneously interpreted such clashes as a continuation of the civil war conflict. O'Duffy's eminent anti-republican role in 1922–3 did not go unnoticed in republican circles, while George Gilmore was to describe O'Duffy's organization as 'a dangerous regrouping of the enemies of the Republic'.[180] Typically, therefore, the anti-fascist fight was tied in with other threads of republican socialist thinking. And if the international struggle against the fascists was held to overlap with the civil war division, so, too, the task of fighting fascism had to be seen as integrally tied to the anti-capitalist crusade. Only 'a revolutionary party of the Irish working class and small farmers' could lead the anti-fascist fight, and the anti-fascist struggle must not be narrowed to an attempt merely 'to save an Irish parliament for Irish capitalism. We must fight fascism, but we must come into this fight under a working-class leadership, opening the road for freedom not merely from imperialism, but from Irish capitalism as well.'[181]

For his part, James Hogan put forward the argument that fascism had proved more appealing than communism 'in the highly organized nations of the west' because of its national, traditional appeal: 'By comparison communism was something alien and cosmopolitan and in its appeal to the class war appeared a murderous and destructive thing.'[182] In the event, neither ideology was

---

[178] The Republican Congress stressed the overriding urgency of combating the fascist menace. For the thinking behind Hogan's *Could Ireland Become Communist?*, see Hogan to Henry, 18 Apr. [1935?], enclosed with QUB Library copy of Hogan, *Could Ireland Become Communist?*, QUB Special Collections Room.

[179] *Republican Congress*, 19 May, 26 May, 2 June, 16 June 1934.

[180] *The Irish Republican Congress* (1978 edn.), 12, 17.

[181] *Republican Congress*, 12 May 1934.   [182] *Modern Democracy*, 7–8.

lastingly to thrive in de Valera's Free State.[183] Contrary to the impression given by Republican Congress whingeing,[184] Fianna Fáil did take strong action against the Blueshirts. The 'National Guard (also or formerly known as the Army Comrades Association)' was 'declared by order of the Executive Council to be an unlawful association'.[185] As Professor Lee has argued, 'The Blueshirt episode permitted Fianna Fáil to pose as, and even to become, constitutionalists, defenders of law, order, and majority rule against a militaristic threat'.[186] O'Duffy, who, in February 1933, had been dismissed from his post as Commissioner of the Garda Siochana,[187] was arrested at the end of the year and brought before the Military Tribunal 'in a case which was to drag on for the next three months'.[188] In contrast to the rival republican and Blueshirt forces, Fianna Fáil further entrenched itself in majoritarian, constitutional authority. Enjoying the state power to which electoral support provided access, the party came increasingly to embody mature political practice within the confines of the southern state. The rowdy clashes between republicans and Blueshirts in the early 1930s[189] helped to bring into clearer focus Fianna Fáil's powerful constitutionalism.

While republicans collided with Blueshirts, they also scrapped among themselves. The breakaway by the Congress had provoked unsurprising hostility from the IRA leadership. On 10 April 1934, the Army Council had issued a statement which referred to the Athlone manifesto and then asserted that

It must be clearly understood that in so far as the statement referred to is an attack on the present social and economic system, and an indictment of the policies of the governments of the six and twenty-six counties, the Army Council is in complete agreement with it. In fact, in this connection, this statement is merely repeating what has been said over and over

[183] On the demise of the Blueshirts, see M. Manning, *The Blueshirts* (Dublin, Gill and Macmillan, 1970), chs. 9–11.
[184] See e.g. 'Sixty Republicans charged in courts and one Blueshirt' (*Republican Congress*, 19 May 1934).
[185] Statement Given to Press (22 Aug. 1933), *Constitution—Special Powers: Establishment of the Tribunal Procedure File*, Files of the Dept. of the Taoiseach, NA S 2437.   [186] *Ireland*, 180.
[187] Meeting of the Executive Council (22 Feb. 1933), Dept. of the Taoiseach, Govt. and Cabinet Minutes, NA G 2/10.
[188] McMahon, *Republicans and Imperialists*, 136.
[189] *An Phoblacht*, 2 Sept., 16 Sept., 30 Sept., 7 Oct. 1933.

by the Army Council in its public pronouncements and through the columns of *An Phoblacht*.

Nevertheless, O'Donnell, Price, and Gilmore had been 'suspended from membership of the army' and were 'awaiting courtmartial'. For, as the Army Council went on to explain, the IRA's leaders strongly objected to the creation of an autonomous rival.

The issue at stake is not contained in the statement issued from Athlone but centres round the formation of a new political party independent of the Irish Republican Army, and under its own leaders. This party will, in course of time, contest elections and enter the Free State parliament. Inevitably it will follow the road which has been travelled by other constitutional parties which, though setting out with good intentions, ended in failure. It is not very long ago since Fianna Fáil leaders told us that they wanted to go into the Free State parliament only for the purpose of smashing it up, but they now hold this institution and the whole Free State machine as sacred.[190]

Republican suspicion of 'politics',[191] therefore, mingled with annoyance at the traitorous establishment of a rival organization.

In fact, IRA anxiety regarding their new rival proved to have been unnecessary. The question of numbers is an awkward one. Coogan claims that he was 'persistently given a figure of 4,000' for the defection from the IRA to the Congress. He also asserts that 'it can be safely assumed' that the IRA had over 30,000 in its ranks in the Free State at this time. These estimates tend to conflict with his subsequent statement that 'all in all the effect of the Congress was to split the IRA down the middle'.[192] This is precisely what did not happen. Even if one accepts the slightly more

[190] Ibid. 14 Apr. 1934.

[191] Republican socialists had been plagued by this anti-political quality of mind before; see e.g. the comments of one inter-war Army Council stalwart that he 'did not agree to the army promoting Saor Eire . . . I objected to it. I saw it as a drift towards politics' (T. O Maoileoin, quoted in MacEoin (ed.), *Survivors*, 101).

[192] Coogan, *The IRA*, 109. The precise numbers involved in the IRA are difficult to determine for this period as a whole. Brady suggests 'a parade strength of perhaps 25,000' for 1925–6, while Bell offers 20–25,000 for the latter part of 1926. John Murphy gives himself more room, claiming that from 1925 until the mid-30s membership was 'somewhere in the region of 15,000 to 30,000'. McInerney's claim that 'about 1927' *An Phoblacht* enjoyed a circulation of approximately 40,000 appears rather generous, as does Geoffrey Coulter's latter-day assertion that circulation grew 'to more than 40,000' after Frank Ryan's assumption of editorial authority. A more accurate index of the scale of IRA support can, perhaps, be found in a letter written by Ryan himself to Joseph McGarrity at the start of 1930.

optimistic claims of Patrick Byrne, it is still evident that the Congress took with it only a minority of the IRA. Byrne puts the number of IRA defectors at 'about 6,000 to 8,000'. He admits the difficulties involved in assessing precise numbers, but estimates that the Congress had 'between 6[,000] to possibly 10,000 paid-up members'.[193] Coming from one of the movement's joint secretaries, such estimates cannot be ignored (though caution must be employed when dealing with such questions). Two things can, however, be asserted with some confidence. First, the Congress was heavily dependent for its membership on IRA converts. Second, the new movement's fundamental claim that its interpretation of republicanism was the genuine one was a view which the majority of IRA members clearly did not share.

It was not that overwhelming bitterness necessarily divided the two factions from one another. As on other occasions, political division could co-exist with bonds of personal respect and friendship. O'Donnell recalled that Moss Twomey had 'strongly opposed our policies'.[194] Yet O'Donnell, Gilmore, and Humphreys all praised Twomey's qualities,[195] and *Republican Congress* items such as the piece offering condolences to Twomey on the death of his mother, or that praising the recently incarcerated Tom Barry,[196] suggest that it was possible for Congress supporters to hate the sin while still being rather partial to the sinner.

There was no ambiguity, however, regarding Congress criticisms of IRA policy. In its first issue, *Republican Congress* carried a self-justifying article which stated:

At the 1933 Convention the first voices of protest against the policy, or lack of policy, of the leadership were heard. The IRA had a revolutionary

With reference to *An Phoblacht*, Ryan stated, 'We had dropped to 4,000 from the 18,000 figure we had in 1925. But, as a result of an intensive circulation drive, we are now printing—and selling—8,000 copies' (C. Brady, *Guardians of the Peace* (Dublin, Gill and Macmillan, 1974), 142–3; Bell, *Secret Army*, 57; J. A. Murphy, 'The New IRA 1925–62', in T. D. Williams (ed.), *Secret Societies in Ireland* (Dublin, Gill and Macmillan, 1973), 153; McInerney, *O'Donnell*, 122; Cronin, *Ryan*, 25; Ryan to McGarrity, 25 Jan. 1930, McGarrity Papers, NLI MS 17,535).

[193] To the author, 12 Apr. 1988.   [194] Quoted in McInerney, *O'Donnell*, 137.
[195] P. O'Donnell, *There Will Be Another Day* (Dublin, Dolmen, 1963), 118; Gilmore, *The Irish Republican Congress* (1978 edn.), 24; Sheila Humphreys, interview with the author, Dublin, 26 Feb. 1987.
[196] *Republican Congress*, 5 May, 12 May 1934. Amicable contact between people on different sides in the 1934 schism was to be retained throughout the decade; see, for example, Cronin, *Ryan*, 105.

programme, and a revolutionary plan. The leadership were postponing the putting into operation of these. That was protested against by some. The leadership answered that it was postponing its programme until a more favourable time, not shelving it. But the shelving was done. And measures were taken by direction of the leadership to stifle opposition to that shelving.[197]

On Sunday 3 June 1934, a meeting was held in College Green (Dublin) at which Andy Cooney, Moss Twomey, Sean MacBride, and Michael Fitzpatrick—all leading figures in the IRA—addressed a republican audience.[198] The following Saturday's issue of *Republican Congress* contained an editorial which claimed that this gathering had witnessed the unwitting clarification by IRA leaders of the 'issues that separated the revolutionary section of the IRA from the present leadership'.

'Wait until we get into power and we will deal with the fascists.' 'Wait until we get into power and you will get a Workers' Republic.' That is the essence of the speeches of the most authoritative of the IRA leaders. Thus are the facts of the present shirked for the possibilities of the future. Thus are the rank and file of the IRA—the most honest minds among Irish youth—kept away from the real revolutionary struggle. Repeatedly, on Sunday, the IRA leaders stressed that the fascist menace is ended. They raised instead the slogan that the real obstacle to the Republic is the armed forces of the two partition governments, and that therefore the urgent task is the perfecting of the military machine. Thus is the physical force idea made cover the retreat from the revolutionary road. Thus are the mistakes of other days repeated.

Emphasis on the centrality of physical force, therefore, underlined the gulf between socialist republicanism and IRA orthodoxy. With increasing urgency of tone, the editorial asserted:

Against the IRA leaders' slogan, 'Fight the state forces,' we raise the slogan, 'Fight fascism.' Against the slogan, 'Concentrate on military affairs,' we raise the slogan, 'Concentrate on revolutionary work.' Against their slogan, 'Wait until we're ready,' we raise the slogan, 'Fight now.' For the Republic cannot be achieved by a 'national salvation army' seizing power and doling out freedom to the masses. But it can be achieved by a mass revolutionary struggle of which the IRA could be the armed vanguard.

[197] *Republican Congress*, 5 May 1934.
[198] *Irish Press*, 4 June 1934; *Republican Congress*, 9 June 1934.

The Congress, therefore, sought popular mobilization on social issues. Using religious metaphor, the article claimed:

Faith without good works is dead. Of what use is the protest of the IRA leaders that they stand for the Workers' Republic, when they do not carry their protestations into practice? They shirk the day-to-day struggles of the working class. They bitterly oppose the unleashing of the people which the Republican Congress will bring about.[199]

The final twelve words were to prove unjustifiably optimistic. But the preceding argument clarified Republican Congress thinking, critical as it was of IRA over-concentration on physical force and reluctance to engage in social, class struggles. Indeed, the Congress explicitly recognized what had been implicit during the post-civil war period: that the IRA was not a viable medium through which to express socialist republicanism. Saor Eire, the Congress's paper observed in May 1934, had been

the high-water mark of the process of radicalization that had been going on within the IRA.... The IRA not only dropped Saor Eire but soon began to shed from the leadership those who had shouldered the organization towards it. All trace of Saor Eire is gone out of army pronouncements during the past year. The lesson of Saor Eire is that the IRA may stagger, that working-class elements in it may even win a pull towards working class ideals, but the power of anti-working-class forces within it will win the second pull.[200]

Religion, so problematic for Saor Eire, posed difficulties also for the Congress. Frank Ryan commented in August 1934 on a priest 'who told me how I'll feel in Hell after I've died for the Congress',[201] and, indeed, anti-Congress sentiment was all too evident among the Catholic clergy. Joseph MacRory was as hostile toward communism in 1934 as he had been three years earlier, stating in April that communists 'were the enemies of God' and that they must be 'conquered' by the Catholic Church.[202] Writing in the *Standard* in September 1934, Revd Michael Burke warned, legitimately enough, that the Republican Congress was in league with the official Communist Party of Ireland. The Athlone manifesto, he claimed, could not have pleased the CPI more 'had it emanated from Russia'. The Congress was propounding communist principles 'week after week': 'The poison has infected a number

---

[199] *Republican Congress*, 9 June 1934.   [200] Ibid. 5 May 1934.
[201] Ibid. 18 Aug. 1934.   [202] *Standard*, 4 May 1934.

of young men and young women who profess allegiance to the faith, but have become bitter critics of the Church and ardent anti-clerics. They despise the social teachings of the Church and scorn the doctrines of the Pope.' The following week, on the eve of the Congress's Rathmines Convention, an editorial in the same paper claimed that the movement was 'bidding farewell to most of the principles that have guided our country to her greatest triumphs in the past'. But the Irish people knew that Christ's teaching was 'an infinitely higher charter for the poor than all the maxims devised in Soviet Russia'. They would, therefore, 'appraise at their true value the glowing, but utterly fallacious, statements they are likely to hear within the coming week'.[203]

Seán O'Faoláin's observation that 'the Irish bishops form as conservative a body of men as may be found in any country'[204] might have seemed to Congress enthusiasts to have been all too apt. On 6 January 1935, Jeremiah Kinane, Bishop of Waterford and Lismore, justified his role in a dispute concerning Frank Edwards, who had been sacked from his teaching post because of his involvement with the Republican Congress. Speaking in Waterford Cathedral, Kinane stated that 'the principles and aims of the Republican Congress movement are opposed to the teaching of the Church. Its principles are socialistic and communistic.'[205] Frank Ryan, already condemned by at least one cleric to a rather Hellish future, publicly protested on Edwards' behalf.[206] But on 11 January Kinane wrote a letter to the *Irish Times* in which he stuck resolutely to his anti-socialist stance, citing papal and divine backing for his political views: 'In accordance with the Catholic teaching as stated by Pope Leo XIII in the Encyclical Quadragesimo anno, the right to own private property has been given to man by God's natural law'.[207] Five days later, the same paper published further clerical condemnation of the Congress, with Rev. W. Byrne asserting that the movement was 'un-Irish, communistic, and anti-Catholic'.[208]

The accusation of being 'un-Irish' reflected one of the problems which the Congress had with clerical condemnation. The movement attempted to claim republican credentials superior to others in the nationalist camp; its assertion that Fianna Fáil could not achieve

[203] Ibid. 21, 28 Sept. 1934.   [204] *De Valera*, 78.
[205] *Irish Catholic*, 12 Jan. 1935.   [206] *Irish Times*, 9 Jan. 1935.
[207] Ibid. 12 Jan. 1935.   [208] Ibid. 17 Jan. 1935.

republican objectives typified this pattern. Yet the strong identification between Irish Catholicism and Irish nationalism, which predated the twentieth century,[209] created problems for nationalists claiming the separatist high ground while being perceived by most Catholic clergy and vast numbers of the laity as exponents of 'un-Catholic' principles. It was not that the Church could mechanically stifle sturdy political opposition; as the Saor Eire episode demonstrated, it was possible for a group such as the IRA to withstand clerical pressure. The point is rather that socialistic argument was considered alien and unconvincing by most Irish people; it was, indeed, perceived by most nationalists to be both un-Irish and anti-Catholic, each quality reinforcing the other. This cannot simply be put down to institutional Catholic hostility toward socialist ideas. The Irish Church was only able to maintain so overwhelmingly anti-socialist a stance precisely because its laity so widely considered socialist argument to be hostile to their worldly, economic interests. The politics of land ownership, for example, helped to sustain institutional Catholic anti-socialism. But it is also true that clerical anti-socialism, which extended well beyond Ireland in this period, helped reinforce the tendencies which emerged out of Irish economic interests and relations. The process was reciprocal, and all the more sturdy for that.

John Whyte has argued:

The years 1923–37 reveal, so far as religious values are concerned, a remarkable consensus in Irish society. There was overwhelming agreement that traditional Catholic values should be maintained, if necessary by legislation. There is no evidence that pressure from the hierarchy was needed to bring this about: it appears to have been spontaneous.[210]

That socialistic ideas were presented as embodying anti-Catholic values, therefore, certainly did nothing to help the cause of the republican left, and the latter's response to the problem was tellingly complicated. For socialist republicans, there *was* no right answer to this awkward question, and their confused and impotent responses reflected the weakness of their position. They had to

---

[209] J. Newsinger, 'Revolution and Catholicism in Ireland, 1848–1923', *European Studies Review*, 9/4 (Oct. 1979), 459–60.

[210] *Church and State in Modern Ireland, 1923–79* (Dublin, Gill and Macmillan, 1984; 1st edn. 1971), 60.

recognize people's religiosity and also the significance of the clergy within Irish society.[211] Moreover, the existence of sympathetic clerics was highlighted,[212] and it was hinted that there was no real conflict between Catholicism and the politics of the republican left. Irish Catholics, according to O'Donnell, were 'slow to face the fact that the defence of Catholicism to which they are often rallied, is a slogan which covers transactions little deserving Catholic support, even though bishops make the call'. Clerical views, it was argued, had worldly origins and involved the defence of worldly causes which deserved no Christian support. O'Donnell argued that episcopal opinions 'on land reform, slum clearance, and the like are inspired by very worldly considerations, and not by whistles from the stars'.[213] Frank Ryan, referring to the Spanish civil war in which he played a much-cited role, claimed that there was 'more Christianity in any one Spanish worker than there is in the whole of the miscalled "Irish Christian Front" '. Ryan had earlier claimed that he resented 'the mingling of religion and of politics'.[214] Yet his Spanish-related reference showed him, rather inconsistently, attempting to claim religious high ground in his own political battles. This double-faced approach reflected harsh truths. It was understandable for the republican left to wish that religion and politics could somehow inhabit separate realms, since the force of religious influence tended so overwhelmingly to work against them. But it was also unsurprising that socialist republicans should attempt to utilize religion for their own purposes, given their recognition that religion was unavoidably significant within Irish life.

Other aspects of republican socialists' response to religious questions similarly reflected the fragility of their situation. Thus, for example, Peadar O'Donnell was able to argue both that people exhibited anti-socialist frenzy because they were driven to it by

[211] P. O'Donnell, *Adrigoole* (London, Jonathan Cape, 1929), 243–4; *On the Edge of the Stream*, (London, Jonathan Cape, 1934), 279; *Salud! An Irishman in Spain* (London, Methuen, 1937), 138; A. Crean, 'Confronting Reality: Social and Political Realism in the Writings of Peadar O'Donnell, 1922–39', M.Phil. thesis (UCD, 1986), 38.

[212] O'Donnell, *There Will Be Another Day* (Dublin, Dolmen, 1963), 108–9.

[213] O'Donnell, *Salud!*, 101, 123. Cf. his comment, in reference to episcopal opposition to republicans in 1922, that 'their pastorals should be put into the same course of study as the newspaper editorials of that day to form, with those editorials, the literature of reaction in a period in Irish history, one deriving from religion as little as the other' (O'Donnell, *There Will Be*, 124).

[214] Cronin, *Ryan*, 26, 89.

the clergy,[215] and also that clergy essentially responded to and followed the pre-existing views of their laity.[216] This apparently contradictory attitude, in fact, pointed to the important fact that while the clergy did indeed often seek to rouse popular passion against socialism, their laity had already, in many cases, arrived at anti-socialistic conclusions themselves. Again, the relationship was mutually reinforcing and, from the republican socialist perspective, all the more bleak as a result. O'Donnell sometimes gave the impression of enjoying clerical disapproval. Thus, having been present at an attack on a church in Spain (during the civil war), he reflected that the 'Dominican Fathers would have proof at last that left republican movements in Ireland were active church-burners; some imp in me rejoices in such thoughts'.[217] The imp had probably adopted the best strategy. For, despite O'Donnell's suggestion that 'it was a shame that we [republicans] had not struck back' against the clergy who had opposed the republican side,[218] there was little that the republican left, at least, could have done to counter clerical hostility.

Far more snug within the mainstream Catholic ethos were de Valera's Fianna Fáil. Not only had the newly empowered government adopted the strategy of using the parliamentary medium, they had also cuddled closely with religious orthodoxy. And, just as the use of parliamentary process drew on the reserves of popular assumption regarding democratic practice,[219] so, too, Fianna Fáil's approach to Catholic Christianity enabled them safely to draw on the wells of popular religious assumption in the twenty-six counties. Sean T. O'Kelly stated in 1933 that the Free State government was 'inspired in its very administrative action by Catholic principles and Catholic doctrine'. O'Kelly—to whom Pius XI expressed specific concern regarding communism—was able to comment, in regard to Pius's social encyclical, that 'in no country was this inspiring pronouncement read and studied with greater eagerness

---

[215] McInerney, *O'Donnell*, 242; P. O'Donnell, 'When a Minority Sulks', *The Bell*, 16/4 (Jan. 1951), 5–6.

[216] P. O'Donnell, 'Liberty Ltd.', *The Bell*, 12/4 (July 1946), 279–80; P. O'Donnell, 'Facts and Fairies', *The Bell*, 13/1 (Oct. 1946), 4.   [217] *Salud!*, 77–8.

[218] Ibid. 152–3.

[219] Coakley rightly notes that 'Britain bequeathed to its neighbouring island . . . its political vocabulary, concepts, institutions, and patterns of behaviour' (J. Coakley, 'Society and Political Culture', in Coakley and Gallagher (eds.), *Politics in the Republic of Ireland*, (Galway, PSAI Press, 1992), 27).

and interest than in Ireland'. In this same October 1933 Geneva speech, O'Kelly outlined various schemes being pursued by the government in an effort to ensure that Irish society was structured on the lines advocated in the encyclical.[220] This reflected and endorsed a smug cultural cosiness which republican socialists were plainly unable to share.

[220] D. Keogh, *The Vatican, the Bishops, and Irish Politics 1919–39* (Cambridge, CUP, 1986), 202–4.

4

Schism, Republican Solipsism, and Spain, 1934–1937

RATHMINES

The Congress is not a new movement—except in the sense that before it was launched the Republican movement had come to a halt. It is better to consider it as the revivifying of an old movement—the movement for national independence.

George Gilmore[1]

Republican Congress: we tried to get the labour movement and working class to lead the national struggle and we failed . . .

George Gilmore[2]

One of the many characteristics which the Republican Congress inherited from the IRA was an unfortunate propensity toward schism. When the Congress gathered in Rathmines Town Hall on 29 and 30 September 1934 for what was to have been its triumphant unleashing, the result was a devastatingly balanced split. This 'shattering blow'[3] had complicated origins. The Rathmines meeting was to adopt a 'Republican resolution' intended to define the Congress's aims, means, and political character. Eight days before the gathering, the Congress's Organizing Bureau decided to replace their original resolution with two alternatives.[4] The Bureau had become divided and the rival statements were to be presented to the Rathmines conference where the issue would be debated and put to the vote.

[1] *The Irish Republican Congress* (New York, United Irish Republican Committees of US, 1935), 8.

[2] Statements in conversation with Anthony Coughlan, recorded by the latter (Coughlan Papers, PP).

[3] P. Byrne, *Memories of the Republican Congress* (London, Connolly Association, n.d.), 12. [4] *Republican Congress*, 29 Sept. 1934.

The three resolutions—the original, that favoured by the majority of the Organizing Bureau, and that favoured by its minority—were in fact very similar. There were four ingredients upon which they variously drew: separatism, socialism, the assertion of working-class incorruptibility, and the programmatic statement of objectives. Each resolution declared itself committed to national independence. Each advocated social struggles which would simultaneously advance the cause of the lower classes and facilitate territorial liberation. Each denounced Irish capitalists as exploitative and anti-national, and sought instead to build on the working classes, whose unique reliability was implied in the original and explicitly stated in the majority and minority resolutions. The latter two statements listed specific objectives, numerous of which were identical.[5]

With such similarities, why the split? The answer emerges more clearly from the Rathmines debate than from the semantic differences between the two rival republican resolutions under scrutiny. In essence, the majority of the Organizing Bureau gave greater prominence to the socialist ingredients in the movement's ideology, the minority to the republican. Both factions were committed to the fusion of socialism and republicanism. They differed, first, over the appropriate slogan with which to adorn and define their struggle and, second, over the appropriate method of organization. The majority—which included Roddy Connolly, Nora Connolly O'Brien, and Michael Price—sought to create in the Congress a new political party which would campaign for a 'Workers' Republic'. In opposition to this, the powerful triumvirate of Gilmore, O'Donnell, and Ryan sponsored the idea of co-ordinating a united front, drawing together various organizations and marching under the banner of an 'Irish Republic'.[6] Sean Nolan, present at Rathmines in a journalistic capacity, subsequently described the stance of the 'Workers' Republic' group as 'a manifestation of leftism'; according to this faction, he continued, 'you had to have the name or nothing'.[7]

Certainly, the Rathmines debate demonstrated that both Connolly and Price were insistent on adherence to their phrase. In Connolly's case there was a family tradition:

---

[5] Ibid. 8, 29 Sept. 1934.   [6] Ibid. 29 Sept. 1934.
[7] Interview with the author, Dublin, 3 Feb. 1988.

The slogan of the Workers' Republic . . . covered the objectives of the workers and small farmers. It was not new. It had a good tradition and has always typified the most revolutionary outlook. It dated from 1896 when it was advanced by the Irish Socialist Republican Party founded by James Connolly. It brought out the greatest force, intensity, passion, and enthusiasm of the Irish working class. It was something the workers, small farmers, and agricultural labourers thoroughly understood. It would weld that trinity together and help make them invincible in the leadership of the struggle against capitalism.[8]

Price did not claim such panacean powers for the slogan. But he was still determined to keep it, saying that he could not subscribe 'to anything less than a declaration that this Congress stands emphatically for the overthrow of capitalism in Ireland and for the enthronement of the Irish Workers' Republic'.[9]

Writing two years later, O'Donnell rather patronizingly dismissed Price's stand as 'a weird stunt' and a 'distraction'.[10] O'Donnell himself had no love for the 'Workers' Republic' phrase: 'I never did enthuse over that slogan. It was too city-minded a term and my world was essentially that of the small farm countryside'.[11] Thus, while the majority resolution sought a restructuring of Irish society 'along the lines of complete working-class supremacy in a Workers' Republic', that to which O'Donnell put his name omitted any reference to this slogan. Instead, the minority resolution closed with the following, rousing peroration: 'The Republican Congress, rallying centre for mass struggles capable of smashing imperialist and native exploiters, calls for a UNITED FRONT of working-class and small farmers so that the submerged nation may be roused to free itself and to free and unite the Irish Republic'.[12]

It was a question of tactics. O'Donnell, Gilmore, and Ryan adopted a primarily republican emphasis not because they were less socialist than their rivals, but because they felt that republicanism offered the framework and language most appropriate to that particular moment. The 'Irish Republic' was considered a preferable banner to that of the 'Workers' Republic' precisely because the former phrase was seen as bringing the actual substance of a workers' republic nearer. In moving the minority resolution

---

[8] *Republican Congress*, 6 Oct. 1934.   [9] Ibid. 13 Oct. 1934.
[10] 'The Irish Struggle Today', *Left Review* (Apr. 1936), 299.
[11] Quoted in M. McInerney, *Peadar O'Donnell: Irish Social Rebel* (Dublin, O'Brien, 1974), 40.   [12] *Republican Congress*, 29 Sept. 1934.

at Rathmines, O'Donnell claimed that very few among his audience would be able to persuade themselves that he stood for anything *except* a workers' republic. But actions rather than words would define this new state.

> It is the struggles we conduct in the picket line, our association with the drive of landless men and small farmers against the ranchers, and such activities that determine the nature of our Republic. We dare not permit the Republican forces to develop or rest apart from active association with work-a-day struggles. We dare not jump through a stage in the fight, raising now the slogan 'Workers' Republic', and leaving Fianna Fáil to escape, saying that they are standing for one kind of Republic, but that we stand for a different one.[13]

George Gilmore later asserted that the 'Real issue [was] not the "Workers' Republic" against the "Republic", but whether there should be a new party or not'.[14] Indeed, the divergence over slogans was interwoven with a split over proposed methods of organization. Peadar O'Donnell was to define his united-front position as one founded on the belief 'that an identifiable working-class vanguard should mobilize all the independence forces'.[15] Behind the 'Irish Republic' slogan, therefore, was the commitment to organize a united front consisting of those who sought independence. What the O'Donnell, Gilmore, and Ryan group aimed at was 'a united front of Republican and Labour organizations for the breaking of the connection with the British empire and the re-establishment of an independent Republic for a united Ireland'.[16] The Congress was to draw together all those who genuinely sought an independent republic. Crucial to this outlook was the view, expressed by George Gilmore, that 'there were people of republican and radical sentiment in all parties and groups, and outside these as well'.[17]

Behind the 'Workers' Republic' slogan lay the desire for a new political party. On 8 June 1934, at 'a mass meeting of Dublin workers' in Cathal Brugha Street, Michael Price had argued that

---

[13] Ibid. 6 Oct. 1934.
[14] Statements in conversation with Anthony Coughlan, recorded by the latter (Coughlan Papers, PP).   [15] Byrne, *Memories*, 12.
[16] G. Gilmore and F. Ryan, Foreword in Gilmore, *The Irish Republican Congress* (1935 edn.), 3.
[17] Statements in conversation with Anthony Coughlan, recorded by the latter (Coughlan Papers, PP).

'a Workers' Revolutionary Party' would emerge from the Republican Congress.[18] Nora Connolly O'Brien later recalled that she
had

> had such great hopes for Republican Congress, only to have it spoiled in
> the effort to create a bogus *united front*. The tradition of my life has been
> Republican; I am a Republican and will always be a Republican. I could
> not tolerate the idea of a *united front* which would not be Republican. We
> had there the makings of a Republican Workers' Party but we wasted it.[19]

While this passage is unambiguous on the issue of Connolly
O'Brien's commitment to a new party and her hostility to the
united front, it does little to explain the reasoning which led her
to this position. Her suggestion that the united front would not be
republican is rather peculiar; the creation of such a front would
undeniably have set the Congress firmly in republican soil. Her
speech at Rathmines perhaps provides a more significant clue
to her thoughts. In this she referred to the claim that one of
the 'greatest things' achieved by the Congress was the conversion
to the movement of 'many sections in the North that had been
hostile and had kept away from the Republican and national
movements'. The reason for this supposed success was that the
movement had made clear 'that the type of Republic we were
fighting for was a Workers' Republic'.[20] It was, in fact, highly unlikely that any 1930s group—particularly one emerging from the
IRA—would be able to persuade a large number of Northern Irish
Protestants that republicanism was good for them. But Connolly
O'Brien plainly believed that six-county hostility to the republic
could be overcome if the latter were only dressed up in an unambiguous 'Workers' Republic' fashion.

In addition to the rival republican resolutions, there were
proposed two accompanying resolutions dealing with organization.
The differences between the two factions were amplified by these
latter, organizational resolutions. The majority group—whose
organizational resolution was described in *Republican Congress* as
containing 'proposals for the setting-up of a Revolutionary Party'—
argued that 'none of the presently constituted organizations' in

---

[18] *Republican Congress*, 16 June 1934.
[19] Quoted in U. MacEoin (ed.), *Survivors* (Dublin, Argenta, 1987; 1st edn. 1980),
213.   [20] *Republican Congress*, 6 Oct. 1934.

Ireland fully satisfied the desires of workers and small farmers, and that the time was now ripe 'for the launching of a new organization' which would 'give expression to the aims and activities of those desirous of achieving an Irish Workers' Republic'. A twenty-person National Executive was to be elected, and this would have the task of ascertaining the best form and manner of launching the new body. Meanwhile, Congress groups were 'to retain their formation, enlarge their membership, and increase their activities'. The minority statement on organization asserted the Congress to be resolved 'that the forces represented by delegates at Congress shall be kept intact and expanded under the name of "The Republican Congress" '. No new party here; rather, there was to be 'an intensified campaign for further Congress Branches'. In its keenness to maintain the existing movement, the framers of this resolution outlined for the Congress a rather elaborate organizational structure comprising local Branches, United Councils, a National Congress, a National Executive, and an Administrative Bureau.[21]

In the Rathmines vote on the rival republican resolutions, 99 people supported the O'Donnell, Gilmore, and Ryan proposal, while 84 backed its rival. The majority resolution on organization was withdrawn by Nora Connolly O'Brien and the united-front alternative agreed to.[22] The united-front approach had won the day. George Gilmore subsequently asserted that it had been O'Donnell and Sean Murray who had thought up the Republican Congress idea,[23] and certainly Murray's CPI was crucial in the Rathmines split. The Party had, in the words of its historian, 'welcomed the Athlone manifesto as the decision of an important section of the IRA to declare for involvement in the social struggles of the people'.[24] But the CPI opposed the idea that the Congress should form a new party. At Rathmines all of the Party's leading members spoke in favour of the O'Donnellite position, and every Party delegate voted for the united-front resolution.[25] George Gilmore later considered that 'perhaps Murray [had been]

---

[21] Ibid. 29 Sept. 1934.   [22] Ibid. 6 Oct., 13 Oct. 1934.

[23] Statements in conversation with Anthony Coughlan, recorded by the latter (Coughlan Papers, PP).

[24] CPI, *Outline History* (Dublin, New Books, n.d.), 22.

[25] M. Milotte, *Communism in Modern Ireland: The Pursuit of the Workers' Republic Since 1916* (Dublin, Gill and Macmillan, 1984), 155.

influenced by [the] Popular Front ideas of the time',[26] and Nora Connolly O'Brien rather sourly claimed that there had been direct communist influence over O'Donnell:

The Communist Party sent Willie Gallacher over from London just before the Congress to persuade O'Donnell to stand for a united front instead of making Republican Congress a political party. Gallacher and O'Donnell were up all night arguing about this point, and finally O'Donnell gave in, and stood for a united front. Even Sean Murray, the leader of the Communist Party of Ireland, did not know about this. It was Willie Gallacher himself who told me about this later. I lost all respect for O'Donnell after this, and have never had any respect for him ever since.[27]

O'Donnell's personal influence at Rathmines was certainly important. Patrick Byrne presented the split as centring on 'whether the Congress should resolve itself into a new revolutionary Socialist Party, or remain as a united front of all progressive forces against fascism'. But, in his own decision on the issue, personal loyalty appears to have conflicted with ideological inclination: 'Personally, I favoured the idea of a new Socialist Party, but loyalty to Peadar, Frank Ryan, and George Gilmore determined my vote. Looking back I think it was a great mistake that we did not go for a Workers' Party.'[28] This certainly fits in with much other evidence regarding the degree of personal, individual influence wielded within early-twentieth-century Irish republican culture.[29] And George Gilmore provided further evidence of the crucial part played by personalities, individual influence, and personal clashes, when he talked of the

key role of Roddy Connolly in causing [the] split in [the] Republican Congress. Mick Price would not have been strong enough or influential enough to do it on his own. He was well-meaning, but swinging from ultra-left positions to quite right-wing ones all the time.... But Roddy was a different character. He had a lot of prestige and was followed by many militants. He was piqued that Sean Murray had become secretary

---

[26] Statements in conversation with Anthony Coughlan, recorded by the latter (Coughlan Papers, PP).

[27] *We Shall Rise Again* (London, Mosquito, 1981), 72.

[28] *Memories*, 11–12. Cf. 'The time was right, the policy was right, and the leadership was right, for a Party to be formed. Although I voted against, much against my inclination, due to loyalty to O'Donnell and Ryan, I was most unhappy' (Patrick Byrne, letter to the author, 12 Apr. 1988).

[29] See e.g. T. P. Coogan, *The IRA* (London, Fontana, 1987; 1st edn. 1970), 64; E. O'Malley, *The Singing Flame* (Dublin, Anvil, 1978), 86.

of the CP—they had both been in the Workers' Revolutionary Groups and Roddy wanted a job. He had a family to support and could hardly have been making much in Bray Technical School. He originally hoped that the Congress, if oriented on a leftward course, might become a kind of rival CP, with himself in charge.[30]

While personal interest and influence played an important role in the Rathmines split, it is also vital to explore the ideological content of the debate in question. The first thing to note is the change of emphasis involved in the September 1934 O'Donnellite position. George Gilmore had been prepared openly to endorse the 'Workers' Republic' in May 1934, and indeed the Congress's paper had proudly and explicitly carried this objective.[31] By September the position was clearly different. Yet the similarities in argument are also striking. There remained the emphasis on the importance of having the correct republican leadership. Frank Ryan, speaking at Rathmines in favour of the united-front approach, argued that 'by adopting the minority resolution, they would initiate a movement that would put the working class at the head of the national struggle'.[32] O'Donnell later argued, again with reference to the united-front view, that 'the central idea of the Republican Congress was that an identifiable working-class vanguard should mobilize all the independence forces. . . . the essential feature of [the Congress] was that it saw itself mobilizing all the independence forces behind a clearly recognizable workers' vanguard'.[33]

Similarly, the successful united-front group maintained their definitive anti-capitalist emphasis. This, indeed, brings us to the problems involved in the position adopted by the O'Donnellites at Rathmines, for theirs was a highly contradictory stance. On the one hand, Gilmore and Ryan presented the proposed united front as drawing together all republican groups, regardless of social outlook, in a struggle to achieve an independent Irish republic. There had, they wrote, been at Rathmines

a section which held the opinion that the Congress ought to differentiate its policy from those of the Fianna Fáil and IRA leaderships. That section wished to adopt the slogan of 'The Workers' Republic' as opposed to

---

[30] Statements in conversation with Anthony Coughlan, recorded by the latter (Coughlan Papers, PP).   [31] *Republican Congress*, 5 May 1934.
[32] Ibid. 13 Oct. 1934.   [33] Byrne, *Memories*, 12.

'The Republic'. It wished to form a new party instead of working for a united front movement. The Congress decided that that was an incorrect approach to the present political situation. It held that the correct line of approach for Republicans, no matter what form of Republic they visualized as their ultimate objective, was a united front of Republican and Labour organizations for the breaking of the connection with the British empire and the re-establishment of an independent Republic for a united Ireland.[34]

Yet it had been argued by the united-front faction at Rathmines that in order to be considered a genuine republican one had to endorse a very specific social outlook indeed. O'Donnell, for example, had criticized de Valera on precisely these grounds: 'My quarrel with de Valera is not that he is not a socialist, for he makes no pretence to be one. My quarrel is that he pretends to be a Republican while actually the interests for which his party acts—Irish capitalism—are across the road to the Republic.'[35] Thus, presumably, those who 'visualized as their ultimate objective' a capitalist republic were held not to be true republicans; instead, they were incapable of achieving the republic, since the interests which they supported blocked the republican advance. Simultaneously, therefore, people were both invited into a united front regardless of their social philosophy, and informed that only an anti-capitalist social philosophy was consistent with being a republican.

This led to a peculiar attitude with regard to Fianna Fáil. The party was asked, as a republican organization, to join a Republican Congress united front; but it was also, as we have just seen, condemned as non-republican owing to its pro-capitalistic leanings. The Congress sought, in Gilmore and Ryan's words, not to 'differentiate its policy' from that of the Fianna Fáil leadership, but rather to draw Fianna Fáil into the proposed united front. Yet the very grounds on which this republican united front was to be based—anti-capitalist, class-conscious struggles—were precisely those which led the O'Donnellites to dismiss the Fianna Fáil leadership as non-republican! This ambiguous approach to Fianna Fáil could only be resolved if it were held that the Congress's united

---

[34] Gilmore and Ryan, Foreword in Gilmore, *The Irish Republican Congress* (1935 edn.), 3.

[35] Quoted in Gilmore, *The Irish Republican Congress* (Cork, CWC, 1978; 1st edn. 1935), 52.

front would win over such numbers of Fianna Fáil supporters that the party's leadership would be forced to convert from a pro-capitalist to an anti-capitalist version of nationalism. In that case, however, de Valera's party was being invited into the Congress only on the condition that it adopted an ideological outlook entirely different from that which it currently held. This made nonsense of the claim that the Congress was not differentiating its policy from that of the Fianna Fáil leadership, or that republicans could unite regardless of the kind of republic which they ultimately envisaged.

Such an approach to Fianna Fáil was based on assumptions which were crucial to the sustenance of socialist republican thinking during these years. It was held that there was only one form of republicanism which could be effective—hence O'Donnell's desire to prevent Fianna Fáil from 'saying that they are standing for one kind of Republic, but that we stand for a different one'. In fact, Fainna Fáil and the Republican left did stand for different republics, the one built around capitalistic development, the other defining itself by its anti-capitalist impetus. But it was vital to socialist republicans that they maintain the view that republican advance could alone be achieved on the basis of anti-capitalist politics. The successful Rathmines minority republican resolution declared that the 'main body of capitalist and financial interests in the country' was 'in alliance with the imperial state'. Those who were pro-capitalist could not, according to the Congress analysis, be true, effective republicans. It was upon those who were exploited under capitalistic arrangements that the Congress aimed to build: 'native' as well as 'imperialist' exploiters were to be smashed, and Irish capitalism would be 'exposed' by a Congress campaign founded on workers and small farmers.[36]

According to the latter-day O'Donnell—not always the most reliable of witnesses—Fianna Fáil had taken 'all the radical and worthwhile elements from Sinn Fein'; in the late 1920s, he continued, he had known that 'there was more radical content in Fianna Fáil than there was in any other organization'.[37] This belief was crucial also to the 1934 united front position. According to the republican left, it was vital 'to rally the Republican masses clear of

---

[36] Gilmore, *The Irish Republican Congress* (1978; 1st edn. 1935), 48–9, 53.
[37] Quoted in MacEoin (ed.), *Survivors*, 32.

Mr de Valera's formula',[38] and O'Donnell was to declare that de Valera himself was 'numb' to the working-class struggle.[39] As we have seen, the Fianna Fáil party's approach was condemned for its agency on behalf of capitalist (and, therefore, non-republican) interests. But while the party line and the party leader were deeply unsound, the membership was held to contain many genuine republicans, and it was on these people that the united-front strategy relied. The 'radical content' of Fianna Fáil had to be set free of de Valera's restricting ideology. The terms 'republicanism' and 'republic', were being claimed for what was, in fact, a particular, class-struggling version of republicanism. O'Donnell typically argued in April 1935 that the radical-social and separatist-republican aspects of the conflict were unavoidably interwoven with one another:

the basis for Congress work is in the worsening conditions and in the growth of Republican feeling in the country ... We know that the well-being of the many cannot be finally organized and guaranteed within the capitalist system. ... Let us keep clearly in mind that our task is to get united action by Republican and working class forces behind industrial and land struggles and against Fascism, and to build up demonstrations for a re-declaration of the Republic.[40]

The proposed drawing of Fianna Fáil to the left was, in fact, distinctly implausible. Fianna Fáil supporters who had rallied so enthusiastically around an explicitly anti-communist and overwhelmingly capitalistic project were hardly likely to be mobilized with equal momentum around a diametrically opposed political programme. In place of a party using twenty-six-county constitutionalism and building on a capitalistic bourgeoisie, Fianna Fáil voters were here expected to endorse anti-constitutional, impossibilistic republicans who defined their republicanism by its very quality of anti-capitalism.

This unlikely sea change was one which O'Donnell, at least, appears to have believed possible well after the failure of the 1930s Republican Congress.[41] It brings us to the heart of the

[38] O'Donnell, 'Irish Struggle', 299.
[39] *There Will Be Another Day* (Dublin, Dolmen, 1963), 14.
[40] *Republican Congress*, 6 Apr. 1935.
[41] Cf. Owen Dudley Edwards's assertion (in relation to the 1950s) that 'Peadar was still convinced of the possibility of recovering Fianna Fail for socialist republicanism' (O. D. Edwards, 'Evangelical Puritanism', *Fortnight*, 290 (Supplement, Dec. 1990), 8.)

Congress's approach and exemplifies the ambiguity which Patterson rightly identifies in the republican left's attitude toward Fianna Fáil. Again, however, Patterson perhaps understates the differences between the O'Donnellites on the one hand and the exponents of de Valera-ism on the other. His suggestions, first, that the left republicans criticized not the Fianna Fáil objectives, but rather the party's capacity to achieve them; and, second, that O'Donnell's intention was that of 'pushing Fianna Fáil to the left rather than displacing it',[42] both need to be brought into sharper focus. To the republican left, the nature of the objectives sought and achieved was dependent on the nature of the struggle to attain them. It was not possible for them to criticize de Valera's capacity to achieve his objective without implying criticism of that objective and its replacement by a different aim. Both the united-front O'Donnellites and Fianna Fáil used the slogan 'the republic', but they meant very different things by that phrase. These differences were reflected in the Congress's emphasis on the correct, class-conscious, nature of the struggle which would lead to the republic. O'Donnell, at Rathmines, set out the connection between the struggle and the outcome in such a way that the differences between his republic and that envisaged by Fianna Fáil were made clear:

The way to build was to create committees of workers and small farmers to conduct working class and small farmer struggles, and to express the political aspirations of these growing forces in increased and urgent campaign to achieve the Republic. In this way Irish capitalism will be exposed, and ever-growing power will rest in our committees of workers and small farmers. A Republic achieved that way becomes a Workers' and Small Farmers' Republic because the organs of struggle become the organs of government, to express the will of those who were the driving force to victory.[43]

Where Fianna Fáil's republic would reflect the pro-capitalist, bourgeois-inclusive alliance sought by that party, O'Donnell's republic would be governed by an alliance of the working classes whose anti-capitalist instincts had qualified them to become true, effective republicans. The different vision of the struggle implied a different vision of the outcome. Both groups used the phrase

---

[42] 'Fianna Fáil and the Working Class: The Origins of the Enigmatic Relationship', *Saothar*, 13 (1988), 84, 86.
[43] Quoted in Gilmore, *The Irish Republican Congress* (1978; 1st edn. 1935), 53.

'the republic', but this label referred to thoroughly divergent objectives. The republican left, therefore, not only brought into question Fianna Fáil's ability to reach the republic, but also offered a different republic as the objective to be sought.

It is also important to note the composition of the groups, which represented, according to the Congress, an embryonic Irish government. O'Donnell's comment that 'the organs of struggle become the organs of government' makes it important to understand the precise nature of the composition of these proposed bodies. According to Gilmore, articulate apologist for the united-front position, the Congress's local groups would certainly draw on a wider pool than on Fianna Fáil alone:

The local branches composed of individual supporters of the Congress movement (irrespective of whether or not they are members of other organizations) will have as one of their tasks the organizing of United Councils representative of local worker, national, unemployed, small farmer, and cultural formations.[44]

The groups which would 'become the organs of government', therefore, were not Fianna Fáil groups. Although Fianna Fáil members would be expected to join such bodies, the groups themselves would be Congress groups, drawing on a wider reservoir than simply de Valera's party. If O'Donnell genuinely meant what he said at Rathmines concerning his vision of the future government of Ireland, then we can assume that Fianna Fáil were indeed to be displaced from power in the Congress's version of the future. While party members, and, hopefully, the party leadership and organization, were to play their part in this formation, the actual government of the new republic would not be a Fianna Fáil one, but rather one comprising the wider forces brought together under the authority and umbrella of the Congress. It was hoped, therefore, that Fianna Fáil would be drawn to the left; but it was also envisaged that governmental power would be taken from it. It was not a case of *either* drawing it to the left *or* displacing it; it was a case of both.

One more point of significance should be acknowledged in relation to the united-front position. In the Rathmines debate Sean Murray stated that

---

[44] *The Irish Republican Congress* (1935 edn.), 22.

Congress should stand for an Irish Republic. . . . I would state the position to be the very opposite to what Michael Price says. He said you cannot get rid of British imperialism until you smash capitalism. I say you cannot smash capitalism until you get rid of British imperialism. Therefore let Congress address itself to the task of fighting for the leadership of the great masses of the Irish people who are fighting for national independence.[45]

Yet Murray's united-front ally, George Gilmore, argued at the same Rathmines conference that 'the united front resolution was based exactly on the Athlone call. "We believe that the Republic of a free united Ireland will never be achieved except by a struggle which uproots capitalism on its way": that formulated the theory for a united-front movement which would overthrow capitalism'.[46] Murray aimed to uproot imperialism prior to dismantling capitalism; his united-front ally, Gilmore, envisaged the reverse process, holding that the republic could only be reached by a struggle which uprooted capitalism 'on its way'. Thus, a certain confusion again characterized the united-front approach.

The stance of the Gilmore, Murray, and O'Donnell group at Rathmines has been cast by various authors in terms of a 'stages' thesis. Mike Milotte, for example, referred to Murray's Rathmines approach as 'a reversion to the "stages" theory of pre-"class against class" days: national freedom *could* be achieved while capitalism still existed; the republic they aimed at was a *capitalist* republic, although by avoiding the prefix its precise class nature was obscured'.[47] This thesis provoked typically boisterous condemnation from Patrick Byrne—'Mike Milotte (*Communism in Modern Ireland*) is talking through his hat. This is pure rubbish'—[48] but Milotte is not alone in espousing this 'stages' interpretation of the united-front position,[49] and, as we have seen, there is certainly some evidence to support him.

Anthony Coughlan has argued that 'Gilmore and O'Donnell accepted the so-called "stages" view, whereby national independence and socialism are two phases of one democratic transformation of society'. He further states that O'Donnell and his colleagues

---

[45] Quoted in Gilmore, *The Irish Republican Congress* (1978 edn.), 54.
[46] *Republican Congress*, 13 Oct. 1934.
[47] *Communism in Modern Ireland*, 156.
[48] Letter to the author, 29 Apr. 1988.
[49] ICO, *The Irish Republican Congress* (London, ICO, 1966), 22–3; C. D. Greaves in *Irish Democrat*, Aug. 1989.

'did not aim to build a socialist organization, but a republican, anti-imperialist one, in which workers, socialists, and the labour movement would be in the lead, but which would contain many non-socialists'.[50] This fits neatly with Gilmore's disdainful attitude toward '-isms'.[51] But, as we have seen, Gilmore's view regarding '-isms' was not shared by all of those who voted for the united front,[52] and Coughlan's dismissal of the socialist nature of the united-front project needs, perhaps, to be qualified. Certainly, as noted, those on that side of the Rathmines split gave less explicit prominence to the socialist aspect of their outlook, and some— Gilmore, in particular—clearly preferred not to interpret their philosophy as socialist. But there is no doubting the influence of socialist ideas on those behind the Congress, including those who advocated the united-front approach. Gilmore himself identified Murray and O'Donnell as the inventors of the Congress movement, and each of them was deeply and undeniably imbued with socialist thinking. And Gilmore's own intellectual framework was massively influenced by James Connolly.[53]

Moreover, while the formal endorsement of socialist ideology was not a part of the united front's immediate policy, there is no question but that the assumptions on which immediate united-front activity was to be based were themselves socialistic. It was as participants in a republican struggle that people were invited to join the united front; but the terms of that republican struggle were specifically socialistic. True republicans could not be pro-capitalist; indeed, capitalism was to be opposed and exposed by the members of the united front, while those who acted on behalf of capitalist interests were defined out of the republican advance. The republican struggle was therefore presented, as it had been earlier presented in documents such as O'Donnell's *For Or Against the Ranchers?*, in terms of class conflict, while the forces driving onward toward the republic were identified in a class-conscious,

---

[50] To the author, 30 May 1991.

[51] Statements in conversation with Anthony Coughlan, recorded by the latter (Coughlan Papers, PP).   [52] Patrick Byrne to the author, 12 Apr. 1988.

[53] Gilmore, *The Irish Republican Congress* (1978 edn.), pp. iii–iv. Members of the republican left often referred to their own socialism and socialist influences: see e.g. O'Donnell, *Monkeys in the Superstructure: Reminiscences of Peadar O'Donnell* (Galway, Salmon, 1986), 24; Patrick Byrne to the author, 12 Apr. 1988; O'Donnell, quoted in S. Cronin, *Frank Ryan: The Search for the Republic* (Dublin, Repsol, 1980), 57.

class-specific way; it was the 'working class and small farmers' who were to achieve the desired republic.[54] Furthermore, these class-specific, class-conscious, anti-capitalist forces would not only be the means by which the republic would be established; they—'the organs of struggle'—would administer and govern the republic once established.

These features of the united-front argument and approach are so imbued with socialist influence, so reliant upon socialist assumption, that it is unhelpful to dismiss them as non-socialist. The September 1934 O'Donnellites displayed a reticence with regard to labels ('Workers' Republic', 'socialism'). But it is clear that the assumptions upon which their republicanism was based—anti-capitalist, (working-)class-conscious, class-struggling assumptions—were those of a socialistic reading of republicanism. To ignore this is to make the same error that the O'Donnellites themselves made: namely, to impute to the terms 'republicanism' and 'republic' a set of values and assumptions which were in fact endorsed only by a minority of the republican movement. Crucial to the socialist republican argument was the belief that republicanism, properly understood, implied a class-struggling, anti-capitalist philosophy. The aim of the united front was to build the republican advance on the foundations of such thinking. According to this view, the de Valera leadership was not truly republican because it acted in the interests of Irish capitalism. It was vital that Fianna Fáil's policy be dismissed as non-republican, and that people accept that the only true republicanism was that imbued with O'Donnellite assumptions. This was why O'Donnell made such a point of warning against Fianna Fáil claiming that it stood for one kind of republic and the Congress for another. According to the republican left, the only way to the republic was their way, and consequently the only kind of republic was that which their struggle would produce. In reality, the Congress zealots merely embodied one particular creed within the wider republican church. What really blocked the path to an independent, united Irish republic was not capitalist political leadership, but rather the sturdy, cross-class anti-republicanism of Ulster unionists. And all sections of the republican movement were impotent to mount that formidable obstacle. To obscure the true, socialist nature of the united-

[54] Gilmore, *The Irish Republican Congress* (1978 edn.), 49.

front position is to blur our understanding of the various factions within the inter-war republican movement.

Clarity of vision on this point reinforces the view of republican socialists' marginality within inter-war Irish nationalism. To perceive the Congress as one particular fraction of nationalist culture highlights the extent to which their assumptions were, indeed, atypical. The question of whether one uprooted imperialism before or after one defeated capitalism was a less important feature of the republican left's argument than their fundamental conviction that the two processes were inextricably linked together. During the inter-war period, socialist republicans offered a variety of scenarios regarding the precise order of their sought-after transformation. As in the case of Gilmore and Murray at Rathmines, allies were not beyond putting simultaneous, contradictory arguments forward on this very point. But what really distinguished the republican socialist outlook was less the exact order of their predicted revolution than the dual, interwoven nature of their creed. In Gilmore's words, 'the oneness of the struggle against national subjection and social oppression in a subject nation has been stressed by James Connolly ... The failure to make that essential oneness a basis for political action has been the great weakness in the republican movements of the nineteenth century and right down to our own day'.[55]

Indeed, from the perspective outlined here by George Gilmore, modern republican movements had proved disappointing. The post-Rathmines experience of the Congress was to demonstrate that this situation continued to obtain: the united-front philosophy failed to resonate significantly amongst republicans and nationalists, and the Congress movement died without leaving a major imprint on Irish political life. Certainly, the Rathmines split did little to improve the group's prospects. The advocates of the united front had won the argument at the conference, but it was a thoroughly Pyrrhic victory. Frank Edwards, a Belfast-born Congress supporter living in Waterford, later referred to the 'disastrous split' which had occurred; Byrne (subsequently) and O'Donnell (at the time) noted that the movement had effectively been 'split down the middle'.[56] Gilmore also drew attention to the damaging effects of the schism.

[55] Ibid. 3.   [56] MacEoin (ed.), *Survivors*, 7, 9; Byrne, *Memories*, 11.

The defeat of the majority republican resolution led to the refusal of Nora Connolly O'Brien, Michael Price, and some others of its supporters to allow their names to go forward for the new Executive. Other resignations followed, and, though the Congress groups continued to work strenuously to carry out the programme of revolutionary work laid down by the Rathmines meeting, it soon became apparent that we had lost that section of the trades union movement whose support was essential to success. The hard core of militants—both of the trades unions and of the republican organizations—with few exceptions remained with the Republican Congress, but most of the well entrenched and comparatively 'safe' men of the trades unions who, restive under the labour leadership, had ventured towards the revolutionary movement, retreated again into their old position.[57]

Gilmore was right in observing that a broad section of trade-union backing was essential. The notion of a radical united front meant little without a significant degree of support from organized labour. In fact, regardless of the Rathmines split, there was little likelihood of the Congress's revolutionary outlook being endorsed by sufficiently large numbers of people—within either the republican or the labour camp—to make the project a viable one. An examination of both the labour and the republican cases demonstrates precisely how marginal the Republican Congress argument actually was.

Any hope of achieving significant support from organized labour was crushed soon after Rathmines. At the Labour Party's fourth annual conference, held in Dublin in October 1934, Roddy Connolly proposed a hybrid motion which drew on both the majority and minority positions of the previous month:

Believing that the dangers which face the workers of this and every other country from capitalism, fascism, international war, and imperialism are too real and serious for us to remain parties to artificial divisions within the working class ranks, we call for a truce among all who stand for an Irish Workers' Republic and a united front against the common enemy. We recommend that in order to achieve united action the Administrative Council invite representatives of the TUC, the Republican movement, and other workers' Republican bodies to exchange views with them upon this question.

In proposing this resolution, Connolly argued that there was no reason why Labour should not consult with the IRA, the

---

[57] *The Irish Republican Congress* (1978 edn.), 57.

Republican Congress, and the Citizen Army: 'these were all movements into which the working class was split up and they were anxious that these bodies should come together with them so as to decide on the best way of attaining their desires'. Significantly, however, the motion was defeated.[58]

For a considerable gulf separated the reformist, constitutional Labour Party from the revolutionary, extra-constitutional tradition represented by Connolly. At the same October conference, the 1916 leader's son had also moved a separate resolution which deplored 'the drastic action' recently taken 'against persons engaged in resisting fascist aggression'; condemned state protection of 'fascist demonstrators'; called for 'a resolute struggle' against any efforts to establish fascist dictatorship in Ireland; and instructed the Administrative Council 'to take every possible step in conjunction with all forces opposing that reactionary dictatorship to combat this great danger to the labour movement'.[59] Behind the rhetoric lay support for the anti-Fine Gael violence which the state was actively opposing.[60]

Appropriately, two of the strongest denunciations of Connolly's approach came from people thoroughly enmeshed within the constitutional apparatus of the Free State. Senator Thomas Johnson (whom Peadar O'Donnell had tried to have deported from Ireland in 1922):

hoped the conference would very emphatically turn down the resolution which, in effect, proposed that the Labour Party should attack its political opponents by violence not because of something they are doing but because of something they are preaching and thinking ... The resolution was an attempt to turn the Labour Party from a political organization into a mass of thugs and garotters and insinuated that no protection should be given to political opponents who differed violently from them. It was suggested that they should attack individuals in the streets because those individuals were wearing uniforms that would probably be an incitement to certain other people and while very reprehensible for general policy, surely it was not the business of the Labour Party to take upon itself police duties.

[58] ILP, *Report of the Proceedings of the Fourth Annual Conference* (25–7 Oct. 1934), 119, 121.   [59] Ibid. 62.
[60] *Republican Congress* had regularly argued that the state both protected 'fascists' and took action against those engaging in 'anti-fascist' activities (*Republican Congress*, 19 May, 26 May, 2 June, 16 June 1934).

Senator Thomas Foran also opposed Connolly's motion. He argued that the Labour Party itself would not be in existence if violence had the capacity to kill a movement. Recalling 'the violent scenes at the inaugural meeting of the Labour Party in the Mansion House some few years ago', he continued that 'had it not been for the intervention of the police force on that occasion' many Labour supporters 'would be looking up at the daisies today'. If Connolly's resolution were adopted, he went on, then 'many of the people who had a real Labour outlook in the Party would not be associated with it'.[61] The senator's comments are highly instructive regarding the dichotomy between that strand of the left which had endorsed and become absorbed within the Free State, and that which had refused to become part of the majoritarian constitutional process. Johnson was, of course, antifascist; but he opposed the kind of autonomous citizen violence which Connolly was endorsing, and he supported the state in prosecuting such street aggression. His vision of democracy involved the notions both that his political opponents should be allowed to express their views, and that the state was the legitimate source of order. If physical action were required against the Blueshirts then the police should be the ones to take it. Foran's words similarly reflected a desire to maintain a certain freedom of political expression via the apparatus of the state: if Labour people had relied on the police to protect their political liberty, then it would be inconsistent to argue against the provision of such protection for others. The Congress had grown out of the IRA, and retained a definite—though comparatively minor—strain of militaristic thinking.[62] Its stand against the Blueshirts was, admittedly, characterized more by street brawling than by full, armed engagements. But both paramilitarism and street-fighting were alien to the vision of people such as Foran.

The discussion on Connolly's resolution had not been completed when the conference adjourned on 25 October. The next morning, the Standing Orders Committee recommended that the motion be replaced by the following: 'Conference condemns emphatically the political and economic manifestations of the fascist movement and, recognizing the danger to political freedom and personal liberty

---

[61] ILP, *Report of the Proceedings of the Fourth Annual Conference*, 64–5.
[62] Byrne, *Memories*, 5.

inherent in every form of dictatorship, pledges the masses of the Irish people to resist its introduction by every available means.' The new motion omitted criticism of state action against anti-fascist agitation. It lacked the demand for an end to the protection of right-wing demonstrators. It contained no aspirations toward a united front, and thereby removed the implication that its acceptance would commit Labour to some form of alliance with such nefarious groups as the Congress and the IRA. The replacement motion did call for people to resist dictatorship 'by every available means'. But while this phrase may have held certain violent (and therefore placatory) connotations for Roddy Connolly, it undoubtedly meant very little in the context of the new resolution. This was, in fact, a vague piece of rhetoric which expressed Labour's genuine opposition to fascism without involving the endorsement of, or participation in, anti-Fine Gael violence. As such, it accorded perfectly with the Free State politics of Johnson and Foran. As such, it was accepted.[63]

The parliamentary road favoured by Thomas Johnson,[64] and the cautious nature of trade-union orthodoxy, both militated against Congress interests. Indeed, while labour figures were prepared to cite James Connolly to rhetorical advantage, the less than encouraging response to Connolly's son's political proposals provides a more accurate index of practical realities for the radical left. Connolly the father was a celebrated prophet, but, like many prophets, he could also be a distinct embarrassment. Charles McCarthy, writing of Irish trade unions in the 1930s, observed that 'Connolly . . . continued to be lauded as a prophet, while his teachings were gingerly put aside'.[65]

Internal schism, and rejection by the Labour Party, were devastating blows for the Congress. But its campaign continued. There was support for strikes and participation in industrial disputes.[66] O'Donnell pushed Congress people who were members of the ITGWU toward 'the initiation and the development of fights for better wages and conditions', and he argued that 'the road of genuine working-class fight is strike action, the sympathetic strike,

[63] ILP, *Report of the Proceedings of the Fourth Annual Conference*, 66.
[64] A. Mitchell, *Labour in Irish Politics 1890–1930: The Irish Labour Movement in an Age of Revolution* (Dublin, Irish Univ. Press, 1974), 206.
[65] 'From Division to Dissension: Irish Trade Unions in the 1930s', *Economic and Social Review*, 5/3 (Apr. 1974), 359.
[66] *Republican Congress*, 6 Oct., 13 Oct. 1934.

the political strike.'[67] Housing struggles continued.[68] Support for the unemployed was maintained.[69] Rural class struggle was advocated.[70] Conflict with the 'fascists' continued to gain favourable coverage, and Congress people were physically engaged in the violence.[71] Emphasis was also placed on the importance of bringing Northern Irish people into the Congress campaign, and of opposing the Northern Irish state,[72] although, typically, nothing serious was achieved here. Indeed, for all the energy displayed by the Congress, little significant progress was made toward its goal of a united, independent, socialist Ireland. The Congress had difficulty enough simply remaining in existence. In February 1936, *Republican Congress* ceased publication owing to a lack of funds which had plagued the movement from its inception;[73] the replacement, *Irish People*, was effectively stillborn.[74] In April 1936 Frank Ryan admitted that the Congress was moribund,[75] and in September of the same year George Gilmore referred to its 'comparative failure'.[76] Patrick Byrne later suggested that the Congress 'just fell apart after the fall of Spain in January 1939',[77] but, as Gilmore and Ryan's 1936 comments show, it had become clear well before this that the movement's ambitious project was not going to be fulfilled.

CUMANN POBLACHTA NA H-EIREANN

The Irish people will be invincible, as they were from 1918 to 1921, when they regain confidence and realize their strength, when they spurn compromise, expediency, and opportunism and stand unflinchingly for the Republic.

Cumann Poblachta na h-Eireann, *Manifesto, Constitution, and Rules*[78]

---

[67] Ibid. 5 Jan. 1935. [68] Ibid. 6 Oct., 13 Oct., 20 Oct. 1934.
[69] Ibid. 6 Oct., 20 Oct., 10 Nov., 24 Nov. 1934.
[70] Ibid. 13 Oct., 17 Nov., 24 Nov. 1934.
[71] Ibid. 6 Oct., 13 Oct., 27 Oct., 3 Nov. 1934. [72] Ibid. 13 Oct., 20 Oct. 1934.
[73] Cronin, *Ryan*, 54, 61; for an example of the movement's rather poignant pleas for financial assistance, see 'A Cry For Help' (*Republican Congress*, 5 May 1934).
[74] *Irish People* ran from 29 Feb. 1936 to 11 Apr. 1936. [75] Cronin, *Ryan*, 65.
[76] Ibid. 70; cf. 'It has been fashionable up till recently in social revolutionary circles to be a member of "the Congress", but it seems now (Autumn, 1936) that this fashion is nearly over' (*Notes on Communism in the Saorstat* (Nov. 1936), MacEntee Papers, ADUCD P67/523 (5)). [77] To the author, 12 Apr. 1988.
[78] *Manifesto, Constitution, and Rules for the Organization*, Coyle O'Donnell Papers, ADUCD P61/10 (1), 4.

> I found out what was in it, and was not in it, / The night they
> murdered Boyle Somerville...
>
> Paul Durcan, 'The Night They Murdered
> Boyle Somerville'[79]

In addition to rejection by the organized labour movement, Congress found itself marginalized within the republican and nationalist world. As we have seen, only a minority of the IRA took the Congress path at the split in the early part of 1934. An examination of developments within contemporary republican culture demonstrates that the post-Rathmines situation was no more benign. On 27 September 1935, Sean MacBride, much criticized by republican socialists for his role in the events of the mid-1930s,[80] addressed a College Green audience in Dublin with the assertion that 'it might be necessary to put forward candidates at elections who would be pledged to the Republic. Steps were being taken to devise the best means of doing these things. Anything done in this direction must be based on the non-recognition of the institutions imposed upon this country'.[81]

The following spring saw the birth of Cumann Poblachta na h-Eireann, a new republican political party founded at a meeting in Dublin on 7 March 1936.[82] The group's objectives were six-fold: first, to bring the 1916 proclamation 'into effective operation and to re-establish and consolidate a government of the Republic of Ireland, representative of the whole of Ireland, based on that proclamation'; second, to 'break the connection with England and the British empire'; third, to establish within the new republic 'a region of social justice based on Christian principles, by a just distribution and effective control of the nation's wealth and resources'; fourth, to end existing governmental machinery—which was declared to be 'in the hands of civil servants'—and to replace it with 'a system of government suited to the particular needs of the people'; fifth, to 'secure international recognition for the Republic of Ireland'; and sixth, to promote the restoration of the Irish language and culture, to promote 'the widest knowledge

---

[79] In E. Longley (ed.), *The Selected Paul Durcan* (Belfast, Blackstaff, 1985; 1st edn. 1982), 31.

[80] 'An Appeal to IRA Volunteers' in CWC, *The Irish Case for Communism* (Cork, CWC, n.d.), 42; Patrick Byrne to the author, 12 Apr. 1988.

[81] *Irish Press*, 28 Sept. 1935.   [82] Coogan, *The IRA*, 115.

of Ireland's history', to make Irish people both aware and proud of 'their traditional and cultural heritage', and to educate people in their 'rights and responsibilities' as citizens of the Irish republic.[83] The new party's manifesto referred to England as 'the never-failing source of all our ills' and Cumann Poblachta, in fact, offered a traditional brew made up of republicanism, platitudinous social aspiration, Gaelicism, and anglophobia. On the awkward question of how its aims were to be realized, the new movement was predictably vague. It was feebly declared that the objectives would be achieved by 'mobilizing the Irish people in Cumann Poblachta na h-Eireann into a disciplined force' which would 'move forward to the immediate restoration of the Republic' and to the achievement of the stated aims.

In practice the new grouping was an abstentionist electoral party. Candidates were to be put forward, but the existing twenty-six and six-county state structures were not to be endorsed. Elected candidates were only to recognize or participate in the deliberations of an assembly claiming to be, and attempting to function as, 'the parliament of the Republic of Ireland, claiming and attempting to enforce its jurisdiction over the whole of Ireland'.[84] Despite these impeccably abstentionist principles, the IRA was far from unanimous in endorsing Cumann Poblachta. At a Convention held in Dublin on 19 May 1936, Moss Twomey appears to have disagreed with Sean MacBride's proposal that the army actively support the new political party. A typical republican walk-out occurred, Twomey leading the charge and being followed by some prominent Dublin officers.[85]

Cumann Poblachta's vague, non-socialistic approach to social issues differed greatly from the class-struggling enthusiasm of the republican left. Taken together with the continuing non-socialistic orthodoxy of the IRA, this underlines the fact that the socialist republican argument remained unconvincing in the eyes of large numbers of republicans. The O'Donnellites might proclaim that theirs was the only true, effective version of republicanism, but their view remained marginal within the republican family. Cumann Poblachta's outlook, indeed, was deeply orthodox; it reflected persistent traits of republican thinking, such as a hostility toward

[83] *Manifesto, Constitution, and Rules*, Coyle O'Donnell Papers, ADUCD, P61/10 (1), 6–7.   [84] Ibid. 4, 7, 11.
[85] Coogan, *The IRA*, 116.

compromise, and a simple belief in the value of the unflinching maintenance of principle. Like Brendan Behan's character, they sometimes gave the impression that they were not 'right' in the head, and thought they were 'still fighting in the Troubles or one of the anti-English campaigns before that'.[86]

The Irish people will be invincible, as they were from 1918 to 1921, when they regain confidence and realize their strength, when they spurn compromise, expediency, and opportunism and stand unflinchingly for the Republic. We appeal to those who, in the past, fought for and served the Republic to take their places again in the struggle and to bring the cause to victory. We appeal especially to young men and women to organize and throw their enthusiasm and generous instincts into the fight for freedom.[87]

Consideration of Cumann Poblachta supports the thesis that 1930s republicans were characterized by a self-referential approach to politics. Indeed, it can be argued that 1930s republicanism might best be understood in terms of the concept of solipsism, defined as the view that self is 'the only thing really existent'.[88] Republicans tended to act as though their own political views, beliefs, and culture were the only really existent ones, and as though those of others could, as a consequence, be ignored. Republicans, to refer back to the telling words of Joseph McGarrity, could 'pay no heed to public clamour' as long as they felt that they were 'doing a national duty'.[89] Cumann Poblachta certainly evinced this self-referential, solipsistic quality.[90] Abstentionism was, by the mid-1930s, an entirely untenable approach unless one ignored the repeatedly expressed electoral preferences of the Irish people. The early years of the independent Irish state had, as we have seen,

---

[86] 'The Hostage', in B. Behan, *The Complete Plays* (London, Methuen, 1978), 129.

[87] Cumann Poblachta na h-Eireann, *Manifesto, Constitution, and Rules*, Coyle O'Donnell Papers, ADUCD P61/10 (1), 4.

[88] *The Shorter Oxford English Dictionary*, ii. 2046.

[89] To de Valera, 2 Oct. 1933, McGarrity Papers, NLI MS 17441.

[90] Though the argument regarding solipsism refers specifically here to Cumann Poblachta, it can also be applied to inter-war republican socialists themselves. Peadar O'Donnell's claim, for example, that the independence movement had grown out of a Connolly-style class awakening of the working classes (*Workers' Republic*, 26 Aug. 1922) did not represent, or even take into serious consideration, actual popular attitudes. Instead, O'Donnell ignored the overwhelming evidence against his thesis, and merely imputed to the Irish working classes a social/national vision derived entirely from reference to his own experience and atypical outlook.

witnessed the increasing legitimation of that state by its elector-ate. By the time of Cumann Poblachta's launch, there had been a clear, unarguable shift away from republican rejection of the state. Abstentionism could be seen, from evidence visible at the time to all but the extraordinarily myopic, to have been superseded by the participationist post-republicanism of Fianna Fáil.

It was only by refusing to notice or acknowledge the reality of this massive shift in nationalist opinion that one could endorse abstentionism as late as 1936. If one examined the actual political life of the state, then abstentionism was plainly a discredited option. But if one refused to consider the existence of political cultures other than one's own, then one could adhere to uncompromised re-publican principles and persist in denying the validity and strength of the independent Irish state. A republican syllogism was em-ployed: the idealized republic was legitimate and inviolable; to acknowledge the legitimacy of the Free State was to profane the republic; therefore one could not acknowledge the legitimacy of Free State structures. According to this self-referential logic, absten-tionism made complete sense. That it made no *political* sense at all was ably demonstrated when Cumann Poblachta ventured into electoral competition. In the Dublin Corporation elections of June 1936, the party fielded five candidates, one in each area. The first received 675 votes (out of a poll of 21,519); the second obtained 482 votes (out of a poll of 32,517); the third managed 720 votes (out of a poll of 32,617); the fourth received 630 votes (from a poll of 21,556); and the fifth obtained 689 votes (out of a poll of 29,733). Not one of these candidates came within 2,000 votes of reaching the quota necessary for election.[91]

Irish democracy, that 'underrated achievement',[92] was able to brush off the abstentionist challenge of its self-referential rivals. Other aspects of Cumann Poblachta further demonstrate its solipsistic quality. Its declared objective of establishing 'a govern-ment of the Republic of Ireland, representative of the whole of Ireland, based on [the 1916] proclamation'[93] is a telling one. The point of reference was a proclamation purporting to represent the

---

[91] *Irish Times*, 2 July 1936.

[92] T. Garvin, 'Unenthusiastic Democrats: The Emergence of Irish Democracy', in R. J. Hill and M. Marsh (eds.), *Modern Irish Democracy: Essays in Honour of Basil Chubb* (Blackrock, Irish Academic Press, 1993), 23.

[93] *Manifesto, Constitution, and Rules*, Coyle O'Donnell Papers, ADUCD P61/10 (1), 6.

people of Ireland but in fact drawn up and proclaimed without concern for a preceding popular mandate. Moreover, the claim that the government based on this proclamation would be 'representative of the whole of Ireland' seems a rather presumptuous one. The whole of Ireland had never sanctioned it, and, as we saw at an earlier stage in our argument, it could hardly be considered a document which reflected the complexity of the 'whole' island's political cultures.

If 1916 was a reference point drawn from a tradition of self-validating legitimacy, then Cumann Poblachta's approach to Gaelicism was further proof of the all-consuming self-obsession of 1930s republican culture. The party aimed to 'promote the restoration of the Irish language and of Irish culture and the widest knowledge of Ireland's history'.[94] Cumann Poblachta's knowledge of Irish history plainly did not stretch to the appreciation that many people in Ireland were hostile to Gaelicization. It was not recognized that there was a certain tension between on the one hand, aspiring toward the absorption of Northern Ireland and, on the other, sustaining definitions of Irishness which effectively excluded the majority of people in Northern Ireland. The only political culture really existent was one's own.

Sean MacBride was Secretary to Cumann Poblachta's Provisional National Council, and his influential role here is interesting. He had been thoroughly involved with the socialist republican Saor Eire organization, yet his approach from 1932 onwards bore little trace of class struggle as the determining quality of republican politics. On the contrary, he appears to have been influential among those who opposed attempts to socialize the IRA during the post-Saor Eire period. As we have seen, MacBride carried with him a certain scepticism about the merits of majority rule. Right or wrong, however, the majority's opinion was decisive in relation to Cumann Poblachta, and MacBride had to wait another decade before helping to establish a party (Clann na Poblachta) which made a serious impression on Irish political life.[95]

By then he, too, had been converted to an acceptance of participative parliamentary methods, casting tacit criticism on the

---

[94] Ibid. 7.
[95] Ibid. 5; *Anti-State Activities Apr. 1929–Oct. 1931*, Files of the Dept. of the Taoiseach, NA S 5864 A. For biographical information on MacBride, see MacBride, quoted in MacEoin (ed.), *Survivors*; *Irish Times*, 16 Jan. 1988; J. J. Lee, *Ireland, 1912–85: Politics and Society* (Cambridge, CUP, 1989).

approach which he had adopted during the 1930s. The important point to note about Cumann Poblachta concerns the persistent republican refusal to acknowledge the reality or validity of political cultures other than one's own. This is a theme which had emerged from MacBride's attitude during his (previously discussed) conversations with de Valera, and it reappeared in the context of this new political party. Cumann Poblachta's abstentionism testified to its refusal to acknowledge the dominant culture of Free State constitutionalism; its sincere absorption in the 1916 myth reflected its false assumption that minority proclamation could, without popular permission or sanction, be extended to cover the occupants of the whole island; its endorsement of Gaelicism exemplified its tendency to look purely at its own culture rather than taking note of the existence of other views. In each of these areas there was a blindness to the reality and validity of political cultures other than its own.

Cumann Poblachta notwithstanding, there remained within the republican movement those who were sceptical about engagement with 'politics'. This trend had been in evidence at the IRA's March 1934 Convention, where one participant had expressed an IRA unit's concern that the Army Council 'were out to try to establish a political party to contest elections—enough attention was not being given to the army from the military point of view'.[96] Peadar O'Donnell himself was hostile to Cumann Poblachta, considering that the IRA would go 'to pieces' if 'a sickly abstentionist party [Cumann Poblachta na h-Eireann] is permitted to develop as a fungus on its body'.[97] O'Donnell's socialist emphasis gave him a particular negative view of MacBride's political party. But in order to appreciate the truly marginal nature of socialist republicanism in this period, it is important to note that among those who disagreed with O'Donnell's social outlook there were those who were extremely wary of anything which deviated too far from the militaristic path. At the IRA's 1934 Convention, one speaker, having argued that 'there is too much stress on the economic policy', contended that 'military preparations is [*sic*] more our job. We should give more consideration to it'.[98]

Certainly, the violence exhibited by the mid-1930s IRA reflected

---

[96] IRA General Army Convention (17 Mar. 1934), Minutes, MacEntee Papers, ADUCD P67/525.　　　　　　　　　　　　[97] 'Irish Struggle', 300.
[98] IRA General Army Convention (17 Mar. 1934), *Minutes*, MacEntee Papers, ADUCD P67/525.

a centre of gravity far removed from O'Donnell's. While the army did not orchestrate any systematic campaign of violence during this period, there were individual incidents—such as the killing of Richard More O'Ferrall in County Longford in February 1935, the shooting of Vice-Admiral Somerville in County Cork in March 1936, and the assassination of John Egan in County Waterford the following month.[99] Each of these highlighted aspects of the spasmodic physical-force pattern characteristic of the IRA in the mid-1930s. Localized, vengeful, and ineffective, they reflected both the absence of any coherent strategy and the resilience of the paramilitaristic mentality from which they resulted. The persistent, all-devouring quality of this approach is intriguingly signalled by a Cumann na mBan report written in 1936. This referred to the organization's September 1934 Convention, at which a 'Social Programme' had been endorsed. The women's organization had 'for many years' supported 'the advancement of a social programme on the lines laid down by James Connolly', and it suggested to the IRA Executive that the army and Cumann na mBan should cooperate to implement the social policy adopted in September 1934. A conference was held between the Executives of the two organizations, and the outcome was a telling one: 'At this conference our plan was fully explained but we found that the co-operation we had hoped to get would not be possible as the army had been committed by its Convention to an intensive training campaign which would fully occupy its members.' Indicating their true priorities, the IRA representatives suggested that other kinds of co-operation be pursued, with Cumann na mBan supporting the armed struggle by working in such areas as communications, medical service, intelligence, and finance.[100]

At its own 1934 Convention, the IRA had heard J. J. Sheehy argue that 'now that de Valera sees that the Blueshirts are finished he hits out at the IRA. We are now in for a hard time'.[101] This proved prophetic enough. De Valera's response to mid-1930s republican violence was unsurprising, given the majoritarian outlook which he had come to endorse. Addressing the Dáil in May

---

[99] *Irish Times*, 11 Feb., 21 Feb. 1935, 25 Mar., 28 Apr. 1936; Coogan, *The IRA*, 120–2.

[100] *Report of Cumann na mBan Convention (15–16 Sept. 1934)* (1936), Coyle O'Donnell Papers, ADUCD P61/7a (3).

[101] IRA General Army Convention (17 Mar. 1934), *Minutes*, MacEntee Papers, ADUCD P67/525.

1935, he defended his use of extraordinary powers to deal with republican–Blueshirt tension by arguing that 'ordinary democratic government' had come under threat:

We were going to have a contest between two groups who were prepared each one to make good its promises and its policy by force. Eventually there was going to be a triumph for one or other, but when the triumph was gained what was going to be the position of the people and what was to be the situation in the country?[102]

Sporadic though it was, IRA violence in the mid-thirties prompted de Valera to take stern action in defence of 'ordinary democratic government'. On 18 June 1936 the IRA was proscribed, its chief of staff having been arrested in the previous month.[103] Twomey— who had for some time been concerned regarding the progress made by the state against his organization—[104] was sentenced on 19 June, by the Special Powers Tribunal, to three years' imprisonment on charges relating to his membership of an unlawful association and his refusal to provide the police with an account of his movements and actions.[105]

If the IRA's persistence with physical force had brought upon them the wrath of the one-time republican symbol, it also demonstrated the marginal standing of socialists within the republican family. Taken together, Cumann Poblachta's abstentionist, non-socialist tactics and the IRA's continuing belief in the primacy of force testified to the peripherality of O'Donnellite thinking. The notion of defining republicanism according to class consciousness and class conflict remained an unconvincing one as far as most republicans were concerned.

SPAIN

For almost four months Christianity has been fighting for its life in Spain. The communists in every country, and their

---

[102] *Dáil Debates*, 56/2091.

[103] Coogan, *The IRA*, 123; *Irish Times*, 22 May 1936.

[104] 'We have endured frightful humiliation from the actions of our own men— [who] when questioned give all the information at their disposal to the police' (IRA General Army Convention (17 Mar. 1934), *Minutes*, MacEntee Papers, ADUCD P67/525).

[105] *Irish Times*, 20 June 1936; *Saorstat Eireann: Constitution (Special Powers) Tribunal* (19 June 1936)—*Attorney General v. Maurice Twomey*, Files of the Dept. of the Taoiseach, NA S 9088.

sympathizers in the press, have propagated the lie that the
fight is one between fascism and democracy. It is not. It is a
fight between the Faith and Antichrist.

Irish Independent[106]

I have been over the entire Basque Province. Not a single
church has been burned or priest or religious molested.

George Gilmore[107]

Writing in April 1937, Peadar O'Donnell argued that trade unions
and republicans should 'unite forces and get themselves a building
open to the left ferment'; he welcomed 'signs of some united action towards this end of a Republican-Labour headquarters. It is
long overdue'.[108] O'Donnell's continuing conviction that republicanism and socialism harmoniously intersected with one another
was complemented by the republican left's view that the republican struggle in Ireland was interwoven with international progressive campaigns. The latter argument was given intriguing
expression during the Spanish civil war. Ireland contributed volunteers to both sides in the conflict,[109] and the fact that these pro-
and anti-Franco contingents were, respectively, led by Eoin O'Duffy
and Frank Ryan gave the expeditions something of the flavour of
Ireland's own civil war. While O'Duffy seems genuinely to have
convinced himself that 'the cause of Franco is the cause of Christian civilization',[110] those of his fellow citizens who supported
the Spanish republicans perceived a more domestic dimension to
the Irish battle over Spain. On 5 November 1936 a meeting, co-
ordinated by George Gilmore and Owen Sheehy-Skeffington, took
place in Dawson Street, Dublin, to expose the *Irish Independent*'s
'drive to organize, under cover of a ramp against the Spanish
government, the anti-Republican forces in Ireland.' Ernie O'Malley
presided at this republican gathering, and Peadar O'Donnell
attempted to set contemporary events in an appropriate Irish

---

[106] 6 Nov. 1936.   [107] *Evening Mail*, 17 Nov. 1936.
[108] *Irish Democrat*, 24 Apr. 1937. The Belfast-published *Irish Democrat* set out
'to express the opinions and demands of the progressive peoples' movement in our
country' (Enclosure to: Murray to O'Malley, 22 Dec. 1936, Cormac O'Malley
Papers, PP); sponsored by the Northern Ireland Socialist Party, the Republican
Congress, and the CPI, it ran from March to December 1937 (CPI, *Outline History*,
28).   [109] *Irish Press*, 14 Dec. 1936.
[110] E. O'Duffy, *Crusade in Spain* (Dublin, Phoenix, 1938), 11.

historical context: 'The *Independent* was viciously conducting a campaign to work up feeling in Ireland so that it could complete the job it had failed to do in 1913, 1916, and 1922'.[111]

As to events in Spain, the Free State opponents of Franco (based around the Republican Congress) sought to persuade their predominantly Catholic fellow citizens that the civil war was not a religious one. Gilmore returned from a visit to Spain proclaiming confidently: 'I have been over the entire Basque Province. Not a single church has been burned or priest or religious molested.'[112] As a result of Gilmore's trip a Basque priest, Father Ramon La-Borda, visited Dublin, and, speaking at a 'crowded' Gaiety Theatre on 17 January 1937, argued that the civil war 'was not religious, nor were the elections before it concerned with religion. The left wing had beaten the right with votes, and now the right was trying to beat them with guns.'[113]

The battle between left and right in the Free State was less spectacular, but was undeniably fierce. Prior to the outbreak of the Spanish conflict, Dublin socialists had found that they risked the fate of New Testament Stephen if they attempted public gatherings,[114] and the civil war did nothing to render this atmosphere more friendly. In April 1937 a Dublin meeting held under the auspices of the pro-Franco Irish Christian Front adopted resolutions calling on the government 'to banish communism completely from our social life' and demanding 'the prohibition of its propaganda or the profession of its doctrines in any shape or form in this country'.[115] Such action was not necessary, given the political powerlessness of the hard left. Atrocity stories about the nasty activities supposedly practised by Spanish communists undoubtedly did little to convert the twenty-six counties to socialism,[116] but there was no sign that such a conversion was going to occur anyway. In this, at least, the *Irish Independent*'s approach to Spain was fairly accurate: in describing its Dawson Street critics as 'a little

---

[111] *Irish Press*, 6 Nov. 1936.   [112] *Evening Mail*, 17 Nov. 1936.
[113] *Irish Times*, 18 Jan. 1937.
[114] Ibid. 14 Apr. 1936; cf. 'Acts of the Apostles' in *The New English Bible* (Oxford, OUP, 1970 edn.), 157.   [115] *Irish Press*, 5 Apr. 1937.
[116] O'Donnell himself referred to 'the national indignation' provoked in Ireland by the atrocity stories, adding that the issue in Ireland had been presented in very simple terms: 'You were either in favour of burning churches and all that or you were against burning churches and all that' (P. O'Donnell, *Salud! An Irishman in Spain* (London, Methuen, 1937), 239).

clique' it aptly identified their status. Even the sturdily optimistic O'Donnell conceded at one point that the Irish conflict over Spain was 'a rather one-sided fight'.[117]

According to O'Donnell, Irish anti-republicans were vociferous in supporting Spanish fascism, while it was Irish republicans who took up the anti-fascist cause.[118] Republicanism, perceived from the perspective of the republican left, not only involved class-struggle, but was itself tied in with international fights for freedom. Thus Frank Ryan—whose involvement in Spain has become so famous that it has been noted by observers as divergent as Eric Hobsbawm and the Pogues—[119] argued that going to Spain represented

a demonstration of the sympathy of revolutionary Ireland with the Spanish people in their fight against international fascism. . . . We want to show that there is a close bond between the democracies of Ireland and Spain. Our fight is the fight of the Spanish people, as it is of all peoples who are the victims of tyranny.[120]

In O'Donnell's view, Ryan had come to see 'Ireland's struggle being one with subject people all over the world',[121] and certainly this accords with Ryan's own vision of what he was doing in Spain. His fight was for 'human liberty': 'If I died in Spain I would die for human liberty as certainly—perhaps more certainly—than I would in Ireland today.' He felt that Ireland must be forced 'to think internationally' and that his participation in Spain's war would contribute to this process.[122] More directly, as we have seen, Ryan held that 'revolutionary Ireland' was bonded sympathetically with the Spanish anti-fascist struggle and with the wider anti-fascist battle of which this particular struggle formed a part.

Yet the truth of the matter was far more complicated. Revolutionary Ireland, in the form of the republican tradition to which Ryan pugnaciously subscribed, faced in a number of conflicting directions during these years in relation to international struggles. As Ryan's own case history amply demonstrates, these directions did not all fall neatly in line with the 'fight against international fascism', with the struggles of 'all peoples who are the victims of

---

[117] Ibid.   [118] Ibid. 239–40, 255–6.

[119] E. J. Hobsbawm, *Nations and Nationalism since 1780: Programme, Myth, Reality* (Cambridge, CUP, 1990); Pogues, 'The Sick Bed of Cuchulainn', in *Rum, Sodomy, and the Lash* (Stiff Records, 1985).

[120] Ryan, quoted in Cronin, *Ryan*, 84.   [121] Quoted ibid. 24.

[122] Quoted ibid. 102, 116.

tyranny', or with those of 'subject people all over the world'. Ryan and his fellow anti-Franco campaigners have repeatedly been celebrated.[123] Yet the importance of Ryan's experiences in relation to his own argument regarding the international connections of 'revolutionary Ireland' lies in precisely the opposite direction from that which he himself sought to stress. Rather than demonstrating, as Ryan himself argued, an automatic bond between Irish separatist enthusiasm and international fights for freedom, Ryan's tragic Spanish and post-Spanish career in fact illustrates the simplistic, inadequate nature of such an argument. In 1936 Ryan had led a body of Irish volunteers who joined the International Brigades; in March 1937 he briefly returned to Ireland, having been wounded the previous month at Jarama; he arrived back in Spain in June 1937; the following March he was captured by Italian troops and imprisoned; in June 1938 he was transferred to Burgos Central Prison for trial on capital charges; there was considerable agitation and intercession on his behalf; and in July 1940 he was escorted to the French border by Spanish police and representatives of the German intelligence agency, Abwehr II.

He was taken via Paris to Berlin, where he was reintroduced to a republican colleague, Sean Russell. Russell had been engaged in talks with the German Foreign Office regarding IRA–German cooperation. His transport back to Ireland was being arranged by Abwehr II. Ryan and Russell set out as passengers on a U-boat which was scheduled to deposit them on the Dingle peninsula on 15 August. On 14 August, however, Russell died, apparently as a result of a perforated duodenal ulcer. Ryan decided to return to Germany. In January 1943 he suffered a stroke. In the autumn he was briefly hospitalized because of a stomach ulcer; his health continued to deteriorate, and in January 1944 he collapsed following an air raid on Berlin. He spent two further weeks in hospital and then went to a Dresden sanatorium. He moved back to Berlin at the end of May 1944, but was soon very ill again, and died on 10 June, in Dresden, of pneumonia.[124]

There was considerable irony in Ryan's having gone to Spain

---

[123] For recent examples, see: M. Longley, 'In Memory of Charles Donnelly', in *Gorse Fires* (London, Martin Secker and Warburg, 1991), 48; E. Egan, 'Ideals Indecently Buried', *Fortnight*, 318 (June 1993), 28–9.

[124] Biographical details from: Cronin, *Ryan*; F. Stuart, 'Frank Ryan in Germany', *The Bell* 16/2 (Nov. 1950) and 16/3 (Dec. 1950); author's interviews with Francis Stuart, Nora Harkin, Sheila Humphreys.

to fight against 'international fascism', only to end up as a 'distinguished guest' in Germany, 'drawing double rations'.[125] The irony appears rather more acute when one considers statements such as that made by Ryan in 1941 that there might arise a situation in which he would 'go as a liaison' from the Germans to de Valera.[126] This certainly sits awkwardly with Peadar O'Donnell's verdict that

All serious Irish revolutionaries saw Ireland's fight for freedom as one with the world struggle of subject nations and oppressed peoples everywhere. . . . It was along this road Frank Ryan travelled to reach his decision to go to Spain where the popularly elected government of the people was under attack by fascist forces.[127]

Eric Hobsbawm has suggested that while from 'the point of view of the antifascist left someone like Frank Ryan was difficult to understand', from 'the point of view of traditional Irish republicanism Ryan could be seen as someone pursuing a consistent policy'.[128] But neither this, nor O'Donnell's thesis, captures the basic difficulty with Ryan's position. An examination of the Russell–Ryan connection clarifies the issue. Ryan had argued that it was natural—indeed, necessary—that the Irish republican tradition be represented in the fight against Franco; hostility toward tyranny and oppression was, in his view, implicit within Irish republicanism, and so republicans in Ireland would naturally have an affinity with the international fight against fascism. Sean Russell's neo-Fenian, conspiratorial opportunism, which will be addressed in more detail in the following chapter, was undiluted by considerations such as those which had taken Ryan to Spain. To Russell's mind, England was at war with Germany and so Germany became a potential and legitimate ally. It is in the tension between these two attitudes that the painful irony of Ryan's position is to be

---

[125] Ryan to Kerney, 6 Nov. 1941, 'Frank Ryan, Sean Russell', Dept. of Foreign Affairs, Secretary's Office Files, NA A20/4.

[126] Ibid. Francis Stuart, with whom Ryan became well acquainted while both were in Berlin, recalls an incident which further raises questions concerning the extent and nature of Ryan's discussions with the authorities who provided his double rations: 'I remember once walking down to the university where I was teaching. [Ryan] accompanied me, and shortly before we parted he said, "You know . . . if Germany wins the war I'll be a member of the next Irish government". And, to some extent, it seemed to me some sort of veiled threat' (Francis Stuart, interview with the author, Dublin, 24 Feb. 1987); cf. G. Elborn, *Francis Stuart: A Life* (Dublin, Raven Arts, 1990), 157.   [127] Foreword in Cronin, *Ryan*, 11–12.

[128] *Nations and Nationalism*, 149.

discerned. For the Ryan–O'Donnell argument that revolutionary, republican Ireland fitted neatly into the paradigm of international opposition to tyranny was flatly contradicted by the activities of the influential Sean Russell. Russell's German alliance—and, less spectacularly, Ryan's contemplation of playing an intermediary role between the fascists and Ireland—both scupper the simplistic thesis that Irish separatist republicanism should automatically be considered within the framework of the international fight against oppression.

Sheila Humphreys commented on the intimacy of the latter-day Ryan–Russell relationship, suggesting in explanation that 'Ireland's freedom came first with the two of them'.[129] Ryan himself stressed the closeness of the relationship: 'He [Sean Russell] and I were always good personal friends—and never more so than during his last days. He died in my arms.'[130] But, sadly for Ryan, Russell's political approach in fact demolished the view that the Irish republican cause was one automatically in harmony with the cause of human liberty. Separatists in Ireland, both in their domestic and in their international outlook, could adopt policies which flatly contradicted the notion of human liberty. Michael O'Riordan has written of the Irish International Brigade volunteers' 'convictions on the necessary relationship between the issue of the national liberation of their own country and the cause of international solidarity'.[131] This was precisely the construction placed by O'Donnell and Ryan upon the Spanish episode. In fact, as Russell's and, to an extent, Ryan's careers amply demonstrate, there was no such 'necessary' connection. Irish republicanism could, on this as on other matters, face in any one of a number of differing directions when it came to the question of human liberty.

In Ireland during 1937 there emerged another crucial case study in which republican socialists found themselves diverging starkly from the ambitions of fellow Irish nationalists. The orthodox culture against which the republican left protested was most powerfully occupied by Fianna Fáil. It appears that it was in the summer of 1936 that the detailed drafting of a new constitution began;[132] a draft

---

[129] Interview with the author, Dublin, 26 Feb. 1987.

[130] Ryan to Kerney, 14 Jan. 1942, 'Frank Ryan, Sean Russell', Dept. of Foreign Affairs, Secretary's Office Files, NA A20/4.

[131] *Connolly Column* (Dublin, New Books, 1979), 63.

[132] S. Faughnan, 'The Jesuits and the Drafting of the Irish Constitution of 1937', *IHS* 26/101 (May 1988), 80.

was published on 1 May 1937 and the constitution was approved by the Dáil in June, passed by referendum in July, and effective from 29 December.[133] Despite considerable advice as to what it should contain, the constitution was definitely de Valera's,[134] serving, as Dermot Keogh has put it, to embody his 'ideals and ideology'.[135] John Murphy has drawn attention to the hybrid nature of this document, one which 'attempted to give expression to two very different notions—the liberal and secular tradition of parliamentary democracy *and* the concept of a state grounded upon Catholic social teaching'.[136] This, indeed, provides a useful starting point for an assessment of the relationship between socialist republican dissidence and the mainstream political culture at this time. Where the 1922 constitution had been 'a typical liberal-democratic document', suitable for a country 'of any religious complexion', its 1937 replacement was distinctly Catholic.[137] De Valera's justification—that '93 per cent. of the people in this part of Ireland and 75 per cent. of the people of Ireland as a whole' were Catholic in allegiance and philosophy—[138] reflected a twenty-six-county pragmatism which contradicted his irredentist aspirations with regard to Northern Ireland. Seán O'Faoláin's (1939) biography of de Valera noted shrewdly that 'no northerner can possibly like such features of southern life, as at present constituted, as its pervasive clerical control; its censorship; its Gaelic revival; its isolationist economic policy', and also observed that

whatever pious aspirations or resolutions may be found in the constitution of Eire about religious tolerance it is a matter of common knowledge to those who care to enquire, or even observe, that the Protestant in the south has as little chance of getting his fair share of public appointments as the Catholic in the north.[139]

But the point was that the nationalist tradition from which de Valera drew sustenance had indeed gained much definition,

---

[133] R. Fanning, *Independent Ireland* (Dublin, Helicon, 1983), 117.

[134] Faughnan, 'The Jesuits', 102.

[135] D. Keogh, *The Vatican, the Bishops, and Irish Politics 1919–1939* (Cambridge, CUP, 1986), 220.

[136] J. A. Murphy, *Ireland in the Twentieth Century* (Dublin, Gill and Macmillan, 1975), 90.

[137] J. Whyte, *Church and State in Modern Ireland, 1923–79* (Dublin, Gill and Macmillan, 1984; 1st edn. 1971), 51–6.

[138] *Dáil Debates* 67: 1890; the 1936 Census recorded that out of a total Free State population of 2,968,420 there were 2,773,920 Catholics (93.4%) (Eire/Ireland, *Census of Population 1936*, vol. iii, 3).

[139] *De Valera* (Harmondsworth, Penguin, 1939), 155–6.

momentum, and meaning from its Catholic identification. It is undeniable that this cut across republican hopes for a harmonious all-Ireland state, a contradiction rendered all the more painful and unhelpful by the 1937 constitution's simultaneous claim over the territory of Northern Ireland. Indeed, while Sean MacBride appears to have been impressed by the document,[140] the republican left protested against it on exactly this issue of sectarian bias. On 22 May 1937 the *Irish Democrat* carried a Republican Congress manifesto dealing with de Valera's draft constitution. Signed by O'Donnell and Ryan, it stated that republicans were opposed to the concept of 'a state or a semi-state church' and were also aware 'that partition will not be overcome unless the terms Catholic and Protestant are merged in the common name of Irishman'. To 'set up the Roman Catholic hierarchy in any position of political privilege except what devotion to the independence of the country and to the general democratic struggle may earn them', the manifesto continued, would be to perpetuate partition. Unwittingly, however, the Congress enthusiasts had touched on precisely the point which undermined their would-be non-sectarian critique. It was precisely because the Catholic church had, during the modern period, been associated with nationalist aspirations and experience that it should be considered so natural by many Irish nationalists to accord it a special place in their vision of Irishness. Devotion 'to the independence of the country' was indeed a quality which the Catholic church in Ireland had a distinctive ability to claim. Thus, even in attempting to present a non-sectarian approach, the republican left indicated the very obstacle which blocked their path in this respect: the overwhelmingly confessional nature of modern Irish political allegiance.

The socialist republican response to the constitution provides an index of other differences between this radical version of republicanism and de Valera's Fianna Fáil-ism. The 1937 document, for example, reflected de Valera's instinctive masculinism,[141] and the O'Donnell/Ryan critique noted that the guarantee to women of equal rights and opportunities—'stated so clearly in the 1916

---

[140] Murphy, *Ireland in the Twentieth Century*, 96; Cronin, *Ryan*, 175.

[141] R. F. Foster, *Modern Ireland 1600–1972* (London, Allen Lane, 1988), 544; Murphy, *Ireland in the Twentieth Century*, 91; O. D. Edwards, *Eamon de Valera* (Cardiff, Univ. of Wales Press, 1987), 32. For protests regarding the position of women under the constitution, see Files of the Dept. of the Taoiseach, NA S 9880; cf. K. Clarke, *Revolutionary Woman: Kathleen Clarke 1878–1972—An Autobiography* (Dublin, O'Brien, 1991), 218–9.

proclamation'—was not included in the draft document published on 1 May: 'Republicans demand that it be openly declared in any constitution for the Irish Republic that equal pay and opportunities for women in industry shall be assured'. A more central plank of republican socialist thinking was reflected in the following passage, also from the Congress manifesto:

The poor of Ireland will receive this constitution with increasing opposition. Within the hearts and minds of the common people of this country the breaking of the connection included the supplanting of the traitor minority who shut them out from land, drove them into exile, and impoverished them at home. The 1916 proclamation was always read to promise just such a triumph of the poor over the small group of rich men who trafficked in their misery. This draft constitution would, if adopted, sound the death-knell of their dreams. For private property is raised here almost to the dignity of a sacrament. . . . Landless men, jobless, under-paid insecure harassed bread winners are guaranteed only their poverty. Tenement dwellers are guaranteed only the smelly over-crowding and the rack renting. The articles on private property are the holdfasts to which the Irish people are to be shackled so that the people's enemies may feel secure.

It was no surprise, argued the manifesto, that there had been no 'national rejoicing' over the draft constitution: 'It does not restore the Republic, but on the contrary it attacks the people's charter, the 1916 proclamation'.[142]

This passage clearly delineates the nature of socialist republican thinking at the end of our period. The myths of the republic were still zealously adhered to, and were still given a (spuriously) radical reading. The 'triumph of the poor' remained an integral part of the left republican vision but, as we saw at an earlier stage of our argument, such a reading of 1916–23 republicanism is too simplistic to stand up to serious scrutiny. Indeed, as the Congress's marginal dissidence within de Valera's Ireland demonstrates, most nationalists rejected the O'Donnellite thesis; the identification of class conflict as the essential dynamic of the struggle for independence still failed to convince most of the nationalist (or, indeed, the republican) faithful.

More broadly, the retention by O'Donnell, Ryan, and their comrades of a strict republican paradigm is itself worthy of

---

[142] *Irish Democrat*, 22 May 1937.

comment. It has repeatedly been shown during this study that the republican left offered a significantly different version of politics from that of their non-socialist colleagues within the republican movement. In terms of their historical analysis, of their current policies, of their programmatic ambitions, and of the republic which they ultimately envisaged, the O'Donnellites represented a distinctive faction within the republican family. But despite their divergence from much republican orthodoxy, and despite their attention to underlying economic and social dynamics, the republican left retained the unbending, all-Ireland, separatist framework which so persistently characterized and limited contemporary nationalist thinking. The mystique of an uncompromised republic continued to haunt, to dazzle, to blur the vision of even those atypical figures who had challenged much of republican orthodoxy with a socially rooted critique. Thus, for example, O'Donnell and Ryan were able to employ undiluted republican rhetoric a decade and a half after the mythic period which their imaginations still inhabited:

If this [1937 draft] constitution had been a call to the people to redeclare the Republic and set up a national assembly to organize and govern it then Ireland would have gone gay. . . . The argument, however, is not that the constitution proclaims the Republic but that it ends the treaty. Men did not die to end the treaty but to defend the Republic, and not merely to defend the Republic but to undo the conquest.[143]

Such tub-thumping, integrity-of-the-republic rhetoric is a useful reminder of the purist republican framework within which figures such as Ryan and O'Donnell continued to work. They were keen to reinterpret republican mythology, not to reject it.

The refusal of most Irish nationalists to be convinced by this reinterpretation condemned republican socialists to marginal impotence. De Valera's non-socialist non-republic was endorsed by popular approval; the republican socialist alternative merely represented the views of a minority rebelling against a society which they were unable to recreate in their own image. But the intellectual deficiencies of the O'Donnellite position are even further uncovered on consideration of what it shared with the wider nationalist outlook. For socialist republicans unequivocally shared with their non-socialist colleagues the paradigm of an all-island,

---

[143] Ibid.

entirely separate Irish republic. That this owed more to romantic sentiment than to serious analysis was evident even at those moments when the republican left tried to present its most Protestant-friendly face. Ryan and O'Donnell's qualification about Catholic/nationalist identification unwittingly reflected the problems in assuming an all-Ireland national framework: even when they attempted non-sectarian poses they hinted at the confessionally divided reality.

The Catholic, Gaelicist, separatist qualities of Irish republicanism rendered the creed (at best) distinctly unappealing to most Irish Protestants during these years. Like other republicans, those of the left were intent on co-opting unionists into a nation and a state against their repeatedly expressed will to the contrary. This calls into question the assumption entertained by the O'Donnellite left that they were fighting a struggle for human liberty. As we have seen, such a thesis was extremely shaky in relation to wider international conflicts. But it was also highly questionable in an Irish context, unless one assumed that island and nation were coextensive, that Irish nationalism was a liberating, progressive force, and that unionists should automatically be denied the right to political choice. The contentious nature of such assumptions required both that their adherents should understand the position of those with whom they disagreed, and also that some convincing, empirically sturdy arguments should be offered in defence of the uncomplicated nationalist paradigm. As has been shown, interwar republican socialists in fact demonstrated a marked lack of comprehension on the subject of unionist attitudes and cultures. What O'Donnellites shared with other members of the republican family, therefore, was a questionable, paradigmatic assumption regarding a united, independent Ireland. Where they overlapped with other republicans, they were on intellectually shaky foundations; where they diverged from their fellow republicans, they found themselves in a marginalized, powerless minority. Viewed in this context, Peadar O'Donnell's latter-day admission of defeat—'I never was on the winning side in any damn thing ever I did'—[144] acknowledges a monumental lack of success at which one should not, perhaps, be entirely surprised.

[144] Speech in Belfast, 7 Apr. 1984.

Conclusion: The Myth of
Irish Socialist Republicanism

THE IRA'S BRITISH BOMBING CAMPAIGN

The organization in Britain is now as perfect as we can make
it. They are just awaiting orders.

Sean Russell (September 1938)[1]

The government of the Republic of Ireland, satisfied with the
prosecution of the war against Britain and with the growing
resistance of the people of this country to the British occupation of Irish territory, demand the continuity of the active
support of all our people so that they may attain the national
objective without further delay.

IRA Radio Broadcast (December 1939)[2]

The IRA's militaristic philosophy was given virtually undiluted
expression at the end of the 1930s following the rise to power
within the organization of the inveterate conspirator, Sean Russell.
Possessed of a long-term paramilitary pedigree,[3] Russell represented the incarnation of uncompromising physical-force republicanism, and it is in this connection that he was significant during
the 1930s. As early as 1936, he had been intriguing with the influential Clan na Gael figure, Joseph McGarrity, about the possibility of 'operations in England'.[4] Russell's tendency to assume
unauthorized powers and to ignore organizational procedure led
to his being court-martialled and suspended by the IRA in January 1937.[5] But his scheme—'a policy of aggressive action in Britain',

---

[1] To McGarrity, 21 Sept. 1938, McGarrity Papers, NLI MS 17485.
[2] Copy, Dec. 1939, Files of the Dept. of the Taoiseach, NA S 11564 A.
[3] For biographical details, see S. Cronin, *Frank Ryan: The Search for the Republic* (Dublin, Repsol, 1980), 169 and R. F. Foster, *Modern Ireland* 1600–1972
(London, Allen Lane, 1988), 548.
[4] Russell to McGarrity, 31 [*sic*] Nov. 1936, McGarrity Papers, NLI MS 17,485.
[5] Ibid. 29 Jan. 1937; Cronin, *Ryan*, 178; J. B. Bell, *The Secret Army: The IRA
1916–79* (Swords, Poolbeg, 1989; 1st edn. 1970), 131.

as one of his colleagues later put it—was approved at an IRA Convention in the spring of 1938, with Russell himself becoming chief of staff.[6]

Funded with United States republican money,[7] the campaign proceeded. On 8 December 1938, the IRA's Army Council was invested with ultimate republican authority when it took over 'the government of the Republic of Ireland' from the Executive Council of Dáil Éireann (the republican body claiming to represent the legitimate governmental authority originally invested in the Second Dáil).[8] Its legitimist credentials unquestionable, the IRA embarked on an ill-conceived and amateurishly implemented bombing spree in Britain. In January 1939 the British Foreign Secretary, Lord Halifax, received an ultimatum from the IRA Army Council, demanding that the British government signify within four days its intention to effect 'the withdrawal of all British armed forces stationed in Ireland'.[9] There followed a series of IRA-created explosions: on 24 July 1939 the British Home Secretary, Samuel Hoare, informed the House of Commons that 127 IRA incidents had taken place in London and the provinces since January. It was clear, he argued, 'that in the early chapters of the campaign the attempt was intended against property and not against human life'. None the less, he continued, 'during the period of these outrages one man was killed in Manchester, one man lost his eye in Piccadilly . . . and 55 persons have been seriously or less seriously injured'.[10]

The most horrific incident was yet to occur: on 25 August 1939 a bomb in Coventry killed five people and injured many more.[11] Although the campaign trickled over into 1940, the Coventry episode stands as its natural epitaph: the person planting the bomb had panicked and left it in an unintended and crowded part of the city; the incident revived anti-republican feeling in Britain; and two people—neither of whom had planted the bomb—were

---

[6] S. Hayes, 'My Strange Story', *The Bell*, 17/4 (July 1951), 12; T. P. Coogan, *The IRA* (London, Fontana, 1987; 1st edn. 1970), 155–6; Cronin, *Ryan*, 178.

[7] Russell to McGarrity, 1 Dec. 1938, McGarrity Papers, NLI, MS 17,485; cf. Copy of IRA Radio Broadcast, Dec. 1939, Files of the Dept. of the Taoiseach, NA S 11564 A.   [8] *Wolfe Tone Weekly*, 17 Dec. 1938.

[9] Coogan, *The IRA*, 164–5.

[10] *House of Commons Official Report*, 350/1049–50.

[11] *Times*, 26 Aug. 1939; Coogan, *The IRA*, 167.

subsequently hanged in connection with the incident.[12] The trag-
edy, ineffectiveness, and farce associated with the campaign should
not, however, cause it to be dismissed lightly. Responses to the
Coventry episode reflected a persistent theme in modern Anglo-
Irish affairs: the capacity for popular mobilization in Ireland on
behalf of those punished for republican activities—activities which
would not in themselves have elicited popular support. Thus in a
letter of 22 December 1939 the Department of the Taoiseach was
informed that Cavan County Council had unanimously adopted a
motion stating 'that the Government of Eire is earnestly requested
to work for the pardon of the two men who are sentenced to be
hanged in connection with charges arising out of explosions at
Coventry'.[13] In the same month Westport Urban District Council
had passed a resolution calling on de Valera and Chamberlain 'to
secure the reprieve of two Irishmen recently condemned to death
in England'. The resolution continued by asserting 'that when such
executions take place, they do not achieve peace'; they would
prove 'a cause of bitterness and combat which both ministers should
understand it is in the interests of their people to avoid at the
present time'.[14]

More importantly, the bombing campaign also provides valuable
insights into a particular kind of republican mind. Sean Russell is
the crucial figure here, for although Joseph McGarrity played a
seed-sowing role,[15] the British episode would not have occurred
without the energetic activity of Russell, the physical force enthusiasts' 'idol'.[16] Russell's mentality is indeed fascinating. His single-
mindedness and sincerity struck numerous contemporaries.[17] Peadar
O'Donnell commented in March 1939 on Russell's 'consistency',
but (significantly) added that he 'had no brains'.[18] Russell certainly

[12] Bell, *Secret Army*, 161–2; Coogan, *The IRA*, 167, 171; on the trial relating to the Coventry explosion, see J. L. D. Fairfield (ed.), *The Trial of Peter Barnes and Others: The IRA Coventry Explosion of 1939* (London, Notable British Trials Series, 1953).
[13] Reilly to Smith, 22 Dec. 1939, Files of the Dept. of the Taoiseach, NA S 11575 A.
[14] *Minutes* of Meeting of Westport Urban District Council (18 Dec. 1939), ibid.
[15] Russell to McGarrity, 31 [*sic*] Nov. 1936, McGarrity Papers, NLI MS 17485.
[16] Hayes, 'My Strange Story', 12.
[17] Ibid. 13; Francis Stuart, interview with the author, Dublin, 24 Feb. 1987; G. Gilmore, *The Irish Republican Congress* (Cork, CWC, 1978; 1st edn. 1935), 25; U. MacEoin (ed.), *Survivors*, (Dublin, Argenta, 1987; 1st edn. 1980), 148, 391.
[18] O'Doherty to McGarrity, 22 Mar. 1939, McGarrity Papers, NLI MS 17472.

displayed appalling political judgement. He predicted that the bombing campaign would either force de Valera to 'take his stand' with the IRA (thereby restoring 'the 1920–1 position'), or lead him to 'interfere' with the army, in which case the 'people would rise in anger against him and rally round' the IRA (again, restoring the 1920–1 situation).[19] Such thinking was wildly inaccurate: de Valera did 'interfere' with the IRA, but the people emphatically did not 'rally round' the army as a result.

The point here is that Russell's preoccupation with his own neo-Fenian conception of republicanism had blinded him to the weight of opinion which backed the very different nationalism espoused by de Valera. Despite the enormous gulf which now separated the IRA from Fianna Fáil, Russell still considered it possible that de Valera might ally with the practitioners of the bombing campaign. Furthermore, it was unimaginable to Russell that de Valera could oppose the IRA without incurring the wrath of the people. Preoccupation with his own conspiratorial culture had sealed his mind, leaving him entirely ignorant of the true marginalization of the late-1930s IRA.

Russell was not alone in exhibiting this solipsistic quality of mind. In August 1940 representatives of the republican group Coras na Poblachta wrote to de Valera and enclosed a document which called for a truce between the government and the IRA; it stated that 'two groups of Irishmen professing the same noble aim, the establishment of the Irish Republic, are in armed conflict. If these groups are sincere there can be no real obstacle to their unity'.[20] To have failed to recognize the enormous differences which had, by 1940, emerged between Fianna Fáil and the IRA required precisely the inward-looking quality of mind which has been identified earlier in our argument as characteristic of 1930s republicanism. Fianna Fáil had proscribed the IRA in 1936 and had, in June 1939, suppressed the army 'in the public interest'.[21] De Valera had, for years, shown exasperation with the IRA, and to imagine that there could be 'no real obstacle to their unity' involved a stubborn and ignorant persistence. The point is this: to the republicans in

---

[19] Hayes, 'My Strange Story', 12–13.

[20] Fitzpatrick/Kennedy to de Valera, 22 Aug. 1940, Files of the Dept. of the Taoiseach, NA S 12069.

[21] *Unlawful Organization (Suppression) Order, 1939* [23 Jun. 1939], Dept. of the Taoiseach: Govt. and Cabinet Minutes, NA G3/3.

Coras na Poblachta it was unimaginable that their commitment to the idealized republic could have become marginalized. Their 1940 document reflected the conviction that 'the Irish people' somehow shared the organization's own zealous vision. With reference to the proposed unity between Fianna Fáil and the IRA, the document declared that, 'the Irish people have the right to demand that a truce shall be declared between them which will enable the whole nation to march forward to the achievement of its full rights'.[22] Content to recognize only their own political logic, Coras na Poblachta failed to appreciate certain crucial political realities: that Fianna Fáil had adopted an irreconcilably different version of nationalist advance; that, in doing so, they had taken most twenty-six-county nationalists with them; and that a sizeable minority of the people of the island refused to be defined as part of the proposed nation at all. Taken together, these considerations dealt a fatal blow to unreconstructed republican ambitions.

In September 1940 Sean MacBride wrote to de Valera, passing on proposals from 'some members of the Old IRA'. The proposals were that the IRA should suspend its activities—including the British bombing campaign—and that the government should 'instruct police to suspend all activities against IRA, to suspend sentences against IRA in prison, and to gradually release prisoners'. A conference was to be initiated between the army and the government 'to explore possibilities of active cooperation towards [the] Republic'. MacBride assured de Valera that 'in case any formal guarantees are required' he had 'been given to understand that these would be forthcoming'.[23] Again, therefore, there was a republican proposal of combined Fianna Fáil and IRA activity directed towards the republic. Despite repeated and unmistakable signs to the contrary, including MacBride's own conversations with de Valera,[24] republicans still failed to acknowledge that their approach differed enormously from, and was openly rejected by, the dominant nationalist culture. Rather than examining the true

[22] Fitzpatrick/Kennedy to de Valera, 22 Aug. 1940, Files of the Dept. of the Taoiseach, NA S 12069.

[23] MacBride to de Valera, 5 Sept. 1940, Files of the Dept. of the Taoiseach, NA S 12069.

[24] Referring to the MacBride/de Valera conversations discussed earlier in this book, MacBride himself stated that de Valera's 'general attitude' had been 'that the IRA should disband itself' (MacBride to McGarrity, 19 Oct. 1933, McGarrity Papers, NLI MS 17456).

range of Irish political aspirations and practices, they preferred instead to look inward and then, wrongly, to imagine that their own views were substantially shared by 'the Irish people'.

If Russell was not unique in his solipsistic approach, he none the less remains the vital figure in terms of the late 1930s bombing episode. From the perspective of the republican left, Russellite neo-Fenianism was a depressing phenomenon. As George Gilmore recognized, 'Sean Russell was not interested in "political" questions. His sole interest was in armaments'.[25] Again, therefore, the centre of republican gravity demonstrated the marginal position occupied by socialist republicans. The O'Donnellite attempt to draw republicanism away from its militaristic focus had failed, with Russell's late-1930s binge of violence providing grisly proof of the failure.

At the heart of Russell's thinking was the capacity to assume the existence of circumstances more convenient than reality: starting from the certainty of his own vision, he went on to create a fictional account of the wider political world. Thus he felt able, in writing to the German ambassador to the United States in October 1936, to style himself as the 'Special Envoy of Ireland to the US' and to speak as a representative of the 'government of the Irish Republic'. In the same letter he wrote that the Free State government 'depends for its very existence on the British parliament whose puppet it is',[26] thereby ignoring the fact that the Free State government in reality depended 'for its very existence' on the support of the Free State people. In a sense, such attitudes reflected a distorted optimism; shortly before the disastrously inept bombing campaign Russell informed McGarrity that it was 'very clear' to him that reasonable success would be achieved.[27] Such woefully inaccurate prophecies smack of absurdity, but the most important point to stress about Russell and the philosophy which he embodied is their deadly seriousness, both in terms of intention and of result. Rumpf and Hepburn are right to state that the bombing campaign marked the IRA's return 'to a traditional policy

[25] Gilmore, *The Irish Republican Congress* (1978 edn.), 25.

[26] Russell to Luther, 25 Oct. 1936, McGarrity Papers, NLI MS 17485.

[27] Russell to McGarrity, 21 Sept. 1938, McGarrity Papers, NLI MS 17485. In fact, there was very little clarity concerning the precise way in which the bombings were supposed to achieve republican objectives; cf. M. L. R. Smith, 'The Role of the Military Instrument in Irish Republican Strategic Thinking: an Evolutionary Analysis', Ph.D. thesis (London, 1991), 152.

of uncomplicated physical force against "England" ', but it is perhaps more vital to emphasize that those within the IRA who orchestrated this campaign had never *departed* from uncomplicated physical force. Russell had remained consistently unimpressed by non-military proposals,[28] exemplifying an anti-political quality of mind which was shared by many within the early-twentieth-century IRA. If Russell's IRA at the end of the 1930s was one which was returning from the wilderness of political experimentation—the Saor Eire, Republican Congress, and Cumann Poblachta na h-Eireann experiments—then Russell himself personified a brand of republicanism to which such experimentation was entirely alien. His was the politics of absolute conviction in a self-legitimized republican crusade, of right and wrong, of straightforward (paramilitary) means by which to achieve an objective which was held to be unquestionably valid. Not all IRA people shared Russell's undiluted militarism; even by the standards of extremism his was an extreme position. But, as already noted, physical force was fundamental to the army's approach. According to official IRA logic, indeed, Russell's neo-Fenian approach seems anything but extraordinary. His bombing campaign was the natural, if revolting, offspring of a philosophy which declared force of arms to be its primary method of struggle.

Though intellectually feeble, the solipsistic approach characteristic of Russell, and indeed of other contemporary republicans, plainly had attractions for its adherents. The self-validating process offered psychological rewards in terms of its comforting certainties and simplicities. Intransigence and simplification—two persistent themes within twentieth-century republican thinking—reinforced the self-propelling potential of 1930s republicanism. Those who remained in the extra-constitutional, post-revolutionary republican rump were factional zealots, guardians of a faith which the majority had rejected. The only way to sustain any kind of momentum was to build a political vision based entirely on one's own tiny culture. Those whose passion remained concentrated on the idealized republic could only continue undisturbed in the faith by imputing to the wider public their own peculiar enthusiasm.

---

[28] E. Rumpf and A. C. Hepburn, *Nationalism and Socialism in Twentieth-Century Ireland* (Liverpool, Liverpool Univ. Press, 1977), 94; Cronin, *Ryan*, 173; P. Byrne, *Memories of the Republican Congress* (London, Connolly Association, n.d.), 3.

Their political arguments were entirely self-sustaining: they simply imputed to 'the Irish people' ideas and aspirations which they themselves fervently held. Since they had no intention of asking what the Irish people actually thought and wanted, they were able to proceed unchallenged in their own delusions.

There was, therefore, a stark contrast between their 'imagined political community',[29] which supposedly held to the faith, and the real, republican, cliquish community by which the faith was in fact maintained. The nation supposedly consisted of the former; in practice it extended only to the latter. Thus, for republican zealots in this period, self effectively became confused with nation; when describing the supposed qualities, ideals, and aspirations of the Irish nation they were in fact merely describing their own. There was a solipsistic assumption that self was the only thing really existent, that the world beyond the republican cult was not valid, and did not, therefore, require serious attention and appraisal. This approach proved self-defeating within the twenty-six counties. The state achieved a solid and practical legitimacy based on the twin foundations of popular sanction and effective independence. Thus republicanism was undermined through the successful adaptation of the very themes which its own rhetoric so loudly proclaimed: independence and the will of the people.

Russell's campaign reflected no grasp either of political realities in Northern Ireland. The roots of partition were simply not understood. Instead of any serious analysis there was offered only violence; the IRA simply attempted to bully a path towards British withdrawal and held, simplistically, that this would result in the successful reunification of the island in a new republic. Again, the reassuring simplicity of republican thinking enabled figures such as Russell to evade the more awkward and complex aspects of political reality. That mainstream nationalists themselves still retained irredentist aspirations was unfortunate in that it encouraged unrealistic republican hopes. More important, however, was the southern state's practical acquiescence in partition. That de Valera's constitution claimed Northern Irish territory undeniably helped to sustain an unhealthy irredentism; that his state effectively adopted a partitionist mentality both rendered the constitutional claim rather

---

[29] B. Anderson, *Imagined Communities: Reflections on the Origin and Spread of Nationalism* (London, Verso, 1983), 15.

less than consistent, and also served further to undermine the Russellite republican position. As we have seen, Russell's hopes that people would rally to the IRA flag (with or without de Valera) reflected his complete misreading of popular attitudes in independent Ireland. Yet again, the republican mind looked only in on itself, failing to acknowledge the nature and implications of wider political conditions and cultures.

The inward-looking approach of republicans in this period is brought into even sharper relief when one examines contemporary governmental responses to republicanism. There emerges a clearly defined contrast between the vision held by republicans (based purely on an imputation of their own assumptions to the wider population) and the outlook characteristic of the government (based more firmly on an appreciation both of popular opinion and of Irish political complexity). Thus, while an IRA radio broadcast of 1939 claimed to speak on behalf of the 'Government of the Republic of Ireland' and asserted that the IRA Army Council's ultimatum to Lord Halifax had been given 'on behalf of the Irish people',[30] the actual government (elected by the actual people) looked on with hostility. The IRA's activities during these years were recorded at some length.[31] One such catalogue listed the army's actions with a certain sneer: 'The following detailed list gives the major crimes and offences against the public safety during the decade 1935 to 1945 of the organization which has assumed the title "IRA" '. It went on to give details of many IRA activities under the headings: 'murders', 'attempted murders', 'attacks on the defence forces or its members', 'attacks on the Garda Siochana or its members', 'attacks on witnesses', 'attacks on civilians', 'armed robberies', 'discoveries of arms dumps', 'cases of arson', 'cases of kidnapping', 'cases of drilling, arms instruction classes, establishing armed camps', and 'cases of association with foreign agents during the war'.[32]

The governmental philosophy which lay behind this cataloguing of gruesome IRA achievements can be deduced from a 1940s memorandum dealing specifically with the republican army. Highlighting the IRA's self-referential approach, the memorandum asserted:

---

[30] Copy of IRA Radio Broadcast, Dec. 1939, Files of the Dept. of the Taoiseach, NA S 11564 A.   [31] See e.g. ibid. 'List of IRA Activities, 1932–41'.
[32] Ibid. 'List of IRA Activities, 1935–45'.

Under the cloak of a profession of patriotism it [the IRA] is aiming at absolute power. It rejects not merely the authority of the government but the whole idea of democracy. It recognizes no standard of right and wrong except its will; and its contempt for the institutions of the state is excelled only by its contempt for the ballot-box.

The government's attitude to the IRA conspiracy had, continued the memorandum, 'never been in doubt'. From the moment it took office, the government had 'made it clear that it was prepared to tolerate no other governmental authority and no other army than the government and the army of the state'. Referring to the mid-1930s, the memorandum stated that:

it had become apparent that those who had refused to respond to the appeal to give up their arms had resolved to use these arms to try and enforce their demands in defiance of the expressed will of the people and that there was in existence an unlawful organization which refused to recognize the right of the people to choose their own governors and had appropriated the title of the IRA so that it might benefit by its historic prestige.

The 1939 bombing campaign was condemned as 'insensate folly': 'a number of acts of terrorism in England directed not against the British forces but against the civilian population, some of whom, women included, lost their lives'.[33]

A memorandum to de Valera in relation to the IRA's 1939 British campaign referred to 'the strong feeling of the Ulster majority upon certain matters in regard to which the feeling among our people is correspondingly strong in the contrary direction'. The memorandum, contained in Sean MacEntee's papers, enjoined de Valera to point out

how this difference of viewpoint accentuates the difficulties of securing a solution of the partition problem which will be acceptable to both parties. . . . Emphasize the consequent lesson that only a well-considered and judicious plan, consistently pursued and authoritatively directed, can attain to such a solution. Repeat what has already been said on several occasions, that a campaign based on violence offers no hope in this direction.[34]

[33] Ibid. 1–4, 'Memorandum on the Policy of the Government with Regard to Offences Against the State'.
[34] 'Memo to Eamon de Valera regarding attitude to be taken up in connection with IRA outrages in GB in 1939', MacEntee Papers, ADUCD P67/529.

It is debatable just how 'well-considered' or 'judicious' Fianna Fáil's own 1930s approach toward Northern Ireland actually was: the mixture of Catholic, Gaelicist, twenty-six-county nationalism with all-island irredentist rhetoric and sentiment might be thought a rather ill-considered and poorly judged political legacy. But such passages as the above do certainly draw attention to the distance which now separated the party from IRA zealotry and paramilitarism. Fianna Fáil's nationalism had come, in practice, to reflect both popular opinion and the limitations of hard-line republican ideology. During the 1930s the party effectively embraced a twenty-six-county, majoritarian, post-republican form of nationalism. Viewed from this perspective, the IRA's refusal to examine political realities beyond the confines of their own culture had to be rejected. If de Valera resented the fact that the IRA had 'butted in' at the end of the 1930s,[35] then this reflected the gulf by which republicans were cut off even from those whose rhetoric might appear to give them encouragement.

SELF-DELUDING MYTHS

The Army Council motion was then put and defeated so that the position is unchanged and no auxiliary is to be organized. Instead a resolution was adopted 'That the army do not launch a political party.'

Report on IRA GAC (March 1934)[36]

It would be a good thing if P[eadar] O'D[onnell] and F[rank] R[yan] had their heads knocked together until they learned sense.

Mary MacSwiney (January 1935)[37]

In 1985, Peadar O'Donnell commented to Kevin O'Higgins's daughter that 'that was a terrible thing about your father's death. ... He should have been let do his job—but then we Irish can never pull together.'[38] In April 1927, *An Phoblacht*—then under Peadar O'Donnell's editorship—had asserted that:

---

[35] Ibid. 530 (21).
[36] 'To: All Camps: The General Army Convention of the IRA ...', McGarrity Papers, NLI MS 17539.
[37] To Brugha, 23 Jan. 1935, Brugha Papers, ADUCD P15/8.
[38] Una O'Higgins O'Malley to the author, 27 Mar., 15 Apr. 1993; *Irish Times*, 6 June 1992.

The general election in the twenty-six counties is only a few months distant. . . . The election will give our people, in one portion of our mutilated motherland, an opportunity of bringing to an end the shameful and disastrous rule of King George's ministerial puppets in Dublin. . . . But the election would do much more if our people are determined to repudiate the imperialists. It would give the government of the Republic authority to smash the so-called treaty, and to place on trial every traitor who sold his country to England, and every murderer and torturer who, in England's interests, shot down or brutally ill-treated Republicans who refused to perjure themselves and worship at the shrine of British imperialism. The Cosgraves, [O']Higgins'[s], Mulcahys, Blythes, and the rest of the traitors who ordered the murder of Republicans, would have to face the music if they were not smuggled out of the country in submarines and warships by the English masters, whose dirty work they have done so well.[39]

The contrast between O'Donnell's latter-day words and his paper's 1927 approach comes into stark relief when one considers the attitude of those who killed Kevin O'Higgins three months after the above *An Phoblacht* piece was published. In the words of one of the killers,

seeing him [O'Higgins] and realizing that it was not a mistake, we were just taken over and incensed with hatred. You can have no idea what it was like, with the memory of the executions, and the sight of him just walking along on his own. We started shooting from the car, then getting out of the car we continued to shoot. We all shot at him; he didn't have a chance.[40]

The threatening, recriminatory prose of O'Donnell's paper plainly helped to sustain precisely that vengeful attitude toward pro-treaty figures which lay behind O'Higgins's killing. This brings us to the heart of inter-war republican socialist culture: one of the persistent themes throughout this book has been the contradictory stance of the republican left with regard to violence. On the one hand, there was repeated stress that violence should not be the central, pivotal feature of republican culture; in O'Donnell's words, the 'heresy of the cult of armed men' had to be overcome.[41] Yet republican socialists also flattered the sensibilities of those committed

---

[39] *An Phoblacht*, 22 Apr. 1927.
[40] Gannon Statement, NA 999/951. Cf. T. de V. White, *Kevin O'Higgins* (Dublin, Anvil, 1986; 1st edn. 1948), 256; MacEoin (ed.), *Survivors*, 34.
[41] *The Gates Flew Open* (London, Jonathan Cape, 1932), 168.

to violence (O'Donnell: 'Success cannot come along any line for this country without recourse to arms at some stage');[42] until the 1934 schism, indeed, they worked within an organization which (more, perhaps, than any other in Ireland) had the right to be considered a cult of armed men. That this was an incoherent approach becomes clear when one considers the mass of contemporary evidence testifying to the militaristic, anti-political centre of gravity within the republican left's chosen vehicle for expression. Constitutionally, as we have seen, the IRA was committed to the primacy and centrality of force; such an approach clearly placed socialist republicans in an extremely marginal position. At the 1934 Convention which witnessed the departure of the O'Donnellites from the army, it was clear that there was strong sentiment in favour of a militarism undiluted by preoccupation with politics or economics: 'enough attention was not being given to the army from the military point of view'; 'there has been far too much stress put upon the social side'.[43]

Such attitudes should not have come as a surprise, given the ethos prevalent in the IRA during the revolutionary period, and given the organization's continuing militaristic orthodoxy during the early years of the Free State's existence. The view outlined by Joseph McGarrity in 1926 serves neatly to encapsulate the physical force approach: 'A silent, persistent up-building of the army will win more respect from the enemy than all the election campaigns imaginable can ever do.'[44] This anti-political quality of mind carried with it depressing implications for those who sought to define republicanism in terms of social argument. For the same reluctance to allow elections to distract from or disrupt the struggle militated equally against the O'Donnellite, class-based vision of republicanism. When the IRA Army Council declared in 1938 that 'the army is above political parties'[45] it reflected a hostility toward politics which was widely prevalent within that inter-war republican movement through which O'Donnellite socialists sought to work. Given the nature of the republican left's political vision, their break with

---

[42] *An Phoblacht*, 21 Jan. 1928.
[43] IRA General Army Convention (17 Mar. 1934), *Minutes*, MacEntee Papers, ADUCD P67/525.
[44] To Aiken, 1 Sept. 1926, McGarrity Papers, NLI MS 17421.
[45] Oglaigh na h-Eireann to the People of Ireland (Oct. 1938), Files of the Dept. of the Taoiseach, NA S 11564 A.

the militaristic, non-socialist IRA in March 1934 appears entirely natural. Their previous immersion in the organization, however, must be seen as rather incongruous. For if the IRA leadership was characterized by 'bankruptcy' in April 1935,[46] then it was also true that (in O'Donnellite terms, at least), the organization as a whole had been virtually bankrupt during its entire existence. The brutal fact is that there was little sense in being a socialist republican in a predominantly non-socialist-republican army. Attempts to persuade the army to define its own approach in terms of class conflict were destined for predictable failure, given the militaristic, anti-social orthodoxy which underpinned the movement.

In this, as in much else, socialist republicans sustained their project through self-deluding myths. James Connolly's socialist republican theory was their intellectual point of reference, but they failed to see that even Connolly's own career demonstrated the inadequacy of his central thesis. Inter-war socialist republicans offered incoherent readings of the 1916–23 revolutionary period; on the basis of these misconstructions they maintained the fiction that republicanism, properly understood, had class conflict at its root. The Irish masses were held to be both socially radical and also instinctively separatist, the two elements of their thinking supposedly interweaving with one another. That this was not the case was demonstrated not only by the increasing marginalization of hardline separatism during our period, but also by the repeated failure of the left even to persuade the republican faithful that their Connollyesque duality made sense. The land annuities episode, the Saor Eire experience, and the fate of the Republican Congress proposals all demonstrated that the IRA route was not a viable one for republican socialists to take.

In some respects, socialist republicans did resemble their non-socialist co-republicans. Mainstream republican hostility toward compromise (aptly captured in Mary MacSwiney's argument that ' "No compromise" is the only sane policy in Ireland')[47] was characteristic also of the republican left. Thus, for example, O'Donnell's celebration of civil-war intransigence echoed that of his non-socialist comrade, Ernie O'Malley.[48] Linked closely into

---

[46] *Republican Congress*, 13 Apr. 1935.
[47] To McGarrity, 12 Apr. 1926, McGarrity Papers, NLI MS 17461.
[48] O'Donnell, *The Gates*, 5; R. English and C. O'Malley (eds.), *Prisoners: The Civil War Letters of Ernie O'Malley* (Swords, Poolbeg, 1991), 35.

the wider republican family,[49] the socialists evinced the same un-flinching commitment to a thirty-two-county national paradigm, the same refusal to take unionism seriously, the same tendency toward a celebration of Gaelicism, and the same anti-treaty hos-tility toward the supposedly illegitimate Free State. In relation to Northern Ireland, the O'Donnellite left unfortunately displayed all too familiar a reluctance to reconsider the rigidity of thirty-two-county republicanism. O'Donnell spoke of northern Pro-testants' 'weird fear of the Catholic church'.[50] But he failed to acknowledge the seriousness of the sectarianism implicit in statements such as Mary MacSwiney's, that a 'social programme in accordance with Catholic principles is quite good enough for any-one'.[51] It was not enough to declare that true republicanism was not sectarian, and simply to dismiss the confessionally rooted quality of so much modern Irish nationalist experience and culture.

Indeed, O'Donnell and his colleagues failed to appreciate the true nature of unionism at all. In March 1934, O'Donnell himself suggested that 'the things that mark off the six counties from the rest is [*sic*] imperialistic finance and factory workers such as you have in Manchester.'[52] Ironically, he had hit on precisely the point: from the unionist perspective, 'such as you have in Manchester' was a phrase which might be judged to establish the appropriate framework for considering unionist opposition to republican claims. As on other occasions, however, O'Donnell failed to see such an irony in his words. Wedded to an all-Ireland, separatist paradigm, republican socialists failed to deal with the complexities of the north-east or with the sturdiness of Ulster unionism. As Henry Patterson has rightly noted: 'For republicans of the left and right, unionism was a reactionary ideology whose mass base had to be explained by assuming a Protestant working class blinded to its own interests.'[53] Indeed, rather than reading the republican left in

[49] On the family connections and cultic intimacy linking the republican left to the wider republican community see, for example, Ryan to Kerney, 14 Jan. 1942, 'Frank Ryan, Sean Russell', Dept. of Foreign Affairs, Secretary's Office Files, A20/4; Cronin, *Ryan*, 109; MacEoin (ed.), *Survivors*, 350–1.

[50] O'Donnell, quoted in M. McInerney, *Peadar O'Donnell: Irish Social Rebel* (Dublin, O'Brien, 1974), 216.

[51] To Brugha, 23 Jan. 1935, Brugha Papers, ADUCD P15/8.

[52] IRA General Army Convention (17 Mar. 1934), *Minutes*, MacEntee Papers, ADUCD P67/525.

[53] *Politics of Illusion: Republicanism and Socialism in Modern Ireland* (London, Hutchinson Radius, 1989), 64.

terms of their iconoclasm[54] it is perhaps more important to stress that they were not iconoclastic enough, regarding the orthodoxies of their own tradition, for them to make credible sense.

Yet inter-war republican socialists undeniably did represent a distinctive fraction within the wider republican family. While they shared many of the limitations of their fellow republicans, they also subjected aspects of the republican tradition to critical scrutiny, and offered a critique of Irish and Anglo-Irish politics which attempted to redefine republican thinking according to radical social argument. In drawing attention to the economic dynamics behind nationalist experience they surely identified crucial questions. The argument of this book, however, has been that their answers to these questions were hopelessly inadequate. Simplistic, incoherent, inconsistent, and self-referential, socialist republicans misrepresented the vital relationship between economics and Irish nationalism. The contrast between Fianna Fáil's less ambitious economic argument and the impossibilistic class struggling of the republican left helps to delineate the complicated impact which economic interest had on nationalist attitudes in this period. Fianna Fáil's more conservative stance drew in social groups between which the republican left sought to foment conflict. Moreover, de Valera's party built on the solid nationalist enthusiasm of many people whom O'Donnellite thinking defined out of the separatist advance. For as during the 1916–23 era, class affiliations could help to determine nationalist conviction and attachment in more complex ways than was allowed for in socialist republican argument. Just as the republican left simplified the complex relationship between nationalists and unionists so, too, they adhered to a model of class-determined nationalist allegiance which was far too rigid to provide an accurate reflection of Irish political realities. There was, in fact, no neat 'oneness' between the national and the social and class struggles. Fianna Fáil's Irish nationalist success demonstrated both the conservatism and the complexity of economic and social nationalism in Ireland during these years.

But the republican left not only argued that national and social conflicts were interwoven in Ireland, but also that the republican cause in Ireland formed part of a wider, international struggle between the forces of liberty and those of oppression. Again,

[54] Cf. O. D. Edwards, 'Evangelical Puritanism', *Fortnight*, 290 (Supplement, Dec. 1990), 8.

however, the situation was more complicated than republican socialist theory suggested. Certainly, many on the republican left did oppose 1930s fascism. But some also found themselves sympathizing with Hitler during the Second World War,[55] and the picture is further complicated the more one explores the evidence. Non-socialist republicans undoubtedly did not fit in with the progressive synergy claimed by the O'Donnellites. Pro-Germanism and anti-Semitism were both evident in republican pronouncements during the war.[56] O'Donnell and Gilmore adopted a very different approach, arguing for 'no truck with any of the belligerents' and 'for the Republic and neutrality'.[57] Frank Ryan's less public voice also backed neutrality: 'In a time of national crisis like this, there must be a unified command. The country comes before party. So, in his neutrality policy—which is the only sane policy under the circumstances—Dev should get 100 per cent support.'[58]

But Ryan's contemplation of a liaison role between the Germans and de Valera rather complicates the supposedly progressive picture; indeed, the very endorsement of neutrality itself reflected the fact that Irish nationalist interests and the international fight against tyranny were not automatically harmonious. Gilmore did, at one stage, try to push de Valera towards entering the war on the allied side, but his comments about the situation immediately prior to the war hardly coincide with the view that Irish republicanism naturally formed part of an internationally progressive alliance: 'I saw a war coming and I knew that all the more republican elements in the Dáil or outside it would tend to back the Germans'.[59] Thus, the central arguments of the republican left, regarding the harmony of national and social struggles within Ireland, and the harmony between Irish republicanism and international progressivism, can both be seen to be unconvincing.

Yet republican socialism has proved more resilient than its

[55] M. Milotte, *Communism in Modern Ireland: The Pursuit of the Workers' Republic Since 1916* (Dublin, Gill and Macmillan, 1984), 183–5.
[56] *War News* (22 Mar. 1940), MacEntee Papers, ADUCD P67/532 (1); copy of IRA Radio Broadcast, Dec. 1939, Files of the Dept. of the Taoiseach, NA S 11564 A.   [57] *Invasion!* (n.d.), Coughlan Papers, PP.
[58] To Kerney, 14 Jan. 1942, 'Frank Ryan, Sean Russell', Dept. of Foreign Affairs, Secretary's Office Files, NA A20/4.
[59] Statements in conversation with Anthony Coughlan, recorded by the latter (Coughlan Papers, PP).

intellectual feebleness and confusion might have led one to expect. The creed has continued to have an attraction for sections of the Irish republican movement even in the modern period.[60] Moreover, numerous commentators have adopted a positive approach which is as intellectually unjustified as it is politically unfortunate. Thus, for example, Philip O'Leary is right to recognize that Peadar O'Donnell's literary work reflected his hatred of passive fatalism and that his characters 'usually battle to shape their own destinies'; he is also correct in arguing that O'Donnell never lost 'either his commitment or his optimism'. But, as we have seen, O'Donnell's literary work and his political projects cannot be understood independently of one another: each is essential to an explanation of the other. So there is little use in identifying O'Donnell's optimism and commitment without assessing the validity or otherwise of the social argument which underlay such enthusiastic faith. O'Donnell's literature has to be understood in relation to the political ambitions which he wanted such writing to serve. O'Leary argues that 'O'Donnell is a passionate believer in the need for leadership drawn from the working class itself', and that he sees neighbourliness 'as a major power for social change',[61] but offers no scrutiny whatsoever of these political views. In fact, our own study has repeatedly demonstrated the inadequacy of O'Donnell's arguments regarding both working-class leadership and the possibilities of radical social change. To present the literature without accompanying criticism of the politics is to allow O'Donnell an unjustified escape.

Similarly, Alexander Gonzalez celebrates O'Donnell's lack of sentimentality, arguing that his novel, *The Big Windows*, 'provides a wealth of detail about glen life, in effect recreating that life for the modern reader to marvel at and to enjoy'.[62] Even allowing for the fact that *The Big Windows* is one of O'Donnell's least didactic works, it is still remarkable that an essay on O'Donnell's depiction of Donegal should not even consider the political implications of

---

[60] See e.g. G. Adams, *The Politics of Irish Freedom* (Dingle, Brandon, 1986), 6–8, 37–8, 90, 93. For an illuminating discussion of more recent socialist republican politics, see Patterson, *Politics of Illusion*.

[61] 'The Donegal of Seamus Ó Grianna and Peadar O'Donnell', *Eire-Ireland*, 23/2 (Summer 1988), 138–9, 144–5, 149.

[62] A. G. Gonzalez, 'Intricacies of Glen Life at the Turn of the Century: The Broad Appeal of Peadar O'Donnell's *The Big Windows*', *Journal of Irish Literature*, 20/3 (Sept. 1991), 26.

his re-creation of community life. As with O'Leary, there is here a separation of the literature from the overarching purpose against which it has to be understood. Such celebration of O'Donnell's portrait of Irish community existence is only possible if one fails to explore his wider communal vision, and to address the problems within it. Nor is such uncritical endorsement characteristic only of literary commentators. One recent observer has argued that 'with regard to the Republican movement it would seem that [the Republican] Congress, if [it] had been somewhat more successful, could have gained for the idea of social and economic liberation, a more secure and coherent position upon the revolutionary Republican agenda.'[63] In fact, it was precisely because the Congress's social and economic outlook was, as we have seen, insecure and incoherent that it was not 'somewhat more successful'.

For the evidence discussed in this book has overwhelmingly testified to the intellectual inadequacy and incoherence of the republican socialists' case. Their view of history, of the relation between class and nation, of the mechanisms of political power, of land, of religion, of political violence, and of Irish unionism have all reflected their incapacity to deal successfully with actual Irish experience. Triumphantly outflanked within the twenty-six counties by Fianna Fáil, they lacked the qualities which suited the latter party for political success. Fianna Fáil's own approach was marred by rhetorical dishonesty, and by severe limitations in economic and in cultural argument. But de Valera's party did reflect the more conservative and more complicated relationship which actually existed between economic interest and nationalist commitment: Fianna Fáil drew on a wider reservoir of social support, and backed a more appropriately conservative project. Moreover, Fianna Fáil's adoption of a majoritarian, compromising, and pragmatic approach toward state power enabled it to reach a maturity which republican socialists preferred to scorn. By adhering to an impossibilistic millenarianism, the republican left effectively remained in political adolescence.

This study has aimed not only to unveil the weakness of the socialist republican argument, but also to depict aspects of the culture which characterized the inter-war republican left. For all of

---

[63] M. Doyle, 'The Republican Congress, 1934: A Study in Irish Radicalism', MA thesis (UCD, 1988), 80.

its deficiencies, republican socialism plainly held sufficient attractions to be able to command the support of a significant minority of republican zealots. This study has highlighted the psychological rewards of the socialist republican outlook. Political simplification justified a refusal to compromise, and thereby sustained a satisfying paradigm of incorruptibility. The belief in having discovered the economic key to Irish politics and to Anglo-Irish relations further deepened the smugness which was so persistent a trait of the republican left in these years. Pearse, de Valera, Collins, Lynch, Macardle, and others could all be patronized for not having perceived the class-based essence of the struggle. This conviction in a social gospel helped to maintain a quasi-religious faith that mass conversion was a realistic prospect. Thus, despite the tiny numbers involved in the cult, the republican left could envisage grand schemes and entertain millenarian expectations. The identification of oppressed nation with oppressed classes, and of the Irish republican struggle with international campaigns against tyranny, served to strengthen the republican socialist sense of victimhood and of righteousness.

Each of these aspects of the republican socialist mentality contributed to its self-sustaining quality. Yet these same characteristics dictated that the approach would, ultimately, prove self-defeating. Simplification, an unwillingness to compromise, a smug and unrealistic posture of incorruptibility, a crude theory of economically determined nationalist momentum, an energetically pursued but wildly over-optimistic radical evangelism—these features of the republican socialist outlook were all, in their own way, crippling. The supposed identification of national and social struggles evaporated on serious inspection, rendering the central socialist republican thesis entirely unconvincing. Inter-war republican socialism, indeed, must be judged illuminating primarily for its deficiencies.

Bibliography

Manuscripts

Unless otherwise stated, PP indicates that the manuscripts are held by the person named in the title of the collection.

Ernest Blythe Papers, ADUCD
Andrew Bonar Law Papers, HLRO
Caithlin Brugha Papers, ADUCD
Daniel Bryan Papers, ADUCD
Brendan Byrne Papers, PP
Jonathan Cape Archives, University of Reading Library
Robert Erskine Childers Papers, TCD
Joe Clarke Papers, NLI
Michael Collins Papers, NLI
Anthony Coughlan Papers, PP (Anthony Coughlan is George Gilmore's literary executor)
Eithne Coyle O'Donnell Papers, ADUCD
Desmond FitzGerald Papers, ADUCD
Mabel FitzGerald Papers, ADUCD
Frank Gallagher Papers, NLI
Nora Harkin Papers, PP
Robert Mitchell Henry Papers, QUB
Sheila Humphreys Papers, ADUCD
Thomas Johnson Papers, NLI
Sean MacEntee Papers, ADUCD
Joseph McGarrity Papers, NLI
Patrick McGilligan Papers, ADUCD
William McMullen Papers, PP (in the possession of Joyce and Terry McMullen)
Mary MacSwiney Papers, ADUCD
Terence MacSwiney Papers, ADUCD
Maurice Moore Papers, NLI
Richard Mulcahy Papers, ADUCD
Sean Murray Papers, PRONI
National Archives, Dublin:
    Files of the Department of the Taoiseach
    Department of the Taoiseach: Government and Cabinet Minutes

Department of Foreign Affairs: Secretary's Office Files Series 'A'
William O'Brien Papers, NLI
Cormac O'Malley Papers, PP
Ernie O'Malley Papers, ADUCD
Eithne Sax Papers, PP
Austin Stack Papers, NLI

Newspapers and Journals

An Phoblacht
An Phoblacht/Republican News
An t-Oglach
Bell
Blueshirt
Catholic Mind
Dublin News
Eire
Evening Mail
Forward
Freeman's Journal
Irish Democrat (Belfast)
Irish Democrat (London)
Irish Freedom
Irish Independent
Irish People
Irish Press
Irish Rosary
Irish Times
Irish Workers' Voice

Irish Workers' Weekly
Kerry News
Leader
Left Review
Limerick Weekly Echo
Munster News
Nation
Republican Congress
Republican File
Saoirse
Shan Van Vocht
Sinn Fein
Sligo-Leitrim Liberator
Standard
The Times (London)
Voice of Labour
Wolfe Tone Weekly
Workers' Republic
Workers' Voice

Books, Articles, and Essays

ADAMS, G., *Falls Memories* (Dingle, Brandon, 1983; 1st edn. 1982).
—— *The Politics of Irish Freedom* (Dingle, Brandon, 1986).
—— *A Pathway to Peace* (Cork, Mercier, 1988).
—— *Cage Eleven* (Dingle, Brandon, 1990).
ADAMS, M. W., *Censorship: The Irish Experience* (Dublin, Scepter, 1968).
AKENSON, D. H., *A Mirror to Kathleen's Face: Education in Independent Ireland 1922–60* (Montreal, McGill-Queen's Univ. Press, 1975).

ALEXANDER, Y., and O'DAY, A. (eds.), *International Studies in Terrorism, ii: Ireland's Terrorist Dilemma* (Dordrecht, Martinus Nijhoff, 1986).

ALLEN, K., *The Politics of James Connolly* (London, Pluto, 1990).

—— 'Forging the Links: Fianna Fáil, the Trade Unions, and the Emergency', *Saothar*, 16 (1991).

ALTER, P., 'Symbols of Irish Nationalism', *Studia Hibernica*, 14 (1974).

ANDERSON, B., *Imagined Communities: Reflections on the Origin and Spread of Nationalism* (London, Verso, 1983).

ANDREW, C., *Secret Service: The Making of the British Intelligence Community* (London, Heinemann, 1985).

ANDREWS, C. S., *Dublin Made Me: An Autobiography* (Cork, Mercier, 1979).

—— *Man of No Property: An Autobiography, ii* (Cork, Mercier, 1982).

ARBLASTER, A., *Viva la Liberta! Politics in Opera* (London, Verso, 1992).

ARENSBERG, C. M., *The Irish Countryman: An Anthropological Study* (London, Macmillan, 1937).

—— and KIMBALL, S. T., *Family and Community in Ireland* (Cambridge, Harvard Univ. Press, 1968).

ARMOUR, W. S., *Facing the Irish Question* (London, Duckworth, 1935).

AUDEN, W. H., *Collected Poems by W. H. Auden* (London, Faber and Faber, 1991).

BAKER, S., 'Nationalist Ideology and the Industrial Policy of Fianna Fáil: The Evidence of the *Irish Press* (1955–1972)', *IPS* 1 (1986).

BALLIETT, C. A., 'The Lives—and Lies—of Maud Gonne', *Eire-Ireland*, 14/3 (Fall 1979).

BARDON, J., *A History of Ulster* (Belfast, Blackstaff, 1992).

BARRY, T., *Guerilla Days in Ireland* (Dublin, Anvil, 1981; 1st edn. 1949).

—— *The Reality of the Anglo-Irish War, 1920–1 in West Cork: Refutations, Corrections, and Comments on Liam Deasy's 'Towards Ireland Free'* (Tralee, Anvil, 1974).

BARTON, B., *Brookeborough: the Making of a Prime Minister* (Belfast, IIS, 1988).

—— 'Relations Between Westminster and Stormont During the Attlee Premiership', *IPS* 7 (1992).

BAX, M., *Harpstrings and Confessions: Machine-Style Politics in the Irish Republic* (Amsterdam, Van Gorcum, 1976).

BEASLAI, P., *Michael Collins and the Making of a New Ireland* (Dublin, Phoenix, 1926).

BECKETT, J. C., *The Making of Modern Ireland 1603–1923* (London, Faber and Faber, 1966).

BEHAN, B., *Borstal Boy* (London, Arrow, 1990; 1st edn. 1958).

—— *Confessions of an Irish Rebel* (London, Arrow, 1991; 1st edn. 1965).

—— *The Scarperer* (London, Arena, 1987; 1st edn. 1966).

BEHAN, B., *The Complete Plays* (London, Methuen, 1978 edn.).

BELL, J. B., 'Ireland and the Spanish Civil War, 1936–9', *Studia Hibernica*, 9 (1969).

—— *The Secret Army: The IRA 1916–79* (Swords, Poolbeg, 1989; 1st edn. 1970).

—— *The Gun in Politics: an Analysis of Irish Political Conflict, 1916–86* (New Brunswick, NJ, Transaction, 1991; 1st edn. 1987).

—— *The Irish Troubles: A Generation of Violence, 1967–92* (Dublin, Gill and Macmillan, 1993).

BELL, T., 'The Situation in Ireland', *Labour Monthly*, 12, 2 (Feb. 1930).

—— 'James Connolly: Some Reminiscences', *Labour Monthly*, 19, 4 (Apr. 1937).

BEW, P., *Land and the National Question in Ireland, 1858–82* (Dublin, Gill and Macmillan, 1978).

—— *C. S. Parnell* (Dublin, Gill and Macmillan, 1980).

—— *Conflict and Conciliation in Ireland, 1890–1910: Parnellites and Radical Agrarians* (Oxford, Clarendon, 1987).

—— 'Sinn Fein, Agrarian Radicalism, and the War of Independence, 1919–21', in Boyce (ed.), *The Revolution in Ireland*.

—— 'Parnell and Davitt', in Boyce and O'Day (eds.), *Parnell in Perspective*.

—— 'The Easter Rising: Lost Leaders and Lost Opportunities', *Irish Review*, 11 (Winter 1991–2).

—— and GIBBON, P., and PATTERSON, H., *The State in Northern Ireland, 1921–72: Political Forces and Social Classes* (Manchester, Manchester Univ. Press, 1979).

BISHOP, P., and MALLIE, E., *The Provisional IRA* (London, Corgi, 1988; 1st edn. 1987).

BLANSHARD, P., *The Irish and Catholic Power: An American Interpretation* (London, Verschoyle, 1954).

BOURKE, M., *John O'Leary: a Study in Irish Separatism* (Tralee, Anvil, 1967).

BOWDEN, T., 'Bloody Sunday: A Reappraisal', *European Studies Review*, 2/1 (Jan. 1972).

BOWMAN, J., *De Valera and the Ulster Question, 1917–1973* (Oxford, Clarendon, 1982).

—— '"The Wolf in Sheep's Clothing": Richard Hayes's Proposal for a New National Library of Ireland, 1959–60', in Hill and Marsh (eds.), *Modern Irish Democracy*.

BOYCE, D. G., *Englishmen and Irish Troubles: British Public Opinion and the Making of Irish Policy, 1918–22* (London, Cape, 1972).

—— ' "Normal Policing": Public Order in Northern Ireland Since Partition', *Eire-Ireland*, 14/4 (Winter 1979).

—— *Nationalism in Ireland* (London, Routledge, 1991; 1st edn. 1982).

—— 'Brahmins and Carnivores: The Irish Historian in Great Britain', *IHS* 25/99 (May 1987).

—— *The Irish Question and British Politics, 1868–1986* (Basingstoke, Macmillan, 1988).

—— (ed.), *The Revolution in Ireland, 1879–1923* (Basingstoke, Macmillan, 1988).

—— *Nineteenth Century Ireland: The Search for Stability* (Dublin, Gill and Macmillan, 1990).

—— ' "Can Anyone Here Imagine . . . ? ": Southern Irish Political Parties and the Northern Ireland Problem', in Roche and Barton (eds.), *The Northern Ireland Question*.

—— and O'DAY, A. (eds.), *Parnell in Perspective* (London, Routledge, 1991).

——, ECCLESHALL, R., and GEOGHEGAN, V. (eds.), *Political Thought in Ireland Since the Seventeenth Century* (London, Routledge, 1993).

BOYD, A., *The Rise of the Irish Trade Unions, 1729–1970* (Tralee, Anvil, 1972).

BOYLAN, H., *Wolfe Tone* (Dublin, Gill and Macmillan, 1981).

BOYLE, A., *The Riddle of Erskine Childers* (London, Hutchinson, 1977).

BOYLE, J. W. (ed.), *Leaders and Workers* (Cork, Mercier, 1978, 1st edn. 1966).

—— *The Irish Labour Movement in the Nineteenth Century* (Washington, Catholic Univ. of America Press, 1988).

BRADLEY, D., 'Speeding the Plough: The Formation of the Federation of Rural Workers, 1944–8', *Saothar*, 11 (1986).

—— *Farm Labourers: Irish Struggle, 1900–76* (Belfast, Athol, 1988).

BRADSHAW, B., 'Nationalism and Historical Scholarship in Modern Ireland', *IHS* 26/104 (Nov. 1989).

BRADY, Ciaran (ed.), *Worsted in the Game: Losers in Irish History* (Dublin, Lilliput, 1989).

BRADY, Conor, *Guardians of the Peace* (Dublin, Gill and Macmillan, 1974).

BRANSON, N., *History of the Communist Party of Great Britain, 1927–41* (London, Lawrence and Wishart, 1985).

BREEN, D., *My Fight for Irish Freedom* (Dublin, Anvil, 1964; 1st edn. 1924).

BRENNAN, M., *The War in Clare, 1911–21: Personal Memoirs of the Irish War of Independence* (Dublin, Four Courts Press, 1980).

BREUILLY, J., *Nationalism and the State* (Manchester, Manchester University Press, 1982).

BRISCOE, R., and HATCH, A., *For the Life of Me* (London, Longmans, 1959).

BRITISH AND IRISH COMMUNIST ORGANIZATION, *Communism in Ireland* (Belfast, BICO, 1977).

BRODY, H., *Inishkillane: Change and Decline in the West of Ireland* (London, Faber and Faber, 1986; 1st edn. 1973).

BROMAGE, M. C., *De Valera and the March of a Nation* (London, Hutchinson, 1956).

BROOKE, R., *Rupert Brooke: the Collected Poems* (London, Papermac, 1992; 1st edn. 1918).

BROWN, M. J., *The Politics of Irish Literature: from Thomas Davis to W. B. Yeats* (London, Allen and Unwin, 1972).

BROWN, T., *Ireland: a Social and Cultural History, 1922–85* (London, Fontana, 1985; 1st edn. 1981).

—— *The Whole Protestant Community: the Making of a Historical Myth* (Derry, Field Day, 1985).

BROWNE, N., *Against the Tide* (Dublin, Gill and Macmillan, 1986).

—— *Church and State in Modern Ireland* (Belfast, QUB Dept. of Politics, 1991).

BRUCE, S., *The Red Hand: Protestant Paramilitaries in Northern Ireland* (Oxford, OUP, 1992).

BUCHAN, J., *The Thirty-Nine Steps* (London, Hodder and Stoughton, 1926; 1st edn. 1915).

—— *Greenmantle* (Harmondsworth, Penguin, 1956; 1st edn. 1916).

—— *Mr Standfast* (Edinburgh, Thomas Nelson, 1923; 1st edn. 1919).

—— *The Three Hostages* (Harmondsworth, Penguin, 1953; 1st edn. 1924).

—— *The Island of Sheep* (Harmondsworth, Penguin, 1956; 1st edn. 1936).

BUCKLAND, P., *The Factory of Grievances: Devolved Government in Northern Ireland, 1921–39* (Dublin, Gill and Macmillan, 1979).

—— *James Craig, Lord Craigavon* (Dublin, Gill and Macmillan, 1980).

—— *A History of Northern Ireland* (Dublin, Gill and Macmillan, 1981).

BUCKLEY, D. N., *James Fintan Lalor: Radical* (Cork, Cork Univ. Press, 1990).

BULL, P., 'The United Irish League and the Reunion of the Irish Parliamentary Party, 1898–1900', *IHS* 26/101 (May 1988).

BUNTING, A., 'The American Molly Childers and the Irish Question', *Eire-Ireland*, 23/2 (Summer 1988).

BURNS, E., *British Imperialism in Ireland* (Dublin, Workers' Books, 1931).

BUTLER, E., *Barry's Flying Column* (London, Leo Cooper, 1971).

BUTLER, H., *Wolfe Tone and the Common Name of Irishman* (Mullingar, Lilliput, 1985).

BYRNE, P., *Memories of the Republican Congress* (London, Connolly Association, n.d.).

CADOGAN GROUP, *Northern Limits: Boundaries of the Attainable in Northern Ireland Politics* (Belfast, Cadogan Group, 1992).

CAHILL, L., *Forgotten Revolution: Limerick Soviet 1919—a Threat to British Power in Ireland* (Dublin, O'Brien, 1990).

CAMPBELL, F., *The Dissenting Voice: Protestant Democracy in Ulster from Plantation to Partition* (Belfast, Blackstaff, 1991).

CANNING, P., *British Policy Towards Ireland, 1921–41* (Oxford, Clarendon, 1985).

CARDOZO, N., *Maud Gonne: Lucky Eyes and a High Heart* (London, Gollancz, 1979).

CARROLL, J. T., *Ireland in the War Years* (Newton Abbot, David and Charles, 1975).

CARTER, R. W. G., and PARKER, A. J. (eds.), *Ireland: Contemporary Perspectives on a Land and its People* (London, Routledge, 1990; 1st edn. 1989).

CARTY, R. K., *Party and Parish Pump: Electoral Politics in Ireland* (Ontario, Wilfrid Laurier Univ. Press, 1981).

CAULFIELD, M., *The Easter Rebellion* (London, Muller, 1964).

CHAVASSE, M., *Terence MacSwiney* (Dublin, Clonmore and Reynolds, 1961).

CHILDERS, R. E., *The Riddle of the Sands: A Record of Secret Service* (Harmondsworth, Penguin, 1978; 1st edn. 1903).

—— 'Law and Order in Ireland', *Studies*, 8 (Dec. 1919).

CHUBB, B., *The Government and Politics of Ireland* (London, Longman, 1992; 1st edn. 1970).

—— *The Politics of the Irish Constitution* (Dublin, Institute of Public Administration, 1991).

CLARK, S., *Social Origins of the Irish Land War* (Princeton, Princeton Univ. Press, 1979).

—— and DONNELLY, J. S. (eds.), *Irish Peasants: Violence and Political Unrest, 1780–1914* (Manchester, Manchester Univ. Press, 1983).

CLARKE, K., *Revolutionary Woman: Kathleen Clarke 1878–1972* (Dublin, O'Brien, 1991).

CLARKSON, J. D., *Labour and Nationalism in Ireland* (New York, AMS Press, 1970; 1st edn. 1925).

CLARKSON, L. A., and GOLDSTROM, J. M. (eds.), *Irish Population, Economy, and Society: Essays in Honour of the Late K. H. Connell* (Oxford, Clarendon, 1981).

CLEARY, A. E., 'The Gaelic League, 1893–1919', *Studies*, 8 (1919).

CLIFFORD, A., *The Constitutional History of Eire/Ireland* (Belfast, Athol, 1987).

CLIFFORD, B., *James Connolly: An Adventurous Socialist* (Cork, Labour Comment, 1984).

CLYDE, T. (ed.), *Ancestral Voices: The Selected Prose of John Hewitt* (Belfast, Blackstaff, 1987).

COAKLEY, J., 'Minor Parties in Irish Political Life, 1922–89', *Economic and Social Review*, 21/3 (1989–90).

COAKLEY, J., (ed.), *The Social Origins of Nationalist Movements* (London, Sage, 1992).

—— and GALLAGHER, M. (eds.), *Politics in the Republic of Ireland* (Galway, PSAI Press, 1992).

COLLINS, M., *The Path to Freedom* (Cork, Mercier, 1968; 1st edn. 922).

COLUM, P., *Arthur Griffith* (Dublin, Browne and Nolan, 1959).

COMERFORD, R. V., *Charles J. Kickham: A Study in Irish Nationalism and Literature* (Portmarnock, Wolfhound, 1979).

—— 'Patriotism as Pastime: The Appeal of Fenianism in the mid-1860s', *IHS* 22/87 (Mar. 1981).

—— *The Fenians in Context* (Dublin, Wolfhound, 1985).

—— 'Comprehending the Fenians', *Saothar*, 17 (1992).

COMMUNIST PARTY OF IRELAND, *Outline History* (Dublin, New Books, n.d.).

CONNELL, K. H., *Irish Peasant Society: Four Historical Essays* (Oxford, Clarendon, 1968).

CONNOLLY, J., *Collected Works, i* (Dublin, New Books, 1987).

—— *Collected Works, ii* (Dublin, New Books, 1988).

CONNOLLY, N., *The Unbroken Tradition* (New York, Boni and Liveright, 1918).

—— (as N. Connolly O'Brien) *Portrait of a Rebel Father* (London, Rich and Cowan, 1935).

—— *We Shall Rise Again* (London, Mosquito, 1981).

—— and NI SHEIDHIR, E. (eds.), *James Connolly Wrote for Today* (Dublin, Irish Freedom Press, 1978).

COOGAN, T. P., *The IRA* (London, Fontana, 1987; 1st edn. 1970).

—— *Michael Collins: A Biography* (London, Hutchinson, 1990).

COONEY, J., *The Crozier and the Dail: Church and State in Ireland, 1922–86* (Cork, Mercier, 1986).

CORISH, P. J., *The Irish Catholic Experience: A Historical Survey* (Dublin, Gill and Macmillan, 1985).

—— (ed.), *Radicals, Rebels, and Establishments* (Belfast, Appletree, 1985).

CORK WORKERS' CLUB, *The Irish Case for Communism* (Cork, CWC, n.d.).

COSGROVE, A., and McGUIRE, J. I. (eds.), *Parliament and Community* (Belfast, Appletree, 1983).

COUGHLAN, A., 'The Social Scene', *Administration*, 14/3 (Autumn 1966).

—— *C. Desmond Greaves, 1913–88: An Obituary Essay* (Dublin, Irish Labour History Society, 1991; 1st edn. 1990).

—— 'A Unitary Irish State', in McGarry and O'Leary (eds.), *The Future of Northern Ireland*.

COXHEAD, E., *Daughters of Erin: Five Women of the Irish Renascence* (London, Secker and Warburg, 1965).

CRADDEN, T., 'The Left in Northern Ireland and the National Question: The "Democratic Alternative" in the 1940s', *Saothar*, 16 (1991).

CRONIN, A., *Dead as Doornails: A Chronicle of Life* (Dublin, Dolmen, 1976).

CRONIN, S., *The Revolutionaries: The Story of Twelve Great Irishmen* (Dublin, Republican Publications, 1971).

—— *The McGarrity Papers* (Tralee, Anvil, 1972).

—— *Marx and the Irish Question* (Dublin, Repsol, 1977).

—— *Young Connolly* (Dublin, Repsol, 1978).

—— *Frank Ryan: The Search for the Republic* (Dublin, Repsol, 1980).

—— *Irish Nationalism: A History of its Roots and Ideology* (Dublin, Academy Press, 1980).

—— *Washington's Irish Policy 1916–1986: Independence, Partition, Neutrality* (Dublin, Anvil, 1987).

CROTTY, R. D., *Irish Agricultural Production: Its Volume and Structure* (Cork, Cork Univ. Press, 1966).

CROZIER, F. P., *Ireland for Ever* (London, Cape, 1932).

CROZIER, M. (ed.), *Cultural Traditions in Northern Ireland: Varieties of Irishness* (Belfast, IIS, 1989).

—— (ed.), *Cultural Traditions in Northern Ireland: Varieties of Britishness* (Belfast, IIS, 1990).

—— (ed.), *Cultural Traditions in Northern Ireland: All Europeans Now?* (Belfast, IIS, 1991).

CULLEN, L. M., *An Economic History of Ireland Since 1660* (London, Batsford, 1972).

CULLEN, M., 'How Radical was Irish Feminism Between 1860 and 1920?' in Corish (ed.), *Radicals, Rebels, and Establishments.*

CUNNINGHAM, V. (ed.), *The Penguin Book of Spanish Civil War Verse* (Harmondsworth, Penguin, 1980).

—— *British Writers of the Thirties* (Oxford, OUP, 1988).

CURRAN, J. M., *The Birth of the Irish Free State, 1921–3* (Alabama, Univ. of Alabama Press, 1980).

DALTON, C., *With the Dublin Brigade, 1917–21* (London, Peter Davies, 1929).

DALY, M. E., *Social and Economic History of Ireland Since 1800* (Dublin, Educational Company of Ireland, 1981).

—— 'An Irish-Ireland for Business?: The Control of Manufactures Acts, 1932 and 1934', *IHS* 24/94 (Nov. 1984).

—— *Industrial Development and Irish National Identity, 1922–39* (Dublin, Gill and Macmillan, 1992).

DANGERFIELD, G., *The Damnable Question: A Study in Anglo-Irish Relations* (Boston, Little and Brown, 1976).

DAVIS, H. B., *Nationalism and Socialism* (New York, Monthly Review Press, 1967).

—— *Toward a Marxist Theory of Nationalism* (New York, Monthly Review Press, 1978).

DAVIS, R., *Arthur Griffith and Non-Violent Sinn Fein* (Dublin, Anvil, 1974).
—— *The Young Ireland Movement* (Dublin, Gill and Macmillan, 1987).
—— *William Smith O'Brien: Ireland—1848—Tasmania* (Dublin, Geography Publications, 1989).
DAVIS, T., *Literary and Historical Essays* (Dublin, James Duffy, 1854).
DAWSON, R., *Red Terror and Green* (London, New English Library, 1972; 1st edn. 1920).
DEANE, S., *A Short History of Irish Literature* (London, Hutchinson, 1986).
—— (ed.), *The Field Day Anthology of Irish Writing*, 3 vols. (Derry, Field Day, 1991).
DEASY, L., *Towards Ireland Free: The West Cork Brigade in the War of Independence, 1917–21* (Dublin, Mercier, 1977).
—— *Brother Against Brother* (Dublin, Mercier, 1982).
DE BLACAM, A. S., *Towards the Republic: A Study of New Ireland's Social and Political Aims* (Dublin, Kiersey, 1918).
—— *What Sinn Fein Stands for: The Irish Republican Movement—Its History, Aims, and Ideals, Examined as to their Significance to the World* (Dublin, Mellifont, 1921).
—— *The Life Story of Wolfe Tone, Set in a Picture of his Times* (Dublin, Talbot, 1935).
—— *The Black North: An Account of the Six Counties of Unrecovered Ireland—Their People, Their Treasures, and Their History* (Dublin, Gill, 1938).
DENMAN, T., 'The Catholic Irish Soldier in the First World War: The "Racial Environment" ', *IHS* 27/108 (Nov. 1991).
—— *Ireland's Unknown Soldiers: The 16th (Irish) Division in the Great War* (Blackrock, Irish Academic Press, 1992).
DEVLIN, P., *Yes We Have No Bananas: Outdoor Relief in Belfast, 1920–39* (Belfast, Blackstaff, 1981).
DONNELLY, C., 'Portrait of a Revolution', *Left Review* (Oct. 1935).
—— 'Connolly and Casement', *Left Review* (Apr. 1936).
DONNELLY, J., *Charlie Donnelly: The Life and Poems* (Dublin, Dedalus, 1987).
DOYLE, D. N., 'The Irish in Chicago', *IHS* 26/103 (May 1989).
DRUDY, P. J. (ed.), *Ireland: Land, Politics, and People* (Cambridge, CUP, 1982).
—— (ed.), *The Irish in America: Emigration, Assimilation, and Impact* (Cambridge, CUP, 1985).
—— (ed.), *Ireland and Britain Since 1922* (Cambridge, CUP, 1986).
DUGGAN, J. P., *Neutral Ireland and the Third Reich* (Dublin, Gill and Macmillan, 1985).
—— *A History of the Irish Army* (Dublin, Gill and Macmillan, 1990).
DUNNE, T., *Theobald Wolfe Tone: Colonial Outsider* (Cork, Tower, 1982).

—— 'New Histories: Beyond "Revisionism"', *Irish Review*, 12 (Spring/ Summer 1992).

DWYER, T. R., *Eamon de Valera* (Dublin, Gill and Macmillan, 1980).

—— *De Valera's Darkest Hour: In Search of National Independence, 1919–32* (Cork, Mercier, 1982).

—— *De Valera's Finest Hour: In Search of National Independence, 1932–59* (Cork, Mercier, 1982).

—— *Strained Relations: Ireland at Peace and the USA at War, 1941–5* (Dublin, Gill and Macmillan, 1988).

—— *De Valera: The Man and the Myths* (Swords, Poolbeg, 1991).

EAGLETON, T., *Nationalism, Colonialism, and Literature: Nationalism— Irony and Commitment* (Derry, Field Day, 1988).

EDWARDS, O. D., *The Mind of an Activist: James Connolly* (Dublin, Gill and Macmillan, 1971).

—— *Eamon de Valera* (Cardiff, Univ. of Wales Press, 1987).

—— 'Evangelical Puritanism', *Fortnight*, 290 (Supplement, Dec. 1990).

—— and RANSOM, B., (eds.), *James Connolly: Selected Political Writings* (London, Cape, 1973).

EDWARDS, R. D., *Patrick Pearse: The Triumph of Failure* (Swords, Poolbeg, 1990; 1st edn. 1977).

—— *James Connolly* (Dublin, Gill and Macmillan, 1981).

ELBORN, G., *Francis Stuart: A Life* (Dublin, Raven Arts, 1990).

ELLIOTT, M., *Watchmen in Sion: The Protestant Idea of Liberty* (Derry, Field Day, 1985).

—— *Wolfe Tone: Prophet of Irish Independence* (New Haven, Yale Univ. Press, 1989).

ELLIOTT, S. (ed.), *Northern Ireland Parliamentary Election Results, 1921–72* (Chichester, Political Reference Publications, 1973).

ELLIS, P. B., *A History of the Irish Working Class* (London, Pluto, 1985; 1st edn. 1972).

—— (ed.), *James Connolly: Selected Writings* (Harmondsworth, Penguin, 1973).

ELLIS, S. G., 'Nationalist Historiography and the English and Gaelic Worlds in the Late Middle Ages', *IHS* 25/97 (May 1986).

—— 'Historiographical Debate: Representations of the Past in Ireland: Whose Past and Whose Present?', *IHS* 27/108 (Nov. 1991).

ELLMANN, R., *Oscar Wilde* (London, Penguin, 1988; 1st edn. 1987).

ENGELS, F., *The Condition of the Working Class in England* (London, Granada, 1969).

ENGLISH, R., 'Peadar O'Donnell: Socialism and the Republic, 1925–37', *Saothar*, 14 (1989).

—— 'Socialism and Republican Schism in Ireland: The Emergence of the Republican Congress in 1934', *IHS* 27/105 (May 1990).

ENGLISH, R., 'Green on Red: Two Case Studies in Early Twentieth Century Irish Republican Thought', in Boyce, Eccleshall, and Geoghegan (eds.), *Political Thought in Ireland Since the Seventeenth Century.*

—— and O'MALLEY, C. (eds.), *Prisoners: The Civil War Letters of Ernie O'Malley* (Swords, Poolbeg, 1991).

FAIRFIELD, J. L. D. (ed.), *The Trial of Peter Barnes and Others: The IRA Coventry Explosion of 1939* (London, Notable British Trials Series, 1953).

FALLON, C. H., *Soul of Fire: A Biography of Mary MacSwiney* (Cork, Mercier, 1986).

FALLON, G., *Sean O'Casey: The Man I Knew* (London, Routledge and Kegan Paul, 1965).

FANNING, R., *The Irish Department of Finance, 1922–58* (Dublin, Institute of Public Administration, 1978).

—— *Independent Ireland* (Dublin, Helicon, 1983).

—— *The Four-Leaved Shamrock: Electoral Politics and the National Imagination in Independent Ireland* (Dublin, National Univ. of Ireland, 1983).

—— ' "The Rule of Order": Eamon de Valera and the IRA, 1923–40', in O'Carroll and Murphy (eds.), *De Valera and His Times.*

FARRELL, B., *The Founding of Dail Eireann: Parliament and Nation Building* (Dublin, Gill and Macmillan, 1971).

—— (ed.), *The Irish Parliamentary Tradition* (Dublin, Gill and Macmillan, 1973).

FARRELL, M., *Northern Ireland: The Orange State* (London, Pluto, 1976).

—— 'The Extraordinary Life and Times of Sean MacBride', *Magill*, 6/3 (Christmas 1982) and 6/4 (Jan. 1983).

FAUGHNAN, S., 'The Jesuits and the Drafting of the Irish Constitution of 1937', *IHS* 26/101 (May 1988).

FEEHAN, J. M., *The Shooting of Michael Collins* (Dublin, Mercier, 1981).

FENNELL, D., *The Revision of Irish Nationalism* (Dublin, Open Air, 1989).

FINNEGAN, R. B., 'The Blueshirts of Ireland During the 1930s: Fascism Inverted', *Eire-Ireland*, 24/2 (Summer 1989).

FISK, R., *In Time of War: Ireland, Ulster, and the Price of Neutrality, 1939–45* (London, Paladin, 1985; 1st edn. 1983).

FITZGERALD, D., *Memoir of Desmond FitzGerald, 1913–16* (London, Routledge and Kegan Paul, 1968).

FITZPATRICK, D., *Politics and Irish Life, 1913–21: Provincial Experience of War and Revolution* (Dublin, Gill and Macmillan, 1977).

—— 'The Geography of Irish Nationalism, 1910–21', *Past and Present*, 78 (Feb. 1978).

—— 'Strikes in Ireland, 1914–21', *Saothar*, 6 (1980).

—— *Irish Emigration, 1801–1921* (Dublin, Economic and Social History Society of Ireland, 1984).

—— (ed.), *Ireland and the First World War* (Mullingar, Lilliput, 1988).

—— (ed.), *Revolution? Ireland, 1917–23* (Dublin, TCD Modern History Department, 1990).

FOLEY, C., *Legion of the Rearguard: The IRA and the Modern Irish State* (London, Pluto, 1992).

FORESTER, M., *Michael Collins: The Lost Leader* (London, Sidgwick and Jackson, 1971).

FOSTER, R. F., *Charles Stewart Parnell: The Man and his Family* (Hassocks, Harvester, 1976).

—— 'We are all Revisionists Now', *Irish Review*, 1 (1986).

—— *Modern Ireland, 1600–1972* (London, Allen Lane, 1988).

—— (ed.), *The Oxford Illustrated History of Ireland* (Oxford, OUP, 1989).

—— 'Varieties of Irishness', in Crozier (ed.), *Cultural Traditions in Northern Ireland: Varieties of Irishness.*

FREYER, G., *Peadar O'Donnell* (Lewisburg, Bucknell University Press, 1973).

—— ' "Big Windows": the Writings of Peadar O'Donnell', *Eire-Ireland*, 11/1 (Spring 1976).

GAILEY, A., *Ireland and the Death of Kindness: The Experience of Constructive Unionism, 1890–1905* (Cork, Cork Univ. Press, 1987).

GALLAGHER, F., *Days of Fear* (London, John Murray, 1928).

GALLAGHER, M., 'Party Solidarity, Exclusivity, and Inter-party Relationships in Ireland, 1922–77: The Evidence of Transfers', *Economic and Social Review*, 10/1 (Oct. 1978).

—— 'Do Ulster Unionists have a Right to Self-Determination?', *IPS* 5 (1990).

GALLAGHER, P., *Paddy the Cope: An Autobiography* (New York, Devin-Adair, 1942).

GARVIN, T., 'Nationalist Elites, Irish Voters, and Irish Political Development: A Comparative Perspective', *Economic and Social Review*, 8/3 (Apr. 1977).

—— *The Evolution of Irish Nationalist Politics* (Dublin, Gill and Macmillan, 1981).

—— 'Priests and Patriots: Irish Separatism and Fear of the Modern, 1890–1914', *IHS* 25/97 (May 1986).

—— 'Anatomy of a Nationalist Revolution: Ireland, 1858–1928', *Comparative Studies in Society and History*, 28 (1986).

—— 'The Politics of Language and Literature in Pre-Independence Ireland', *IPS* 2 (1987).

—— *Nationalist Revolutionaries in Ireland, 1858–1928* (Oxford, Clarendon, 1987).

—— 'Defenders, Ribbonmen, and Others: Underground Political Networks in Pre-Famine Ireland', in Philpin (ed.), *Nationalism and Popular Protest in Ireland.*

GARVIN, T., 'Unenthusiastic Democrats: The Emergence of Irish Democracy', in Hill and Marsh (eds.), *Modern Irish Democracy*.

GAUGHAN, J. A., *Austin Stack: Portrait of a Separatist* (Mount Merrion, Kingdom Books, 1977).

—— *Thomas Johnson* (Mount Merrion, Kingdom Books, 1980).

GELLNER, E., *Nations and Nationalism* (Oxford, Basil Blackwell, 1983).

GEOGHEGAN, V., 'The Emergence and Submergence of Irish Socialism, 1821–51', in Boyce, Eccleshall, and Geoghegan (eds.), *Political Thought in Ireland Since the Seventeenth Century*.

GIBBON, P., *The Origins of Ulster Unionism: The Formation of Popular Protestant Politics and Ideology in Nineteenth Century Ireland* (Manchester, Manchester Univ. Press, 1975).

GIBBONS, L., 'Identity Without a Centre: Allegory, History, and Irish Nationalism', *Cultural Studies*, 6/3 (Oct. 1992).

GILMORE, G., *The Irish Republican Congress* (New York, United Irish Republican Committees of US, 1935).

—— 'The Republic and the Protestants', *The Bell*, 16/5 (Feb. 1951).

—— *Labour and the Republican Movement* (Dublin, Repsol, n.d.; 1st edn. 1966).

—— *The Relevance of James Connolly in Ireland Today* (Dublin, Fodhla Printing Co., n.d. [1970?]).

—— *The Irish Republican Congress* (Cork, CWC, 1978).

GIRVIN, B., 'Industrialization and the Irish Working Class Since 1922', *Saothar*, 10 (1984).

GLANDON, V. E., *Arthur Griffith and the Advanced Nationalist Press: Ireland, 1900–22* (New York, Peter Lang, 1985).

GONNE MACBRIDE, M., *A Servant of the Queen: Reminiscences* (London, Gollancz, 1974; 1st edn. 1938).

GONZALEZ, A. G., 'Intricacies of Glen Life at the Turn of the Century: The Broad Appeal of Peadar O'Donnell's *The Big Windows*', *Journal of Irish Literature*, 20/3 (Sept. 1991).

GRAY, T., *Mr Smyllie Sir* (Dublin, Gill and Macmillan, 1991).

GREAVES, C. D., *The Life and Times of James Connolly* (London, Lawrence and Wishart, 1972; 1st edn. 1961).

—— *Liam Mellows and the Irish Revolution* (London, Lawrence and Wishart, 1971).

—— *Sean O'Casey: Politics and Art* (London, Lawrence and Wishart, 1979).

—— *The Irish Transport and General Workers' Union: The Formative Years, 1909–23* (Dublin, Gill and Macmillan, 1982).

—— 'Connolly and Easter Week: A Rejoinder to John Newsinger', *Science and Society*, 48/2 (Summer 1984).

—— *1916 as History: The Myth of the Blood Sacrifice* (Dublin, Fulcrum, 1991).

GRIFFIN, B., 'Social Aspects of Fenianism in Connacht and Leinster', *Eire-Ireland*, 21/1 (Spring 1986).

GROGAN, G. F., *The Noblest Agitator: Daniel O'Connell and the German Catholic Movement, 1830–50* (Dublin, Veritas, 1991).

HACKETT, F., *Ireland: A Study in Nationalism* (New York, Huebsch, 1920).

HARBINSON, J. F., *The Ulster Unionist Party, 1882–1973: Its Development and Organization* (Belfast, Blackstaff, 1973).

HARKNESS, D. W., *The Restless Dominion: The Irish Free State and the British Commonwealth of Nations, 1921–31* (London, Macmillan, 1969).

—— *History and the Irish: An Inaugural Lecture Delivered Before The Queen's University of Belfast on 5 May 1976* (Belfast, QUB, 1976).

—— *Northern Ireland Since 1920* (Dublin, Helicon, 1983).

HART, P., 'Youth Culture and the Cork IRA', in Fitzpatrick (ed.), *Revolution?*.

—— 'Michael Collins and the Assassination of Sir Henry Wilson', *IHS* 28/110 (Nov. 1992).

HARTLEY, S., *The Irish Question as a Problem in British Foreign Policy, 1914–18* (London, Macmillan, 1987).

HARVEY, A. D., 'Who Were the Auxiliaries?', *Historical Journal*, 35/3 (1992).

HAVERTY, A., *Constance Markievicz: An Independent Life* (London, Pandora, 1988).

HAYES, S., 'My Strange Story', *The Bell*, 17/4 (July 1951).

HAYES-MCCOY, G. A. (ed.), *Historical Studies* x (Dublin, Gill and Macmillan, 1976).

HAZELKORN, E., '*Capital* and the Irish Question', *Science and Society*, 44/3 (Fall 1980).

—— 'Reconsidering Marx and Engels on Ireland', *Saothar*, 9 (1983).

HEPBURN, A. C., 'The IRA in Historical Perspective', *L'Irlande Politique et Sociale*, 1/1 (1985).

HIGGINS, M. D., 'Liam O'Flaherty and Peadar O'Donnell: Images of Rural Community', *Crane Bag*, 9/1 (1985).

HILL, R. J., and MARSH, M. (eds.), *Modern Irish Democracy: Essays in Honour of Basil Chubb* (Blackrock, Irish Academic Press, 1993).

HOBSBAWM, E. J., *Nations and Nationalism Since 1780: Programme, Myth, Reality* (Cambridge, CUP, 1990).

HOBSON, B., *Ireland Yesterday and Tomorrow* (Tralee, Anvil, 1968).

HOFFMAN, J., 'James Connolly and the Theory of Historical Materialism', *Saothar*, 2 (1976).

HOGAN, J., *Could Ireland Become Communist? The Facts of the Case* (Dublin, Cahill, n.d. [1935?]).

—— *Modern Democracy* (Cork, Cork Univ. Press, 1938).

—— *Election and Representation in Ireland* (Cork, Cork Univ. Press, 1945).

HOLMES, C., 'The British Government and Brendan Behan, 1941–54: The Persistence of the Prevention of Violence Act', *Saothar*, 14 (1989).

HOPKINSON, M., *Green Against Green: The Irish Civil War* (Dublin, Gill and Macmillan, 1988).

—— 'The Craig-Collins Pacts of 1922: Two Attempted Reforms of the Northern Ireland Government', *IHS*, 27/106 (Nov. 1990).

HOPPEN, K. T., *Ireland Since 1800: Conflict and Conformity* (London, Longman, 1989).

HOWELL, D., *A Lost Left: Three Studies in Socialism and Nationalism* (Manchester, Manchester Univ. Press, 1986).

HUTCHINSON, J., *The Dynamics of Cultural Nationalism: The Gaelic Revival and the Creation of the Irish Nation State* (London, Allen and Unwin, 1987).

HUTTON, S., and STEWART, P. (eds.), *Ireland's Histories: Aspects of State, Society, and Ideology* (London, Routledge, 1991).

HYDE, H. M., *Carson: The Life of Sir Edward Carson, Lord Carson of Duncairn* (London, Constable, 1987; 1st edn. 1953).

INGLIS, B., *Roger Casement* (Belfast, Blackstaff, 1993; 1st edn. 1973).

IRISH COMMUNIST ORGANIZATION, *The Irish Republican Congress* (London, ICO, 1966).

JACKSON, A., 'Irish Unionism and the Russellite Threat, 1894–1906', *IHS* 25/100 (Nov. 1987).

—— *The Ulster Party: Irish Unionists in the House of Commons, 1884–1911* (Oxford, Clarendon, 1989).

—— 'Unionist Myths, 1912–85', *Past and Present*, 136 (Aug. 1992).

JACKSON, T. A., *Ireland Her Own: An Outline History of the Irish Struggle for National Freedom and Independence* (London, Lawrence and Wishart, 1971; 1st edn. 1947).

JAMESON, F., *Nationalism, Colonialism, and Literature: Modernism and Imperialism* (Derry, Field Day, 1988).

JOHNSON, D. S., 'The Economic History of Ireland Between the Wars', *Irish Economic and Social History*, 1 (1974).

JORDAN, A. J., *Major John MacBride, 1865–1916* (Westport, Westport Historical Society, 1991).

KARSTEN, P., 'Irish Soldiers in the British Army, 1792–1922: Suborned or Subordinate?', *Journal of Social History*, 17 (1983).

KEARNEY, R. (ed.), *The Irish Mind: Exploring Intellectual Traditions* (Dublin, Wolfhound, 1985).

KEENA, C., *Gerry Adams: A Biography* (Cork, Mercier, 1990).

KELLEY, K. J., *The Longest War: Northern Ireland and the IRA* (London, Zed, 1988; 1st edn. 1982).

KELLY, J., 'The Fifth Bell: Race and Class in Yeats's Political Thought' in Komesu and Sekine (eds.), *Irish Writers and Politics*.

KEMMY, J., 'The Limerick Soviet', *Saothar*, 2 (1976).

KENNEDY, D., *The Widening Gulf: Northern Attitudes to the Independent Irish State, 1919–49* (Belfast, Blackstaff, 1988).

KENNEDY, L., *The Modern Industrialization of Ireland, 1940–88* (Dundalk, Dundalgan, 1989).

—— 'Modern Ireland: Post-Colonial Society or Post-Colonial Pretensions?', *Irish Review*, 13 (Winter 1992–93).

—— and OLLERENSHAW, P. (eds.), *An Economic History of Ulster* (Manchester, Manchester Univ. Press, 1985).

KEOGH, D., *The Rise of the Irish Working Class: The Dublin Trade Union Movement and Labour Leadership, 1890–1914* (Belfast, Appletree, 1982).

—— 'De Valera, the Catholic Church, and the "Red Scare", 1931–2', in O'Carroll and Murphy (eds.), *De Valera and His Times.*

—— *The Vatican, the Bishops, and Irish Politics, 1919–1939* (Cambridge, CUP, 1986).

—— 'Mannix, de Valera, and Irish Nationalism', in O'Brien and Travers (eds.), *The Irish Emigrant Experience in Australia.*

KOMESU, O., and SEKINE, M. (eds.), *Irish Writers and Politics* (Gerrards Cross, Colin Smythe, 1990).

LAFFAN, M., 'The Unification of Sinn Fein in 1917', *IHS* 17/67 (Mar. 1971).

—— 'Violence and Terror in Twentieth Century Ireland: IRB and IRA', in Mommsen and Hirschfield (eds.), *Social Protest.*

—— *The Partition of Ireland, 1911–25* (Dundalk, Dundalgan, 1983).

—— ' "Labour Must Wait": Ireland's Conservative Revolution', in Corish (ed.), *Radicals, Rebels, and Establishments.*

LARKIN, E., 'Socialism and Catholicism in Ireland', *Church History*, 33/4 (Dec. 1964).

—— *James Larkin: Irish Labour Leader, 1876–1947* (London, Routledge and Kegan Paul, 1965).

—— 'Socialism and Catholicism in Ireland', *Studies*, 74/293 (1985).

LAWLOR, S., *Britain and Ireland 1914–23* (Dublin, Gill and Macmillan, 1983).

LEE, J. J., *The Modernization of Irish Society, 1848–1918* (Dublin, Gill and Macmillan, 1973).

—— 'Irish Nationalism and Socialism: Rumpf Reconsidered', *Saothar*, 6 (1980).

—— *Ireland, 1912–85: Politics and Society* (Cambridge, CUP, 1989).

LENIN, V. I., *British Labour and British Imperialism: A Compilation of Writings by Lenin on Britain* (London, Lawrence and Wishart, 1969).

LEVENSON, L., and NATTERSTAD, J. H., *Hanna Sheehy-Skeffington: Irish Feminist* (Syracuse, Syracuse Univ. Press, 1986).

LEVENSON, S., *James Connolly: A Biography* (London, Martin Brian and O'Keeffe, 1977).

—— *Maud Gonne* (London, Cassell, 1977).

LONGLEY, E. (ed.), *The Selected Paul Durcan* (Belfast, Blackstaff, 1985; 1st edn. 1982).

LONGLEY, M., *Gorse Fires* (London, Martin Secker and Warburg, 1991).

LUDDY, M., and MURPHY, C. (eds.), *Women Surviving: Studies in Irish Women's History in the Nineteenth and Twentieth Centuries* (Swords, Poolbeg, 1989).

LYNCH, P., 'The Social Revolution that Never Was', in Williams (ed.), *The Irish Struggle*.

LYONS, F. S. L., *Ireland Since the Famine* (London, Fontana, 1973; 1st edn. 1971).

—— *Charles Stewart Parnell* (London, Fontana, 1978; 1st edn. 1977).

—— *Culture and Anarchy in Ireland, 1890–1939* (Oxford, OUP, 1982; 1st edn. 1979).

MACARDLE, D., *Tragedies of Kerry, 1922–3* (Dublin, Irish Freedom Press, 1988; 1st edn. 1924).

—— *The Irish Republic: A Documented Chronicle of the Anglo-Irish Conflict and the Partitioning of Ireland, with a Detailed Account of the Period, 1916–1923* (London, Gollancz, 1937).

MAIR, P., *The Changing Irish Party System: Organizations, Ideology, and Electoral Competition* (London, Pinter, 1987).

MANNING, M., *The Blueshirts* (Dublin, Gill and Macmillan, 1970).

MANSERGH, N., *The Irish Question, 1840–1921* (London, Unwin University Books, 1965).

—— *The Unresolved Question: The Anglo-Irish Settlement and its Undoing, 1912–72* (London, Yale Univ. Press, 1991).

MARKIEVICZ, C., *Prison Letters of Countess Markievicz* (London, Virago, 1987; 1st edn. 1934).

MARX, K., *Capital: A Critique of Political Economy*, 3 vols. (London, Lawrence and Wishart, 1954–9 edn.).

—— *The Eighteenth Brumaire of Louis Bonaparte* (Moscow, Progress, 1954 edn.).

—— and ENGELS, F., *Ireland and the Irish Question* (London, Lawrence and Wishart, 1971).

—— and ENGELS, F., *Manifesto of the Communist Party* (Moscow, Progress, 1977 edn.).

MACBRIDE, S., *A Message to the Irish People* (Cork, Mercier, 1985).

McCARTHY, C., 'From Division to Dissension: Irish Trade Unions in the Nineteen Thirties', *Economic and Social Review*, 5/3 (Apr. 1974) and 5/4 (July 1974).

McCAUGHAN, M., *Steel Ships and Iron Men: Shipbuilding in Belfast, 1894–1912* (Belfast, Friar's Bush, 1989).

McDermott, F., *Taking the Long Perspective: Democracy and "Terrorism" in Ireland: The Writings of W. E. H. Lecky and After* (Sandycove, Glendale, 1991).

MacDonagh, O., *Ireland: The Union and its Aftermath* (London, Allen and Unwin, 1977).

—— *States of Mind: A Study of Anglo-Irish Conflict, 1780–1980* (London, Allen and Unwin, 1983).

—— *O'Connell: The Life of Daniel O'Connell, 1775–1847* (London, Weidenfeld and Nicolson, 1991).

MacEoin, U. (ed.), *Survivors* (Dublin, Argenta, 1987; 1st edn. 1980).

MacEvilly, M., 'Sean MacBride and the Republican Motor Launch *St George*', *Irish Sword*, 16/62 (1984).

McGarry, J., and O'Leary, B. (eds.), *The Future of Northern Ireland* (Oxford, Clarendon, 1990).

McInerney, M., *Peadar O'Donnell: Irish Social Rebel* (Dublin, O'Brien, 1974).

McKenna, L., *The Social Teachings of James Connolly* (Dublin, Veritas, 1991).

McLellan, D., *The Thought of Karl Marx: An Introduction* (London, Macmillan, 1971; 1980 edn.).

McKenzie, F. A., *The Irish Rebellion: What Happened—and Why* (London, C. Arthur Pearson, 1916).

McMahon, D., *Republicans and Imperialists: Anglo-Irish Relations in the 1930s* (New Haven, Yale Univ. Press, 1984).

MacMahon, J. A., 'Catholic Clergy and the Social Question, 1891–1916', *Studies*, 70/283 (1981).

MacManus, F. (ed.), *The Years of the Great Test* (Cork, Mercier, 1978; 1st edn. 1967).

MacMillan, G. M., *State, Society, and Authority in Ireland: The Foundations of the Modern State* (Dublin, Gill and Macmillan, 1993).

McMullan, G., 'The Irish Bank "Strike", 1919', *Saothar*, 5 (1979).

McMullen, W., Introduction to *The Workers' Republic* (1951) in Connolly, *Collected Works, ii.*

MacNeice, L., *Collected Poems* (London, Faber and Faber, 1979; 1st edn. 1966).

Meenan, J., *The Irish Economy Since 1922* (Liverpool, Liverpool Univ. Press, 1970).

Metscher, P., *Republicanism and Socialism in Ireland: A Study in the Relationship of Politics and Ideology from the United Irishmen to James Connolly* (Frankfurt, Peter Lang, 1986).

Miller, K. A., *Emigrants and Exiles: Ireland and the Irish Exodus to North America* (Oxford, OUP, 1985).

Milotte, M., *Communism in Modern Ireland: The Pursuit of the Workers' Republic Since 1916* (Dublin, Gill and Macmillan, 1984).

MITCHELL, A., *Labour in Irish Politics, 1890–1930: The Irish Labour Movement in an Age of Revolution* (Dublin, Irish Univ. Press, 1974).

MOKYR, J., *Why Ireland Starved: A Quantitative and Analytical History of the Irish Economy, 1800–50* (London, Allen and Unwin, 1983).

MOMMSEN, W. J., and HIRSCHFIELD, G. (eds.), *Social Protest, Violence, and Terror in Nineteenth and Twentieth Century Europe* (London, Macmillan, 1982).

MOODY, T. W. (ed.), *The Fenian Movement* (Cork, Mercier, 1978; 1st edn. 1968).

—— *Davitt and Irish Revolution, 1846–82* (Oxford, Clarendon, 1981).

MORAN, S. F., 'Patrick Pearse and the European Revolt Against Reason', *Journal of the History of Ideas*, 50 (1989).

MORGAN, A., 'Connolly and Connollyism: The Making of a Myth', *Irish Review*, 5 (1988).

—— *James Connolly: A Political Biography* (Manchester, Manchester Univ. Press, 1988).

—— *Labour and Partition: The Belfast Working Class, 1905–23* (London, Pluto, 1990).

—— and PURDIE, B. (eds.), *Ireland: Divided Nation, Divided Class* (London, Ink Links, 1980).

MOYNIHAN, M. (ed.), *Speeches and Statements of Eamon de Valera, 1917–73* (Dublin, Gill and Macmillan, 1980).

MUENGER, E. A., *The British Military Dilemma in Ireland: Occupation Politics, 1886–1914* (Dublin, Gill and Macmillan, 1991).

MUNCK, R., and ROLSTON, B., 'Oral History and Social Conflict: Belfast in the 1930s', *Oral History Review*, 13 (1985).

——, ROLSTON, B., and MOORE, G., *Belfast in the Thirties: An Oral History* (Belfast, Blackstaff, 1987).

MURPHY, B. P., *Patrick Pearse and the Lost Republican Ideal* (Dublin, James Duffy, 1991).

MURPHY, J. A., 'The New IRA, 1925–62', in Williams (ed.), *Secret Societies*.

—— *Ireland in the Twentieth Century* (Dublin, Gill and Macmillan, 1975).

—— 'The Achievement of Eamon de Valera', in O'Carroll and Murphy (eds.), *De Valera and His Times*.

MURPHY, R., 'Walter Long and the Making of the Government of Ireland Act, 1919–20', *IHS* 25/97 (May 1986).

MURPHY, W. M., *The Parnell Myth and Irish Politics, 1891–1956* (New York, Peter Lang, 1986).

MURRAY, P., 'Electoral Politics and the Dublin Working Class Before the First World War', *Saothar*, 6 (1980).

MURRAY, S., 'The Irish Case For Communism' (1933), in CWC, *The Irish Case*.

NEARY, J. P., and O'GRADA, C., 'Protection, Economic War, and Structural Change: The 1930s in Ireland', *IHS* 27/107 (May 1991).

NEESON, E., *The Civil War, 1922–3* (Swords, Poolbeg, 1989; 1st edn. 1966).

NEVIN, D., 'Radical Movements in the Twenties and Thirties', in Williams (ed.), *Secret Societies.*

NEWEY, V., and THOMPSON, A. (eds.), *Literature and Nationalism* (Liverpool, Liverpool Univ. Press, 1991).

NEWSINGER, J., ' "I Bring Not Peace But a Sword": The Religious Motif in the Irish War of Independence', *Journal of Contemporary History*, 13/3 (July 1978).

—— 'Old Chartists, Fenians, and New Socialists', *Eire-Ireland*, 17/2 (Summer 1982).

—— 'James Connolly and the Easter Rising', *Science and Society*, 47/2 (Summer 1983).

—— 'Connolly and His Biographers', *IPS* 5 (1990).

—— 'Fenianism Revisited: Pastime or Revolutionary Movement?', *Saothar*, 17 (1992).

NI DHONNCHADHA, M., and DORGAN, T. (eds.), *Revising the Rising* (Derry, Field Day, 1991).

NIMNI, E., *Marxism and Nationalism: Theoretical Origins of a Political Crisis* (London, Pluto, 1991).

O'BRIEN, C. C., *God Land: Reflections on Religion and Nationalism* (Cambridge, Harvard Univ. Press, 1988).

O'BRIEN, F., *The Poor Mouth* (London, Paladin, 1988; 1st edn. 1941).

O'BRIEN, J., and TRAVERS, P. (eds.), *The Irish Emigrant Experience in Australia* (Swords, Poolbeg, 1991).

O'BRIEN, W., *Forth the Banners Go* (Dublin, Three Candles, 1969).

O'BROIN, L., *Revolutionary Underground: The Story of the Irish Republican Brotherhood, 1858–1924* (Dublin, Gill and Macmillan, 1976).

—— *W. E. Wylie and the Irish Revolution, 1916–21* (Dublin, Gill and Macmillan, 1989).

O'BUACHALLA, S. (ed.), *The Letters of P. H. Pearse* (Gerrards Cross, Colin Smythe, 1980).

O'CALLAGHAN, M. M., 'Language, Nationality, and Cultural Identity in the Irish Free State, 1922–7: The *Irish Statesman* and the *Catholic Bulletin* Reappraised', *IHS* 24/94 (Nov. 1984).

O'CALLAGHAN, S., *The Easter Lily: The Story of the IRA* (London, Allan Wingate, 1956).

O'CARROLL, J. P., and MURPHY, J. A. (eds.), *De Valera and His Times* (Cork, Cork Univ. Press, 1986; 1st edn. 1983).

O'CASEY, S., (as P. O'Cathasaigh,) *The Story of the Irish Citizen Army* (Dublin, Talbot, 1971; 1st edn. 1919).

—— *Three Plays: Juno and the Paycock, The Shadow of a Gunman, The Plough and the Stars* (London, Pan Books, 1980 edn.).

O'CATHAOIR, B., *John Blake Dillon: Young Irelander* (Dublin, Irish Academic Press, 1991).

O'CONNELL, M. R., *Daniel O'Connell: The Man and his Politics* (Blackrock, Irish Academic Press, 1990).

O'CONNOR, B., *With Michael Collins in the Fight for Irish Independence* (London, Davies, 1929).

O'CONNOR, E., 'Agrarian Unrest and the Labour Movement in County Waterford, 1917–23', *Saothar*, 6 (1980).

—— 'An Age of Agitation', *Saothar*, 9 (1983).

—— *Syndicalism in Ireland, 1917–23* (Cork, Cork Univ. Press, 1988).

—— *A Labour History of Waterford* (Waterford, Waterford Trades Council, 1989).

—— *A Labour History of Ireland, 1824–1960* (Dublin, Gill and Macmillan, 1992).

O'CONNOR, F., *The Big Fellow: Michael Collins and the Irish Revolution* (Swords, Poolbeg, 1979; 1st edn. 1937).

O'CONNOR, U., *Brendan Behan* (London, Hamilton, 1970).

O'DOHERTY, E., *An Illustrated History of the IRA* (Cork, Mercier, 1985).

O'DONNELL, P., *Storm: A Story of the Irish War* (Dublin, Talbot, n.d. [1926?]).

—— *Islanders* (Cork, Mercier, 1963; 1st edn. 1927).

—— *Adrigoole* (London, Jonathan Cape, 1929).

—— *The Knife* (Dublin, Irish Humanities Centre, 1980; 1st edn. 1930).

—— *For or Against the Ranchers? Irish Working Farmers in the Economic War* (Westport, Mayo News, n.d. [1932?]).

—— *The Gates Flew Open* (London, Jonathan Cape, 1932).

—— *Wrack: A Play in Six Scenes* (London, Jonathan Cape, 1933).

—— *On the Edge of the Stream* (London, Jonathan Cape, 1934).

—— 'The Irish Struggle Today', *Left Review* (Apr. 1936).

—— *Salud! An Irishman in Spain* (London, Methuen, 1937).

—— *The Big Windows* (Dublin, O'Brien, 1983; 1st edn. 1955).

—— *There Will Be Another Day* (Dublin, Dolmen, 1963).

—— *Proud Island* (Dublin, O'Brien, 1977; 1st edn. 1975).

—— *Monkeys in the Superstructure: Reminiscences of Peadar O'Donnell* (Galway, Salmon, 1986).

—— *Not Yet Emmet* (Dublin, New Books, n.d.).

—— Pieces in *The Bell* (1940–1954).

O'DONOGHUE, F., *No Other Law: The Story of Liam Lynch and the Irish Republican Army, 1916–23* (Dublin, Irish Press, 1954).

O'DOWD, A., *Meitheal: A Study of Cooperative Labour in Rural Ireland* (Dublin, Folklore Council of Ireland, 1981).

O'DUFFY, E., *Crusade in Spain* (Dublin, Brown and Nolan, 1938).

O'FAOLÁIN, S., *De Valera* (Harmondsworth, Penguin, 1939).

—— *The Irish* (Harmondsworth, Penguin, 1980; 1st edn. 1947).

O'FARRELL, Padraic, *Who's Who in the Irish War of Independence, 1916–21* (Dublin, Mercier, 1980).

—— *The Sean MacEoin Story* (Dublin, Mercier, 1981).

—— *The Ernie O'Malley Story* (Cork, Mercier, 1983).

O'FARRELL, Patrick, *England and Ireland Since 1800* (Oxford, OUP, 1975).

O'FLAHERTY, L., *The Informer* (London, Jonathan Cape, 1925).

—— *Mr Gilhooley* (Dublin, Wolfhound, 1991; 1st edn. 1926).

—— *The Assassin* (Dublin, Wolfhound, 1988; 1st edn. 1928).

—— *Insurrection* (Dublin, Wolfhound, 1993; 1st edn. 1950).

O'HALLORAN, C., *Partition and the Limits of Irish Nationalism: An Ideology Under Stress* (Dublin, Gill and Macmillan, 1987).

O'HALPIN, E., *The Decline of the Union: British Government in Ireland, 1892–1920* (Dublin, Gill and Macmillan, 1987).

—— 'Intelligence and Security in Ireland, 1922–45', *Intelligence and International Security*, 5/1 (1990).

O'LEARY, C., *Irish Elections, 1918–77: Parties, Voters, and Proportional Representation* (Dublin, Gill and Macmillan, 1979).

O'LEARY, P., 'The Donegal of Seamus O'Grianna and Peadar O'Donnell', *Eire-Ireland*, 23/2 (Summer, 1988).

O'LOUGHLIN, M., *Frank Ryan: Journey to the Centre* (Dublin, Raven Arts, 1987).

O'LUING, S., *I Die in a Good Cause: A Study of Thomas Ashe, Idealist and Revolutionary* (Tralee, Anvil, 1970).

O'MALLEY, E., *On Another Man's Wound* (Dublin, Anvil, 1979; 1st edn. 1936).

—— *The Singing Flame* (Dublin, Anvil, 1978).

—— *Raids and Rallies* (Dublin, Anvil, 1982).

O'NEILL, B., *The War for the Land in Ireland* (London, Lawrence, 1933).

O'NEILL, T. P., 'In Search of a Political Path: Irish Republicanism, 1922 to 1927', in Hayes-McCoy (ed.), *Historical Studies*.

O'RAHILLY, A., *Winding the Clock: O'Rahilly and the 1916 Rising* (Dublin, Lilliput, 1991).

O'RIAIN, L. P., *Doctor Socialism and the Irish Hypochondriac* (Dublin, Socialist Party of Ireland, n.d. [1909?]).

O'RIORDAN, M., *Connolly Column* (Dublin, New Books, 1979).

ORMSBY, F. (ed.), *The Collected Poems of John Hewitt* (Belfast, Blackstaff, 1992; 1st edn. 1991).

O'ROURKE, K., 'Burn Everything British but their Coal: The Anglo-Irish Economic War of the 1930s', *Journal of Economic History*, 51/2 (1991).

ORWELL, G., *Down and Out in Paris and London* (Harmondsworth, Penguin, 1966; 1st edn. 1933).

—— *Burmese Days* (Harmondsworth, Penguin, 1967; 1st edn. 1934).

ORWELL, G., *Keep the Aspidistra Flying* (Harmondsworth, Penguin, 1962; 1st edn. 1936).

—— *Homage to Catalonia* (Harmondsworth, Penguin, 1966; 1st edn. 1938).

—— *Coming Up for Air* (Harmondsworth, Penguin, 1962; 1st edn. 1939).

—— *Animal Farm* (Harmondsworth, Penguin, 1951; 1st edn. 1945).

—— *Nineteen Eighty-Four* (Harmondsworth, Penguin, 1954; 1st edn. 1949).

O'TOOLE, F., 'A Portrait of Peadar O'Donnell as an Old Soldier', *Magill*, 6/5 (Feb. 1983).

O'TUATHAIGH, M. A. G., 'The Land Question, Politics, and Irish Society, 1922–60', in Drudy (ed.), *Ireland: Land, Politics, and People.*

PAINE, T., *Rights of Man* (London, Watts, 1937; 1st edn. 1791–92).

PAKENHAM, F., and O'NEILL, T. P., *Eamon de Valera* (Dublin, Gill and Macmillan, 1970).

PATTERSON, H., 'James Larkin and the Belfast Dockers' and Carters' Strike of 1907', *Saothar*, 4 (1978).

—— *Class Conflict and Sectarianism: The Protestant Working Class and the Belfast Labour Movement, 1868–1920* (Belfast, Blackstaff, 1980).

—— 'Fianna Fail and the Working Class: The Origins of the Enigmatic Relationship', *Saothar*, 13 (1988).

—— *The Politics of Illusion: Republicanism and Socialism in Modern Ireland* (London, Hutchinson Radius, 1989).

PAUL, W., *The Irish Crisis (1921): The British Communist Stand on Irish Self-Determination* (Cork, CWC, 1986; 1st edn. 1921).

PAULIN, T., *Ireland and the English Crisis* (Newcastle, Bloodaxe, 1985).

PEARSE, P. H., *Political Writings and Speeches* (Dublin, Phoenix, n.d.).

PHILPIN, C. H. E. (ed.), *Nationalism and Popular Protest in Ireland* (Cambridge, CUP, 1987).

PRAGER, J., *Building Democracy in Ireland: Political Order and Cultural Integration in a Newly Independent Nation* (Cambridge, CUP, 1986).

PROBERT, B., *Beyond Orange and Green* (Dublin, Academy Press, 1978).

PURDIE, B., *Politics in the Streets: The Origin of the Civil Rights Movement in Northern Ireland* (Belfast, Blackstaff, 1990).

PYNE, P., 'The Third Sinn Fein Party, 1923–6', *Economic and Social Review*, 1/1 (Oct. 1969) and 1/2 (Jan. 1970).

—— 'The New Irish State and the Decline of the Republican Sinn Fein Party, 1923–6', *Eire-Ireland*, 11/3 (1976).

RANSOM, B., *Connolly's Marxism* (London, Pluto, 1980).

RICHARDS, S., 'Polemics on the Past: The Return to the Source in Irish Literary Revivals', *History Workshop*, 31 (1991).

ROCHE, P. J., and BARTON, B. (eds.), *The Northern Ireland Question: Myth and Reality* (Aldershot, Avebury, 1991).

ROSE, P. L., *Wagner: Race and Revolution* (London, Faber and Faber, 1992).

ROULSTON, C., '"Accentuating the National Issue'. Social Republicanism and the Communist Party of Ireland', *IPS* 6 (1991).

ROWTHORN, B., and WAYNE, N., *Northern Ireland: The Political Economy of Conflict* (Cambridge, Polity, 1988).

ROYAL IRISH ACADEMY, *Ireland After the Union: Proceedings of the Second Joint Meeting of the Royal Irish Academy and the British Academy, London, 1986* (Oxford, OUP, 1989).

RUMPF, E., and HEPBURN, A. C., *Nationalism and Socialism in Twentieth Century Ireland* (Liverpool, Liverpool Univ. Press, 1977).

RYAN, D., *James Connolly: His Lifework and Writings* (Dublin, Talbot, 1924).

RYAN, F., (as Seachranaidhe) *Easter Week and After* (Dublin, National Publicity Committee, n.d. [1928?]).

RYAN, M., *The Tom Barry Story* (Dublin, Mercier, 1982).

—— *Liam Lynch: The Real Chief* (Cork, Mercier, 1986).

—— *The Day Michael Collins was Shot* (Swords, Poolbeg, 1989).

SAID, E., *Nationalism, Colonialism, and Literature: Yeats and Decolonization* (Derry, Field Day, 1988).

SANTAMARIA, B. A., *Daniel Mannix: The Quality of Leadership* (Melbourne, Melbourne Univ. Press, 1984).

SCHMITT, D. E., *The Irony of Irish Democracy: The Impact of Political Culture on Administrative and Democratic Political Development in Ireland* (London, Heath, 1973).

SCHWARZMANTEL, J., 'Class and Nation: Problems of Socialist Nationalism', *Political Studies*, 35 (1987).

SEEDORF, M. F., 'Defending Reprisals: Sir Hamar Greenwood and the "Troubles", 1920–1', *Eire-Ireland* 25/4 (Winter 1990).

SHANNON, C. B., *Arthur J. Balfour and Ireland, 1874–1922* (Washington, Catholic Univ. Press of America, 1988).

SHAW, F., 'The Canon of Irish History: A Challenge', *Studies*, 61/242 (Summer 1972).

SHAW, G. B., *Plays Pleasant* (Harmondsworth, Penguin, 1946; 1st edn. 1898).

SHEEHY SKEFFINGTON, A., *Skeff: A Life of Owen Sheehy Skeffington, 1909–70* (Dublin, Lilliput, 1991).

SHEERAN, P. F., *The Novels of Liam O'Flaherty: A Study in Romantic Realism* (Dublin, Wolfhound, 1976).

SIMKINS, P., *Kitchener's Army: The Raising of the New Armies, 1914–16* (Manchester, Manchester Univ. Press, 1988).

SMITH, A. D., *The Ethnic Origins of Nations* (Oxford, Basil Blackwell, 1986).

—— *National Identity* (London, Penguin, 1991).

SMITH, F. B. (ed.), *Ireland, England, and Australia: Essays in Honour of Oliver MacDonagh* (Canberra, Australian National Univ., 1990).

SMITH, J. A., *John Buchan: A Biography* (London, Rupert Hart-Davis, 1965).

SMYTH, J., *The Men of No Property: Irish Radicals and Popular Politics in the Late Eighteenth Century* (Dublin, Gill and Macmillan, 1992).

STEINBECK, J., *Tortilla Flat* (Harmondsworth, Penguin, 1950; 1st edn. 1935).

—— *In Dubious Battle* (London, Pan, 1978; 1st edn. 1936).

—— *Of Mice and Men* (London, Mandarin, 1992; 1st edn. 1937).

—— *The Grapes of Wrath* (London, Pan, 1975; 1st edn. 1939).

—— *Cannery Row* (London, Pan, 1974; 1st edn. 1945).

STEPHENS, J., *The Insurrection in Dublin* (Gerrards Cross, Colin Smythe, 1992; 1st edn. 1916).

STEVENSON, J. A., 'Clashing Personalities: James Connolly and Daniel de Leon, 1896–1909', *Eire-Ireland*, 25/3 (Fall 1990).

STEWART, A. T. Q., *The Ulster Crisis: Resistance to Home Rule, 1912–14* (London, Faber and Faber, 1969).

—— *The Narrow Ground: Aspects of Ulster, 1609–1969* (London, Faber and Faber, 1977).

—— *A Deeper Silence: The Hidden Origins of the United Irishmen* (London, Faber and Faber, 1993).

STRAUSS, E., *Irish Nationalism and British Democracy* (London, Methuen, 1951).

STUART, F., 'Frank Ryan in Germany', *The Bell*, 16/2 (Nov. 1950) and 16/3 (Dec. 1950).

—— *Black List: Section H* (Harmondsworth, Penguin, 1982; 1st edn. 1971).

SWIFT, J. P., *John Swift: An Irish Dissident* (Dublin, Gill and Macmillan, 1991).

SYNGE, J. M., *The Playboy of the Western World/Riders to the Sea* (London, George Allen and Unwin, 1962 edn.).

TARPEY, M. V., 'Joseph McGarrity, Fighter for Irish Freedom', *Studia Hibernica*, 11 (1971).

TAYLOR, R., *Michael Collins* (London, Four Square, 1961; 1st edn. 1958).

THOMPSON, W. I., *The Imagination of an Insurrection: Dublin, Easter 1916—A Study of an Ideological Movement* (West Stockbridge, Lindisfarne Press, 1982; 1st edn. 1967).

THORNLEY, D., 'The Development of the Irish Labour Movement', *Christus Rex*, 18 (1964).

TIERNEY, M., *Eoin MacNeill* (Oxford, Clarendon, 1980).

TODD, J., 'Two Traditions in Unionist Political Culture', *IPS* 2 (1987).

—— 'Northern Irish Nationalist Political Culture', *IPS* 5 (1990).

TONE, T. W., *The Autobiography of Theobald Wolfe Tone, 1763–98*, ii vols. (London, T. Fisher Unwin, 1893).

TOUHILL, B. M., *William Smith O'Brien and his Revolutionary Companions in Penal Exile* (Columbia, Univ. of Missouri Press, 1981).

TOWNSHEND, C., *The British Campaign in Ireland, 1919–21: The Development of Political and Military Policies* (Oxford, OUP, 1975).

—— 'The Irish Railway Strike of 1920: Industrial Action and Civil Resistance in the Struggle for Independence', *IHS* 21/83 (Mar. 1979).

—— 'The Irish Republican Army and the Development of Guerrilla Warfare, 1916–21', *English Historical Review*, 94 (1979).

—— 'Bloody Sunday: Michael Collins Speaks', *European Studies Review*, 9 (1979).

—— 'Martial Law: Legal and Administrative Problems of Civil Emergency in Britain and the Empire, 1800–1940', *Historical Journal*, 25 (1982).

—— *Political Violence in Ireland: Government and Resistance Since 1848* (Oxford, Clarendon, 1984; 1st edn. 1983).

—— *Britain's Civil Wars: Counterinsurgency in the Twentieth Century* (London, Faber and Faber, 1986).

—— 'British Policy in Ireland, 1906–21', in Boyce (ed.), *The Revolution in Ireland*.

—— (ed.), *Consensus in Ireland: Approaches and Recessions* (Oxford, Clarendon, 1988).

VALIULIS, M. G., *Almost a Rebellion: The Irish Army Mutiny of 1924* (Cork, Tower Books, 1985).

—— *Portrait of a Revolutionary: General Richard Mulcahy and the Founding of the Irish Free State* (Blackrock, Irish Academic Press, 1992).

WALKER, B. M., (ed.), *Parliamentary Election Results in Ireland, 1801–1922* (Dublin, Royal Irish Academy, 1978).

—— *Ulster Politics: The Formative Years, 1868–86* (Belfast, Ulster Historical Foundation, 1989).

—— '1641, 1689, 1690, and All That: The Unionist Sense of History', *Irish Review*, 12 (Spring/Summer 1992).

WALKER, G., 'The Northern Ireland Labour Party in the 1920s', *Saothar*, 10 (1984).

—— *The Politics of Frustration: Harry Midgley and the Failure of Labour in Northern Ireland* (Manchester, Manchester Univ. Press, 1985).

—— 'Review Article: Irish Nationalism and the Uses of History', *Past and Present*, 126 (Feb. 1990).

—— 'Old History: Protestant Ulster in Lee's *Ireland*', *Irish Review*, 12 (Spring/Summer 1992).

—— ' "The Irish Dr Goebbels": Frank Gallagher and Irish Republican Propaganda', *Journal of Contemporary History*, 27 (1992).

WARD, M., *Unmanageable Revolutionaries: Women and Irish Nationalism* (London, Pluto, 1983).

—— *Maud Gonne: Ireland's Joan of Arc* (London, Pandora, 1990).

—— *The Missing Sex: Putting Women into Irish History* (Dublin, Attic, 1991).

WEST, N., *MI5: British Security Service Operations, 1909–45* (London, Triad, 1983; 1st edn. 1981).

WEST, T., *Horace Plunkett, Cooperation and Politics: an Irish Biography* (Gerrards Cross, Colin Smythe, 1986).

WHITE, J., *Minority Report: The Protestant Community in the Irish Republic* (Dublin, Gill and Macmillan, 1975).

WHITE, T. de V., *Kevin O'Higgins* (Dublin, Anvil, 1986; 1st edn. 1948).

WHYTE, J., *Church and State in Modern Ireland, 1923–79* (Dublin, Gill and Macmillan, 1984; 1st edn. 1971).

—— *Interpreting Northern Ireland* (Oxford, Clarendon, 1990).

WILLIAMS, T. D. (ed.), *The Irish Struggle, 1916–26* (London, Routledge and Kegan Paul, 1966).

—— (ed.), *Secret Societies in Ireland* (Dublin, Gill and Macmillan, 1973).

WINSTANLEY, M. J., *Ireland and the Land Question, 1800–1922* (London, Methuen, 1984).

YEATS, W. B., ed. A. N. Jeffares, *Selected Poetry* (London, Pan, 1974; 1st edn. 1962).

YOUNG, J. D., 'John MacLean, Socialism, and the Easter Rising', *Saothar*, 16 (1991).

YOUNGER, C., *Ireland's Civil War* (Glasgow, Fontana, 1979; 1st edn. 1968).

—— *Arthur Griffith* (Dublin, Gill and Macmillan, 1981).

ZNEIMER, J., *The Literary Vision of Liam O'Flaherty* (Syracuse, Syracuse Univ. Press, 1970).

Theses

BANTA, M. M., 'The Red Scare in the Irish Free State, 1925–37', M.A. thesis (UCD, 1982).

BRUTON, S., 'Peadar O'Donnell: Republican Socialist Visionary', M.A. thesis (UCD, 1988).

CAMPBELL, C., '"Ablaze with Hope": An Introduction to the Life and Novels of Peadar O'Donnell', M.A. thesis (QUB, 1991).

CREAN, A., 'Confronting Reality: Social and Political Realism in the Writings of Peadar O'Donnell, 1922–39', M.Phil. thesis (UCD, 1986).

DOYLE, M., 'The Republican Congress: A Study in Irish Radicalism', M.A. thesis (UCD, 1988).

DUNPHY, R., 'Class, Power, and the Fianna Fail Party: A Study of Hegemony in Irish Politics, 1923–48', D.Phil. thesis (European Univ. Institute, Florence, 1988).

MCHUGH, J. P., 'Voices of the Rearguard: A Study of *An Phoblacht*—Irish Republican Thought in the Post-Revolutionary Era, 1923–37', M.A. thesis (UCD, 1983).

SMITH, M. L. R., 'The Role of the Military Instrument in Irish Republican Strategic Thinking: An Evolutionary Analysis', Ph.D. thesis (London, 1991).

Other Miscellaneous Sources

DÁIL ÉIREANN, *Dail Debates.*
HOUSE OF COMMONS, *Parliamentary Debates.*
ILP, *Annual Reports.*
ILPTUC, *Annual Reports.*
ITUC, *Annual Reports.*
Irish Catholic Directory and Almanac.
IRISH FREE STATE, *Statistical Abstracts.*
—— *Census of Population, 1926.*
—— *Census of Population, 1936.*
—— *Commission of Inquiry into Banking, Currency, and Credit, 1938: Reports.*
—— *Commission of Inquiry into Banking, Currency, and Credit: Memoranda and Minutes of Evidence.*

Index